George N. Curzon

Problems of the Far East

Japan-Korea-China

George N. Curzon

Problems of the Far East
Japan-Korea-China

ISBN/EAN: 9783743395114

Manufactured in Europe, USA, Canada, Australia, Japa

Cover: Foto ©ninafisch / pixelio.de

Manufactured and distributed by brebook publishing software (www.brebook.com)

George N. Curzon

Problems of the Far East

PROBLEMS
OF
THE FAR EAST

BY THE RIGHT HON.
GEORGE N. CURZON. M.P.

LATE FELLOW OF ALL SOULS COLLEGE, OXFORD, AUTHOR
OF 'RUSSIA IN CENTRAL ASIA' AND 'PERSIA,' AND GOLD
MEDALLIST OF THE ROYAL GEOGRAPHICAL SOCIETY

JAPAN—KOREA—CHINA

NEW AND REVISED EDITION

'And first we must begin with Asia, to which the first place is due, as being the place of the first Men, first Religion, first Cities, Empires, Arts; where the most things mentioned in Scripture were done; the place where Paradise was seated, the Arke rested, the Law was given, and whence the Gospell proceeded; the place which did beare Him in His flesh, that by His Word beareth up all things.'

PURCHAS, *His Pilgrimes*

Westminster
ARCHIBALD CONSTABLE AND CO.
14 PARLIAMENT STREET

MDCCCXCVI

All rights reserved

Edinburgh: T. and A. CONSTABLE, Printers to Her Majesty

TO THOSE

WHO BELIEVE THAT THE BRITISH EMPIRE

IS, UNDER PROVIDENCE, THE GREATEST INSTRUMENT FOR GOOD

THAT THE WORLD HAS SEEN

AND WHO HOLD, WITH THE WRITER, THAT

ITS WORK IN THE FAR EAST IS NOT YET ACCOMPLISHED

THIS BOOK IS INSCRIBED

PREFACE TO NEW AND REVISED EDITION

THE first edition of this work appeared in August 1894, within a few weeks of the firing of the first shot in the Far Eastern War. Of the three nations who had furnished its subject matter, two were the protagonists, and the third was the victim in that eventful struggle. There was good fortune, therefore, in the moment of publication. But if this coincidence was undesigned, it was attended by a more than proportionate risk. For the book itself was less a history, or a narrative, or a criticism, than it was a forecast, entered into with only so much confidence as was born of a patient examination of facts upon the spot, but in ignorance of how soon it would be subjected to the rough test of experience. The fact that I am able to issue a fourth edition of the book —after the conclusion of a war that was seismic both in its character and consequences—in substantially the same guise as it originally wore, with alterations and additions that, while required to bring it up to date, only confirm my former argument, is to me a consolatory vindication of my venture then, and may, I hope, be regarded by others as a sufficient ground for republication now. For the causes that, during the intervening year, have brought about the collapse of China, the sufferings of Korea, and the victory of Japan, are the facts which this volume originally endeavoured to set forth, and which, so far from being rendered obsolete by the war, have been endowed thereby with a fresh vitality. The Far Eastern Question has not been closed, but, on the contrary, has been reopened by its termination; and so much of my former prophecy as remains unfulfilled I am encouraged once more to submit, though with less trembling, to the hidden touchstone of the future.

The central theme of these pages, when first published, was the utter rottenness of Chinese administration, and the certainty of military disaster in the case of conflict with a well-equipped foe; the confident ambitions and swelling power of Young Japan; the corrupt though picturesque imbecility of Korea; and the onerous responsibilities likely to be entailed upon Great Britain in the inevitable readjustment of Eastern Asia. So little were these conditions appreciated at the time that the most thoughtful of English newspapers thus criticised my argument :—

'Though Mr. Curzon is a diligent collector of facts, and deserves every credit for his praiseworthy attempts to understand the problems with which he is confronted, he does not show any very strong grasp either of the great issues at stake in the Far East, or as to the relative power and capacity of the two nations which are now confronting each other. As Mr. Curzon's conclusions are necessarily prophetic in their nature, it is not, of course, possible as yet to prove him mistaken ; but it cannot be said that he shows that instinctive appreciation of international affairs which is requisite for those who undertake to diagnose the conditions of three such kingdoms as Japan, Korea, and China. . . . In spite of Mr. Curzon, we believe that the weight of opinion is on the side of those who hold, as we do, that China could, if hard put to it, organise a most formidable fighting force. Does Mr. Curzon remember what

Lord Wolseley has said on the subject? He has expressed his opinion that the one danger of the Anglo-Saxon race was meeting the Chinese in war, and this is no abstract opinion, for Lord Wolseley helped to beat the Chinese under the walls of Peking. "They possess every military virtue," said Lord Wolseley of the Chinese. Mr. Curzon infers that the Chinese are a very unwarlike people. The world will, we think, prefer the verdict of a soldier who has met the Chinese in battle, to that of a civilian who has done little but sniff the evil odours of Peking, and, as he would doubtless be the first to admit, has nothing that can be called first-hand knowledge of China.'

Somehow or other 'the evil odours of Peking seem, after all, to have left a correct impression upon my civilian nostrils; and so fair-minded a critic as the *Spectator* will not, I am sure, grudge to a writer who has dared to prophesy the rare satisfaction of success.

In this New Edition, which has been carefully revised throughout, I have corrected a few mistakes that had crept into the first, and have introduced a good deal of additional matter, supplied or suggested by the events of the past year. The Revision Treaty between Great Britain and Japan, and the Treaty of Peace between Japan and China, are printed as appendices; and in a fresh chapter I have endeavoured to sum up the main issues of the recent conflict, and to forecast its bearing upon the Asiatic situation. I should add that the greater part of this chapter was written before the late change of Government in England, and that it has been composed in entire independence of official information or authority.

The Far East, which a year ago was an uncommon, has since become a familiar phrase in the terminology of International Politics. Its problems, which suggested to me the title of this book, are and will remain problems for many a year to come. Just, however, as these pages, in their original form, were the last description, in point of time, of an era that has since irretrievably vanished; so in their revised shape they may invite perusal as the first account that has appeared since the war of the new world that has been generated amid the clash of arms. Not merely, therefore, do they relate the past, but they relate to the future. In that future I am confirmed, instead of shaken, by all that has occurred, in the belief with which I before concluded, that a great part remains to be played, if the energy and the courage and the sagacity are still forthcoming, by the Government and the people of my own country.

GEORGE N. CURZON.

PREFACE TO THE FIRST EDITION

THE work of which I here publish the first part, though the outcome of two journeys round the world in 1887-88 and in 1892-93, does not pretend to be a book of travel. Rather is it an attempt to examine, in a comparative light, the political, social, and economic conditions of the kingdoms and principalities of the Far East. By this title I signify the countries that lie between India and the Pacific Ocean. They include both the best known and the least known of Oriental nations—Japan and China in the former category; Korea, Tongking, Annam, Cochin China, Cambogia, and Siam in the latter. In respect of race, religion, and habits, Burma should fall within the same class; but since it is now an integral portion of the Indian Empire, it will be purposely excluded from this survey.

The above-mentioned countries have each their special features of climate, scenery, architecture, religion, and life, differentiating them from each other, and still more from the rest of the world. To the traveller these idiosyncrasies cannot fail to appeal; nor can he be indifferent to the atmosphere of romance in which those fanciful regions, when once he has left them, appear ever afterwards to float. To such æsthetic impressions I would profess no invulnerability; and the descriptions which will be found in these pages of the capitals of Korea and China, and of other scenes, will prove the completeness of my occasional surrender. On the whole, however, I have relegated these aspects of my journeys to the background, and have preferred to discuss the problems, perhaps less superficially interesting, but incomparably more important, and vastly more abstruse, which are suggested by the national character, resources, and organisation of those countries as affected by their intercourse with foreign or Western Powers. What is the part which they are now playing, or are capable of playing, on the international stage? What is the political future that may, without foolhardiness of prediction, be anticipated for the peoples and lands of the Far East?

In preparing and comparing my observations upon these countries, I very early found that to attempt to deal with the political features of eight different States within the compass of a single volume could only be achieved at the expense both of unity and exactitude—a conviction which was fortified by the natural subdivision of my subject into a twofold heading. Japan, Korea, and China, suggest a number of problems, substantially similar if not actually interconnected. Their maritime outlook is towards the Pacific Ocean. The remaining countries of the Far East are in a different stage of evolution; and partly owing to their intrinsic weakness, partly to the degree in which they have already been brought under European control, illustrate a different argument. They are also alike in turning a backward gaze upon the Indian Seas. Following this natural classification, I have confined the present volume to the examination of the three first-mentioned States, reserving for a future work the territories of the Indo-Chinese peninsula.

In the case of Japan I must confess to having departed widely from the accepted model of treatment. There will be found nothing in these pages of the Japan of temples, tea-houses, and bric-à-brac—that infinitesimal segment of the national existence which the traveller is so prone to mistake for the whole, and by doing which he fills the educated Japanese with such unspeakable indignation. I have been more interested in the efforts of a nation, still in pupilage, to assume the manners of the full-grown man, in the constitutional struggles through which Japan is passing, in her relations with foreign Powers, and in the future that awaits her immense ambitions.

Similarly in China I have been more concerned with the internal structure of that mysterious archaism, with the policy of its rulers, the strength or weakness of its resources, and with the pulse that throbs so defiantly beneath the bosom of its amazing people, than with the sights and scenes of Treaty Ports, or the superficial features of native existence. In Korea I hope that I may claim in some respects to break almost new ground. In the few and singularly inadequate accounts of that kingdom that have appeared in Europe, and that have left it, next to Tibet, the least known part of Asia, no serious endeavour has been made to examine its political status—a question of great complexity and of international importance—or to determine its bearing upon surrounding States; and I doubt whether to most persons at home Korea is known except as a land of white clothes and black hats. If a disproportionate space may appear to have been allotted to its treatment, as compared with that of China and Japan, it will be because of an intrinsic novelty that is not yet exhausted, and of a general ignorance that in view of present events deserves to be appeased.

If, in spite of a good deal of descriptive matter that may perhaps interest or assist both the reader and the traveller, it be objected that the trail of politics is over all this work, I answer that such is the principal claim that I venture to make for it. Other writers of great ability have recorded their impressions of the social or artistic sides of Eastern life. But, in their interest in the governed, they have too frequently forgotten the government; nor does the photograph of a fleeting moment lend much assistance to the forecast of a wider future. For myself, in essaying this more ambitious task, I can honestly disclaim, on the several occasions when I have travelled in the East, any *a priori* prepossession for this or prejudice against that people. I have no anterior theory to support, and no party interest, unless the British Empire be a party interest, to serve. But to my vision all the nations of the East seem to group themselves as sections or parts, of varying age and utility, in the most wonderful piece of natural and human mechanism that the world now presents, namely, the political evolution of the Asiatic Continent. What function is fulfilled by each in the movement of this vast machine, how far they individually retard its progress or contribute to the collective thunder of its wheels, is to me the most absorbing of problems. What will become of this great fabric in the future, whether its minor atoms will break up and split asunder, thereby adding to the already formidable strain upon the larger units, whether the slow heart of the East will still continue to palpitate beneath the superimposed restraints of Western force or example, or whether, as has been predicted, some tremendous cataclysm may be expected, in which the tide of human conquest shall once more be rolled back from East to West, are speculations to the solution of which I have no fonder wish than to subscribe my humble quota of knowledge.

Finally, these volumes are part of that scheme of work, now nearly half realised, which ten years ago I first set before myself in the examination of the different aspects of the Asiatic problem. What I have already endeavoured to

PREFACE TO THE FIRST EDITION

do for Russia in Central Asia, and for Persia, or the countries on this side of India, *i.e.* the Near East—what I hope to be able to do hereafter for two other little-known Asiatic regions, directly bordering upon India, *i.e.* the Central East—I attempt to do in this volume, and in that which will follow it, for the countries lying beyond India, *i.e.* the Far East. As I proceed with this undertaking, the true fulcrum of Asiatic dominion seems to me increasingly to lie in the Empire of Hindustan. The secret of the mastery of the world, is, if only they knew it, in the possession of the British people.

No Englishman need grudge the splendid achievements and possessions of the mighty Power whose hand is outstretched over the entire north of Asia, from the Ural Mountains to the Pacific. He need not be jealous of the new-born Asiatic zeal of our next-door neighbour in Europe. He may respect alike the hoary pride of China and the impetuous exuberance of renascent Japan. But he will find that the best hope of salvation for the old and moribund in Asia, the wisest lessons for the emancipated and new, are still to be derived from the ascendency of British character, and under the shelter, where so required, of British dominion. If in the slightest degree I succeed in bringing home this conviction to the minds of my countrymen at home, I shall never regret the years of travel and of writing which I have devoted and hope still to devote to this congenial task.

My sincere thanks are due, for revision or advice in different parts of this work, to Mr. Cecil Spring-Rice, of H.B.M's Diplomatic Service, the delightful companion of my later journeys; to Mr. W. C. Hillier, H.M. Consul-General in Korea; and to Mr. J. N. Jordan, of the British Legation at Peking.

July 1894.

CONTENTS

CHAPTER I
THE FAR EAST

The enchantment of Asia—Her products—Homogeneousness—Contact with civilisation—Moral lessons—The Far East—Its idiosyncrasies—India the pivot 1

JAPAN

CHAPTER II
THE EVOLUTION OF MODERN JAPAN

Japanese railways—The streets of Tokio—The Diet—Public opinion—Parliamentary symptoms—Rocks ahead—The Ministers and Parliament—The Ministry of All the Talents—Expectations—Session of 1892-93—Session of 1893—The crisis—General Elections of 1894—Real points at issue—1. Clan government—Oligarchy *v.* Democracy—2. Position of the Sovereign—3. Ministerial responsibility—The issue—Japanese Navy—Army—Corroborative opinion—Finances—Trade—Manufacturing industries—Attitude of Japanese towards foreigners—Schoolboy patriotism—Chances of Christianity in Japan 13

CHAPTER III
JAPAN AND THE POWERS

Treaty Revision—History of the Treaties—Postponement of Revision—The case of Japan—The case of the Powers—Previous attempts at Revision. Count Inouye, 1882-87—Count Okuma, 1888-89—Viscount Aoki, 1890—Bases of settlement—Position of the Codes—Further Postponement—Address to the Throne in 1893—Anti-Mixed residence agitation—The Chinese Question—Agitation against foreign ownership of property—Other demands—Prospects of settlement—The Treaty of July, 1894 51

APPENDIX TO CHAPTER III

I.—Treaty of Commerce and Navigation between Great Britain and
   Japan (July 1894) 70
II.—Protocol 79

KOREA

CHAPTER IV

LIFE AND TRAVEL IN KOREA

The fascination of Korea—Literature of the subject—The Treaty
Ports—Fusan—Gensan—Chemulpo—The Korean people—Total
population—Ethnology and language—National character—The
extremes of society—Necessities of travel—Visit to the Diamond
Mountains—Korean monks—Monastic life and habits—Buildings
—Korean religion—Spirit-worship and Confucianism—Conditions
of travel—Sport—Peasant life—Rural habits—Memorial tablets—
Tombs—Wayfarers—The Korean inn 85

CHAPTER V

THE CAPITAL AND COURT OF KOREA

Name of the capital—Walls and gates of Soul—Its situation—Beacon-
fires—Population and streets—Dirt and ditches—Houses—Street-
life and costume—Dancing-girls—Hats—Amusements—The Big
Bell—Shops—Stone pagoda and pillar—Temples—Red Arrow
Gate—The painted Buddha—Execution-place—Royal fortresses—
Sovereignty in Korea—Royal Palaces—East, or New Palace—
West, or Old Palace—Great Hall of Audience—Summer Palace—
The King of Korea—The Tai Wen Kun—The King's reign—His
character—The Queen—The Crown Prince—Theory of monarchy
—Audience with the Foreign Minister—Court dress and etiquette
—Audience with the King—Royal procession—Korean army—
State review 118

CHAPTER VI

POLITICAL AND COMMERCIAL SYMPTOMS IN KOREA

An Asiatic microcosm—Korean administration—Revenue and debt—
Foreign Treaties—Foreign advisers—Projects and speculations—
The currency—New Mint and silver coinage—Banks—Obstacles to
commercial development—Means of communication—Roads—
River Navigation—Coast Navigation—Railways—Growth of trade
—Steamship service—Customs service—Smuggling—Native Stand-

CONTENTS xix

PAGE

point—Mines and Minerals—Gold—Future prospects—Missionary work in Korea—1. Persecution—2. Toleration—English Protestant Mission—Native sentiment 165

CHAPTER VII

THE POLITICAL FUTURE OF KOREA

Anomalous political status of Korea—Connection with Japan—Tribute Missions—Friction and rupture—Recovery of influence—Treaty of 1876—Convention of Tientsin in 1885—Commercial ascendency—Political bluster—True policy of Japan—Outbreak of war—Connection with China—Existing evidences of Korean vassalage—Death of the Queen Dowager in 1890 Thread of Chinese policy. 1. Repudiation — 2. Neutralisation — Terms of the Treaties — Question of envoys—Question of troops at Soul—3. Practical sovereignty—The Chinese Resident—Position of the King—Justification of Li Hung Chang—Connection with Russia—Aggressive designs—*Ad interim* plans—Attitude of Great Britain—Occupation of Port Hamilton in 1885—The other Powers—The carcase and the eagles 18

CHINA

CHAPTER VIII

THE COUNTRY AND CAPITAL OF CHINA

Transition to China—Tientsin—The Viceroy Li Hung Chang—Interview—Journey to Peking—Chinese rural life—Entrance to Peking—Ground-plan—The three Pekings—Panorama of the streets—Native practitioners—The Imperial Palace—The Emperor Tung Chih—The two Empresses-Regent—The Empress Dowager—The Emperor Kuang Hsu—Palace routine—The Temple of Heaven—Difficulty of admission—The Annual Sacrifice—The Observatory—Examination building—Drum and Bell Towers—Temple of Confucius—Hall of the Classics—Great Lama Temple—Outside the walls—The Great Bell—The Summer Palace—Yuan-ming-yuan—Wan-shou-shan—The Great Wall—The Ming Tombs—British Legation 221

CHAPTER IX

CHINA AND THE POWERS

Relations between Chinese and Europeans—The Tsungli Yamen—A Board of Delay—Chinese diplomacy—The Right of Audience—History—English embassies. Lord Macartney in 1793—Lord

Amherst in 1816—Interval—Audience with Tung Chih in 1873 and 1874—Audience with Kuang Hsu in 1891—Subsequent audiences—Summary of achievement—True significance of the dispute—Foreign policy of China—Attitude towards Russia— China and the Pamirs—Russia in 1895—Attitude towards Great Britain—Anglo-Chinese Trade—Opium Question—Missionary Question—Protestant Missions—Their good service—Sowing the seed—Objections and drawbacks—1. Religious and doctrinal. Hostility to Chinese ethics—Disputes as to name of the Deity— As to the form of religion—Unrevised translations of the Scriptures —Christian dogma—Irresponsible itinerancy—2. Political. History of the Treaties—Subsequent understanding—Imperial Edict of 1891—Chinese sentiments—The appeal for gunboats—Privileges claimed for converts—An *imperium in imperio*—Plea of Political agitation—3. Practical. Mission life—Employment of women— Situation of Buildings—Refusal of converts to subscribe—Belief in witchcraft—Horrible charges—Summing up—Results—The right policy. Respect for the Treaties—Stricter precautions— Choice of material 260

CHAPTER X

THE SO-CALLED AWAKENING OF CHINA

Is China awake?—A tactical surrender—Railways in China—Manchurian Railway—Line to Peking—Great Trunk Line—Hankow Line and factories—Formosa Railway—New Schemes—Other communications—Military reform—The Manchu and National Armies—Discipline—Native officers—European officers—Cost— Alleged successes—General Gordon's opinion—General Prjevalski —Colonel Bell—The Chinese Navy—The false and the real dangers —The mercenaries of Europe—The Press in China—Native enterprise—The curse of officialism—The Mandarinate—The Chinese standpoint—The picture of progress—The reality of standstill . 311

CHAPTER XI

MONASTICISM IN CHINA

Chinese Buddhism—Its superstitious sanction—Contradictory opinion of monks—Its explanation—Original conception of monasticism —Its inversion—A spiritual insurance—Ostracism of the cloister— Popular odium—Common imposture—Different classes of recruits —Means of subsistence—Monastic Temples—Entrance gateway— Main temple—Service—*Vox et praterea nihil*—Tenants of glass houses—Procession—Reliquary—Domestic premises—Cremation . 343

THE PROSPECT

CHAPTER XII

AFTER THE WAR

Responsibility for the War—An Eastern Vendetta—Secondary motives—Japanese patriotism and preparations—Japan on the battlefield—Causes of Chinese disaster—Civil corruption—Military incapacity—The Chinese soldier—Effects of the war—1. Upon China. The possible—The probable—2. Upon Korea. Need for reform—Japanese efforts—Proclamation of Korean Independence—A rain of Reforms—Japanning all round—Pak and the Queen—Passive Resistance—The King—Count Inouye's Confession—Japanese Failure—The Power in the Background—3. Upon Japan. The revolt of Asia—Commercial and industrial expansion . . 361

CHAPTER XIII

THE DESTINIES OF THE FAR EAST

Summary—The future of Japan—The Great Britain of the Far East—Future of China—The Chinese as aliens—The theory of Chinese resurrection—Mr. Pearson's arguments in its favour—The new march of the Mongols—Lords of the future—Objection of unoccupied area at home—Reasons for disputing Mr. Pearson—Alleged successes of China—The Colonial question—Character of Chinese colonists—Military weakness of China—Chinese reconquest impossible—The dream of social apotheosis—Influence of national character—Lessons of history—Danger of rebellion—The real destiny—Race and empire—Is Japan the enemy? . . 390

CHAPTER XIV

GREAT BRITAIN IN THE FAR EAST

The *rôle* of Great Britain—Reflex influence upon England—Commercial supremacy of Great Britain—Our rivals—Contraction of business—Christian Missions—English life in the Far East—The Press—Domestic life—English character—British diplomacy—British representatives—Suggested libraries of special reference—Diplomatic anomalies—Future of Great Britain in the Far East—The English language 413

APPENDIX

	PAGE
I.—Treaty of Shimonoseki between Japan and China (April 1895)	429
II.—Imperial Rescript (May 1895)	434

INDEX 437

LIST OF ILLUSTRATIONS

FULL-PAGE ILLUSTRATIONS

		PAGE
HIS MAJESTY LI HSI, KING OF KOREA	*Frontispiece*	
THE JAPANESE HOUSES OF PARLIAMENT AT TOKIO	*To face*	14
JAPANESE HOUSE OF PEERS	,,	16
JAPANESE HOUSE OF REPRESENTATIVES	,,	20
THE KING IN STATE PROCESSION	,,	158
KOREAN CAVALRY AND ROYAL STANDARD	,,	162
MODERN-DRILLED KOREAN INFANTRY	,,	164
TEMPLE AND ALTAR OF HEAVEN	,,	244
GREAT WALL OF CHINA	,,	256

ILLUSTRATIONS IN TEXT

	PAGE
MARQUIS ITO	24
PORT AND JAPANESE SETTLEMENT OF FUSAN	89
GATE OF NATIVE TOWN, FUSAN	91
PORT OF CHEMULPO	93
KOREAN SCHOOLMASTER AND BOYS	95
A KOREAN MAGISTRACY	99
KEUM KANG SAN, OR DIAMOND MOUNTAINS	102
MONASTERY OF CHANG AN SA IN THE DIAMOND MOUNTAINS	104
ABBOT OF A KOREAN MONASTERY	106
STREET IN A KOREAN VILLAGE	113
A KOREAN PEASANT FAMILY	114
SOUTH GATE OF SÖUL	119
EAST GATE AND WALL OF SÖUL	121

	PAGE
MOUNTAIN OF POUK HAN	122
BEACON TOWER ON NAM SAN	123
GROUND-PLAN OF SÖUL	125
THE CITY AND OLD PALACE, SÖUL	127
KOREAN SECRETARIES	128
KOREAN WAITING-MAID	129
THE KING'S BAND	131
KOREAN MOURNER	132
TEMPLE OF THE GOD OF WAR AT SÖUL	138
ARCHWAY OF THE CHINESE COMMISSIONERS	139
THE CITY AND NEW PALACE, SÖUL	143
GATEWAY OF THE OLD PALACE	144
GREAT HALL OF AUDIENCE	145
INTERIOR OF THE OLD PALACE	147
THE TAI WEN KUN	149
THE CROWN PRINCE	153
A KOREAN MINISTER	157
A KOREAN COLONEL	160
LI HUNG CHANG	224
WALLS AND GATES OF PEKING	231
STREET IN PEKING	234
SOUTHERN ALTAR OF HEAVEN	246

MAPS

KOREA AND PEKING	*To face* 216
JAPAN, KOREA, AND CHINA	*At the end*

CHAPTER I

THE FAR EAST

> The youth who daily farther from the East
> Must travel, still is Nature's priest,
> And by the vision splendid
> Is on his way attended.
> WORDSWORTH: *Ode on Intimations of Immortality.*

ASIA has always appeared to me to possess a fascination which no country or empire in Europe, still less any part of the Western Hemisphere, can claim. It is believed by many to have been the cradle of our race, and the birthplace of our language, just as it certainly has been the hearthstone of our religion, and the fountainhead of the best of our ideas. Wide as is the chasm that now severs us, with its philosophy our thought is still interpenetrated. The Asian continent has supplied a scene for the principal events, and a stage for the most prominent figures, in history. Of Asian parentage is that force which, more than any other influence, has transformed and glorified mankind—viz. the belief in a single Deity. Five of the six greatest moral teachers that the world has seen—Moses, Buddha, Confucius, Jesus, and Mohammed— were born of Asian parents, and lived upon Asian soil. Roughly speaking, their creeds may be said to have divided the conquest of the universe. The most famous or the wisest of kings—Solomon, Nebuchadnezzar, Cyrus, Timur, Baber, Akbar—have sat upon Asian thrones. Thither the

The enchantment of Asia.

greatest conqueror of the Old World turned aside for the sole theatre befitting so enormous an ambition. '*Cette vieille Europe m'ennuie*' expressed the half-formed kindred aspiration of the greatest conqueror of modern times. The three most populous existing empires—Great Britain, Russia, and China—are Asian empires; and it is because they are not merely European but Asian, that the two former are included in the category. From Asia also have sprung the most terrible phenomena by which humanity has ever been scourged—the Turki Nadir Shah, Sultan Mahmud of Ghuzni, the Mongol Jinghiz Khan.

Yet for such crimes as these has Asia paid to us no mean compensation. For to her we owe the noblest product of all literature, in the Old Testament of the Hebrew Scriptures; the sweetest of lyrics, in the epithalamium of a Jewish king; the embryos of modern knowledge, in the empiricism of Arabian geometers and metaphysicians. In Asia the drama was born. There the greatest writer of antiquity chose a scene for his immortal epic. There, too, the mariner's compass first guided men over the pathless waters. In our own times alone it is with her aid that we have arrived at the evolution of three new sciences—comparative mythology, comparative jurisprudence, and philology. From Asia we have received the architecture of the Moslem—that most spiritual and refined of human conceptions—the porcelain of China, the faïence of Persia, Rhodes, and Damascus, the infinitely ingenious art of Japan. On her soil were reared the most astonishing of all cities, Babylon; the most princely of palaces, Persepolis; the stateliest of temples, Angkor Wat: the loveliest of tombs, the Taj Mahal. There too may be found the most wonderful of Nature's productions; the loftiest mountains on the surface of the globe, the most

Her products.

renowned, if not also the largest, of rivers, the most entrancing of landscapes. In the heart of Asia lies to this day the one mystery which the nineteenth century has still left for the twentieth to explore—viz. the Tibetan oracle of Lhasa.

Of course, in displaying this panorama of Asian wonders or Asian charms, while claiming for her an individuality which her vast extent, her historic antiquity, and her geographical features go far to explain, I do not claim for her any absolute unity of product or form. On the contrary, the distinctions of race, irrespective of climate, are perhaps more profound in Asia than in any other continent. There is, on the whole, less exterior resemblance between a Japanese and a Persian than there is between a Prussian and a Spaniard. A Dutchman is more like a Greek than a Turkoman is like a Malay. There is a wider gap between the finest Aryan type and the aboriginal barbarian in the recesses of Saghalin, Formosa, or Laos, than there is, for example, between the Egyptian and the Hottentot, or between the Frenchman and the Lap. Not less marked are the distinctions of language and habits, of caste and creed. The Western world in the Feudal Ages was less sundered and split up than is Hindustan at the present moment. And yet, after visiting almost every part of Asia, I seem, as soon as I taste her atmosphere or come within range of her influence, to observe a certain homogeneousness of expression, a certain similarity of character, certain common features of political and still more of social organisation, certain identical strains in the composition of man, that differentiate her structure from anything in Europe or even in America, and invest her with a distinction peculiarly her own. The sensation is strengthened by the impression left upon most minds since

Homogeneousness.

the days of childhood by the two best books that have ever been written upon the East—viz. the Old Testament and the Arabian Nights. If I strive still further to analyse it, I find that in scenery, as I have elsewhere endeavoured to explain,[1] the dominant note of Asian individuality is contrast, in character a general indifference to truth and respect for successful wile, in deportment dignity, in society the rigid maintenance of the family union, in government the mute acquiescence of the governed, in administration and justice the open corruption of administrators and judges, and in every-day life a statuesque and inexhaustible patience, which attaches no value to time, and wages unappeasable warfare against hurry.

The impact between this solid amalgam of character and habit, and the elastic and insinuating force which we denominate civilisation, is a phenomenon which now in many countries I have set myself to examine, and which, I venture to think, surpasses all others in human interest. In Asia the combat is between antagonists who are fairly matched. It resembles one of those ancient contests between the *gladiator* and the *retiarius*, the man with the rude blade and the man with the supple net, that filled with straining crowds the Imperial arena at Rome. For though craft and agility and superior science will, in the long run, generally get the better of crude force and the naked weapon, yet there are moments when, in the twinkling of an eye, the tables are turned, when the swordsman slashes the netman in twain, when the untutored Oriental makes short shrift with the subtleties and sophistries of the West. If Japan, for instance, illustrates the easy victory of the European, China so far registers an equal triumph for the Asiatic. In Africa and America,

Contact with civilisation.

[1] Vide *Persia and the Persian Question*, vol. i. pp. 13-15.

where no serious contest has been possible, because of the vast moral and intellectual disparity between the organisms engaged, but where civilisation advances like the incoming tide over the castles built by children with wooden spades in the sand, the spectacle is devoid of any such interest.

The same train of reflection may lead us to avoid a common pitfall of writers upon the East—viz. the tendency to depreciate that which we do not ourselves sympathise with or understand, and which we are therefore prone to mistake for a mark of inferiority or degradation. *Moral lessons.* Mankind has built for its moral habitation different structures in different lands and times. It has adopted many divergent styles of architecture, and has entertained widely opposite views upon material, ornament, and design. Sometimes the fabric would seem to have been erected all aslant, or even to have been turned topsy-turvy in the course of construction. And yet, just as there are certain common laws observed in all building that has endured, so there are points of contact in all civilisations, common principles which lie at the root of every morality, however contradictory its external manifestations. It is among the ancient races of Central Asia and in China that these reflections are chiefly borne home to the traveller's mind. When he meets with civilisation as old as, nay older than our own, when he encounters a history whose heroes have been among the great men of all time, religions whose prophets have altered the course of the world's progress, codes of morals which have endured for centuries and still hold millions within their adamantine grip, a learning which anticipated many of the proudest discoveries of modern science, and a social organisation which has in places solved the very problem of reconciling individual liberty with collective force, whereupon the new-fledged democracies

of the West are expending their virgin energies—he feels
that it is absurd for him to censure, and impertinent in him
to condemn. The East has not yet exhausted its lessons for
us, and Europe may still sit at the feet of her elder sister.

No introduction is needed in presenting the Far East to
an English audience,[1] since, on the whole, it is better known
to them already than the Near East, or than the
Central East, if these geographical distinctions
may be permitted. Asia Minor, the Caucasus,
Persia, Beluchistan, and Transcaspia, are each a *terra incognita*
to the majority of our countrymen compared with the coasts
of China and the cities of Japan. The situation of these,
on or near to the ocean highways, and the advanced state
of civilisation to which their inhabitants have attained and
which has long attracted the notice of Europe, and the
extent to which they have in recent years been made accessible by steam-traffic by land and sea, have diverted
thither the stream of travel, and have familiarised men
with Tokio and Canton who have never been to Syracuse or
Moscow. Comfort too plays a great part in the discrimina-
tion of travel. Were there a railroad from the Caspian to
Teheran, more people would visit the capital of the Shah.
Were there an hotel at Baghdad, we might shortly hear of
Cook's parties to the ruins of Babylon. Nevertheless there
are portions of the Far East which the precise dearth of
those communications of which I have been speaking has
still left isolated and almost unknown. The number of

---

[1] It may have been forgotten by most readers, but it is nevertheless the fact, that the historical connection of England with the Far East was antecedent to her connection with India. The East India Trading Company had trading stations in the Malay Peninsula, in Sumatra, Java, and Borneo, before they had opened a single factory in Hindustan, the spice trade being the bait that drew them so far afield. The British advance of the past century has therefore been merely a reappearance upon a scene where the English flag first flew nearly three hundred years ago.

Englishmen who have travelled in the interior of Korea may
be counted upon the fingers of the two hands. I know of
none who have selected Annam as the scene of their explora-
tions. Perhaps, therefore, in including them in my survey
of the Far East, I may help to fill a gap, at the same time
that I subserve the symmetry of my own plan.

There are certain main distinctions which separate this
region from those parts of the Asian continent that border
upon the Mediterranean and the Arabian Sea.
Much of it, comprising the whole of the Indo- *Its idio-syncrasies.*
Chinese peninsula, lies south of the Tropic of
Cancer, and accordingly presents us with a climate, peoples,
and a vegetation, upon which the sun has looked, and which
possess characteristics of their own. Greater heat has produced less capacity of resistance; and just as in India all
the masculine races have their habitat above the 24th degree
of latitude, so in the Far East is there the greatest contrast
between the peoples of China, Korea, and Japan, lying
north of that parallel, and those of Burma, Siam, Malaysia,
and Annam, which lie below it. The one class has retained
its virility and its freedom, the second has already undergone
or is in course of undergoing absorption. Throughout the
Far East there is abundance of water, and the scorched
and sullen deserts that lay their leprous touch upon
Persia, Central Asia, and Mongolia, are nowhere reproduced.
In the Near East, *i.e.* west of the Indus and the Oxus,
there are absolutely only two rivers of any importance, the
Tigris and the Euphrates; and the main reason of the backwardness of those countries is the dearth both of moisture
and of means of communication which the absence of rivers
entails. A further striking difference, of incalculable importance in its effect upon national development, is that of
religion. Western Asia is in the unyielding and pitiless

clutch of Islam, which opposes a Cyclopean wall of resistance to innovation or reform. In Eastern Asia we encounter only the mild faith of the Indian prince, more or less overlaid with superstition and idolatry, or sapped by scepticism and decay; and the strange conglomerate of ethics and demonolatry which stands for religion in China and its once dependent states. Neither of these agencies is overtly hostile to Western influence, though both, when aroused, are capable of putting forth a tacit weight of antagonism that must be felt to be appreciated. Finally, whereas in the Near East population is sparse and inadequate, in the Far East it is crowded upon the soil, cultivating the well-soaked lands with close diligence or massed behind city-walls in seething aggregations of humanity. These conditions augment the complexity of the problem which their political future involves.

Midway between the two flanks of the continent whose rival differences I have sketched lies India, sharing the features, both good and evil, of both. She has wide, waterless, and untilled plains; but she also has throbbing hives of human labour and life. Her surface is marked both by mighty rivers and by Saharas of sand. Among her peoples are Mohammedans of both schools, mixed up with diverse and pagan creeds. Of her races some have always subsisted by the sword alone; to others the ploughshare is the only known implement of iron. She combines the rigours of eternal snow with the luxuriant flame of the tropics. Within her borders may be studied every one of the problems with which the rest of Asia challenges our concern. But her central and commanding position is nowhere better seen than in the political influence which she exercises over the destinies of her neighbours near and far, and the extent to which their fortunes revolve

<small>India the pivot.</small>

upon an Indian axis. The independence of Afghanistan, the continued national existence of Persia, the maintenance of Turkish rule at Baghdad, are one and all dependent upon Calcutta. Nay, the radiating circle of her influence overlaps the adjoining continents, and affects alike the fate of the Bosphorus and the destinies of Egypt. Nor is the effect less remarkable if examined upon the eastern side, to which in this book I am about to invite attention. It is from jealousy of India and to impair the position which India gives to Great Britain in the Far East that France has again embarked upon an Asiatic career, and is advancing from the south-east with steps that faithfully correspond with those of Russia upon the north-west. The heritage of the Indian Empire has within the last ten years made us the land-neighbours of China, and has multiplied threefold the area of our diplomacy at Peking. Even the fortunes of remote Korea are in a manner bound up with the politics of Hindustan, seeing that it is by the same foe that, in the last resort, both are threatened, and that the tactics which aim at the appropriation of the smaller unit have as their ulterior objective the detriment of the greater. Such and so supreme is the position enjoyed in the Asian continent by the Empire of the Kaiser-i-Hind. Towards her, or into her orbit, a centripetal force, which none appears able to resist, draws every wandering star. Just as it may be said that the Eastern Question in Europe turns upon the dismemberment of Turkey, so the Eastern Question in Asia turns upon the continued solidarity of Hindustan. In what relation to that problem stand the countries and peoples of the Far East, what is their present political condition, and in what way they are engaged in constructing the history, or reconstructing the maps of the future, it is my object in these pages to determine.

JAPAN

'Much have I travelled in the realms of gold,
And many goodly states and kingdoms seen,
Round many Eastern islands have I been.'

J. KEATS.

CHAPTER II

THE EVOLUTION OF MODERN JAPAN

Me vestigia terrent,
Omnia te adversum spectantia, nulla retrorsum.
HORACE, *Ep.* I. i. 74–5.

DURING the five years that elapsed between my first and second visits to Japan, in 1887 and in 1892, I found that many things had changed. The Europeanisation of the country proceeds apace, though perhaps with a slightly less headlong rapidity than before. In 1887 short lines of railway ran only in the neighbourhood of the two capitals, Tokio and Kioto, and of the Treaty Ports, Kobe and Yokohama. Now it is possible to travel by rail within a single day from Tokio to Kioto, and also from Tokio to Aomori on the northern coast; 1980 miles of the iron road are recorded as already open to traffic; and a great programme of railway construction, according to which a sum of £8,500,000 is to be spent upon further extensions during the next twelve years, has received the sanction of the Diet. In a few years' time those to whom the discomforts of a marine voyage are inadequately compensated by the fairy landscapes of the Inland Sea, will be able to travel overland, without leaving their compartment, from Kioto to Shimonoseki; while there is a talk of bridging the Straits that bear the latter name with a fabric that shall excel in monstrosity even the Forth Bridge. From Tokio to

Japanese railways.

Nagasaki it will then be as commonplace an incident to travel by rail as it is from London to Wick; and the *jinriksha* will relapse into the dusty limbo of the postillion and the stage-coach. Where the 'iron horse' has rushed in, it may be certain that minor forms of Western invention will not fear to tread. In Tokio tramways clatter along the

The streets of Tokio. streets; gas flames in some of the principal highways; and the electric light is uniformly employed in the public buildings, in many of the residences of ministers and nobles, in the tea-houses which figure so largely in the holiday life of the Japanese gentleman, and in quite a number of stores and even small shops. Telephones and telegraphs stretch a web of wires overhead. The long picturesque lines of *yashikis* or fortified city residences of the feudal lords and their sworded retainers, that covered so great an area within the moats, have almost all disappeared, and have been replaced by public offices of showy European architecture and imposing dimensions. An immense pile of scaffolding, surrounding a space much larger than the Law Courts on the Strand in London, conceals what will presently be known as the new Ministry and Courts of Justice, where will be dispensed a jurisprudence that has been borrowed, with a truly Japanese eclecticism, from the codes of half the nations of Europe. The perpetual bugle-note, and the sight of neat figures in white cotton uniforms and black boots, are indicative of a national army, whose mobilised strength in time of peace is 56,000, and whose discipline, physique, and weapons are the admiration of European critics. Out in Tokio Bay the smart white hulls of gunboats, lying at anchor, represent a navy whose creation has forcibly stirred the national ardour, and which is destined in the future to be no mean factor in the politics of the Pacific. Finally, after a twenty years' travail, Japan

THE JAPANESE HOUSES OF PARLIAMENT AT TOKIO

has given birth to a Parliamentary Constitution; and an unpretentious but roomy temporary structure, built of wood, like its predecessor which was burnt down in 1891, and with no trace of native art or architecture about it, accommodates the nominees of royalty or the representatives of the people, who, in the two Chambers, created by the Constitution of February 1889, and respectively entitled the House of Peers and the House of Representatives, constitute the Imperial Diet of Japan, and are swiftly introducing her people to the amenities of Parliamentary existence—obstruction within the Chamber, platform oratory out of doors—to the phenomena of Radical and Progressive parties, and to the time-honoured *palaestra* of begging and refusing supplies.[1]

In the five years of its existence, since its first meeting in November 1890, the Japanese Diet has passed through eight sessions and four General Elections. The two Houses meet in Chambers identical in size and design, almost the only difference being the presence of the Imperial throne behind the President's

The Diet.

[1] The Japanese Diet approximates more closely to the Prussian than to any other European or foreign model. The House of Peers is partly hereditary, partly nominated, and partly elected. Under the first heading come the Imperial Princes and the higher nobility sitting in their own right; the second category is composed of persons nominated by the Emperor for meritorious services to the State, or for erudition. The members of both these classes sit for life. Under the third heading are included the bulk of the peerage, sitting only for a term of seven years, and consisting of a number of counts, viscounts, and barons, elected by their own orders, and of representatives of the various provinces, returned, subject to the approbation of the Emperor, by small electoral bodies composed only of the highest taxpayers. The House of Peers, thus constituted, contains at the present time 270 members. The Lower House, which contains 300 members, and sits for four years, being bound to assemble at least once every year for a session of three months, is wholly elective, and is composed of the representatives of the principal prefectures and towns, returned in the proportion of one to every 128,000 of the people, upon a taxpaying, residential, and age franchise, the qualification for electors being the possession of land of the taxable value of $600, or of an annual income of $1000, a twelve months' residence, and the minimum age of twenty-five.

chair in the House of Peers. Their ground-plan has been borrowed from that of the bulk of foreign Legislative Chambers, the seats and desks of the members being ranged in the arc of a circle fronting a raised platform, upon which are the presidential chair, the speaker's tribune, the desk of the official reporters, and—a speciality of the Japanese Diet—on either side of this centre a row of seats occupied by the Ministers or delegated officials of the various departments, who are in the Chamber, yet not of it, and who sit there not compulsorily, but of their own option, and without votes, to defend their departments, to make speeches, or answer questions.[1] The Japanese appear to have acquired with characteristic facility the external features of Parliamentary conduct. They make excellent speeches, frequently of great length, and marked by graces of style as well as by quickness of reasoning. On the whole, considering how immature is the Lower House, and how inevitably, as I shall presently explain, it is by its constitution afflicted with the vices of an irresponsible Opposition, it succeeded till lately in conducting its operations with a

---

[1] The merely optional attendance of ministers in the Lower House has excited an already perceptible irritation among the champions of Parliamentary omnipotence and ministerial responsibility. For instance, the published Report of the Proceedings during the session of 1892-93 contained the following interesting passages. A motion was made by a private member, and was carried, that the President be asked to inquire when the Cabinet Ministers could be in their places. Subsequently, the Government replied, with some curtness, that ministers having the power to attend whenever they pleased, there was no necessity for members to put themselves to the trouble of asking them. On a later occasion a member said he believed that some of the ministers were in an anteroom, and requested that a secretary might be sent to see, as in that case he desired to make an urgency motion. Finally the urgency motion, so moved, was carried, on the ground that the Cabinet had ignored its responsibility to the Emperor, the country, and the Diet. The main reason, other than constitutional law and practice, for the absence of ministers, is that the House of Peers meets between 10 and 11 A.M., and the House of Representatives at 1.15 P.M., i.e. at hours when the ministers are at work in their offices.

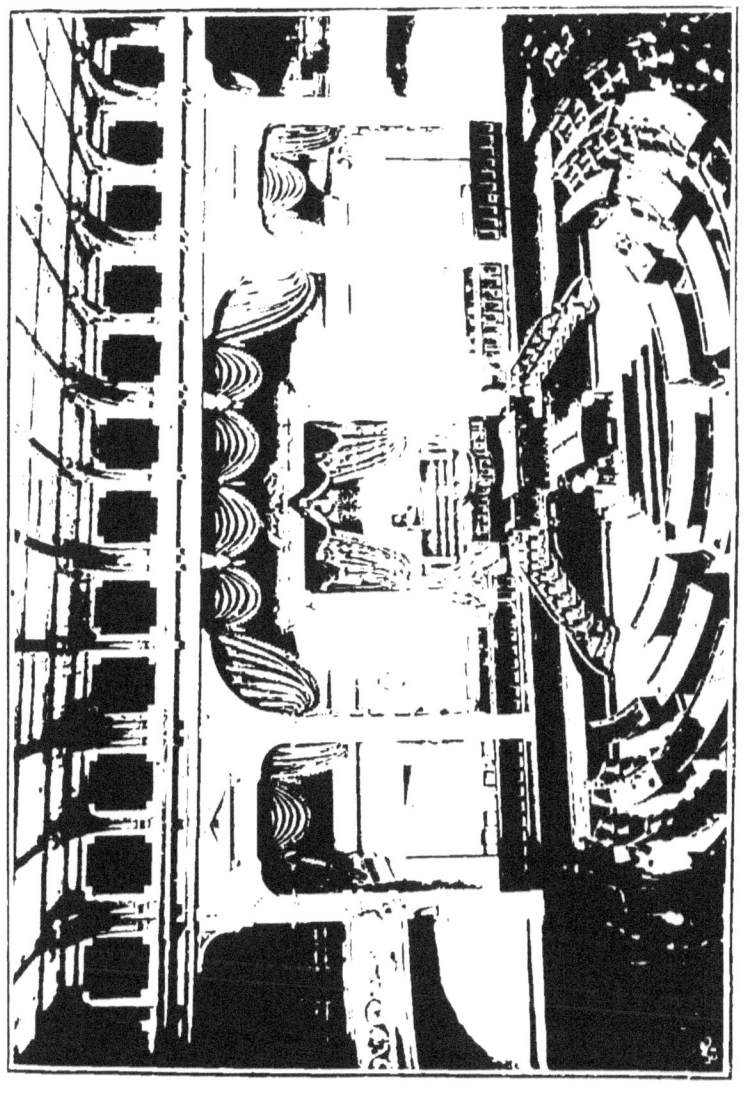

JAPANESE HOUSE OF PEERS

creditable decorum. Very full and accurate reports of the speeches are published by a Government staff of reporters, whose stenographic attainments are on a par with the most highly-trained experts of Europe or America; and a condensed version of the debates in English appears in the columns of the *Japan Daily Mail* from the able pen of its well-known editor, Captain Brinkley.

The new Parliamentary *régime* has developed a prodigious mushroom growth of native journals, few enjoying at all an extensive circulation, but each attached to the creed of some party or section, or inspired by some leader. In this way is being manufactured, with almost bewildering haste, a body of public opinion whose movements it is impossible to forecast, and with which Japanese statesmen already find it difficult to grapple. In the country we read of political clubs, of large meetings held in theatres and public places, of eloquent speeches, of cheering audiences, of the virtues and the wickedness of public men; and we realise that in Japan, as elsewhere, Demos, having found belated articulation, is repeating, for the comfort of the scientific historian, the familiar and venerable accents.

Public opinion.

There are other evidences that Japan is in the bondage of a universal law. Though the level of political intelligence in the Chamber is reasonably high, it does not appear that that of character or prestige is equally so. The attraction of a salary (for each member of both Houses[1] receives a compulsory yearly allowance of $800, equivalent at the present rate of exchange to less than £100 a year—no inconsiderable income in Japan) is

Parliamentary symptoms.

[1] Except the *ex officio* and hereditary Peers, *i.e.* the Princes and Marquises. The Imperial Princes are in receipt of personal grants from the Emperor; but the remaining Princes and Marquises have no salaries, and are in some cases poor.

not believed to add much to the popularity of a political career, since it is estimated that, though a member receives $800 annually, he has to spend $2000 at least, and since, also, the strongest discredit attaches, theoretically, to any suspicion of pecuniary motives. But the system of education organised after the fall of Feudalism—a system based on the aspiration of bridging, with all possible rapidity, the gulf that centuries of isolation had produced in Japanese knowledge—proved disproportionate to the practical needs of the nation, and called into existence a set of youths who regarded official and political life as the only sphere befitting their superior attainments. From the ranks of this class there has gradually been formed a numerous body of professional politicians, who find in platform and Parliamentary publicity a compensation for the closed doors of rank or office. These individuals are in a position of perpetual freedom and no responsibility; they can enjoy the luxury of attacking and paralysing every Government in turn; and, whilst by their votes they can neither form nor oust a Ministry, they can fetter its limbs with any number of Lilliputian cords. The predominance of this class at first deterred many of the older and more influential men from offering themselves for election; but there are signs that their reluctance is yielding to the necessities of the situation. It may be said, indeed, that the Parliamentary experiment is being watched by the more stable elements of the community from a suspicious though narrowing distance, and that a sense of national obligation to the highest duties of citizenship has not yet been at all widely aroused.

At the same time, charges of Government nepotism and electoral tyranny are freely bandied about. It is alleged that the Imperial nominations to Life-peerages, which are reserved by the Constitution for the

Rocks ahead.

reward of distinguished public service or erudition, are distributed among Ministerial adherents. At the General Election early in 1892 official interference appears to have been openly and flagrantly exercised. At least, such was the declared opinion of both houses of the Diet; for, whilst the Lower House only failed to pass by three votes a motion for a memorial to the Throne, declaring that in the elections administrative officials had wantonly perverted the authority of their office by tempting and inveigling voters or by resorting to force for their compulsion—and seeking to fix the responsibility upon the Government—a motion which, if carried, would have amounted to a direct direct vote of censure — both Houses passed by large majorities a representation to the Government urging them to punish the implicated officials; and the new Cabinet so far accepted the instruction as to dismiss five of these offenders from their posts. The General Elections of 1892 and 1894 were also distinguished by a good deal of rioting, and by a notable percentage of broken heads. We may detect similar reproductions, as yet in miniature, of Western forms, in the commencement of an agitation for the reduction of the franchise, which is now based upon a high assessment to direct taxation; while the *minimum* age limit of members of Parliament—viz. thirty years—implies a mistrust of precocious genius which is naturally distasteful to the self-conceit of young Japan.

None of these 'Rocks ahead,' however, can be compared for seriousness with the main question of the relations of the Chamber with the Government, which reproduce in a different but not less acute form the controversial *impasse* that is from time to time presented in England, not between the House of Commons and the Ministry, but between a Radical majority

<small>The Ministers and Parliament.</small>

in the House of Commons and a Conservative majority in the House of Lords. Japan, though governed by party men, is not blessed or cursed with party government. The Ministers in Japan, like the President's Cabinet in America, are the nominees and servants of the Emperor. They are not responsible to the Diet, and can remain in office as long as the Sovereign honours them with his confidence. But whereas in America a majority hostile to the Executive in both Houses is a phenomenon extremely rare in occurrence, and certain to be terminated in a short period of time, in Japan there is no *a priori* reason why such a situation should not exist in the first place, or be indefinitely prolonged. The theory of the Japanese Constitution, therefore, being the rule of a Government legislating through two Chambers, but not responsible to either, and treating their representations with comparative indifference, it may readily be understood that the popular Chamber at any rate, which rests solely upon election, though on a narrow franchise, becomes an almost automatic machine of opposition. There is a more or less rough subdivision of parties, with supposed supporters or adversaries of the Government. But these do not in either or any case sit in groups; nor can their votes be relied upon with any certainty, the 'Below the gangway' attitude being as popular in Tokio as it is in Northampton. The largest combination in the House of 1892 only numbered 96 out of a total of 300; and the two main sections of the Radical party are irreconcilably opposed. So far the Japanese House of Representatives has rendered itself as disagreeable to successive Governments as it could, obstructing their measures, defeating their budgets, and generally betraying an attitude that might have been studied in Irish academies. Nor can I imagine a more fruitful occupation for the student, be he partial or prejudiced, of representative

JAPANESE HOUSE OF REPRESENTATIVES

institutions, than a perusal of the proceedings of the Lower
House of the Japanese Diet during its last six sessions.
There will be much to interest and inform him; some
things to reassure; but not a little to dispirit and dismay.

At the time of my visit in September 1892, a new
Ministry had recently assumed the seals of office, and as I

MARQUIS ITO

revise these pages (1895) is still in power. Count Ito, the
Minister President, or Prime Minister, is probably the best-
known Japanese statesman outside his own country;
the adventurous exploit of his early career, when,
with his life-long friend and colleague Count
Inouye, he was smuggled in disguise on board an English

The Minis-
try of All
the Talents.

vessel for conveyance to England, there to study the manners and institutions of the West, being as familiar to most foreigners as is the part which he subsequently played in the Restoration, and as a pioneer in the evolution of Modern Japan. In his own country his experience, his tact, and his individual responsibility for the new Parliamentary Constitution,[1] render him the most respected and influential of Japanese public men. Already once Prime Minister and President of the Privy Council, and the first President of the House of Peers, he now returned after an interval in which he had seen other Ministers come and go in the preliminary flux consequent upon a new order of things, in order to mould into durable shape the offspring of his own political creation, and to endeavour to give something like stability to the administration of his country. With him were associated in the Cabinet his old friend Count Inouye, a former Minister for Foreign Affairs, and, perhaps, the most daring and original of Japanese statesmen;[2] Count Yamagata, himself a former Premier, to whom was entrusted the portfolio of Justice;[3] and Viscount Mutsu, a travelled and highly-accomplished statesman, who had represented his country at Washington before being transferred to the Foreign Office.[4] The only public man of the

[1] Count Ito has himself published a learned commentary on the Japanese Constitution, which has been translated into English and is published in Tokio. Since the war he has been made a Marquis.

[2] After the preliminary successes of Japan in the recent war, Count Inouye was sent in the autumn of 1894 to Korea to organise the new Government, and to superintend the introduction of the so-called reforms. The experience of a year's dictatorship has left him a wiser, and probably a sadder, man. But he is still engaged upon the hopeless task.

[3] Count Yamagata, with the rank of Field-Marshal was invested with supreme command of the Japanese forces in Korea after the victory of Ping-yang in September 1894, and subsequently led the army corps that invaded Manchuria. He was afterwards made a Marquis.

[4] In earlier life Viscount Mutsu was implicated in the Satsuma Rebellion, and was sentenced to ten years' imprisonment, before being pardoned and released.

very first rank who was outside the new ministry was Count Okuma, the author of the famous attempt at Treaty Revision that culminated in an attempt upon his life, and who, for no very well ascertained reason other than that he is the acknowledged leader of the Progressionist party in the House of Representatives, was supposed to be more or less in opposition. The new Government might almost claim to be a Ministry of All the Talents; and, undoubtedly, the summons of Count Ito by the Emperor upon the fall of the Matsukata Cabinet in the summer of 1892, and the composition of his Administration, had excited the liveliest satisfaction in political circles in Japan. A few caustic censures on Clan government scarcely broke the general consensus, on the one hand, of congratulation that the true leaders had at length consented to lead, on the other hand of judgment held in suspense until they had shown of what stuff they were made. I enjoyed the pleasure on several occasions of meeting and conversing on the political situation with Counts Ito and Inouye, and with Viscount Mutsu; and a foreigner may perhaps be allowed without impertinence to compliment the country that can produce such public men.

The question of the hour was the attitude to be adopted by the Government towards Parliament when it should meet that body in November. In the Session of 1891-92, the Budget had been so systematically opposed that it was never passed at all, and recourse had to be made to an article in the Constitution, admitting in such a case (with wise foresight of the idiosyncrasies of Japanese character) of the readoption of the estimates of the previous year.[1] The repetition of such a rebuff could

Expectations.

[1] It is amusing, in the light of what has actually happened, to read Count Ito's sanguine commentary upon this article of the Constitution (No. LXXI.): 'When the Diet has not voted on the Budget, or the Budget has not been brought into actual existence, the result will be, in extreme cases,

not lightly be endured by the strongest Government that modern Japan could produce; and public opinion exhausted itself in surmise as to the probable bearing of Count Ito and his colleagues towards this obstreperous nursling. How was it to be controlled—by a policy of cuffs, or by a programme of caresses? Should the Ministry rule in despite of the Chamber, or should it make terms with the latter, and treat it with that assumption of deference that is so grateful to injured pride? The answer that was returned to these questions by the experiences of the two Sessions of 1892-93 and 1893 sheds so luminous a ray both upon the internal polity of modern Japan, and upon the dangers by which it is threatened, that I make no apology for referring to them.

The actual facts were as follows. The Government met Parliament with a programme whose two chief items were a scheme for the reassessment of the Land-tax—a time-honoured grievance in Japan ever since the Restoration [1]—which scheme would involve a reduction of $3,750,000 in the revenue so raised; and a plan for the increase of the Navy by

Session of 1892-3.

the destruction of the national existence; and, in ordinary ones, the paralysis of the machinery of the Administration. *But such a state of affairs being possible only in countries where democratic principles are taken as the basis of their political institutions, it is incompatible with a polity like ours.*'

[1] After the Revolution in 1868, the Japanese farmers, who were in theory though not in practice tenants-at-will, received certificates of ownership, with freedom of transfer and sale. Henceforward they paid their rent as a direct tax to the Government, which had resumed possession of the national property. Since the days of the Shogunate the tax has been reduced by one-half, while the proportion which it bears to the entire revenue has largely diminished, owing to the increase of receipts from other sources of taxation. Nevertheless the one great domestic question in Japan is the reform of the land-tax, promised by every Government and introduced in every Session. The assessment is said to be both obsolete and unequal; the State as rent-collector is not prone to mercy; and the tax being paid, not, as formerly, in kind, but in cash, is seriously affected by the fluctuations in the price of grain.

the expenditure of $16,000,000, to be spread over seven years, the appropriation required for these two purposes being raised by an increase of the tobacco-tax, the *saké*-tax, and the income-tax. From the very first the House showed its temper in the most uncompromising fashion. The two sections of the Opposition, the Kaishinto or Progressionists, under Count Okuma, and the Jiyuto or extreme Radicals, under Count Itagaki, gleefully joined hands in order to embarrass the Government. The new taxes were refused; a private bill for the immediate reduction of the land-tax, independently of reassessment, was carried by the Lower House; even the Upper Chamber passed a representation in favour of the reduction of all official salaries (with the exception of those in the military, naval, diplomatic, and consular departments) from 12 per cent. to 7 per cent. of the total revenue, and of the dismissal of superfluous officials; and when the Budget was finally introduced in the House of Representatives its items were ruthlessly cut down, wholesale reductions were made in official salaries, and the appropriations for the new shipbuilding programme were absolutely refused. Three times did the inexorable Opposition send back the amended Budget to the Government; three times the Government refused to accept it. Then came the crisis. The leader of the Opposition moved the adoption of a representation to the Throne, which was tantamount to a vote of want of confidence in the Ministry. But no sooner had he opened his speech than the President had placed in his hands an Imperial Rescript, ordering (under the terms of an article in the Constitution) a special adjournment of the Diet for fifteen days. An attempt at compromise in the interval resulted in failure; and when the House met again, the same resolution was moved, and in spite of a temperate and conciliatory speech from the Prime

Minister was carried by a majority of 181 to 103. Three days later an Imperial message was read out in both Chambers, in which the Emperor pointed out, in language of reproachful solemnity, that the spectacle of discord presented by the Parliamentary conflict was one by which the spirits of his Ancestors were likely to be much disturbed;[1] and that to end the crisis and recall the nation to its duties in the matter of the national defences, where 'a single day's neglect might involve a century's regret,' he proposed to surrender, during the space of six years, one-tenth of his Civil List, or the sum of $300,000 annually; at the same time directing all military and civil officials to contribute a similar proportion for the same period.[2] To this Rescript a loyal reply was voted; and a Committee of the Lower House was appointed to confer with the Government. The latter practically gave way on the main points, pledging themselves to sweeping administrative reforms, and to a large reduction both of officials and of official salaries, as well as to special reforms in the Naval Department. The Budget was then passed, and the crisis was temporarily at an end. From the conflict the Government had only emerged

[1] The belief in an immemorial antiquity of the Imperial Throne, and an immense and ceremonious respect for the Imperial Ancestors, supply an archaic framework in which the brand-new Japanese Constitution sometimes looks strangely out of place. The Preamble of the latter begins with the words: 'Having, by virtue of the glories of Our Ancestors, ascended the throne of a lineal succession unbroken for ages eternal.' Article 1. repeats the same consolatory fiction, while projecting it into an endless future: 'The Empire of Japan shall be reigned over and governed by a line of Emperors unbroken for ages eternal.' In the Imperial oath, taken at the promulgation of the new Constitution, the Emperor said: 'That we have been so fortunate in our reign, in keeping with the tendency of the times, as to accomplish this work, we owe to the glorious spirits of the Imperial Founder of our House, and of our other Imperial Ancestors.'

[2] According to Article x. of the Constitution, 'The Emperor determines the organisation of the different branches of the Administration, and the salaries of all civil and military officials, and appoints and dismisses the same.'

by the personal intervention of the Emperor, and by a capitulation on many important points to their adversaries. In the compromise the latter were the real victors.

In the ensuing Session, which opened in November 1893, the crisis arrived with even greater rapidity, and demanded a more drastic solution. No sooner had the Diet assembled than the Lower House proceeded to pass, by a large majority, a vote of want of confidence in its Speaker or President, on the scarcely concealed ground that, though originally appointed by the Radicals as a Radical partisan, he had falsified expectations by showing an unbecoming inclination to favour the Government. The President, who had been elected for four years, declined to resign; and the House accordingly voted an address to the Throne on the subject and adjourned. In the end this particular quarrel, the importation of the Emperor into which was a symptom of the advanced state of Parliamentary disorganisation, terminated in the expulsion of the recalcitrant official by the appointment of a successor in his place. Meanwhile the House of Representatives, having, so to speak, tasted blood, proceeded to gratify an even more dangerous appetite. Unable to wreak that personal vengeance upon the Government which a majority of its members desired, they addressed the Throne on two subjects—(1) on Official Discipline and the Status of Ministers, practically demanding the dismissal of the Cabinet; and (2) on the strict enforcement of the Foreign Treaties—a part of the petty and vexatious policy recently instituted by the Opposition in order to embarrass the Government and to force Treaty Revision upon their own terms. After this step the sittings of the House were again suspended; and Count Ito, in presenting the address to the Throne, requested, as a matter of form, to be relieved of the discharge of

Session of 1893.

duties which a majority of the Chamber were bent upon rendering impossible.

A few days later the Emperor replied, in a statesmanlike Rescript, declining to dismiss his Ministers, a prerogative which, he remarked, appertained, not to the Diet, but to the Crown; and refusing to depart from the policy hitherto pursued towards foreigners, which had been liberal and progressive. Anything tending to interrupt the consummation of that policy would be contrary to the Imperial wishes. Retrograde and vexatious proposals such as those suggested would alienate Foreign Powers, and were incompatible with the spirit of civilisation. Upon the reassembling of the House, these views were enforced in a singularly temperate and dignified speech by the Foreign Minister, Viscount Mutsu; which however did not prevent the occurrence of violent scenes, and the use of opprobrious and disgraceful language. The Diet was forthwith prorogued for a fortnight; but it was obvious that a repetition of adjournments was a palliative that had already lost its efficacy; and, on the last day but one of the year appeared an Imperial Decree dissolving the Diet. Like many European forerunners, the Japanese Government had realised that the only purgative for a factious and discredited Parliament is an appeal to the people. Simultaneously they asserted and strengthened the authority of the Executive by dissolving the Great Japan Society —an anti-foreign Association that had been formed for the purpose of agitating against the Revision of the Treaties except upon terms inequitable to the foreigner—and prohibited political societies.

The progress of the General Election, which lasted for two months, was attended with scenes of violence and even bloodshed, in which the *soshi* or professional rowdies, who are ready, for a consideration, to let out their services to either party in Japan, played a prominent part. On March 1 the elections took place, the result being that the Government failed to better their condition, the aggregate of the various Opposition parties being sufficient to render them impotent in the Diet, and to secure for Japan a continuance of those constitutional struggles which, at a moment when all parties should combine to lay firm the bases of the new polity, threaten to jeopardise its very existence, and to convince the world that the Japanese are at present in too featherheaded and wayward a mood to be able to work out even their own salvation. When the new session opened in May the Ministry was vehemently assailed, its bills were rejected, and a vote of want of confidence in the Government was within five votes of being carried. Realising that with such a Chamber legislation, or even government, was impossible, Count Ito again advised the Emperor to dissolve the Diet. And thus, for the second time within a single year, Japan was plunged in the throes of a General Election. The outbreak of war in the summer of 1894, and the sense of national patriotism which it aroused in no ordinary degree, had the effect for a time of stifling these dissensions; and at the General Election the Government strengthened its position, though still remaining in a position of numerical inferiority to the opposing groups. Now that the war is over, the constitutional volcano may be expected again to become active. *General Elections of 1894.*

These events are interesting, and I have narrated them, less as incidents in a Parliamentary drama than because of the explanation that lies behind. They are symptoms of the threefold problem by which Japanese statesmen and the Japanese nation are now confronted, and which will not, in all likelihood, be *Real points at issue.*

solved without a great strain, if not actual jeopardy to the Constitution itself. The principles involved, or the questions at issue, are these: the ancestral conflict between democratic and oligarchical ideas in government; the part to be played in a so-called Constitutional *régime* by the Sovereign; and the relation of ministerial responsibility to a Parliamentary system. They are problems about which European States have been fighting (and in some cases are still fighting) for hundreds of years; and now that our own analogous conflicts are for the most part over, we may contemplate, with the sententious satisfaction of maturity, the almost identical struggles of impetuous youth.

In refusing the appropriations asked for the shipbuilding programme in 1893, the Opposition speakers were careful to explain that it was from no stint of patriotism or disbelief in the need of a powerful navy that they took that step. The administration of the Naval Department they held to be corrupt and bad, but, as one speaker said, 'the head and front of all the reforms needed was to free the navy from the dominant influence of the Satsuma clan.' On another occasion another speaker remarked: 'A man could not become head of the Home Office, or of the Railway Bureau, unless he were of Choshiu origin, or head of the War Department, or the Navy, unless he were of the Satsuma clan.' These observations introduce us to a curious feature in the Japanese system, rarely noticed by European writers, but nevertheless exercising a predominant and conservative force in the midst of a welter of change, viz. the continued dominion of the old Clan system, which has prevailed in Japan ever since, just as it had done for centuries before, the Revolution. Ieyasu, the founder of the last or Tokugawa family of Shoguns in 1603, was practically the head of a northern confederacy,

1. Clan government.

which defeated and held in subordination the clans of the south and south-west. Two and a half centuries later the decline of the Tokugawa Shogunate gave to these the chance of a long-postponed revenge. Raising the cry of the restoration of the legitimate Sovereign and the expulsion of foreigners, they rallied around themselves all the disaffected and patriotic elements in the country, and carried their purpose. Satsuma, Choshiu, Tosa, and Hizen were the four principal clans concerned in this successful revolution, which re-established the ascendency of the South over the North. In their hands the new government, though outwardly based on European ideas, was in reality administered on the old Japanese system, namely, by a territorial clique. The Satsuma rebellion showed that one great section of the victorious clan cared only for the old system, and not at all for the new principles. It was defeated, and the Progressive policy prevailed. Nevertheless, under a Western exterior the victors have always clung tightly to the traditional methods, and have retained an almost unchallenged supremacy, alike in the formation of Cabinets and the distribution of patronage. In the old days, no doubt, this was due to the importance of powerful princes or nobles backed by formidable aggregations of armed men. It is now the triumph, not of territorial influence, but of a civil and military hierarchy, largely organised upon the privilege of birth. The army, and still more the navy, which in the background play a very important part in the politics of modern Japan, and which are the real mainstay of the Government against the subversive tendencies of Parliamentary majorities or demagogic Radicalism, are principally officered by men belonging to the chief clans; the present Cabinet is mainly recruited from the same sources; and the cry of the Opposition is to a large extent well founded, that to be a clansman is to possess the key to the doors of official promotion.

In reality the conflict is only a Japanese version of the familiar duel between a powerful and disciplined oligarchy and an ambitious but as yet imperfectly organised democracy. It is essentially the same historical phenomenon that was presented by the contest of the Gracchi with the Senate in the expiring century of the Roman Republic; and that was reproduced in our own country in the popular struggle against what is commonly called Whig ascendency in the first quarter of the present century. The Cabinet of Count Ito is in English political terminology a Whig Cabinet, composed of members of the great Whig families, the Cavendishes and Russells of modern Japan (though without their pedigrees), and sustained by the patronage which the Japanese equivalents to rotten boroughs afford. The system possesses that desperate tenacity which is the result of inherited ability and conscious worth. It has the authority which prescription and possession unite to confer, and it is undoubtedly in conformity with the history and the most cherished traditions of the people. A long time may yet elapse before it disappears; but ultimately, in face of an opposition which complains with some truth that it is being deluded by the mere semblance of liberty and outward form of change, it seems destined to perish, as did the influence of the Whig oligarchy in England.

Oligarchy v. Democracy.

It will have been noticed that in each of the three Parliamentary sessions of which I have spoken, the majority of the Lower House, profiting by the liberty conceded by an article in the Constitution,[1] addressed frequent representations to the Throne,

2. Position of the Sovereign.

---

[1] Article XLIX. 'Both Houses of the Imperial Diet may respectively present addresses to the Emperor.'

in a sense hostile to the Government of the day; and further, that in the Session of 1892-93 a settlement of the political deadlock was only obtained by the direct intervention of the Emperor. This habit of erecting the Sovereign into an outside court of appeal against the Executive is both in open divergence from the spirit, even though permitted by the letter, of the Constitution, and, if persisted in, cannot fail to cause trouble in the future. Count Ito in his Commentary on the Constitution evidently never contemplated such an abuse of the prerogative of memorial when he thus explained its application :—

'The meaning of the word "addresses" includes the reply to an Imperial speech in the Diet, addresses of congratulation or of condolence, representations of opinion, petitions and the like. In transmitting the writing, proper forms of respect must be observed. The dignity of the Emperor must not be infringed by any proceeding implying coercion.'

Still more serious however in its consequences, if too frequently repeated, must be the personal descent of the Sovereign, as a sort of Attic *deus ex machina*, on to the Parliamentary stage. The Emperor cannot perpetually be extricating his Ministers from difficulty, and the Diet from a deadlock, by a surrender of part of his Civil List; nor should his interposition in the disputes of the Chambers come to be regarded as the sole possible exit from a *cul de sac*, carefully prepared in advance by an Opposition ostentatiously devoid of any sense of responsibility. The Throne occupies a very singular and unique position in the polity of modern Japan. Still enveloped in the dignity of a limitless past, and not yet wholly stripped of the halo of a once divine sanction, it stands out in the breathless turmoil of Japanese evolution as the single element of unshaken stability, the rallying-point of all parties, the common oracle of warring social and political creeds. To the Japanese the Emperor is the personification of that intense and perfervid spirit of patriotism which, alone of Eastern peoples, they appear to feel. He is identified with their beautiful islands, with their immemorial language, with their ancestral religion. He represents the triumph of no conquering race, of no alien caste, and of no compulsory creed. His forefathers created Japan for the Japanese to inhabit, and for their descendants to rule. So little in Japan are men predisposed to question the Imperial sanctity, that it may be said to be almost independent of the personality of the Sovereign. Just, however, as the Gods of Olympus, when they descended from their misty heights, were found to be men of like passions with men, and ended by becoming the personifications merely of exaggerated human attributes or lusts, so will the prestige that still clings to the Mikado's authority and name be rapidly dissipated by their employment on the battle-ground of parties or in the strife of factions. The strength and safeguard of the Throne lies in its entire severance from the political arena. For centuries, while his practical authority was a figment, the Emperor never lost his hold upon the public imagination, because of the mysterious and awe-inspiring background in which he lived. Rival combatants used his name while they fought, and his prerogatives after they had conquered. The clans rose and fell, but the Imperial power, though held in suspense, remained. Whilst this is no longer either possible or wise, yet the attitude of reserve and withdrawal is still, under a Parliamentary *régime*, the true secret of Imperial strength. The Emperor's function is to support his Cabinet, who, under the Japanese Constitution, are his own servants and nominees, and to entertain no address that brings him down, so to speak, from the throne, or that touches his prerogatives as fixed by law. Any modification or alteration of them should proceed from his own initiative, and not at the dictation of the Diet. Nor should such a course be attended by any insuperable difficulty, seeing that this is the theory of the Imperial prerogative plainly contemplated by the framers of the new Constitution, and that the latter is guarded with the peculiar jealousy attaching to a written instrument by a people who claim to see in it the embodiment of all constitutional wisdom, and who are sensible enough to recognise the danger of beginning to tamper with so delicate a fabric.

A more imminent and less easily soluble problem is that presented by the open combat between the Executive and the Parliamentary majority. It is obvious from recent experience that the Government, except under the strain of national danger, has little hold over the Diet, and but slight control over public opinion. Weekly it has seen itself flouted, insulted, and crippled by a combination of parties powerless to eject it, and incapable of replacing it if ejected. The Address to the Throne presented by the majority of the House of Representatives in February 1893 contained the following definition of the situation and account of its origin :—

_{3. Ministerial responsibility.}

'Humble reflection leads your Majesty's servants to conclude that the chief object of representative government is to promote concord between high and low, and to secure their co-operation in aid of the State. Hence there can be no profounder or greater desideratum than that the Legislature and the Administration should occupy towards each other an attitude of thorough sincerity, and should achieve the reality of harmonious co-operation. But ever since the opening of the Diet, the Legislature and the Administration have been wanting in concord, all their projects have been impeded, all their capabilities marred, so that in the sequel they have failed to secure for the country the benefits of progressive development in concert with the advance of the age.

Your Majesty's servants acknowledge that the insufficiency of their own zeal is in part responsible for these things, but they believe that the chief cause is to be sought in the Cabinet's failure to discharge its functions. . . . The origin of the friction between the Government and the Diet, and of the discord between officials and people, extends to a remote time. Unless accumulated abuses be removed, and the reality of representative government achieved, the nation will lapse into a state of decline. . . . Your Majesty's servants gave expression to the desire of the people, but the Cabinet utterly declined to listen, and thus prevented us from discharging our legislative function of consent. Such is not the proper course to adopt in adjusting the finances of the Empire and carrying out the administration of the State. Your Majesty's servants apprehend that, so long as they are associated with such a Cabinet, it will be impossible for them to discharge the trust reposed in them by your Majesty above, and to give expression to the desires of the people below.'

Here is a sufficiently plain statement, though couched in somewhat circumlocutory language, of the demand by the popular Chamber for Party Government upon the accepted European lines. Such a demand is wholly inconsistent with both the spirit and the letter of the new Constitution. Ministerial responsibility is there defined as existing towards the Emperor alone, and is thus explained by Count Ito in his Commentary :—

'Who is it except the Sovereign, that can appoint, dismiss, and punish a Minister of State? The appointment and dismissal of them having been included by the Constitution in the sovereign power of the Emperor, it is only a legitimate consequence, that the power of deciding as to the responsibility of Ministers is withheld from the Diet. But the Diet may put questions to the Ministers and demand open answers from them before the public, and it may also present addresses to the Sovereign setting forth its opinions. Moreover, although the Emperor reserves to himself in the Constitution the right of appointing his Ministers at his pleasure, in making an appointment the susceptibilities of the public mind must also be taken into consideration. This may be regarded as an indirect method of controlling the responsibility of Ministers.'

What the 'susceptibilities of the public mind' demand in Japan is not however a remote and indirect voice in the appointment of Ministers, but a direct voice in their dismissal; and the chasm that separates the two parties is one that no concessions on either side appear likely to fill. Prior to the opening of the second Session of 1893 the Government testified their recognition of this fact by publishing an announcement that until a party (not an accidental or momentary combination of parties) appeared in the House with an absolute majority on its side, they would neither surrender their power nor share it with any section, however influential; and that they would regard no vote of censure or rejection of their proposals, but would remain in office until men appeared with authority to take it from them.

This bold acceptance of the challenge to war à outrance might seem to some an impolitic defiance of the enemy; and in any country where the Parliamentary system was more developed, or political training more widely diffused, it might be the premonitory symptom of ultimate defeat. In Japan itself there exists a strong party who see in the so-called popular demand a movement which will not lose, but will, on the contrary, gain force until it has secured its object and revolutionised the Constitution. But there are opposing considerations that may justify a more sanguine forecast. First of these is the respect, before spoken of, for the written Constitution. Further, the prominent men in Japan are almost unanimously in favour of the existing law, and the cohesion of the Clan and Court party will not easily be broken down. Thirdly, the Japanese are as yet too ignorant of Party Government to be able to work any such system as is demanded without risk of total collapse; the Opposition is so split up by personal animosities as to render the creation of a working majority out of its ranks highly improbable; whilst the

The issue.

Radical party in particular is so far much too wanting in dignity or prestige to justify the granting of concessions that might transform the intemperate filibusters of the ballot-box and the tribune into portfolio politicians. Finally, the analogy of foreign States suggests that a *modus vivendi* will ultimately be established in the Chamber itself, by an organised Government party less amenable than now to the shifting currents of popular caprice. In the meanwhile, however, we may expect a period of political fermentation, and even of chaos, by which such an issue may be for some time retarded, and from which the Constitution itself may not escape unscathed.

Among the respects in which the advance of modern Japan has been most rapid, though until the recent war scarcely appreciated by foreigners, is the development of the military and naval forces of the Empire. Aspiring to play a predominant part in the politics of Eastern Asia, she has spared no effort and shrunk from no sacrifice to place herself in the matter of armed equipment upon a level with her possible competitors. The Japanese are born sailors; and a country with so extensive and vulnerable a seaboard could in no case afford to neglect its maritime defences. About their Navy the patriotism of the Japanese is as easily aroused as is our own in Great Britain; and although the administration of the Naval Department is the subject of acrimonious party conflict, there is no disagreement upon the broad Imperial policy of a largely increased naval outlay. When in 1893 the strength of the Japanese Navy amounted to 40 vessels and 50,000 tons, and the Government laid down the standard of national requirement as 120,000 tons, there were some among the extreme Radical party who would have preferred to see this figure raised to 150,000. The sums contributed by the Emperor in the crisis of 1893, and ordered to be deducted from the salaries of all military and civil officials, were specially ear-marked from the start for the construction of new battleships of the first rank. An order amounting to £2,000,000 was placed in England; and now that the war is over, it is in contemplation very largely to increase that branch of the national forces to which in the main Japan owed her decisive victory; and Count Ito's boast to me that the Japanese fleet was the next strongest to that of China in the Northern Pacific, and was far more serviceable for action, was more than justified by events. It is largely by the offer of the alliance of her Navy that Japan hopes in the future to control the balance of power in the Far East. Simultaneously the maritime defences of the country, which have been executed under the superintendence of a distinguished Italian engineer, have reached a formidable state of proficiency; and we are not likely to have any 'Shimonoseki bombardment' in the future.

Not less satisfactory or admirable is the spectacle presented by the reorganised Army of modern Japan. With a mobilised peace-footing of between 50,000 and 60,000 men, with a first reserve of 89,000, and a second reserve of 104,500, armed, equipped, and drilled according to the highest standard of nineteenth-century requirement, and moreover economically and honestly administered, the Japanese Army need not shrink from the test of comparison, in point of efficiency, with the forces of European States. Lest, however, my appreciation should be attributed to the uninstructed partiality of the civilian eye, let me quote an English military authority, Colonel E. G. Barrow, who visited Japan shortly before the war. Confessing that he was 'fairly astonished by the marvellous picture which military Japan presents,' he amplifies this statement as follows:—[1]

[1] *United Service Magazine*, September 1893.

'The officers of the Japanese Army have mostly passed through the Imperial Military School, and may therefore be held to be of much the same stamp professionally as the generality of officers of European armies. The barracks are two-storeyed wooden buildings, with airy, well-ventilated rooms, and scrupulously clean. The store-rooms are, however, the really striking feature of the Japanese military system. In completeness and in arrangement there is nothing better to be found in Europe. . . . As regards the troops, the infantry are very good- better even than some European infantry I could name; the artillery good, or at least fair; and the cavalry indifferent. This is scarcely to be wondered at. The Japanese are not an equestrian race; their horse possesses neither of the charging qualities of speed or weight; and, finally, the physical aspect of the country is not one that could ever hope for the development of good cavalry. . . . The army is not a paper sham, but a complete living organisation, framed on the best models, and as a rule thoroughly adapted to the requirements of the country. . . . Here we have an army of 75,000 men, capable of being trebled in war, which costs only about $17,000,000, or, approximately, £2,500,000. . . . The Japanese soldier has discipline, perseverance, and great endurance. Has he valour also?'

To the latter question no one who is acquainted with the many striking pages in Japanese history can hesitate to return an affirmative answer. There is no nation in the world, of anything like comparable antiquity, whose annals exhibit a more brilliant record of personal valour and patriotic devotion. For over a thousand years there have been sung in Japan some verses that fitly express the high ideal of feudal and national loyalty that has always been entertained by the Japanese soldier :—

> 'Is my path upon the ocean yonder?
> Let the waves my shipwrecked body hide!
> Must I over plain and mountain wander?
> Let my slain corpse 'neath the grass abide!
>   Where'er I cease,
>   For me no peace
>   Of last release,
> I shall perish by my liege-lord's side!'

Nor could any people have enacted the tragedy of the Forty-seven Ronins, or maintained for centuries the strange but heroic code of honour involved in *hara kiri*, without possessing a superlative though misdirected form of human courage.[1]

A still more recent work by an English military critic contains an equally discriminating but not less laudatory verdict upon the Japanese Army.[2] The author describes the cavalry as poor, for the reasons before-mentioned, but the infantry as quite excellent, the drill as smart and efficient, the armament as good, and the barrack accommodation as admirable. He supplies figures, derived from official sources, of the numerical strength of the various battalions, regiments, brigades, and divisions; and he gives the total strength of the Territorial Army and Reserves combined as 228,850 men. If his views of what the Japanese Army may be expected to do in the field of international action are in excess of all probability, his testimony to its practical efficiency as a fighting machine is sufficiently authoritative to merit quotation.

Corroborative opinion.

Finally, there is the experience of the recent war, in which, though the Japanese never encountered a serious resistance nor fought a critical battle, there is a general consensus of opinion that they displayed the highest qualities of organisation, discipline, and courage, qualities indeed which merited a more worthy foe.

[1] For many instances of such courage, *vide* A. B. Mitford's *Tales of Old Japan*. With them may be compared the comparatively recent incident that concluded the sanguinary Satsuma Rebellion in 1877. Old Saigo, with a band of devoted adherents, made his way from the East, where his army had been cut off, to his native place, Kagoshima. There, entrenched on a hill above the town, he and his men fought till they perished. When he fell, wounded, he prayed his devoted friends to cut off his head. They complied, and then committed suicide. The dead bodies were found together.

[2] *On Short Leave to Japan.* By Captain G. J. Younghusband. London, 1894. Chap. xvii.

To a sympathiser with Japan not the least gratifying among the evidences of her progress are the signs of a quite uncommon financial prosperity. Money is plentiful in the country. There is a great circulation in notes, and a large reserve in specie in the banks. The Government has a handsome surplus at its command; and, inasmuch as the bulk of the taxes are levied by fixed laws, the economies resulting from the recent administrative reforms, which have already produced an annual reduction of $8,000,000, will considerably swell this total. In consequence of the profitable year's trade in 1892, all good stocks rose in value from 20 to 30 per cent. There has further been a very rapid development of Government credit, as illustrated by the conditions of the National Debt. Bonds paying a high rate of interest have either been converted into 5 per cent. bonds or have been paid off without option of conversion. The only portion of the Debt which is still located outside of Japan is a sum of £750,000, which was raised in 1873 and will mature in 1897. Upon this 7 per cent. interest is paid in gold, equivalent to Japan to 13 per cent. on the original capital. The interest on the remainder of the Debt is paid in silver. The total internal debt amounts to $252,000,000, to the payment of principal and interest upon which $22,000,000 are applied annually. Japanese statesmen have fortunately formed a very high conception of the value both of national credit and of financial retrenchment; and the suspicion of extravagance or corruption is one that arouses an immediate *furore* in the Chamber. It is to be regretted that in their dealings with foreigners the standard of commercial morality that is commonly observed by Japanese merchants is neither so blameless in theory nor so inflexible in practice.

Finances.

As regards the Trade of Japan, I will not here reproduce statistics that may be found in Consular publications, but will merely notice certain salient characteristics. Her foreign trade has increased so rapidly that its total sterling value, which in 1892 stood at £23,800,000, is nearly double that of 1884, and five and a half times as much as that of 1867. The share in this total that is claimed by the British Empire (*i.e.* Great Britain, India, and the Colonies) is by far the largest, amounting to over £8,250,000; although these figures represent a steady recent decline, the proportion, which in 1890 was 41 per cent. of the whole, having, mainly owing to the greatly increased export of silk and tea to the United States, fallen to 35 per cent. in 1892. In shipping, however, Great Britain easily retains her predominance; the total tonnage of British vessels trading with Japan exceeding that of all other countries, including Japan itself, put together. Of the total merchandise imported into and exported from Japan in 1892, 58 per cent. was carried in British bottoms. The German proportion in the same year was 10 per cent.; while the figure that is held to justify the lofty commercial aspirations of France in the Far East was only 13 per cent.

A more remarkable development of Japanese commerce is the advance of her own manufacturing industries. Japan is rapidly becoming her own purveyor, particularly of cotton clothing. The simultaneous process is observed in her Custom Returns of a great increase in the import of raw material, and a corresponding decrease in that of manufactured goods. In 1892 she imported eleven times the quantity of raw cotton imported in 1887; while since 1888 her import of manufactured cottons has decreased 44 per cent. In the last five years her export of goods manufactured in her own looms has been quadrupled. That this process has been very much accelerated by the recent changes in Indian currency there can be no doubt. Just as India has hitherto profited in her competition with Lancashire, so will Japan now profit in her competition with Bombay. She is rapidly extending her plant, and in the course of last year had doubled her number of spindles. Especially will she profit in her export of manufactured cottons to China. Both are silver-standard countries, and in both wages are paid in silver; and when her superior proximity, her low rate of wages, and the cheapness of coal, are taken into account,[1] Manchester and Bombay alike should find in her a most formidable competitor. There is even a talk in Japan of still further stimulating this natural movement by abolishing both the import duty on raw cotton and the export duty on the manufactured article. European merchants are for the moment somewhat nonplussed by this Japanese development. But it may be pointed out to them that any falling off in foreign imports which may result from native competition should be more than compensated by the increased purchasing power of Japan in respect of foreign articles, such as machinery, which she cannot provide herself. Among the other resources which Japan is turning to good account in her industrial expansion is her coal. Japanese coal is now exported everywhere throughout the Far East, the total export having been estimated at over 1,000,000 tons in the year; it is burned on the majority of steamers between Yokohama and Singapore, and it may be said to have driven the Australian product from the Eastern market.

---

[1] The wages of a cotton operative in Japan are from 10 to 20 cents (*i.e.* 3d. to 6d.) a day. Japanese coal is delivered at the mills for 82½ (*i.e.* 6s. 3d.) a ton.

Among the questions which are much discussed, alike by foreigners and residents, and about which very contrary opinions are expressed, not merely at different times, but by different writers at the same time, is the general attitude of the Japanese people, and particularly of the rising generation, towards foreigners. It should not be inferred, because Japan has recognised that Europe is ahead of herself in many branches of knowledge and resources of civilisation, and that she must go to Germany for her guns, to France, Germany, and England for her law, to England for her railways—that she is therefore an indiscriminate admirer of that which she imitates, or that the Western man is an idol in her social pantheon. On the contrary, the more she has assimilated European excellences the more critical she has become of European defects; whilst the at times precipitate rapidity of her own advance has produced a reactionary wave, which occasionally assumes serious proportions. The existence of such a feeling is by no means surprising when we remember the forces by which it is recruited. Among these may be counted the latent Conservatism in the national character, which, though but little expressed, still smoulders with an internal combustion that, like those sudden shocks of nature that wreck the Japanese landscape, now and then breaks forth in a passionate vendetta of outrage or assassination; the inordinate vanity of the people, fostered at once by their illustrious antiquity and by the ease with which they seem to have planted themselves in the forefront of the files of time; the indiscreet rapidity with which they have been asked to swallow, almost in the same gulp, a foreign dress, a foreign language, and a foreign religion; and a consciousness of national strength that resents the suspicion of having bartered its birthright to aliens. Political in-

Attitude of Japanese towards foreigners.

cidents—a proposal of Treaty Revision on terms at all derogatory to the national dignity, the not too sensitive and sometimes brutal candour of the European Press, the resolutions passed at a meeting of foreign merchants—may excite this feeling to a white heat of fury. At other times it slumbers.

In 1891 it seemed for a time to have experienced a sharp inflammation, but afterwards to have subsided. Towards the close of 1893 it underwent a brisk revival, in consequence of the judgment of the British Supreme Court at Shanghai, reversing the decision of the inferior Court at Yokohama in the case of the collision of the P. and O. steamship *Ravenna* with the Japanese cruiser *Chishima* in Japanese waters. This judgment, which was adverse to the Japanese claims, was criticised as though it were a deliberate exhibition of foreign malevolence, directed against the expanding ambitions of Young Japan. Foreigners, including some old and well-known residents, were openly insulted in the streets of the capital, while the native police made not the slightest effort to interfere; and a sharp reminder required to be addressed to the latter of their elementary duties. Another manifestation is the boycotting of foreign manufactures, even when the corresponding native articles are of greatly inferior quality. In 1892 an attempt was actually made upon the life of a well-known native merchant, because he had advocated the use of foreign pipes for the Tokio water-works. These emotions find their chief exponents among the student class, many of whom, under the tuition of American missionaries, have imbibed American notions of democracy, and whose smattering of universal knowledge seems likely to create a considerable element of danger. Perhaps the most innocent form is the continuous dismissal of foreigners from posts in the

THE EVOLUTION OF MODERN JAPAN 47

public service, or in the employ of business firms, their places being filled by Japanese specially educated, though not uniformly fitted, for the purpose.[1] Serious though these individual ebullitions undoubtedly are, the best authorities do not seem to anticipate any very perilous developments of this phase of national resuscitation; and it may probably be regarded as the best safety-valve for humours that might otherwise require a more tempestuous outlet.

A collateral illustration of the same thoughtless and sometimes foolish patriotism is the passionate excitement displayed by the Japanese at any assertion, however extravagant or ridiculous, of the national spirit. Schoolboy patriotism. In this respect they may be termed the Frenchmen of the Far East. In the course of 1893 there occurred three illustrations of this unseasonable ardour. A young lieutenant organised a project for forming a fishing and marauding colony on one of the Kurile Islands; and when he started from Tokio with thirty volunteer companions in a number of open row-boats upon this scatterbrained quest, the populace crowded the wharves of the Sumida, and gave an ovation to the departing hero as though he were Nelson embarking at Portsmouth to take command of the Mediterranean Fleet. Presently came the retributory sequel. The lieutenant encountered a storm. Two of his boats were swamped, and seventeen of the would-be colonists were drowned. The second instance was that of a Japanese military *attaché* at St. Petersburg, who rode overland from that place to Vladivostok. When he landed in Japan he was received with as much honour as though he were Moltke returning from the Franco-German campaign. One trembles

[1] In July 1893 the total number of foreigners in the employ of the Japanese Government, which a few years ago stood at several hundreds, was only 72, of whom 33 were British, 14 Germans, 10 Americans, and 5 French.

to think what will be the fate reserved for a genuine
Japanese hero, should such a one ever appear. The third
example was even more puerile. In pursuit of a forward
policy as regards Korea, the Government was persuaded in
1892 to send a new Minister to that Court. This individual,
having insulted the King of Korea, and quarrelled with
his Ministers, was very shortly recalled ; but, owing to his
name being popularly associated with a policy of so-called
courage and energy, in other words with the daring
diplomacy of gunboats and bounce, he was entertained and
toasted at a great banquet at Tokio upon his return.
How widespread and indeed universal these feelings were,
was shown by the spirit with which the war with China,
as soon as declared, was taken up, by the public contributions that at once flowed in, and by the cheerful alacrity
with which even the severest sacrifices were submitted to
in the vindication of what was conceived to be the national
honour. The strain involved by the campaign, and the
reaction following upon profound exertion, coupled with the
check subsequently imposed upon Japanese ambitions by
the combined pressure of France, Russia, and Germany,
may have exercised a sobering influence upon Japanese
statesmen. But upon the public it is doubtful whether
any such effect has been produced ; and the national
temperament, elated with the pride of conspicuous achievement, will be liable at intervals to sudden outbreaks of
impetuous Chauvinism.

It is probable that these pyrotechnics of a somewhat
schoolboy patriotism, which are not unnatural in the case,
either of a country like Japan that is tentatively winning
its way to greatness, or of one like France that is smarting
under the memory of a great national humiliation, will
diminish in proportion as Japan secures the recognition at

which she is aiming, and acquires the self-control that is born of conscious strength. At present they bring a smile to the lip even of the most impassioned apologist for national delirium.

A further question, much agitated by foreigners, and especially by English and Americans, is the likelihood of Christianity being adopted as the national religion of Japan. A combination of circumstances —the disestablishment of Buddhism in the present reign, the reasonable character and general freedom from superstition of the people, the admitted indifference to older creeds of the upper classes, and the unhampered field opened to the labours of the foreign missionary societies —has led many to suppose that here, at least, the Church of Christ is sure of a magnificent spoil, and that Japan is trembling on the brink of a mighty regeneration. If I do not share these anticipations it is not from any denial either of the strenuous exertions of the reapers, or of the intrinsic richness of the harvest. But, though the State in Japan has withdrawn its sanction from Buddhism, the stream of the common people does not appear to have been one whit diverted from its crumbling, but still hallowed, shrines; and in the clapping of hands and short prayer before the gilded altar, and the practical sermons of the bonzes, the lower classes still find what is to them an adequate salvation. At the old capital, Kioto, there had been building for many years, out of private subscriptions only, and there has since been completed and opened, what is by far the largest Buddhist temple in all Japan. Nor can a people be described as without faith who yearly send forth tens of thousands of pilgrims to climb the sacred summits of Fuji, 12,300 feet high, and of Nantaisan.

Chances of Christianity in Japan.

On the other hand, with the upper and lettered classes,

the advance of knowledge has brought a widespread scepticism, and a reluctance to accept a dogma that eludes the test of material analysis. Neither can I think that the missionary army, though it enters the field with banners waving and soldiers chanting, utilises its strength to the best advantage by dividing its host into so many conflicting and sometimes hostile brigades. I find in the directory that at Tokio alone there are represented thirty-one different missionary churches, societies, sects, or denominations, with an aggregate of 300 male and female missionaries. When Episcopalians, Presbyterians, Baptists, Evangelicals, Lutherans, Church of England, Methodists, Reformed, Russian Orthodox, Quakers, Unitarians, and Universalists appear simultaneously upon the scene, each claiming to hold the keys of Heaven in their hand, it cannot be thought surprising if the Japanese, who have hardly made up their minds that they want a Heaven at all, are somewhat bewildered by the multiplicity of volunteer doorkeepers. Were the ethical teachings of the Bible to be offered to them in a systematised body of precept and of prayer they might turn a willing ear. Nay, I doubt not that a committee of Japanese experts would undertake to-morrow the codification of the moral, just as they have already done that of the civil and criminal law; and that they would turn out for the edification of their fellow-countrymen an admirable synthesis of the ethics of all time. Who shall say whether the new Japan may not yet undertake this momentous task? In the meantime the omens appear to be against the official or popular selection of any professed branch of Christian theology.

CHAPTER III

JAPAN AND THE POWERS

*And statesmen at her council met
Who knew the seasons when to take
Occasion by the hand and make
The bounds of freedom wider yet.*
   TENNYSON.

EVER since the Restoration, and with a progress that has advanced by leaps and bounds during recent years, as the nation has increased in stature and acquired no modest or shrinking estimate of its own importance, the biggest political question in Japan has been Treaty Revision. For a long while dwarfed by the more serious imminence of domestic problems, and retarded by the immaturity and inexperience of the new *régime*, sinking at times into a complete background, but at others sweeping all before it on a tide of popular emotion, it has exercised much the same disturbing and seismic influence upon Japanese politics as has the Home Rule question in Great Britain. It has made and it has upset Ministries, and might even do so again. At the time of my visit it confronted the strongest Government that Japan could produce with a problem which even its strength, it was feared, would prove unequal to solve; and although these expectations were belied by events, and the first Treaty with a European Power conceding Revision was signed with England in July 1894, yet this Treaty, under the terms of agreement, not having yet come into operation, and depending for its ultimate enactment upon the future proceedings of other Powers, this question cannot be considered as finally settled; and it may not therefore be inopportune to reprint in these pages the discussion which appeared in the original edition, the more so as the argument therein contained may supply a test by which the actual Treaty (printed as an appendix) may be judged in the interval that will precede its coming into actual operation.

History of the Treaties.
The Treaties which until superseded by the English and similar Treaties, now in course of negotiation with the other Powers, still regulate the commercial relations of Japan with foreign countries, and which provide for the residence in the Treaty Ports, and for the separate jurisdiction there of foreign subjects, were concluded at various periods with no fewer than eighteen signatory Powers,[1] since the first American Treaty was signed by Commodore Perry in 1855. Roughly speaking, the contract between the two parties was in each case as follows. Japan consented to open a limited number of ports to foreign trade and residence.[2] There only were the subjects of the contracting Powers permitted to live, to trade, to buy or sell property, or to engage in industrial enterprise. Outside the narrow limits of the settlements all these privileges were forbidden; nor was travel or movement permitted without a passport. On the other hand, inside the pale the subjects of foreign Powers were exempted from Japanese jurisdiction,

[1] These are Great Britain, France, Germany, Austria, Russia, Italy, Belgium, Holland, Spain, Portugal, Switzerland, Sweden, Denmark, America, Peru, Mexico, Hawaii, and China.

[2] The Open Ports are Yedo (Tokio), Kanagawa (Yokohama), Hiogo (Kobe), Osaka, Hakodate, Nagasaki, and Niigata. The following ports were subsequently opened in 1890 to Japanese exporters of grain, rice, flour, sulphur, and coal:—Shimonoseki, Moji, Hakata, Karatsu, Kuchinotsu, Misumi, Yokkaichi, Fushiki, Kushiro, Naha, Mororan, and Otaru. The numbers of resident foreigners in the Treaty Ports, on January 1, 1894, were as follows:— British 1458, Americans 700, Germans 416, French 349.

except, of course, when suing Japanese subjects, and were amenable only to their own Consular Courts—a prerogative commonly described as the Extra-territorial system; while the Customs tariff on foreign trade was fixed at a nominal 5 per cent. *ad valorem* on the majority of foreign imports, together with a duty of 5 per cent. on exports. Such is the system under which Japanese association with the outer world has been conducted, at least upon Japanese soil, for nearly forty years; from which for years she made so many abortive efforts to escape; and under which she proclaimed, with yearly increasing insistence, that it was incompatible with her national dignity to continue.

Conscious that the terms of original agreement could not be permanently stereotyped, a clause in the English Treaty, concluded by Lord Elgin in 1858, provided for future revision, upon the notice of either of the high contracting Powers, in 1872.[1] But when 1872 arrived neither party was in a position to move; and on the various occasions later, when revision was seriously attempted, the endeavour resulted in failure owing to the difficulty of reconciling the conflicting claims of the foreign Powers, who were averse to stepping down from their pinnacle of vantage without either a definite *quid pro quo*, or at least a guarantee that they would not suffer by the surrender; and of Japan, who, with a natural consciousness of her steadily improving position and of the obligations of what she termed her 'sovereign rights,' whittled away one by one the counter concessions which she was at first prepared to make, and even talked about exacting conditions herself. Hence the deadlock in which, sooner or later, negotiations

<small>Postponement of Revision.</small>

[1] Art. XXII.—'It is agreed that either of the high contracting parties, on giving one year's notice to the other, may demand a revision on or after July 1, 1872, with a view to the insertion of such amendments as experience shall prove to be desirable.'

were always involved. For my own part I never shared the feelings of either of those schools between which public opinion, as represented in books and newspapers about Japan, seems to have been divided—namely, those, on the one hand, the sentimental side of whose nature, inflamed, if they were Japanese, by patriotism, if they were foreigners, by contact with an engaging people and a pretty country, revolted against what they described as a great national wrong, whereby Japan was cheated out of her birthright, and was kept in perpetual exile in the tents of Edom, or, on the other hand, those who argued for the strict letter of the treaties *ad æternum*, and declined to make the smallest concession to the vast change that forty years had effected in the status of modern Japan. The former attitude was adopted—naturally enough—by Japanese writers; foolishly, as it seemed to me, by the majority of English and American tourists in Japan, who, without an inkling of what was going on behind the scenes, or of the labours of those whom they condemned, pronounced *ex cathedrâ* upon a situation of which they really knew as little as, for example, they might do of the difference between old and modern lacquer. The second or ultra-Conservative attitude was and still is taken up by many of the merchant class in the Treaty Ports, who, for perfectly honourable but selfish reasons, would like to maintain the *status quo* as long as they can. As a matter of fact, there was quite sufficient justice on both sides of the controversy to admit of temperate discussion and of amicable agreement; and the energies of the true friends of Japan were properly directed to minimising the points of friction and broadening the basis of possible compromise, instead of sharpening their blades for a further barren encounter.

With approximate fairness the two cases may be thus stated. Japan demanded Judicial autonomy and she de-

manded Tariff autonomy, from both of which, as already
explained, she was excluded by the Treaties. She demanded the former, because it was derogatory
to the dignity of a civilised Power to have alien *The case of Japan.*
courts of justice sitting within her territories, and
because she claimed to have acquired a jurisprudence based
upon the best European models. She demanded the latter,
because she was precluded from utilising her imports and
exports, except upon certain narrowly prescribed lines, as an
expanding source of Imperial revenue. Upon her imports
she has hitherto made an average of about $4\frac{1}{2}$ per cent. in
customs, and has been compelled in consequence to fix her
export duties at a higher figure than she would wish. She
desired to raise the former with a view to reducing the latter,
and the Land-tax in addition. Extra-territoriality being
abolished, the foreign settlements and municipalities would
lose their present character and would, so to speak, 'fall in'
to the Japanese Government, which would probably issue
new leases for the land held by foreigners therein, similar to
the leases held by Japanese. If she could get these main
concessions (she would, of course, like a few more thrown in),
Japan was prepared to open the entire country to foreigners.
She took her stand, therefore, ignoring the existing Treaties,
upon the solid facts of her attained position and prestige,
and upon an appeal to the enlightened sympathies of foreign
nations.

The merchants, on the other hand, for whom the Powers,
through their ministers, are the official spokesmen, have not
been particularly keen about the opening up of the
country, in which they do not see the prospect of *The case of the Powers.*
great mercantile advantage to themselves; they
are averse to the conditions under which they hold land in
the settlements (as the result of a covenant with the Japanese

Government) being altered or assimilated to native custom without their consent; and they are genuinely alarmed at the proposed abolition of Consular jurisdiction and the settlement of all cases, in which they may be concerned as litigants, in Japanese courts and before Japanese judges. They point to the admitted facts that the reorganised courts have not been long established, and that the bench, though occupied by Japanese who have been partially educated in Western Universities, lacks alike the tradition and the distinction of European judiciaries. They contend that miscarriage of justice would result, in the main from the ignorance, sometimes, perhaps, from the prejudice, of native judges. They fear the risk and complexity of processes before a strange court in a strange language; and they resent the possible subjection of their lives and homes to the domiciliary visits of native policemen. Moreover, they have a very well-founded distrust, not merely of the administration of Japanese law, but of the law itself, particularly in such points as the law of evidence and the law of contract, which are interpreted in Japan in a manner little in harmony with European ideas. Finally, they can point in support of their alarms to the constant diplomatic troubles arising out of 'miscarriage of justice' in the small independent States of the New World. Some of their papers have published very wild and silly articles about the inherent incapacity of the Japanese for the exercise of judicial authority of any kind; although I suspect that many of the British merchants who may be involved as litigants in the courts of the petty South American Republics would not so very greatly object to a change of venue to the courts of modern Japan. But though these more extravagant diatribes may be disregarded, there is undoubtedly a solid substratum of truth in the apprehensions of the foreign trading community, and any attempt to precipitate too hasty a solution could only involve the Japanese Government itself in difficulties which it had not contemplated.

In what quarter, then, did the solution lie? The answer was to be found in a brief examination of the various proposals for Treaty Revision that had so far been made by Japanese statesmen to the foreign representatives, or *vice versâ*. Their history had been one of unbroken disappointment and failure; but it was also marked by certain signs of progressive development in which there was hope for the future. Three times in the last twelve years had Japanese Foreign Ministers made overtures to the Treaty Powers. The first of these was Count Inouye, the present Minister for Home Affairs, who in 1882 originally suggested the ultimate abolition of Consular jurisdiction and the *ad interim* discussion of terms. A preliminary conference was summoned in 1882, and memoranda, prepared by the British and the Japanese Governments, were successively submitted. The negotiations continued till, in 1886, the actual conference of all the Treaty Powers met in Tokio, when a definite scheme, initiated by the British and German Governments, was propounded, and passed through many of the preliminary stages both of examination and acceptance. There were to be a large number of foreign judges on the Japanese bench, the conditions of whose appointment and removal evoked much hostile criticism in the native Press. The promised codes and future amendments therein were to be submitted to the Foreign Powers—an additional source of national irritation. It was not surprising that upon these points the negotiations at length broke down in 1887, although it was to be regretted that the opportunity was lost of effecting a settlement on conditions even a contracted edition of which was far more

Previous attempts at Revision. Count Inouye, 1882-87.

favourable to the scruples of foreigners than any later treaty was likely to be.

Undeterred by the failure of his predecessor, Count Okuma resumed negotiations in 1888 ; but, having learned by ex-

Count Okuma, 1888-89. perience the mistake of dealing with a Round Table at which the representatives of eighteen nations, with conflicting interests, were seated in conclave, he approached the Powers individually, offering, in place of an elaborate scheme of courts with foreign judges, the presence of a majority of foreign assessors in the Supreme Courts in cases where foreigners were concerned. A space of three years was to elapse between the promulgation of the promised codes and the final abolition of Consular jurisdiction. Upon these lines the United States, Germany, and Russia had already signed treaties ; and Great Britain, the vast preponderance of whose commercial interests in Japan renders her in every case the arbiter of the situation, was within measurable distance of the same end, the nature and extent of the securities to be given for the administration of justice to foreigners being one of the few points still undetermined, when, public opinion having been already gravely excited in Japan at the proposed appointment of alien judges, and being further inflamed by the promulgation of the new Parliamentary Constitution and the impending elections for the first Diet, an attempt was made with a dynamite bomb upon the life of Count Okuma in October 1889. The statesman escaped, though seriously mutilated. The would-be assassin killed himself. But his ulterior object had already been gained, for, at the very Cabinet Council in leaving which the bomb was thrown at Count Okuma, a decision had been arrived at, on the advice of Count Yamagata, who had just returned from a special mission to Europe, to suspend negotiations. Once more, accordingly, was Treaty Revision dropped like a hot coal from the baffled fingers of the plenipotentiaries at Tokio. Nor could this renewed failure be fairly set down to cowardice, seeing that public sentiment, though not behind the assassin, was in open sympathy with the motives that had actuated him to a deed which was the more significant that it by no means stands alone in the annals of modern Japan.

Since that date the opening of the Japanese Diet, and the rapid growth both of national self-respect and of ill-marshalled but powerful public opinion which it has produced, combined to render a settlement not more easy, while they have provided Japanese statesmen with an armoury of defensive pleas which a purely irresponsible Government could not previously employ. Nevertheless, Viscount Aoki, Foreign Minister in the succeeding Government, gallantly re-entered the lists in 1890; and his overtures, which were naturally directed in the first place to the removal of the lingering vestiges of British opposition, were met in the most favourable spirit by the administration of Lord Salisbury; since which it only rested with the Japanese Government itself, by the fulfilment of conditions which it had more than once admitted to be reasonable, to enter upon the fruition of the long struggle for complete national autonomy whose successive stages I have described.

Viscount Aoki, 1890.

What would be the leading features of any such solution will have been manifest from what has already been said. In the first place, the full text of the entire Civil and Commercial Codes under which it is proposed that foreigners shall in future reside and conduct their business, must be promulgated, translated, and put into satisfactory operation. No nation could with justice call upon the subjects of another, even within its own territories,

Bases of settlement.

to exchange a position of judicial security, established by treaty and ratified by long and successful experience, for the dubious protection of an inchoate, an imperfect, or an ill-comprehended body of law. Secondly, a period must elapse in which the new codes thus promulgated should be tested by practical operation, the judges becoming accustomed to the exposition of rules which involve in many cases a complete revolution in Japanese customary law, and the new law itself acquiring public respect by pure and consistent interpretation. Not until after such a probationary period could foreigners reasonably be expected to yield to the Japanese demand for complete judicial autonomy.[1] Thirdly, these conditions having been realised, the final abandonment of extra-territorial jurisdiction might fitly be made to synchronise with the entire opening up of the country. Other points might well become the subject of diplomatic *pourparlers* and of intermediate agreement. Such, for instance, were an *ad interim* extension of the present passport system in return for a revision of the tariff; and the novel but intelligible Japanese demand, of which I shall presently speak, that foreigners shall not be allowed to own real property or to buy shares in Japanese banks, railways, or shipping companies.

There were a multitude of obstacles, however, that required to be overcome before any such settlement could

---

[1] The problem that has already arisen in Japan was anticipated by Sir Harry Parkes in his Treaty with Korea, where it is hardly likely ever to arise; for a protocol to the Treaty (which was signed November 26, 1883) contains these words:—'It is hereby declared that the right of extraterritorial jurisdiction over British subjects in Korea, granted by this treaty, shall be relinquished when, in the judgment of the British Government, the laws and legal procedure of Korea shall have been so far modified and reformed as to remove the objections which now exist to British subjects being placed under Korean jurisdiction, and Korean judges shall have attained similar legal qualifications and a similar independent position to those of British judges.'

be arrived at. The first of these was the Parliamentary position of the Codes themselves. Though the process of Japanese judicial reform has been conducted with commendable rapidity, the goal of even approximate finality is yet far distant. It was in 1872 that the modern judicial system was first organised and courts and judges established; both being subjected to a thorough reorganisation in 1890. In the interval the Codes have one by one been evolved. The Criminal Code and the Code of Criminal Procedure were promulgated in 1880, and have now for some time been in operation. The Code of Civil Procedure was promulgated in 1890, and came into operation in 1891. As regards the Civil and Commercial Codes, however, the situation is less advanced. When I was in Japan in 1892 the Commercial Code had already been promulgated, but not yet translated; and the date of its operation, originally fixed for January 1, 1890, stood postponed till January 1, 1893. Those portions of the incomplete Civil Code that had been published stood similarly postponed. In the Session of the Diet of 1892, however, the drift of popular opinion was clearly indicated by the passing with much enthusiasm by both Houses of a bill, introduced by a private member, for further postponing the operation of both codes till December 1896, in order to submit them in Japanese interests to a thorough overhauling It was with little effect that Viscount Enomoto, then Minister for Foreign Affairs, pointed out the intimate connection between the Codes and the subject of Treaty Revision, and urged the Chamber not once more to slam the door in the face of those who had at length shown such a temperate willingness to open it. Conservative alarm at the innovations introduced by the new Codes, particularly in the law of inheritance and in other matters

Position of the Codes.

affecting family life, and at the subversion of the immemorial religious traditions of the country, joined hands with the Radical aspirations of Young Japan to settle the question of Treaties, not as the Powers like, but upon her own terms and on a footing of absolute equality; and the bill was carried by majorities of more than two to one in both Chambers.

This bill had not received either the assent or veto of the Emperor when Count Ito's Cabinet was formed, and much speculation was indulged in as to the advice which he would give to the Sovereign. As it turned out, the postponement was accepted by the Government on the ground that the Codes stood greatly in need of amendment, but with a proviso that such parts of them as were amended to the satisfaction of a Special Commission appointed for the purpose and of the Diet, might come into operation at any time. Subsequently, early in 1893, a large portion of the Commercial Code, dealing with the law of partnership and companies, of bills of exchange, promissory notes, and cheques, and with the law of bankruptcy, was passed, and came into force in July 1893. It will be seen, therefore, that the Codes are only slowly, and by piecemeal, coming into operation, and that the test of the practical working of the entire revised law is one whose possible application still lies in the future.

Further postponement.

In the same Session (February 1893) the attitude of the Lower House on the whole question of Treaty Revision was shown by an address to the Throne, which, after being debated in secret session, was voted by 135 to 121. It contained these words, which are significant as showing not the wisdom, but the temper of the Assembly :—

Address to the Throne in 1893.

'The unfair Treaties remain unrevised. The consequence is

that our jurisdiction does not extend to foreigners living within
our borders, nor do we possess tariff autonomy. No trespasses on
our national rights can be greater than these; and whenever our
thoughts dwell upon the subject we are constrained to bitter
regrets. The exercise of the extra-territorial system enables
foreigners to obey only their own laws and to be subjected to
their own judiciary within the territories of this Empire. Yet we,
in their countries, are compelled to obey their laws and submit
to their jurisdiction. Further, the restrictions imposed in respect
of customs tariff disable us from exercising our natural right to
tax imported goods, whereas foreign countries impose heavy duties
on goods exported by us. Thus our judicial and fiscal rights
being alike impaired, foreigners are enabled to behave in an
arbitrary manner. The result must be that our commerce and
industries will daily deteriorate, that the national wealth will
decrease, and that in the end there will be no means of recuperat-
ing our resources.[1] The fault of concluding such treaties must
be attributed to the fact that the people of your Majesty's realm,
both high and low, were basking in tranquillity and peace,[2] and,
as the country had been isolated for a long time, the Ministers of
State were entirely ignorant of foreign conditions. . . . The right
of concluding treaties belongs to the prerogatives of your Majesty;
and we, your Majesty's servants, are not permitted to interfere
with it. But since your Majesty has made oath to the gods in
heaven above and in the earth beneath, to manage all the affairs
of the nation and to administer the Empire in accordance with
popular opinion, we, your Majesty's servants, representing the
Lower House of the Diet and the opinion of the people of the
realm, may be permitted humbly to express our opinions. They
are:—Firstly, that the extra-territorial system be abolished;
secondly, that the Empire's tariff autonomy be recovered; thirdly,
that the privilege of taking part in the coasting trade be reserved;
and, fourthly, that all foreign interference in our domestic
administration be removed.'

Such then was the attitude of the Popular Chamber. But
a far more serious obstacle to successful negotiation consisted
in the ill-digested but formidable body of public opinion

[1] Of course this is quite fantastic, the Treaties having so far had a precisely opposite effect, in building up the commercial prosperity and wealth
of modern Japan.
[2] Equally absurd and untrue.

that was called into existence and organised throughout
the country by the reactionary party, and which threatened
by the irrational extravagance of its demands to
ruin the prospects of Treaty Revision altogether.
Although it must have been obvious that Revision could only result from mutual concessions,
Japan recovering her judicial and tariff autonomy at the price
of freely opening the country to foreigners, an association
named the Great Japan Union was started in 1892, and,
until its suppression at the end of 1893, conducted a furious
agitation against what is called Mixed Residence in any form
in the interior. In other words, foreigners were to surrender
everything now guaranteed to them by the Treaties, but to
get nothing whatever in return. In the settlements they
were to be subject to Japanese laws and jurisdiction, while
outside their borders they were not to be permitted to live
or move or have their being. A milder party existed which
proposed to sanction mixed residence in all other parts of
the country except Yezo (the Northern Island) and certain
other specified islands; but this compromise, which was quite
illogical and indefensible in itself, did not satisfy the patriots
of the Great Japan Union, who were bent upon making their
country and cause ridiculous in the face of mankind. For,
on the one hand, their agitation, which was based upon an
unreasoning dread of foreign competition, involved a confession of weakness in ludicrous contrast to the vanity by which
its authors were inspired. Secondly, it showed a complete
ignorance of and indifference towards all that foreigners have
done for Japan under the Treaties, in creating its trade, in
teaching it the secrets of manufacture and industry, in con-
verting swampy hamlets or fishing villages into magnificent
and flourishing towns, in pouring daily wages into Japanese
pockets, and in leaving the lion's share of the profits of

Anti-Mixed Residence agitation.

commerce in Japanese hands. Thirdly, it proposed to deprive foreigners of the very privileges which in the dominions of their respective governments the Japanese already enjoy. Fourthly, it was inconsistent with the example set by Japan herself, when, in order to acquire a convenient precedent for Treaty relationship with a foreign State without extra-territorial jurisdiction, she concluded, in 1888-89, a treaty with Mexico (although there were no Mexican subjects in Japan), conceding the privilege of Mixed Residence without any restrictions,[1] and containing also a most-favoured-nation clause, extending the same privileges to any nation willing to accept the same conditions. Finally, this policy was one of midsummer madness, since, if persisted in, its only effect could have been to stiffen the backs of the Treaty Powers (whose subjects it was proposed to subject to this puerile inequality), and so to postpone the Revision to the Greek Kalends. A certain section of the extreme party was, however, so well aware of this that they proposed to seize the opportunity thus deliberately manufactured, in order to repudiate the Treaties altogether, ignoring the ignominy that would attach to their country if she started upon her independent career with the brand of repudiation upon her brow, as well as the humiliating results of a probable naval demonstration of the Foreign Powers who had been so rashly insulted.

It should be added that the Mixed Residence question was somewhat complicated by the inclusion among the Treaty Powers of Japan's most formidable industrial rival, China.

---

[1] Article IV. of the Treaty granted to the Mexicans 'the privilege of coming, remaining, and residing in all parts of Japanese territories and possessions, of there hiring and occupying houses and warehouses, of there trading by wholesale and retail in all kinds of products, manufactures, and merchandise of lawful commerce, and, finally, of there engaging and pursuing all other lawful occupations.'

Were the privileges of free residence and trade in the interior extended without reserve to the frugal and laborious subjects of the Celestial Empire, there might be some ground for alarm on the part of Japan at the competition of so powerful an antagonist.[1] On the other hand, the Chinese Treaty with Japan contained no most-favoured-nation clause; so that privileges conceded to other foreigners could not be claimed as a right by her, and revision, if desired, need only be effected as a matter of separate arrangement.

<small>The Chinese Question.</small>

A further agitation sprang up, in 1891-92, against the ownership by foreigners, as a condition or consequence of Treaty Revision, of real or personal property outside the pale of the settlements. The forms of investment commonly specified under this would-be prohibition were lands, mines, railways, canals, waterworks, docks, and shares. This particular outcome of native susceptibilities was due to a not unfounded alarm that the superior wealth of foreigners might enable them, unless carefully guarded by law, to acquire a commanding hold upon the national resources, and that Japan might some day find herself in the disastrous position of an Asiatic Peru. It was not impossible that in the first instance there might be some danger in the speculative rush of foreign capital for a new form of investment; although, in the long run, natives would enjoy an advantage with which no foreigner could compete. It was clear, however, that means ought to be found without great difficulty of reconciling these apprehensions with the reasonable demands of foreign residents possessing a large stake in the fortunes of the country, and capable of rendering it increased service in the future.

<small>Agitation against foreign ownership of property.</small>

---

[1] There are at present in the Treaty Ports of Japan, where alone they are permitted to reside, 4500 male and 1050 female Chinese, or three-fifths of the entire foreign population.

The prohibition of the coasting trade to foreigners was another of the conditions that were suggested by the alarms of the new school that combined in such equal proportions timidity with bravado. In the event of their extreme demands not being conceded, and of the Government continuing to shrink, as it was bound to do, from a policy of repudiation, they further proposed a warfare of petty revenge upon the subjects of the recalcitrant Powers, which was to take the form of a refusal of passports, minute restrictions upon the issue of game licenses, limitations upon the facilities of railroad and steamboat traffic, upon the postal and telegraphic services, and upon the foreign Press, and a strict enforcement of the existing laws as regards tenure of property and industrial investment in the interior, which had occasionally been eluded by foreigners sheltering themselves under Japanese names. *Other demands.*

These were the main difficulties with which the path of Treaty Revision was beset. Arranging them side by side and observing, on the one hand, the ignorance and vanity of the extreme Reactionaries in Japan, the pretensions of the Diet, the openly avowed desire of the Opposition to embarrass the Government, and the difficulty experienced by the latter in placing any curb upon public opinion; on the other hand, the genuine alarm of the foreign merchants, the mutual jealousies of the various Treaty Powers, and the unfortunate enmity which the postponement of revision was likely to create between natives and foreigners; it was obvious that here was a problem requiring on both sides the exercise of great tact and statesmanship. On some points, concessions to Japanese sentiment were clearly possible. But on the broad questions of the Codes and of Mixed Residence no settlement that attempted an unnatural or patchwork compromise was *Prospects of settlement.*

feasible, or, even if feasible, was likely to be permanent; while to expect foreigners, with the best will in the world towards Japan, voluntarily to strip themselves of all the safeguards which Treaty enactments have given them, and to hand themselves over as a *corpus vile* for the experiments of Japanese Jacobins or neophytes in political economy, was to presuppose an innocence on their part to which previous history would afford no parallel. Fortunately neither the leading statesmen of Japan, nor the most responsible organs of the native Press, showed any real sympathy with the Extremists. Count Ito's plan was to approach the several Governments with separate and confidential communications, hoping to extract from the complacency or the needs of one a concession which should act as a precedent for similar terms with the others. Nevertheless Great Britain remained, as she had all along been, the pivot of the situation—no slight proof of her commanding influence on the destinies of distant Asia. And it was to secure her assent to a definite plan of Revision that the efforts of the Japanese Ministers were in the main directed. The announcement on the very day that these pages originally left my hand (July 30, 1894) that Lord Rosebery's Government had concluded a Revision Treaty with Japan, which was shortly afterwards ratified, and has since been followed by a Supplementary Convention regulating the future tariff, was a proof of the conciliatory and generous spirit in which the Japanese advances had been met, and of Great Britain's desire to welcome into the comity of nations a Power with whom we share so many common relationships, and whose ambitions present such striking features of analogy to our own deeds.

Upon the Treaty itself, which is printed below, and which has been variously described by the two parties previously distinguished as an act of statesmanlike magnanimity and of pusillanimous surrender, I will not here comment, preferring that its contents should be judged in the light of the reasoning already displayed in this chapter. At least, however, this credit must, without dispute, be conceded to Great Britain, and should never be forgotten by Japan, that, first of all the Great Powers, at a period anterior to the Chino-Japanese war of 1894-95, and consequently under no stress of expediency, emulation, or self-seeking, but of her own free-will and with ungrudging hand, England assisted Japan to strike off from herself the shackles of a past to which she had proved herself superior, and which is every day fading into a more rapid oblivion.

The Treaty of July 1894.

APPENDIX TO CHAPTER III

1. TREATY OF COMMERCE AND NAVIGATION BETWEEN GREAT BRITAIN AND JAPAN. (*Signed at London, July 16, 1894; ratified at Tokio, August 25, 1894.*)

ARTICLE I.—The subjects of each of the two High Contracting Parties shall have full liberty to enter, travel, or reside in any part of the dominions and possessions of the other Contracting Party, and shall enjoy full and perfect protection for their persons and property.

They shall have free and easy access to the Courts of Justice in pursuit and defence of their rights; they shall be at liberty equally with native subjects to choose and employ lawyers, advocates, and representatives to pursue and defend their rights before such Courts, and in all other matters connected with the administration of justice they shall enjoy all the rights and privileges enjoyed by native subjects.

In whatever relates to rights of residence and travel; to the possession of goods and effects of any kind; to the succession to personal estate, by will or otherwise, and the disposal of property of any sort in any manner whatsoever which they may lawfully acquire, the subjects of each Contracting Party shall enjoy in the dominions and possessions of the other the same privileges, liberties, and rights, and shall be subject to no higher imposts or charges in these respects than native subjects, or subjects or citizens of the most favoured nation. The subjects of each of the Contracting Parties shall enjoy in the dominions and possessions of the other entire liberty of conscience, and, subject to the Laws, Ordinances, and Regulations, shall enjoy the right of private or public exercise of their worship, and also the right of burying their respective countrymen according to their religious customs, in such suitable and convenient places as may be established and maintained for that purpose.

They shall not be compelled, under any pretext whatsoever, to pay any charges or taxes other or higher than those that are, or may be, paid by native subjects, or subjects or citizens of the most favoured nation.

ARTICLE II.—The subjects of either of the Contracting Parties residing in the dominions and possessions of the other shall be exempted from all compulsory military service whatsoever, whether in the army, navy, National Guard, or militia; from all contributions imposed in lieu of personal service; and from all forced loans or military exactions or contributions.

ARTICLE III.—There shall be reciprocal freedom of commerce and navigation between the dominions and possessions of the two High Contracting Parties.

The subjects of each of the High Contracting Parties may trade in any part of the dominions and possessions of the other by wholesale or retail in all kinds of produce, manufactures, and merchandise of lawful commerce, either in person or by agents, singly, or in partnerships with foreigners or native subjects; and they may there own or hire and occupy the houses, manufactories, warehouses, shops, and premises which may be necessary for them, and lease land for residential and commercial purposes, conforming themselves to the Laws, Police and Customs Regulations of the country like native subjects.

They shall have liberty freely to come with their ships and cargoes to all places, ports, and rivers in the dominions and possessions of the other which are or may be opened to foreign commerce, and shall enjoy, respectively, the same treatment in matters of commerce and navigation as native subjects, or subjects or citizens of the most favoured nation, without having to pay taxes, imposts, or duties, of whatever nature or under whatever denomination, levied in the name or for the profit of the Government, public functionaries, private individuals, Corporations, or establishments of any kind, other or greater than those paid by native subjects, or subjects or citizens of the most favoured nation, subject always to the Laws, Ordinances, and Regulations of each country.

ARTICLE IV.—The dwellings, manufactories, warehouses, and shops of the subjects of each of the High Contracting Parties in the dominions and possessions of the other, and all premises appertaining thereto destined for purposes of residence or commerce, shall be respected.

It shall not be allowable to proceed to make a search of, or a domiciliary visit to, such dwellings and premises, or to examine or inspect books, papers, or accounts, except under the conditions and with the forms prescribed by the Laws, Ordinances, and Regulations for subjects of the country.

Article V. No other or higher duties shall be imposed on the importation into the dominions and possessions of Her Britannic Majesty of any article, the produce or manufacture of the dominions and possessions of His Majesty the Emperor of Japan, from whatever place arriving; and no other or higher duties shall be imposed on the importation into the dominions and possessions of His Majesty the Emperor of Japan of any article, the produce or manufacture of the dominions and possessions of Her Britannic Majesty, from whatever place arriving, than on the like article produced or manufactured in any other foreign country; nor shall any prohibition be maintained or imposed on the importation of any article, the produce or manufacture of the dominions and possessions of either of the High Contracting Parties, into the dominions and possessions of the other, from whatever place arriving, which shall not equally extend to the importation of the like article, being the produce or manufacture of any other country. This last provision is not applicable to the sanitary and other prohibitions occasioned by the necessity of protecting the safety of persons, or of cattle, or of plants useful to agriculture.

Article VI.—No other or higher duties or charges shall be imposed in the dominions and possessions of either of the High Contracting Parties on the exportation of any article to the dominions and possessions of the other than such as are, or may be, payable on the exportation of the like article to any other foreign country; nor shall any prohibition be imposed on the exportation of any article from the dominions and possessions of either of the two Contracting Parties to the dominions and possessions of the other which shall not equally extend to the exportation of the like article to any other country.

Article VII.—The subjects of each of the High Contracting Parties shall enjoy in the dominions and possessions of the other exemption from all transit duties, and a perfect equality of treatment with native subjects in all that relates to warehousing, bounties, facilities, and drawbacks.

ARTICLE VIII.—All articles which are or may be legally imported into the ports of the dominions and possessions of His Majesty the Emperor of Japan in Japanese vessels may likewise be imported into those ports in British vessels, without being liable to any other or higher duties or charges of whatever denomination than if such articles were imported in Japanese vessels; and reciprocally, all articles which are or may be legally imported into the ports of the dominions and possessions of Her Britannic Majesty in British vessels may likewise be imported into those ports in Japanese vessels, without being liable to any other or higher duties or charges of whatever denomination than if such articles were imported in British vessels. Such reciprocal equality of treatment shall take effect without distinction, whether such articles come directly from the place of origin or from any other place.

In the same manner there shall be perfect equality of treatment in regard to exportation, so that the same export duties shall be paid and the same bounties and drawbacks allowed in the dominions and possessions of either of the High Contracting Parties on the exportation of any article which is or may be legally exported therefrom, whether such exportation shall take place in Japanese or in British vessels, and whatever may be the place of destination, whether a port of either of the Contracting Parties or of any third Power.

ARTICLE IX.—No duties of tonnage, harbour, pilotage, lighthouse, quarantine, or other similar or corresponding duties of whatever nature or under whatever denomination, levied in the name or for the profit of the Government, public functionaries, private individuals, Corporations, or establishments of any kind, shall be imposed in the ports of the dominions and possessions of either country upon the vessels of the other country which shall not equally and under the same conditions be imposed in the like cases on national vessels in general or vessels of the most favoured nation. Such equality of treatment shall apply reciprocally to the respective vessels, from whatever port or place they may arrive, and whatever may be their place of destination.

ARTICLE X.—In all that regards the stationing, loading, and unloading of vessels in the ports, basins, docks, roadsteads, harbours, or rivers of the dominions and possessions of the two countries, no privilege shall be granted to national vessels which shall not be equally granted to vessels of the other country; the intention of the High Contracting Parties being that in this respect also the respective vessels shall be treated on the footing of perfect equality.

ARTICLE XI.—The coasting trade of both the High Contracting Parties is excepted from the provisions of the present Treaty, and shall be regulated according to the Laws, Ordinances, and Regulations of Japan and of Great Britain respectively. It is, however, understood that Japanese subjects in the dominions and possessions of Her Britannic Majesty, and British subjects in the dominions and possessions of His Majesty the Emperor of Japan, shall enjoy in this respect the rights which are or may be granted under such Laws, Ordinances, and Regulations to the subjects or citizens of any other country.

A Japanese vessel laden in a foreign country with cargo, destined for two or more ports in the dominions and possessions of Her Britannic Majesty, and a British vessel laden in a foreign country with cargo destined for two or more ports in the dominions and possessions of His Majesty the Emperor of Japan, may discharge a portion of her cargo at one port, and continue her voyage to the other port or ports of destination where foreign trade is permitted, for the purpose of landing the remainder of her original cargo there, subject always to the Laws and Custom-house Regulations of the two countries.

The Japanese Government, however, agrees to allow British vessels to continue, as heretofore, for the period of the duration of the present Treaty, to carry cargo between the existing open ports of the Empire, excepting to or from the ports of Osaka, Niigata and Ebisu-minato.

ARTICLE XII.—Any ship of war or merchant-vessel of either of the High Contracting Parties which may be compelled by stress of weather, or by reason of any other distress, to take shelter in a port of the other, shall be at liberty to refit therein, to procure all necessary supplies, and to put to sea again, without paying any dues other than such as would be payable by national vessels. In case, however, the master of a merchant-vessel should be under the necessity of disposing of a part of his cargo in order to defray the expenses, he shall be bound to conform to the Regulations and Tariffs of the place to which he may have come.

If any ship of war or merchant-vessel of one of the Contracting Parties should run aground or be wrecked upon the coasts of the other, the local authorities shall inform the Consul-General, Consul, Vice-Consul, or Consular Agent of the district of the occurrence, or if there be no such Consular officer, they shall inform the Consul-General, Consul, Vice-Consul, or Consular Agent of the nearest district.

All proceedings relative to the salvage of Japanese vessels wrecked or cast on shore in the territorial waters of Her Britannic Majesty shall take place in accordance with the Laws, Ordinances, and Regulations of Great Britain, and reciprocally, all measures of salvage relative to British vessels wrecked or cast on shore in the territorial waters of His Majesty the Emperor of Japan shall take place in accordance with the Laws, Ordinances, and Regulations of Japan.

Such stranded or wrecked ship or vessel, and all parts thereof, and all furnitures and appurtenances belonging thereunto, and all goods and merchandise saved therefrom, including those which may have been cast into the sea, or the proceeds thereof, if sold, as well as all papers found on board such stranded or wrecked ship or vessel, shall be given up to the owners or their agents, when claimed by them. If such owners or agents are not on the spot, the same shall be delivered to the respective Consuls-General, Consuls, Vice-Consuls, or Consular Agents upon being claimed by them within the period fixed by the laws of the country, and such Consular officers, owners, or agents shall pay only the expenses incurred in the preservation of the property, together with the salvage or other expenses which would have been payable in the case of a wreck of a national vessel.

The goods and merchandise saved from the wreck shall be exempt from all the duties of the Customs unless cleared for consumption, in which case they shall pay the ordinary duties.

When a ship or vessel belonging to the subjects of one of the Contracting Parties is stranded or wrecked in the territories of the other, the respective Consuls-General, Consuls, Vice-Consuls, and Consular Agents shall be authorised, in case the owner or master, or other agent of the owner, is not present, to lend their official assistance in order to afford the necessary assistance to the subjects of the respective States. The same rule shall apply in case the owner, master, or other agent is present, but requires such assistance to be given.

ARTICLE XIII.—All vessels which, according to Japanese law, are to be deemed Japanese vessels, and all vessels which, according to British law, are to be deemed British vessels, shall for the purposes of this Treaty be deemed Japanese and British vessels respectively.

ARTICLE XIV.—The Consuls-General, Consuls, Vice-Consuls, and Consular Agents of each of the Contracting Parties, residing in the dominions and possessions of the other, shall receive from the local authorities such assistance as can by law be given to them for the recovery of deserters from the vessels of their respective countries.

It is understood that this stipulation shall not apply to the subjects of the country where the desertion takes place.

ARTICLE XV.—The High Contracting Parties agree that, in all that concerns commerce and navigation, any privilege, favour, or immunity which either Contracting Party has actually granted, or may hereafter grant, to the Government, ships, subjects, or citizens of any other State, shall be extended immediately and unconditionally to the Government, ships, subjects, or citizens of the other Contracting Party, it being their intention that the trade and navigation of each country shall be placed, in all respects, by the other on the footing of the most favoured nation.

ARTICLE XVI.—Each of the High Contracting Parties may appoint Consuls-General, Consuls, Vice-Consuls, Pro-Consuls, and Consular Agents in all the ports, cities, and places of the other, except in those where it may not be convenient to recognise such officers.

This exception, however, shall not be made in regard to one of the Contracting Parties without being made likewise in regard to every other Power.

The Consuls-General, Consuls, Vice-Consuls, Pro-Consuls, and Consular Agents may exercise all functions, and shall enjoy all privileges, exemptions, and immunities which are, or may hereafter be, granted to Consular officers of the most favoured nation.

ARTICLE XVII.—The subjects of each of the High Contracting Parties shall enjoy in the dominions and possessions of the other the same protection as native subjects in regard to patents, trade-marks, and designs, upon fulfilment of the formalities prescribed by law.

ARTICLE XVIII.—Her Britannic Majesty's Government, so far as they are concerned, give their consent to the following arrangement:—

The several foreign Settlements in Japan shall be incorporated with the respective Japanese Communes, and shall thenceforth form part of the general municipal system of Japan.

The competent Japanese authorities shall thereupon assume all municipal obligations and duties in respect thereof, and the common funds and property, if any, belonging to such Settlements, shall at the same time be transferred to the said Japanese authorities.

When such incorporation takes place the existing leases in perpetuity under which property is now held in the said Settlements shall be confirmed, and no conditions whatsoever other than those contained in such existing leases shall be imposed in respect of such property. It is, however, understood that the Consular authorities mentioned in the same are in all cases to be replaced by the Japanese authorities.

All lands which may previously have been granted by the Japanese Government free of rent for the public purposes of the said Settlements shall, subject to the right of eminent domain, be permanently reserved free of all taxes and charges for the public purposes for which they were originally set apart.

ARTICLE XIX.—The stipulations of the present Treaty shall be applicable, so far as the laws permit, to all the Colonies and foreign possessions of Her Britannic Majesty, excepting to those hereinafter named, that is to say, except to India, the Dominion of Canada, Newfoundland, The Cape, Natal, New South Wales, Victoria, Queensland, Tasmania, South Australia, Western Australia, New Zealand.

Provided always that the stipulations of the present Treaty shall be made applicable to any of the above-named Colonies or foreign possessions on whose behalf notice to that effect shall have been given to the Japanese Government by her Britannic Majesty's Representative at Tokio within two years from the date of the exchange of ratifications of the present Treaty.[1]

ARTICLE XX.—The present Treaty shall, from the date it comes into force, be substituted in place of the Conventions respectively of the 23rd day of the 8th month of the 7th year of Kayei, corresponding to the 14th day of October, 1854, and of the 13th day of the 5th month of the 2nd year of Keiou, corresponding to the 25th day of June, 1866, the Treaty of the 18th day of the 7th month of the 5th year of Ansei, corresponding to the 26th day of August, 1858, and all Arrangements and Agreements subsidiary thereto

[1] To this Article was attached a note, signed by the Japanese Plenipotentiary, and containing an assurance that any of the above-mentioned British Colonies and foreign possessions, upon acceding to the Treaty, should not be bound by the stipulations of Article II.

concluded or existing between the High Contracting Parties; and from the same date such Conventions, Treaty, Arrangements, and Agreements shall cease to be binding, and, in consequence, the jurisdiction then exercised by British Courts in Japan, and all the exceptional privileges, exemptions, and immunities then enjoyed by British subjects as a part of or appurtenant to such jurisdiction, shall absolutely and without notice cease and determine, and thereafter all such jurisdiction shall be assumed and exercised by Japanese Courts.

ARTICLE XXI.— The present Treaty shall not take effect until at least five years after its signature. It shall come into force one year after His Imperial Japanese Majesty's Government shall have given notice to Her Britannic Majesty's Government of its wish to have the same brought into operation.[1] Such notice may be given at any time after the expiration of four years from the date hereof. The Treaty shall remain in force for the period of twelve years from the date it goes into operation.

Either High Contracting Party shall have the right, at any time after eleven years shall have elapsed from the date this Treaty takes effect, to give notice to the other of its intention to terminate the same, and at the expiration of twelve months after such notice is given this Treaty shall wholly cease and determine.

ARTICLE XXII.—The present Treaty shall be ratified, and the ratifications thereof shall be exchanged at Tokio as soon as possible, and not later than six months from the present date.

In witness whereof the respective Plenipotentiaries have signed the same and have affixed thereto the seal of their arms.

Done at London, in duplicate, this sixteenth day of July, in the year of our Lord one thousand eight hundred and ninety-four.

KIMBERLEY.
AOKI.

---

[1] In a supplementary note, the Japanese Plenipotentiary gave an assurance that the Japanese Government would not issue this notice until those portions of the Codes which are at present in abeyance should be brought into actual force.

II.—Protocol.

The Government of Her Majesty the Queen of Great Britain and Ireland and Empress of India, and the Government of His Majesty the Emperor of Japan, deeming it advisable in the interests of both countries to regulate certain special matters of mutual concern, apart from the Treaty of Commerce and Navigation signed this day, have, through their respective Plenipotentiaries, agreed upon the following stipulations:—

1. It is agreed by the Contracting Parties that one month after the exchange of the ratifications of the Treaty of Commerce and Navigation signed this day, the Import Tariff hereunto annexed,[1] shall, subject to the provisions of Article XXIII. of the Treaty of 1858 at present subsisting between the Contracting Parties, as long as the said Treaty remains in force and thereafter, subject to the provisions of Articles V. and XV. of the Treaty signed this day, be applicable to the articles therein enumerated, being the growth, produce, or manufacture of the dominions and possessions of Her Britannic Majesty upon importation into Japan. But nothing contained in this Protocol, or the Tariff hereunto annexed, shall be held to limit or qualify the right of the Japanese Government to restrict or to prohibit the importation of adulterated drugs, medicines, food, or beverages: indecent or obscene prints, paintings, books, cards, lithographic or other engravings, photographs, or any other indecent or obscene articles; articles in violation of patent, trade-mark, or copyright laws of Japan; or any other article which for sanitary reasons, or in view of public security or morals, might offer any danger.

The *ad valorem* duties established by the said Tariff shall, so far as may be deemed practicable, be converted into specific duties by a Supplementary Convention, which shall be concluded between the two Governments within six months from the date of this Protocol: the medium prices, as shown by the Japanese Customs Returns during the six calendar months preceding the date of the present Protocol, with the addition of the cost of insurance and transportation from the place of purchase, production, or fabrication, to the port of discharge, as well as commission, if any, shall be taken as the basis for such conversion. In the event of the Supplementary Convention not having come into force before the expiration of the

[1] This Tariff was printed as an annex to the Protocol, but is not here reproduced.

period fixed for the said Tariff to take effect, *ad valorem* duties in conformity with the rule recited at the end of the said Tariff shall, in the meantime, be levied.

In respect of articles not enumerated in the said Tariff, the General Statutory Tariff of Japan for the time being in force shall, from the same time, apply, subject, as aforesaid, to the provisions of Article XXIII. of the Treaty of 1858 and Articles v. and xv. of the Treaty signed this day respectively.

From the date the Tariffs aforesaid take effect, the Import Tariff now in operation in Japan in respect of goods and merchandise imported into Japan by British subjects shall cease to be binding.

In all other respects the stipulations of the existing Treaties and Conventions shall be maintained unconditionally until the time when the Treaty of Commerce and Navigation signed this day comes into force.

2. The Japanese Government, pending the opening of the country to British subjects, agrees to extend the existing passport system in such a manner as to allow British subjects, on the production of a certificate of recommendation from the British Representative in Tokio, or from any of Her Majesty's Consuls at the open ports in Japan, to obtain upon application passports available for any part of the country, and for any period not exceeding twelve months, from the Imperial Japanese Foreign Office in Tokio, or from the chief authorities in the Prefecture in which an open port is situated; it being understood that the existing Rules and Regulations governing British subjects who visit the interior of the Empire are to be maintained.

3. The Japanese Government undertakes, before the cessation of British Consular jurisdiction in Japan, to join the International Conventions for the Protection of Industrial Property and Copyright.

4. It is understood between the two High Contracting Parties that, if Japan think it necessary at any time to levy an additional duty on the production or manufacture of refined sugar in Japan, an increased customs duty equivalent in amount may be levied on British refined sugar when imported into Japan, so long as such additional excise tax or inland duty continues to be raised.

Provided always that British refined sugar shall in this respect be entitled to the treatment accorded to refined sugar being the produce or manufacture of the most favoured nation.

5. The undersigned Plenipotentiaries have agreed that this Protocol shall be submitted to the two High Contracting Parties at

the same time as the Treaty of Commerce and Navigation signed this day, and that when the said Treaty is ratified the agreements contained in the Protocol shall also equally be considered as approved, without the necessity of a further formal ratification.

It is also agreed that this Protocol shall terminate at the same time the said Treaty ceases to be binding.

In witness whereof the respective Plenipotentiaries have signed the same, and have affixed thereto the seal of their arms.

Done at London, in duplicate, this sixteenth day of July, in the year of our Lord one thousand eight hundred and ninety-four.

KIMBERLEY.
AOKI.

KOREA

'L'Orient ! L'Orient ! qu'y voyez-vous, poètes ?
 Tournez vers l'Orient vos esprits et vos yeux !
 Hélas ! ont répondu leurs voix longtemps muettes,
 Nous voyons bien là-bas un jour mystérieux.'

      Victor Hugo : *Chants de Crépuscule*.

CHAPTER IV

LIFE AND TRAVEL IN KOREA

Where upon Apennine slopes with the chestnut the oak-trees immingle,
Where amid odorous copse bridle-paths wander and wind,
Where under mulberry-branches the diligent rivulet sparkles,
Or amid cotton and maize peasants their water-works ply.

A. H. CLOUGH: *Amours de Voyage*.

FROM the best known and most visited I pass to the least known and least visited of the countries of the Far East. The name of Korea[1] is one that, until the recent war, was still wrapped in so much mystery to the bulk of Englishmen at home, and the phenomena that it presented were at once so interesting, and, for so weak and ill-developed a country, so relatively important, that there were but few places at that time appealing more strongly to the traveller's thirst for the novel. The spectacle of a country possessing an historical antiquity, contemporaneous, as alleged, with that of Thebes and Babylon,[2] but owning no ruins; boasting a separate, if not an independent national existence for centuries, and yet devoid of all external symptoms of strength; retaining latest of all the kingdoms

The fascination of Korea.

---

[1] The name Korea, the veritable form of which is Kori or Koryo (Chinese Kaoli, Japanese Koraï), was originally the name of one of the three sovereignties into which, before its union, the peninsula was divided. The Portuguese transferred this name to the whole country, and called it Coria. Later, the French Jesuits called it, in French, La Corée; whence has arisen the ignorant and detestable habit of speaking of 'The Korea.' The native and official name of the country since 1392 A.D. is Chosen (*lit.* Tsio-sien, Chinese Chao-sien), *i.e.* 'Freshness, or serenity, of the morning.'

[2] The Koreans claim as their first king Ki Tsze, who emigrated from China, and founded a dynasty at Pyong-yang in 1122 B.C.

of the East the title to successful exclusion of the foreigner, and yet animated by no real hostility to aliens; containing beautiful natural scenery still virgin to the traveller's foot; claiming to have given to Japan her letters, her science, her religion, and her art, and yet bereft of almost all vestiges of these herself; inhabited by a people of physical vigour but moral inertness; well-endowed with resources, yet crippled for want of funds—such a spectacle is one to which I know no counterpart even in Asia, the continent of contrasts, and which from a distance had long and powerfully affected my imagination. A bridge between Japan and China, Korea is nevertheless profoundly unlike either. It has lacked the virile training of the Feudal System in Japan, and the incentives to industry supplied by the crowded existence of China. Its indifference to religion has left it without the splendid temples that adorn the former country, without the stubborn self-sufficiency of character developed by Confucianism in the latter. Japan swept it clear of all that was beautiful or ancient in the famous invasion of Hideyoshi (or Fidejosi, commonly called Taikosama) three centuries ago—an affliction from which it has never recovered. China's policy, until interrupted by recent events, has been to keep it in a state of tutelage ever since. Placed in an unfortunate geographical position midway between the two nations, Korea has been, like Issachar, the strong ass couching between two burdens. Suddenly, at the end of the nineteenth century, it wakes up from its long sleep to find the alarum of the nations sounding at its gates; the plenipotentiaries of great Powers appear in its ports to solicit or to demand reciprocal treaties; it enters the comity of civilised peoples; and, still half stupefied by its long repose, relaxes but slowly beneath the doubtful rays of Western civilisation.

In the examination of this country and its people, the

traveller or student has not the advantage, open to him in most other parts of the world, of an adequate literature composed by competent writers. Owing to the long and absolute seclusion of Korea, no foreigners beyond a few heroic Roman Catholic missionaries, who, in the latter part at any rate of their sojourn, carried their lives in their hands, had penetrated into the interior of the peninsula or become domiciled there, anterior to the first opening of the country twenty years ago.[1] A French compilation by Père Dallet, in whose hands were placed the materials thus acquired, appeared in 1874, and has almost ever since provided the substance of European knowledge about Korea, of whose people, and institutions, and life, it presents a minute and absorbing picture;[2] although, being based upon documents extending over the previous half-century, it relates to a time and describes customs which have

Literature of the subject.

[1] The single notable exception was Hendrik Hamel, a Dutchman, and supercargo of the ship *Sparker*, or 'Sparrow-hawk,' who was wrecked, with thirty-five of the crew (including a Scotchman, John Bosket) upon the island of Quelpart, while making for the Dutch factory at Nagasaki, in 1653. They were conveyed to Sôul in 1654, and were imprisoned in different parts of the country till 1666, when a few of the survivors succeeded in making their escape by sea to the island of Goto, and thence to Japan. Hamel wrote an account of their experiences, which was first published in 1668, at Rotterdam, and was then translated into French and English, and included in Astley's, Pinkerton's, and Churchill's Collections of Voyages. For a long time doubt was cast upon its authenticity; but, though the author was a man of no great education, and might have told us much more, his narrative, such as it is, has been amply confirmed by later knowledge, and is highly interesting. It is curious that, when Hamel's party were wrecked, there was already in Sôul another Dutchman, Jan Jansson Weltevree, who, with two of his fellow-countrymen, had been kept prisoners by the Koreans since 1627, when they had been sent ashore from the *Jacht Ouderkerke*, to get water and provisions. Not even these, however, were the first Europeans to set foot in Korea. This distinction belongs to a Portuguese Jesuit, Gregorio de Cespedes, who was sent over by Hideyoshi, in 1594, as chaplain to his second expedition against Korea, which was commanded by a Japanese Christian, Dom Augustin Konishi Yukinaga, and contained many Christians in its ranks. The only relics of the Dutch captives that have, so far, been discovered were two Dutch vessels, unearthed at Sôul in 1886.

[2] *Histoire de l'Église de Corée.* 2 vols. Paris, 1874.

now passed out of recollection or have ceased to prevail; whilst, being compiled by a writer who had not himself set foot in Korea, it lacks the advantage of first-hand editorial revision. Since 1876, the date of the first Treaty, the two most useful works on the country have also been the productions of authors who have never set foot within its borders. *The Hermit Nation*, by Mr. W. E. Griffis, an American, is a scholarly compilation of its past history, mainly from Japanese sources, and a careful, though frequently obsolete description of its habits and customs. The other work, by a Scotch Presbyterian missionary, Rev. J. Ross, who lived long at Newchwang, is also in the main historical.[1] The narratives of the few foreign travellers who have explored the country since its opening are as a rule scattered in the journals of Geographical Societies, in Government reports, or in publications neither easily accessible nor generally known. By far the most meritorious of these, and, within a narrow space, the most vivid and accurate account of Korean life life and character that I have seen, is a report written by Mr. C. W. Campbell, of the British Consular Service, and printed as a Parliamentary paper in 1891.[2] The earlier work by one of his predecessors, Mr. W. R. Carles, contains much interesting information, but is on the whole disappointing.[3] Much more so is the rhapsodical production of an American writer, Mr. P. Lowell.[4] The recent war gave birth to a plentiful crop of literature dealing with the country. But of this much was second-hand and the greater part ephemeral.

The foreign visitor to Korea will naturally first land upon its shores at one of the three Treaty Ports of Fusan, Gensan, and Chemulpo. As I visited and stayed at each of these,

[1] *History of Corea, Ancient and Modern.* Paisley, 1880.
[2] China. No. 2. (1891).   [3] *Life in Korea.* London, 1888.
[4] *Choson. The Land of the Morning Calm.* London, 1886.

I may append a paragraph upon their characteristics.
Fusan is upon the south-east coast, opposite to and
within sight of the Japanese islands of Tsushima The Treaty
(The Twins). Gensan is upon the east coast, Ports.
about half-way between Fusan and Vladivostok. Chemulpo
is upon the west coast, and is the port of the capital, Söul.
A greater variation can hardly be imagined than between

PORT AND JAPANESE SETTLEMENT OF FUSAN

the eastern and western shores of the peninsula. The
former are mountainous, the spurs of the Korean Apennines
reaching down in many places to the water's edge, and are
pierced by a few fine harbours, in which there is but a
weak tide, and which are open all the year round. On the
west coast, which is laved by the Yellow Sea of China,
there are, on the contrary, only shallow and tortuous inlets,
shielded by an archipelago of islands, and either filled or

bared by a tide that rises from 25 to 40 feet, and is frequently frozen in winter.

<small>Fusan.</small> The harbours of Fusan and Gensan are alike in being situated at the bottom of deep and sheltered bays, which could provide anchorage for immense armadas, and which are visited by a yearly increasing mercantile marine, flying the Japanese, the Chinese, and the Russian flags. Fusan,[1] as the port nearest to Japan, has retained for centuries a more than nominal connection with the neighbouring Power, having been from early times a fief of the daimio or lord of Tsushima,[2] until, in 1876, it became a trading port constituted by treaty between the two Powers. A flourishing Japanese community containing over 5000 Japanese subjects (exclusive of a floating population of 6000 Japanese fishermen) is the modern heir of the former military and trading colony, and is settled round the base of a knoll, crowned with a clump of cryptomerias—an obvious importation from over the sea—and with two dilapidated Japanese temples, just opposite to the large

---

[1] Fusan is the Japanese, Pusan the Korean name, signifying *pot* or *kettle* mountain, presumably from the outline of the knoll upon the shore.

[2] It was in the year 1443 that, by an agreement between the Prince of Tsushima and the Prefect of Tongnai (near Fusan), the first Japanese settlement was made at the latter port. The tribute-embassies from Korea to Japan always sailed from Fusan when starting for the Shogun's court at Kamakura, and there also landed the two successive invading armies of Hideyoshi, in 1592 and 1593. Even after the evacuation of the country by the Japanese, it remained in their hands, a garrison of 300 men being permanently quartered there behind a stockade, the only Japanese colony in the world; until, after the Revolution in 1868, it passed, with the other feudal properties of Japan, into the hands of the Mikado. Its formal opening as a Treaty Port in 1876 was a recognition of the resumption of Korean ownership, although the Japanese settlement, for which a nominal head-rent of $50 is supposed to be paid, remains practically a Japanese possession, being administered by the Japanese Consul, and a municipal council. In 1894 part of the Japanese expeditionary force landed at Fusan, but was recalled, before proceeding far into the interior, there being no necessity for a southern advance.

LIFE AND TRAVEL IN KOREA 91

hilly island called by the Europeans Deer Island, which shelters the southern side of the bay.[1] A little to the north of this town is a new Chinese settlement, the latter people having recently broken ground in Fusan, though handicapped as yet by the superior start and numbers of their rivals. Northward again is the original Japanese settlement, known as Kuk-wan; while a little beyond lies

GATE OF NATIVE TOWN, FUSAN

the Korean town surrounded by a stone wall and possessing the ruins of a castle, outside whose gates are a squalid native hamlet and bazaar. The background is formed by wild and desolate hills, with a thin fringe of firs bristling on the skyline, and bright red terraces of cultivated soil below.

[1] The Koreans call this island Tetsuye, the Isle of Enchanting View, or Maki, the Isle of Green Pastures (because it was ἱππόβατος, or a horse-rearing place).

Gensan[1] is situated in the southern hollow of the remarkable inlet in the eastern coast, called, from the British navigator who first surveyed it in 1797, Broughton Bay.[2] A deeper, and even finer indentation of the same bay, sheltered by the Nakimoff peninsula, is the well-known Port Lazareff, first surveyed and named by the Russians in 1854, and ever since believed to have been regarded by that people, from their ice-bound quarters at Vladivostok,[3] with a more than envious eye. The entire bay is fourteen miles in length, from two to six in width, and has a depth of from six to twelve fathoms. Seawards its entrance is masked by an archipelago of islets. As we steam up the bay, the Japanese settlement founded in 1879, and now containing over 700 colonists, may be seen clustered at the base of a hill upon the right. Some mile and a half to the south, and a little way inland, a cloud of smoke indicates the situation of the native town, which contains 13,000 inhabitants. Wooded hills frame a picturesque background, and vapour-caps hide the mountains inland. A less vigorous trade is here conducted by both Japanese and Chinese (the latter having only recently entered the field) with the northern provinces, the populous towns in which are more easily reached from the western coast, and will ultimately be more naturally served from the river-port of Pyong-yang (or Ping-yang), as soon as the latter is opened to foreign commerce, or as the Korean coasting marine becomes equal to its supply.

[Gensan.]

[1] Gensan is the Japanese, Yuensan the Chinese, and Wonsan the Korean version of the name; the difference arising from the different pronunciation by the three peoples of the same Chinese ideographs.

[2] *Vide* Captain W. R. Broughton's *Voyage of Discovery to the North Pacific Ocean*. London, 1804.

[3] During 1893 an attempt was made with a steam ice-crusher to keep the harbour of Vladivostok open the whole year round; but only met with qualified success.

Chemulpo[1] has few natural aptitudes as a port beyond its situation on the estuary of the southern branch of the river Han, or Han-kiang, upon which stands the Korean capital, and its consequent proximity to the main centre of population. The river journey is fifty-four miles in length to Mapu, the landing-place for Söul, which lies

Chemulpo.

PORT OF CHEMULPO

three miles farther on. The land-march to Söul is an uninviting stretch of twenty-six miles. In 1883, when Chemulpo was first opened to foreign trade, there was only a fishing hamlet with fifteen Korean huts on the site, where now may be seen a prosperous town containing over 3000 foreigners, of whom 2500 are Japanese, 600 Chinamen, and over twenty Europeans, as well as a native population of

[1] Chemulpo (signifying 'Various-articles-river-bank') is the name of the settlement formerly known and spoken of in the Treaties, from the name of the nearest magistracy, five miles away, as Japanese Jinsen or Ninsen, Chinese Jenchuan, Korean Inchiun or Inchon, signifying 'Benevolent streams.'

about equal numbers. There are a European club, several billiard-saloons and restaurants, and some excellent Chinese stores. The outer anchorage is some two miles from the shore, for the tide runs out here for miles (with a rise and fall of 25 to 30 feet), leaving an exposed waste of mud-flats and a narrow channel, in which steamers of light draught rest upon the ooze. The busy streets and harbour are indications of a rapidly-advancing trade, which promises further expansion in the near future.

The first glimpse of the Korean coast, at or near any of these ports, which is mountainous, but little wooded, and relatively bare, gives no idea of the timbered heights and smiling valleys which may be encountered in the interior; but the first sight of its white-robed people, whose figures, if stationary, might be mistaken at a distance for white mileposts or tombstones, if moving, for a colony of swans, acquaints us with a national type and dress that are quite unique. A dirty people who insist upon dressing in white is a first peculiarity; a people inhabiting a northern, and in winter a very rigorous latitude, who yet insist upon wearing cotton (even though it be wadded in winter) all the year round, is a second; a people who always wear hats, and have a headpiece accommodated to every situation and almost every incident in life, is a third. But all these combine to make the wearers picturesque; while as to Korean standards of comfort we have nothing to do but to wonder. As to their physique, the men are stalwart, well-built, and bear themselves with a manly air, though of docile and sometimes timid expression. The hair is worn long, but is twisted into a topknot, protected by the crown of the aforementioned hat.[1] The women, of whom

_{The Korean people.}

---

[1] This is the old Chinese fashion under the Mings, which was copied, with other Chinese habits, in Korea, but which was abolished by the Manchus in China.

those belonging to the upper classes are not visible, but the
poorer among whom may be seen by hundreds engaged in
manual labour in the houses, streets and fields, cannot be
described as beautiful. They have a peculiar arrangement
of dress by which a short white bodice covers the shoulders,
but leaves the breasts entirely exposed; while voluminous
petticoats, very full at the hips, depend from a waist just
below the armpits, and all but conceal coarse white or brown

KOREAN SCHOOLMASTER AND BOYS

pantaloons below. Their hair is black, and is wound in a
big coil round the temples, supplying a welcome contrast to
the greasy though fascinating coiffure of the females of Japan.
Indeed, if the men of the two nations are unlike—the tall,
robust, good-looking, idle Korean, and the diminutive, ugly,
nimble, indomitable Japanese—still more so are the women
—the hard-visaged, strong-limbed, masterful housewife of
Korea, and the shuffling, knock-kneed, laughing, bewitching
Japanese damsel. The Korean boy, indeed, might more

easily be taken to represent the gentler sex, since, until he is engaged to be married, he wears his hair parted in the middle and hanging in a long plait down his back.

Of this people, the males among whom exceed the females, there are believed to be about 11,000,000 in Korea, an area very similar in extent to Great Britain.[1] I give this total as a mean, possessing a probable approximation to truth, between the two extremes of 7,000,000 and 28,000,000, both of which have figured in recent publications,[2] and which illustrate the prevailing ignorance about a country and a population that have not as yet passed through the mill of the statistician. Marrying at an early age, prone to large families, and undiminished for many years by war or famine, the Korean population ought to be on the increase were it not that the infant mortality is enormous, and that the death-rate from epidemics, against which no precautions are taken, and which sweep over the country every third or fourth year, is certainly high. On the other hand, the large tracts of uncultivated and almost uninhabited country that still await the ploughshare and the peasant will accommodate an expansion that cannot fail to disappoint the Malthusian enthusiast for many years to come.

<small>Total population.</small>

The Koreans belong unmistakably to the Mongolian stock,

---

[1] The best estimate appears to be 80,000-90,000 square miles. But some place it as high as 100,000-120,000.

[2] Evêque Daveluy, in 1847, gave 3,598,880 males, 3,745,481 females; total 7,344,361. Oppert, in 1867, gave 15,000,000-16,000,000. Père Dallet, in 1874, gave 10,000,000. Japanese statistics, in 1881, gave 16,227,885. Griffis, in 1882, gave 12,000,000. Sir H. Parkes, in 1883, gave 8,000,000-10,000,000. An obviously supposititious census, in 1884, is quoted as having given 28,007,401. The latest Government census, cited in the *Statesman's Year-Book*, is 10,528,937. Varat, the most recent foreign writer, names 16,000,000-18,000,000. On the other hand, the Chinese figures, in a work entitled *Important Facts relating to the Eastern Stockade*, are 3,310,704 males, 3,259,401 females; total 6,570,105.

occupying a sort of intermediate stage between the Mongolian Tartar and the Japanese. It is impossible to confound them either with the latter or with the Chinese; and a Korean would, to any one who has travelled in the country, be a known man in any city in the world. It has been supposed by some writers, who have observed a different variety with blue eyes and fair hair in Korea itself, that there is also a Caucasian element in the stock; but I am not aware that this hypothesis has found any scientific confirmation.[1] Their language is of the Turanian family, with the addition of many Chinese words; and they may be said to possess two syllabaries or alphabets—the Nido or Korean syllabary, which gives a phonetic value to some 250 Chinese ideographs in common use, and which was invented by Syel Chong, a famous scholar and priest, 1100 years ago; and the popular Korean alphabet, or script, which was first promulgated by royal decree in 1447 A.D., and is still used by the lower orders.[2] If one does not either speak or understand Korean oneself, it is always possible to communicate with a Korean by using the Chinese symbols, which he equally employs. On the other hand, among the upper and lettered classes, Chinese itself is the invariable vehicle both of speech and correspondence, just as it is also the official language employed in Government publications, proclamations, examinations, and decrees.

Ethnology and language.

Of the people so constituted there appears to be but one opinion as to the national character and physique. While an invigorating climate has made them naturally

---

[1] May it not, perhaps, be attributable to the twelve years' residence in Korea of the Dutchman Hamel and his companions, two centuries ago?

[2] The most interesting evidence of the early development of Korea is Sir E. Satow's demonstration that the Koreans printed from movable metallic types two centuries before they were known in Europe. He possesses a Korean reprint of the Chinese *Confucian Table-Talk*, which was printed in 1317 A.D. in this fashion.

long-lived and strong, their habits of life and morals [1] have rendered them subject to many forms of ailment and disease; while their want of contact with the world and their servitude to a form of government which has never either encouraged or admitted of individual enterprise, but which has reduced all except the privileged class to a dead level of uncomplaining poverty, have left them inert, listless, and apathetic. As individuals they possess many attractive characteristics — the upper classes being polite, cultivated, friendly to foreigners, and priding themselves on correct deportment; while the lower orders are good-tempered, though very excitable, cheerful, and talkative. Beyond a certain point, however, both classes relapse into a similar indifference, which takes the form of an indolent protest against action of any kind. The politician in Söul remains civil, but is wholly deaf to persuasion. The coolie works one day and dawdles away his wages upon the two next. The *mapu*, or ostler, takes his own time about his own and his pack-pony's meals, and no reasoning or compulsion in the world would disturb him from his complacent languor. These idiosyncrasies may only be interesting to the unconcerned student of national character, but they are of capital importance in their bearing upon national life. When, further, they are crystallised into hardness and are inflamed by the habits of an upper and official class — which subsists by extortion, and prohibits, outside its own limits, either the exercise of surplus activity or the accumulation of wealth — they explain how it is that the Korean people remain poor amid stores of unprobed wealth, lethargic where there should otherwise be a hundred

[margin: National character.]

---

[1] Polygamy may be said to prevail; for whilst most Koreans only have one wife, they keep as many concubines as their circumstances permit. Among the lower orders there is neither cleanliness nor decency, and many vices prevail.

incentives to diligence, nerveless in the face either of competition or of peril. I have seen a Korean coolie carrying a weight that would make the stoutest ox stagger, and yet I have seen three Koreans lazily employed in turning up the soil with a single shovel, by an arrangement of ropes that wasted the labour of three men without augmenting the strength of one.

A KOREAN MAGISTRACY

So it is in every department of the national existence. An immense reserve of masculine force is diverted from the field of labour and is lost to the nation by being absorbed into the *yamens*, or offices of the local magistrates and prefects, where their function, instead of invigorating the blood of the country, is to suck that of their fellow-countrymen.[1] The population of Korea

The extremes of society.

[1] Mr. Carles, in one of his Reports (Corea, No. 2, 1885), mentioned the province of Pyong-an-do as having 44 magistracies, with an average of 400 official hangers-on in each, having nothing to do but to police the district and to collect taxes—in all, a total of 17,600 men.

may, indeed, be roughly divided into two classes—the upper or official, entitled *yangban*,[1] whose position or gentility is a bar to work, and who, therefore, must subsist upon others; and the great residuum, whose business it is to be subsisted upon, and to filch from the produce of their labour the slender necessities of existence for themselves. Poverty in the sense of destitution there is not; but poverty in the sense of having no surplus beyond the bare means of livelihood and of the paralysis of all enterprise is almost universal. Any less indolent people might be expected to rebel; and occasional magisterial encroachments beyond the limits of practice or endurance result in short-lived spasms of mutiny, in the course of which an offending official is seized and, perhaps (as happened once in 1891) is burned alive. But ordinarily this implies too great an exertion; the people are unarmed and very helpless, and the system is mutely acquiesced in, unless pushed to intolerable extremes.

For travelling in the interior of Korea it is advisable to invoke some sort of official assistance. Otherwise the poverty

---

[1] Literally *Nyang-pan*, or Two Orders (civil and military), who constitute the aristocracy of birth, descending from an aristocracy of office. Mr. Campbell, in his Report, gives the best account of them:—'The *nyang-pan* enjoys many of the usual privileges of nobility. He is exempt from arrest, except by command of the King or the governor of the province in which he resides, and then he is not liable to personal punishment, except for the gravest crimes, such as treason or extortion. He wields an autocratic sway over the inmates of his house, and has full license to resent any real or fancied insult levelled at him by the *ha-in*, *i.e.* "low men," the proletariat, just as he pleases. At the same time, the *nyang-pan* lies under one great obligation, *noblesse oblige*; he cannot perform any menial work, or engage in any trade or industrial occupation. Outside the public service, teaching is the only form of employment open to him. If he seeks any other, he sinks irrevocably to the level of his occupation. There is no law laid down on the point. The penalty is enforced socially, and is part of the unwritten code of *nyang-pan* etiquette. These privileges and obligations have naturally influenced the character of the class, so that the officeless *nyang-pan*, no matter how poor, is proud and punctilious as a Spanish hidalgo, not above negotiating a loan with the most shameless effrontery, yet keen to resent the slightest shade of disrespect from an inferior.'

of the country renders it difficult in parts for the stranger to procure either beasts of burden, lodging, or food. The Foreign Office at Söul issues a document known as a *kuan-chow*, which authorises the bearer to employ Government couriers and ponies, and to put up at Government inns and *yamens*, and which calls for fodder, chickens, and torches at night, to be forthcoming. The natives frequently endeavour to circumvent this order by hiding away everything in their possession, and protesting the entire nakedness of the land. Its production at a magistracy is consequently very often necessary, since it is an imperative mandate to the local official to bestir himself in the interests of the bearer, who may otherwise report his indifference at Söul. Without a *kuan-chow* I might never have started from Gensan, where there was a conspiracy among the owners of ponies to refuse all their animals, except at preposterous rates, that was only overcome after a two days' delay and a somewhat stormy interview, *kuan-chow* in hand, with the *locum tenens* at the local *yamen*.

_{Necessities of travel.}

Travel in the heart of a country brings the stranger into contact with a type of humanity more primitive, but also more representative of the national character, than that encountered in the capital or in large cities, whilst it also discloses features of natural scenery of which the residents in towns or the frequenters of high routes alone may remain permanently ignorant. Both these advantages were derivable from the circuitous journey which I took from Gensan to the capital. The familiar route between these places is 550 li, or 170 miles, in length, and, with the exception of one splendid mountain-crossing, traverses a landscape never without interest, though lacking in the higher elements of grandeur or romance. A divergence, however, of a few days from the track brought

_{Visit to the Diamond Mountains.}

me into a region which less than half-a-dozen Europeans have yet visited, and which contains some of the most renowned scenery in Korea, as well as the picturesque and venerable relics of the disestablished Buddhist religion, which for 1000 years before the foundation of the present dynasty, in about 1400 A.D., was the official and popular cult of the

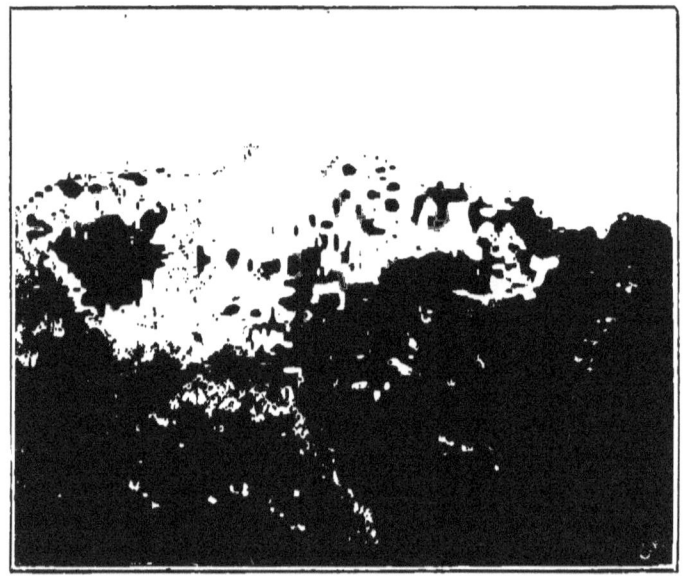

KEUM KANG SAN, OR DIAMOND MOUNTAINS

country. This region is known as the Keum Kang San, or Diamond Mountains; and there—amid mountain valleys and recesses whose superb forest mantle rivals in amplitude, while it excels in autumnal tints of maple and chestnut, the garniture of Californian cañons, where rushing, crystal-clear torrents dance through every glen, and far skywards bare splintered crags lift their horns above the foliage—are scattered a number of monasteries, whose buildings are in some cases

many centuries old, and whose dwindling congregation of
inmates perform in these secluded retreats, secure from any
intrusion save that of the itinerant pilgrim, the stereotyped
devotions before gilded images of Buddha and his disciples,
in which they themselves, in common with the mass of their
countrymen, have long ceased to believe. By lovers of the
picturesque nothing more enchanting than these monastic
retreats can anywhere be found; nor will the discovery
that, while every prospect pleases, man alone is vile—even
though his depravity assume, as is credibly alleged of the
Korean bonzes, the most profligate expression, or, as it did
in my own experience, the more modest form of larceny of
one's personal effects—deter the traveller from keen appreciation of surroundings so romantic.

Surprise may be felt that in a country where the cloister
is so generally and not unjustly despised, it should yet
succeed, in spite of popular scepticism and official
neglect, in attracting to itself a sufficient number   Korean
of recruits. The answer lies in the incurable   monks.
laziness of the people. The monks, who do but little in the
way of manual labour, beyond occasionally tilling the plots
of ground attached to the monasteries, or making sandals,
subsist in the main upon the charity of others—an occupation
in which the Korean finds an enchantment that personal
exertion can never supply. Hither, therefore, retire those
who have nothing to do, or still more, who want to do
nothing; bachelors who cannot marry or widowers who do
not want to marry again; children of whom their families
want to get quit, or who want to get quit of their families;
sometimes fugitives from justice to whom the Buddhist
monastery is like the Jewish City of Refuge; perhaps, here
and there, though not once in a hundred times, an individual
who desires to forsake the world, and to surrender himself

wholly to study and devotion. Hither also comes the Korean sight-seer, the local equivalent to the English Bank Holiday young man on a bicycle—a character very common among the Koreans, who cultivate a keen eye for scenery, and who love nothing better than a *kukyeng*, or pleasure-trip in the country, where they can shirk all business and dawdle along as the humour seizes them; living upon and, where possible, abusing the hospitality of others, and halting as

MONASTERY OF CHANG AN SA IN THE DIAMOND MOUNTAINS

they mount each successive crest, and a new outlook opens before them, to expatiate upon its beauty, to deposit a stone or hang up a rag in the little wayside shrine erected to the local genius or deity, and, if they be sufficiently educated, either to quote the rhapsodies of some previous poet or to compose a stanza themselves. How deeply ingrained in the people is this semi-æsthetic, semi-superstitious nature-worship may be illustrated by the case of Paik-tu-San (White Peak Mountain), the celebrated mountain on the northern frontier, with its gleaming white crown, and with the unfathomed lake in the hollow of its crater. Every year an official deputation starts forth from Hamheung, the nearest seat of provincial government, and when it arrives at a point beyond Unchong, near the Yalu River, from whence the first view of the sacred crest is obtained, makes genuflexions, lays out its offerings, and retires. That the monasteries have for long been visited far more for pleasure's sake than for duty is also evident from the remark of Hamel 240 years ago:—

'The Nobles frequent the Monasteries very much to divert themselves there with common Women or others they carry with them, because they are generally deliciously seated, and very pleasant for Prospect and fine Gardens. So that they might better be called Pleasure-houses than Temples, which is to be understood of the common monasteries, where the religious men love to drink hard.'

A full night's sleep is not easy of attainment in a Korean monastery, even though one's bed be spread on the floor of one of the sacred halls, and at the foot, as often happens, of the high altar. Before the first glimmer of dawn some pious monk, anxious to anticipate his fellows, begins to walk round the courts, tapping a drum, and singing the most lugubrious and discordant of chants. Then somebody else begins to clap, clap, upon a brass gong. Next the big drum on the platform over the entrance is beaten to a frantic tune; and finally every bell, gong, and drum in the establishment are set going at once. This is the common experience of all who sojourn in Buddhist monasteries, where a scrupulous adherence to ritual prevails, and where the outside of the cup and platter is much more thought of than the character of the inward parts.

Monastic life and habits.

The internal arrangements of these monasteries, of which there are said to be nearly forty, along with a few nunneries, in the Diamond Mountains,[1] and of which I also visited the chief or metropolitan monastery of Sak Wang Sa,

Buildings. about twenty miles from Gensan, are commonly the same. Adjoining, sometimes over, the entrance, is a roofed platform or terrace, the pillars and sides of which are thickly hung with the votive or subscription tablets of former pilgrims. Here is usually placed

ABBOT OF A KOREAN MONASTERY

a gigantic drum, reposing upon the back of a painted wooden monster. Hard by a big bronze bell hangs behind a grille. The central court, into which one first enters, contains the principal shrine or temple, usually at the upper end, and subsidiary shrines or guest-chambers on either side. All are of the same pattern—low detached

[1] The accompanying photographs of scenery in the Keum Kang San were taken by Mr. C. W. Campbell.

buildings, with heavy tiled roofs and overhanging eaves, closed by screens, or shutters, or doors along the front. Inside is a single gloomy chamber or hall, the richly-carved and painted ceiling of which is sustained by large red pillars. Opposite the entrance is the main altar, a green or pink gauze veil hanging in front of which but half conceals the gilded figures of seated or standing Buddhas behind, while all round the sides are ranged grotesque and grinning images, usually in painted clay, of other demigods, saints, or heroes. A low stool stands in front of the main altar, and supports a copy of the liturgy and a small brass bell. Thereat, when the hour strikes for morning or evening prayer, a monk, hastily pulling a grey robe and red hood over his white dress, kneels down on a mat, intones a prayer in a language which he does not understand, touches the ground with his forehead, and strikes the brass bell with a small deer's horn. Smaller replicas of the same sanctuary, dedicated to different deities, stand in the neighbouring courts.

The Korean form of Buddhism is, it will thus be seen, closely akin to the Chinese, and is widely divorced from that which found favour in the more artistic atmosphere of Japan. Its hideously bedaubed temples, which only become tolerable with age, and its multiform, grotesque, and barbarous images have little in common with the beauty of Ikegami or the glories of Nikko, or even with the less æsthetic attractions of Asakusa. Essentially Chinese, too, is the manner in which the original faith has been overlaid with anthropomorphic or demonolatrous superstitions, and has had grafted on to it an entire pantheon of semi-deified heroes. Nevertheless, it is a welcome relief to alight upon the shrines even of a dishonoured and moribund faith in a country where no

Korean religion.

popular cult appears to exist save that of spirits, dictated in most cases by nervous apprehension of the forces of nature, and where, as the old Dutch navigator put it, 'as for Religion, the Coresians have scarcely any.'

To these superstitions is the Korean peasant peculiarly prone. Outside his villages are seen wooden distance-posts carved into the hideous and grinning likeness of a human head, in order to propitiate the evil spirits.[1] Of similar application are the bronze figures of monsters that appear upon the roofs of palaces and city gates, the rags and ropes that are tied to the boughs of trees (supposed, in Korean demonology, to be the particular abode of spirits), and the stones that are heaped together on the summits of hill-roads, in passing which our native camp-followers would invariably bow and expectorate. Female sorceresses and soothsayers, to cast horoscopes, and to determine the propitious moment for any important action, are also in great request.[2] In

Spirit-worship and Confucianism.

---

[1] These images are commonly from 4 to 8 feet in height. Their lower part consists of a roughly-hewn log or post, on the front of which is an inscription in Chinese characters, while the upper part is carved into the likeness of a grotesque head, with features besmeared with red paint, white eye-balls, and huge grinning mouth. Their original purpose appears to have been that of mile-stones to record distances, in which case they are called *Chang* or *Jang-sung*; but when planted in rows at the entrance and exit of villages they are also called *Syong-sal-mak*, and are regarded as tutelary guardians against evil spirits. Chang-sung is said to have been the name of a notorious Korean criminal in bygone days. This individual was a general or official of high rank, who, according to different versions of the same legend, murdered his wife and daughter, or married his own daughter, who, for her part, committed suicide. Detected and seized, he was put to death by the King, and the likeness of his head was carved as a warning upon the distance-posts throughout the country. A somewhat analogous idea is represented in the Korean practice, at certain seasons of the year, of making little straw effigies, about 1½ foot in height, in the likeness of some disliked individual, inserting a few loose cash inside, along with a short prayer, and then burning the whole thing as a scape-goat, or presenting it to a beggar, who will gladly appropriate the gift for the sake of the coins.

[2] Outside the walls of Sôul I visited the house of a sorceress—a big black

Sönl I heard a story of a sick man who was supposed to be possessed by a devil, but was successfully cured by an English mission doctor, who affected to drive out the evil spirit, which was forthwith pursued down the street by a large crowd and 'run to ground' in the mission compound. Among the upper classes the only vital form of religion is ancestor worship, developed by familiarity with Confucianism and by long connection with the Chinese. A man has no higher ambition than to leave male descendants who may worship his *manes* and offer sacrifice at his grave. An outcome of the same ethical system is the sense of filial piety, which would have rendered Æneas a typical Chinaman, of unquestioning obedience to the sovereign, and of duty to the aged and to friends. No Buddhist monks are allowed inside the cities—a prohibition which is said to have originated in the Japanese invasion 300 years ago, when the invaders crept into some of the towns in monastic disguise—although the King, in the neighbourhood of the capital, has one or more secure mountain retreats, whither, in time of danger, he flees to the protection of a monkish garrison.

Travelling in Korea is best undertaken in the autumn months of the year. The climate is then perfect—a warm sun by day and refreshing coolness at night. In the winter deep snow falls and the cold is excessive. The summer heats are equally unpleasant. *Conditions of travel.* There are no made roads in the country, and the tracks are mere bridle-paths, of greater or less width, according to the extent to which they are trodden. In a country that is as

woman with a forbidding countenance and an enormous black hair wig, which she put on and off, at the same time that she donned different coloured robes, waltzing slowly round the while to the sound of drums and gongs, and droning a horrible chant, much to the consternation of the large crowd who had come to consult her, bringing big tables piled with sweetmeats, but who were evidently very much frightened by her incantations, and plied her with anxious and tearful entreaties.

plentifully sprinkled with mountains as a ploughed field is with ridges, these are frequently steep and stony in the extreme, and in the out-of-the-way parts which I visited the track was not unfrequently the precipitous and boulder-strewn bed of a mountain torrent, amid and over the jagged rocks of which none but a Korean pony could pick his way. A wonderful little animal indeed is the latter. With the exception of the ox, which is the beast of heavy burden, and the donkey, which is much affected by the impecunious gentry, no other pack or riding animal is known. Rarely more than eleven hands high, combative and vicious, always kicking or fighting when he can, he will yet, with a burden of 150 lbs. or 200 lbs. upon his back, cover a distance of some thirty miles per diem; and provided he has his slush of beans and chopped straw, boiled in water, three times a day, before starting, at noon, and in the evening, he emerges very little the worse at the end of a lengthy journey. Each pony is attended by its own *mapu*, or driver, and the humours of these individuals, who sing and smoke and crack jokes and quarrel all the day long, are among the alleviations of travel. If the destination be not reached before nightfall the bearers of official passports have the right to torchbearers from each village. Long before reaching the latter, tremendous shouts of ' *Usa, usa!* ' (torch), are raised by the *mapus* or *yamen*-runners; and if upon arrival the Government linkmen are not forthcoming with their torches—made of a lopped pine-log or a truss of straw—they are roused from their slumbers or hiding with cuffs and violent imprecations. In a few moments half-a-dozen torches are ignited, and amid waving banners of flame the cavalcade disappears into the night.

Sport is a further and agreeable concomitant of journeying, although, as in every country in the world, not much game can be seen except by divergence from the hurried track of travel. Pheasants abound in the undergrowth on the mountains. In the winter months every variety of wild-fowl, from wild geese and swans to wild duck, teal, waterhen, plover, and snipe, swarm along the coast and rivers or in the soaking rice-plots. The natives either snare them or shoot them sitting; and the spectacle of a rocketing mallard brought down from a great height in the air is greeted by them with frantic shouts of admiration and delight. Turkey bustards, cranes, herons, pink and white ibis are also encountered, and there is a large eagle, whose tail-feathers are much prized by the Chinese for fans. But the richness of the Korean covert lies rather in fur and skin than in feather. Hares, foxes, badgers, wild cat, wild boar, bears, sables, ermin, and otter in the far north, and different kinds of deer (which are hunted for the medicinal properties supposed in China to belong to the horns of the young buck) are to be found in the scrub on the mountains. Leopards are quite common, and in the winter months sometimes venture even inside the walls of Söul. Their skins, costing about $10 each, are part of the official insignia of the court. But the tiger is the king of Korean quarries. He is of great size; and I saw, while in Korea, some splendid skins.[1] His haunt is the wooded mountain-slopes near the east coast, and the entire belt of country northwards as far as the forests on the Yalu, where man-eaters are not uncommon. In winter time tigers have more than once come down into the settlement at Gensan and carried off a victim; I even heard there of a European who, going out to dine, met a tiger walking down the middle of the road; and when I was at Chang An Sa (the Hall of Eternal Peace), the principal of the Keum Kang San monasteries, one was said to

Sport.

---

[1] Only some 30-40 of these are exported in each year. The price rose in 1893 from $22 to $41, i.e. £1, 1s.

patrol the quadrangle every night, and we came across their spoor and droppings. The King maintains a body of royal tiger-hunters, who capture them by means of pits and traps, the commonest of these being a sort of big wooden cage constructed of timbers and stones, rather like a gigantic mouse-trap. A pig is tied up inside, and the entrance of the tiger releases the door and confines the beast, who is then despatched with spears. The natives, however, regard the animal with an overpowering apprehension, and there is an old Chinese saying that 'The Koreans hunt the tiger during one half of the year, while the tiger hunts the Koreans during the other half.' They will not travel singly at night, but go abroad in company, brandishing torches and striking gongs. They are also most reluctant to act as beaters; whence, perhaps, it arises that, common as the tiger is in Korea, I have rarely heard of a European who has bagged one to his own rifle. I am sometimes asked by sportsmen as to the charms or chances of a Korean expedition. As regards wild-fowl shooting, the great nuisance is that there is no means of disposing of the slain, and after a time mere slaughter palls; while, as regards big game, the difficulties and hardships of travel, accommodation, food, and following will probably send back the sportsman with a much worse appetite than when he started.

Thus wayfaring through the country one sees much of peasant life and agriculture. The villages are collections of mud-huts, thatched with straw (over which, as a rule, runs a climbing gourd), warmed by flues running beneath the floors, and surrounded for protection or seclusion by a wattled fence of branches or reeds. On the clay floor outside are usually seen drying a matful of red chillies, or of millet and rice grains fresh threshed by the flail; long strings of tobacco leaves, sus-

pended in festoons, have been picked from the garden plot
hard by, from which also a few castor-oil plants are rarely
absent. A small stye of black and abominable little pigs
usually fronts the road, on which the children are disporting
themselves in a state of comparative nudity. Inside, the
dour-visaged females are performing the work of the household, or are grinding, threshing, or winnowing the grain on

STREET IN A KOREAN VILLAGE

the open threshold. The men are away in the rice-fields or
among the crops of millet, beans, and buckwheat, which are
the staple cereal produce of the country. Cultivation is
assiduous, but not close. Hundreds of acres of cultivable
but uncleared soil alternate with the tilled patches; and
coarse grasses wave where the yellow grain should be ripen-
ing for the garner.

I saw no carts or wagons on my journeys, although they
are used in the north, near Ham-heung, and in a few other

114 KOREA

places. The ox, which is the familiar beast of burden, sometimes drags after him a rude wooden sled. More commonly a sort of wooden rack is fitted on to his back, and is packed with firewood for fuel. Men do not, as in Japan and China, carry burdens on bamboo poles, but in wooden racks, called *chi-kai*, upon their backs. They rest themselves by sitting down, in which

<small>Rural habits.</small>

A KOREAN PEASANT FAMILY

position the rack, having a wooden peg or leg, stands upright upon the ground. The long thin pipe of the country, between two and three feet in length, when not between the lips of its owner, is stuck in his collar at the back of his neck, and protrudes sideways into the air. When a pony is shod it is thrown down upon its back, and its legs tied together at the fetlock by a rope.

Outside towns of any size may commonly be seen a number of stones, or tablets (sometimes of iron or copper), bearing inscriptions in Chinese characters. These are erected either in connection with some historical event, or more frequently in honour of a local governor, who has earned the gratitude of the people, not for justice or clemency, which are not expected, but for wielding with no more than ordinary severity his prerogative of squeeze; or of a successful local candidate at the literary examinations, or of some public benefactor, or of a virtuous wife who has found in suicide the sole consolation for the loss of her spouse. Memorial tablets.

Chinese influence is visible everywhere, notably in the disposition of the dead. The Royal Tombs are at a distance of ten miles from the east gate of Sŏul; but they are on a modest scale compared with the mausoleums of Peking and Hué. Mandarins' graves are frequently marked by a stone table or altar for offerings, and a *stele* or pillar, bearing the epitaph of the deceased. Sometimes, after the Chinese fashion, stone effigies of warriors or animals are added, or a saddled stone horse, in case the spirit of the defunct should care to take a ride, or a small column in case it should have been metamorphosed into a bird and should require a perch. The commonest form of grave, however, is a large, circular, grassy mound, usually placed upon the side of a hill or summit of a little knoll, and surrounded with Scotch firs. The site is selected after consultation with a soothsayer, is visited every year on fixed days, and is ever afterwards kept inviolate from the spade or plough. The environs of Sŏul are sprinkled with thousands of such graves. Tombs.

Officialism, which is the curse of the country, is not without its effect even upon the fortunes of travel. Such an incubus is the travelling mandarin, who quarters himself where he pleases and exacts rations for which he never pays, that the villagers flee from an official passport as from the pest. Though I paid for everything, chickens and eggs were constantly refused me, on the plea that none were forthcoming, but really, I suppose, from fear that, on the strength of the *kuan-chow*, I should appropriate without payment whatever was produced. Under these circumstances, it is necessary to carry almost everything with one, in the form of tinned provisions. In the out-of-the-way parts few wayfarers are encountered; but near the capital the road will be crowded with officials, tucked up in small and comfortless sedans, with candidates going up to or returning from the examinations, with pilgrims, traders, professional players or mountebanks, beggars, picnickers, and impecunious vagabonds of every quality and style.

These are the picturesque sides and spectacles of Korean travel. There are some who would find in the Korean inn, which is the unavoidable resting-place at night, a more than compensating pain. There are no good inns in the country, because there is no class to patronise them. The officials and *yangbans*, as I have shown, quarter themselves on the magistracies. The peasant accepts the rude hospitality of his kind, and the village inn is only the compulsory resort of the residuum. Surrounding a small and filthy courtyard, to which access is gained by a gateway from the street, is on one side a long shed with a wooden trough, from which the ponies suck their sodden food; on another side is the earthenware vat, and the furnace by which it is cooked; opening off in a single, small, low-roofed room, usually 8 feet square, unadorned by any furniture save one or two dilapidated straw mats and some wooden blocks to serve as pillows. There the traveller must eat, undress, dress, wash and sleep as well as he can. He is fortunate if the surrounding filth is not the parent of even more vexatious enemies to slumber. Nevertheless, I have wooed and won a royal sleep in the Korean inn; wherefore let me not unduly abuse it.

CHAPTER V

THE CAPITAL AND COURT OF KOREA

Beautiful for situation is Mount Zion. On the side of the north is the city of the Great King. Walk about Zion, and go round about her: tell the towers thereof. Mark ye well her bulwarks, consider her palaces; that ye may tell it to the generations following. *Psalm* xlviii. 2, 12, 13.

AMONG the unexpected features of Korea is the possession of a capital that, as regards size and population, may fairly be counted one of the great cities of the East. I have spelled the name Söul;[1] but I should say in advance that I have never met two persons, even scholars, who pronounced the name in exactly the same way. Seoul, Syool, Sawull, Sowul, are among the more popular phonetic transliterations. That the word is a dissyllable seems to be certain; but not even on the lips of Koreans does the precise equivalent to the vowel-sounds employed make itself apparent. Perhaps to an English ear the true pronunciation is best conveyed by saying that the way in which an Irishman pronounces the immortal part of him fairly represents the sound.

<small>Name of the capital.</small>

To those who bear in mind the Chinese connection of Korea, upon which I shall so frequently have to insist, it will be no surprise to learn that Söul is in most exterior respects a Chinese city. Indeed, it was first made the

---

[1] The name signifies 'capital city.' Compare the Chinese Pe-king and Nan-king, *i.e.* northern and southern capitals, and the Japanese Tokio and Saikio (Kioto), *i.e.* eastern and western capitals. Söul is the Sior of Hendrik Hamel.

capital of the Korean kingdom exactly five centuries ago
by Ni Taijo, the founder of the reigning house,[1] a monarch
who in everything aped the Chinese model, at
that time, and, we may also say now, the sole standard of majesty or fashion to the petty surrounding
States. He built the stone wall, over twenty feet high, with
battlements and loopholes for archers, by which the city is

Walls and
gates of
Soul.

SOUTH GATE OF SÖUL.

surrounded; and he made the eight great gates, consisting
of a tunnelled passage in the wall, surmounted by a single
or a double-storeyed projecting tiled pavilion, by which
access is still gained to the interior.[2] Like the gates of

[1] The regalia and robes of state of Ni Taijo are still preserved in the
metropolitan monastery of Sak Wang Sa, which he founded in memory of
his 'call' to rule from this spot. The monastery is superbly situated in a
romantic wooden gorge, about twenty miles from Gensan.

[2] They are situated two on the north, one on the north-east, one on the
east, one on the south-east, two on the south-west, and one on the west.
The main gates are the east and west.

Peking, these have names of swelling import—the Gate of Elevated Humanity, the Gate of High Ceremony, and the Gate of Bright Amiability. As at Peking, also, the heavy wooden doors, sheathed and clamped with iron, are shut soon after sunset, the keys being taken to the King's Palace, and deposited with His Majesty, or, when the Chinese Commissioners are in Söul, with the latter.[1] No bribe can then open them, and the only method of ingress is by climbing, with the aid of a friendly hand with a rope, a dilapidated portion of the wall. Just before my visit a British admiral, being a few minutes too late, had been compelled to enter in this not unnautical fashion; whereat the Korean dignitaries could not make up their minds whether to be more shocked or amused.

The entire space circumscribed by the wall is not built over, for the latter climbs with antelope-like facility the scarp of the various rocky hills and mountains by which the city proper is surrounded, and includes much ground which could by no possibility admit of human dwelling. In fact, the wall may be said merely to embrace a defensible area, in the midst and lowlying portions of which has been placed a great human hive. The situation of the city, thus nestling in a trough between high hills, is therefore picturesque in the extreme, and would appear to have been specially designed for the purpose, were it not that the confined atmosphere in summer operating upon a densely-crowded mass of dwellings where the most contemptuous disregard of sanitary law prevails, renders it at that time a nursery of pestilence and sickness. Unlike the scenery which I have described in the last chapter as prevailing in the more northerly and eastern parts of Korea, the hills surrounding Söul are bare, arid, and uninviting.

Its situation.

[1] An interesting collateral admission of Chinese suzerainty.

THE CAPITAL AND COURT OF KOREA 121

The disintegrated granite of which they are composed does not admit of much vegetation, while such verdure as once adorned their slopes has in large measure been swept away. A scanty growth of timber clothes the north hill, called Pouk San, which, very much like Lycabettus at Athens, rises to a sharp elevation behind the Royal Palace. But the other

EAST GATE AND WALL OF SÖUL

hills are almost treeless, with the exception of Nam San, which is splendidly timbered up to its summit, 800 feet above the city on the south. Further away on the northern side the nearer elevations are dominated by the imposing mass of the Mountain of Pouk Han, whose gleaming grey pinnacles protrude themselves from sterile lower slopes.

It is worth while to climb Nam San; for from there is a wild and gloomy outlook over mountains rolling like grey billows on every side; while along the widening valley between them the river Han pushes its broad and shining coils to the sea. On the top of Nam San, too, are four beacon-towers—circular structures built of big stones, in whose interior tall piles of leaves and brushwood are nightly set ablaze, to signal to the capital the message of peace and security or the reverse, which, like the bale-fires of Troy, is supposed to have been passed

Beacon-fires.

MOUNTAIN OF POUK HAN

from peak to peak from the southern confines of the kingdom. On the north-west side another tall and three-pointed hill—known as Sam Kok San, or Three-peaked Hill, which the French in their expedition of 1866 called the Cock's Comb, because of the fiery red which it blushed at the early dawn—flashes an answering gleam from the opposite quarter; nor has this primitive form of telegraphy been nominally abandoned (though it is believed to have fallen into practical disuse), except on the lines where it has been replaced by the electric wire. A special code of signals depending on the number, position, and sequence of the beacon-fires, is employed in times of danger to announce to the capital the scene or moment of invasion and the fortunes of combat in the provinces. Towards nightfall the eye of the visitor, unaccustomed to the novelty, insists on turning

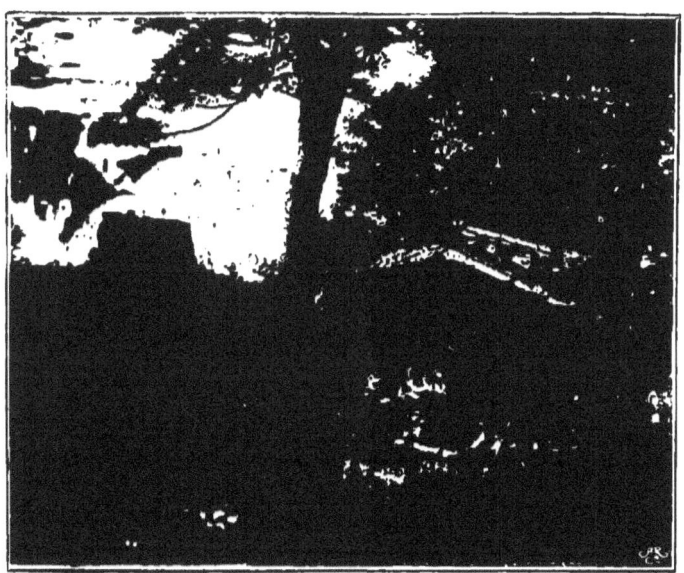

BEACON TOWER ON NAM SAN

skywards, and is not satisfied till 'the reassuring spark glimmers brightly from each sentinel peak.

Within the space thus enclosed and built over is contained a population, the various estimates of whose numerical total range from 150,000 to 300,000. An official calculation has placed the number of houses at 30,000, and we may accept 200,000 as a probable total for their inmates.[1] The bulk of these are crowded in

<small>Population and streets.</small>

[1] On the other hand, the Chinese publication, *Important Facts relating to the Eastern Stockade*, gives the number of houses as 46,565, and of inhabitants as 202,639.

thatched hovels, lining narrow and fetid lanes; but in singular and truly Oriental contrast are the main streets, three in number, one of which runs from the Palace to meet the second, which intersects the city from east to west, while the third strikes off from the latter to the south gate. Each of these is of a breadth and amplitude that would dignify a European capital, being at least fifty yards wide and smoothly gravelled; but even here the native love of crowding and squalor is allowed to assert itself, for the roadway is encroached upon by rows of rude straw-thatched shanties that have been erected by poverty-stricken squatters on either hand, encumbering the passage, and reducing the space available for locomotion to a narrow strip in the middle. When the King goes out, or when any state function of great solemnity takes place, all these improvised tenements are pulled down beforehand (but re-erected directly afterwards); and I own that I was far from sorry to see a large block of them blazing merrily one night, both because the street for a brief space resumed its proper dimensions, and from the insight which the spectacle afforded into the manners of the natives. Some of them sat on the neighbouring housetops, praying to the spirits to arrest the conflagration, which they made no effort to retard; others adopted a remedy by one stage more practical, seeing that they ran about with small pots, bowls, and even teacups, filled with water, which they dashed with sanguine futility upon the flames. But had it not been for the privately organised fire-brigade maintained by the Chinese Resident for the protection of the Chinese quarter, in or near to which the burning houses lay, there seemed no plausible reason why the conflagration should ever have stopped until it had reduced the entire city to ashes.

In the maps Sōul is made to stand upon the river Han;

and when I had read in history-books of the French and American frigates steaming up the river to threaten or attack it, I had pictured to myself a scene and a site not unlike the Nile at Khartum. But, as a matter of fact, the river is between three and four miles away; and the only local substitute for it is a narrow canal, which may be an Abana or a Pharpar in the rainy season,

Dirt and ditches.

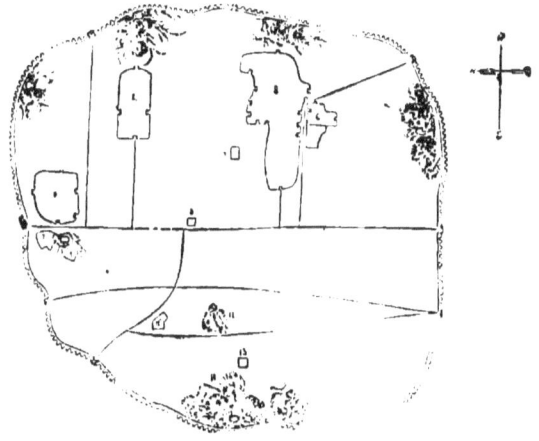

GROUND PLAN OF SÖUL

1. Palace
2. Old Palace (residence of King)
3. Big Bell
4. House of Tai Wen Kun
5. New Palace
6. Palace
7. Russian Legation
8. American Legation
9. Customs
10. British Legation
11. Chinese Residency
12. French R.C. Mission and Church
13. Japanese Legation
14. Nam San

but which, when I saw it, was merely a filthy and shallow sewer, in which the Korean urchins appeared to find pleasure in paddling. Each street or alley, moreover, has an open gutter running upon either side, and containing all the refuse of human and animal life. Söul is consequently a noisome and malodorous place; and exploration among its labyrinthine alleys is as disagreeable to the nostril as it is bewildering to the eye. A few elevations spring up from the general level of the city basin; and these have been opportunely occupied by foreigners with a superior appreciation of site, the British, Russian, and Japanese Legations and the French Catholic Establishment being from any altitude the most conspicious objects in the town. A settlement of 1000 Japanese is in acute competition with an even larger and increasing colony of Chinamen. Nearly 100 Europeans and Americans represent the remainder of the foreign community; but this admixture makes little superficial impression upon the white-coated, white-trousered, white-socked mass of humanity that swarms to and fro in the thronged thoroughfares of the city.

The public buildings of Sŏul are remarkable for their paucity and insignificance. With the exception of the great hooded roofs of the Audience Halls in the Palaces, the whole city, when seen from above, presents an almost even level of tiled roof-tops, packed so closely together that it looks as though a man might step from one to the other. The narrow alleys between them cannot be discerned, and only the white riband of the three principal streets, rendered whiter still by the white dresses of the Koreans, strutting up and down by the hundred, breaks the brown monotony. Even when we descend into the town, we find no beauty in the exterior of the houses; for they are, as a rule, constructed of a mixture of mud, paper, and wood; although those which are more strongly built have walls made of round stones, which are tied round and held together by plaited straw in lieu of the too expensive luxury of mortar. There are no windows in the housefronts—only lifting or sliding screens; and whatever of neatness or elegance exists in the abode is concealed in the interior, where the private dwellings, unseen from the street, are ranged round small courts. The houses of all classes are uniformly built either on platforms or on raised floors, for the purpose of warming

Houses.

THE CAPITAL AND COURT OF KOREA 127

by means of flues running underneath from a single furnace that serves the entire building. At the other end the smoke escapes by a blackened hole in the wall, usually into the street, where it adds to the æsthetic pains of perambulation. There is nowhere in the city anything in the least resembling the elaborate carved and gilded woodwork that adorns the shop-fronts in Peking, or even the monumental painted sign-

THE CITY AND OLD PALACE, SÖUL

boards of Canton. Another obstacle to street embellishment has been the existence of crude and foolish sumptuary laws, prohibiting the erection of houses of more than a certain size or beyond a fixed outlay.

For these drawbacks, however, Söul does its best to atone by two properties of unquestioned and more creditable individuality — viz. a singular and picturesque street-life, and a Court which is alternately dignified and comic, and sometimes both at the same time. Why the Koreans should all dress in white

Street-life and costume.

cotton no one seems able to say. It is not a fashion imposed
by conquest, like the pigtail in China; nor by smartness, like
the Albanian petticoat; nor by dignity, like the Roman toga;
nor by serviceableness, like the Highland kilt; not even by
the vulgar criterion of comfort, like the European trouser.
The colour cannot have been designed to resist the sun, because in winter there is not too much sun to resist; nor can

KOREAN SECRETARIES

the material have been selected for its lightness, since in the
cold weather it is only rendered wearable by being thickly
wadded with cotton-wool. I can only attribute the phenomenon, therefore, to one of those inexplicable freaks of
fortune, which have endowed the world, for instance, with
the crinoline and the top-hat; although, whatever the cause
of its original introduction, I harbour a secret suspicion that
the white cotton garments of the men are now maintained
by them for the excellent purpose they serve in keeping the

women busy. All day long, as you are walking in the streets of Sŏul, you will hear a mysterious tap, tap, tap, emerging from the closed shutters of the houses. This is the housewife who is at work indoors with a wooden cylinder with which she beats, beats, beats, her husband's white cotton clothes, in order to give them the peculiar gloss which

KOREAN WAITING-MAID

masculine fashion affects in Korea. The clothes are always taken to pieces in advance, and after the washing are either loosely stitched with thread, or are pasted together with starch. Over their white cotton drawers, which terminate in a kind of padded stocking, the men of the middle classes wear an outer tunic or skirt of similar material, which is split up at the sides, and looks very much like a nightshirt.

Secretaries and persons in civil employ wear over this a similar semi-transparent garment in black. The women of the lower orders are also as entirely clad in white as a class of English girls going to a Confirmation Service; but in the upper classes a gown of green, or crimson, or purple, instead of hanging from the shoulders, is drawn up over the head, with the sleeves hanging down in two long lappets behind, and is held closely together in front, admitting only a fugitive glimpse of black eyes behind. The most astonishing Korean coiffure is that of the Abigail or waiting-maid, and of all female attendants in the Palace, who wear a colossal erection upon their heads made of greasy black hair twisted in plaits, bigger by far than the artificial head-dress of an old Egyptian Pharaoh, or the wig of an English Lord Chancellor. This adornment is made up from the clippings or combings of boys' pigtails, which are dyed black, and sold in tresses at the cost of about 3s. a coil, each coil being one yard long and of the thickness of a finger. Upon the summit of this an enormous tray reposes as safely as upon a four-legged table.

Another peculiar coiffure is that of the King's dancing-girls, or *corps de ballet*, who are a regular feature at every Korean entertainment. These girls, who are called 'Ki-saing,' correspond to the Geisha of Japan. Companies of them exist in every town of any size, combining prostitution with the pursuit of their profession. Many of them are far from bad-looking, the type of feature being much more regular, even if wanting in the feminine attractiveness of the Japanese girl. The national dance, which is performed to the strains of a slow plaintive music evoked by a seated band, is monotonous in character and interminable in length.[1] Like all the dances

Dancing-girls.

---

[1] The photograph of the King's band was taken by Captain Castle, of H.M.S. *Leander*, in 1893.

of the Far East, it consists of a series of postures free from
indelicacy, and some of them not without grace, and has
been described as 'a not unpleasing mixture of minuet and
quadrille, with a dash of the reel towards the finish.' The
Koreans will sit and gaze at it in rapt ecstasy for hours at a
stretch.

THE KING'S BAND

It is as a country of hats that Korea has attained the
widest external fame, and in the course of a single stroll the
streets of Söul will afford material for an extensive
classification. The ordinary headpiece is a twofold
structure; for the outer hat, broad-brimmed and with slightly
conical crown, not unlike the old market-hat of the Welsh-
woman—though made of a material more delicate than
Wales ever saw—namely, among the upper classes split
bamboo fibres, woven together and lacquered black, and
among the lower orders a cheaper variety of the same, or
horsehair—is only the exterior covering or superstructure of

Hats.

a skull-cap and fillet of the same material, which is pressed around the temples, in order to hold in place the uncut hair of the men, drawn upwards and tied in a knot upon the crown. The exterior hat is kept on by a riband or string of amber and cornelian beads beneath the chin. Then there are hats for every rank, occupation, and even phase of life. The youth, when he is betrothed, wears, till his marriage, a smart fabrication of straw.

The successful candidate at one of the literary examinations is distinguished by two wires adorned with coloured rosettes, which project like hoops or *antennæ* over the summit of his hat. Peasants and bull-drivers are remarkable for colossal penthouses of plaited straw, which almost conceal the features, and whose circumference embraces the full width of the shoulders.

KOREAN MOURNER

Perhaps the mourner has the worst time; for, not only must he wear a somewhat similar extinguisher, hexagonal at the brim, but for a period of one, two, or three years, according to his relationship with the deceased, he is compelled to don a hempen robe, tied by a cord round the waist, and to carry in front of his mouth a small hempen screen between two sticks, in order, I believe, to keep at a proper distance the spirit of the departed.[1] During the period of mourning, prescribed

---

[1] This dress was worn for disguise by the Roman Catholic missionaries during the Christian persecution.

by an inflexible regulation, he is further forbidden to marry, or indulge in any of the lighter occupations of life; and instances have occurred of ill-starred bridegrooms, a continuous mortality among whose relations has left them stranded high and dry for years on the sad sands of celibacy, their *fiancées* meanwhile growing grey and ill-favoured before their eyes. Monks have a hat peculiar to their order, made of rush-matting, with a hexagonal brim, and terminating in a conical apex; while there is a separate long narrow straw fabric for nuns. The Korean soldiers also have a distinguishing hat, made of black horsehair felt, tied on with coloured tape ribands; a superior variety of the same article, adorned with plumes, makes of their officers a wondrous sight. It is only, however, when we reach the grades of court and official society that the Korean hatmaker achieves his greatest masterpieces. Thus, for the governor of a province he supplies a sort of mitre of gilt pasteboard; while for ministers and officials generally are prescribed various degrees of headpiece, constructed with receding stages, like a Doge's cap of state, and fitted with wings or paddles projecting from the back. Even the royal lackeys have a headpiece, consisting of a small bamboo structure, stuck on sideways, with a huge bunch of artificial flowers at the back, which is only less fantastic than the harlequin's cap of the Shah's runners at Teheran.

With nine out of every ten persons clad in white, and with the entire ten adorned with these astonishing varieties of headgear, it may readily be imagined that street-life in Söul is not exactly the same, for instance, as in London or New York. Nor are there any carriages or wheeled vehicles, of whatsoever description, to suggest a Western parallel. Locomotion is

<small>Amusements.</small>

entirely pedestrian, save for such persons, usually of high estate, as are perched upon the backs of the diminutive Korean ponies, clinging with difficulty to the pommel of a saddle, which lifts them almost as high above the back of the animal as the latter is above the ground; or as are borne along by shouting attendants in open chairs or sedans. Next to ponies the most familiar animals encountered in the streets of Söul are magnificent bulls, marching along under vast stacks of brushwood, and behaving themselves with a docility that is quite extraordinary. They are the only other beast of burden known to the country, are highly prized, and fetch comparatively heavy prices. Children abound everywhere, and derive a peculiar gratification from sporting in the gutters. They are frequently clad in pink or some other bright colour, and are usually engaged in flying small rectangular painted kites, made of the wonderful oiled paper of the country.[1] Kite-fighting consists in drawing one kite sharply across another when at a great height in the air, so as to sever the rival string. Another popular urban amusement is stone-throwing. Different parts of the capital,

[1] The Korean paper is the most remarkable native manufacture. It is made from more than one material, though usually from the inner bark of a mulberry-tree; but there is hardly anything in Korea that cannot be made of it. After it has been soaked in oil of sesame it becomes both exceedingly durable and waterproof. As such it is used instead of carpets on the floors, instead of paper on the walls, instead of glass in the windows, and instead of white-wash on the ceilings. Clothes, hats, shoes, tobacco-pouches, and fans are made of it; so are umbrellas, lanterns, and kites. Rooms are divided by paper screens; clothes are kept in paper chests; men travel with paper trunks; children play with paper toys. Then there are the ordinary purposes of writing and printing; and so frugal are the Koreans, that even the examination-papers of the candidates in the literary examinations, instead of being thrown away, are disposed of for a few coppers, and subsequently do duty as improvised macintosh capes on the shoulders of the coolies, who go marching along in the rain, innocently parading the maxims of Confucius on their backs. The principal manufactory is in a valley watered by a stream outside the north gate of Söul; and a steam paper-mill, with foreign machinery, has just been erected at Yang-hwa-chin on the Han, four miles below the capital.

which is divided into five quarters or wards, or different villages, wage fierce warfare on an open space of ground, driving each other backwards and forwards with showers of missiles. These contests are conducted with great ferocity, and frequently result in loss of life. Even with the advance of civilisation their savagery has scarcely abated; though the sport, which has nothing to recommend it, is said to be less popular than of yore. It is not unlike the custom, still prevailing in one or two English places, of an annual football match in the main street between two parts of a town, in which every one who likes may take part.

A history of sack and siege has left very few relics of antiquity either in the capital or in its neighbourhood; but, such as they are, I will describe them. At the junction of the two main streets, under a roofed pavilion, known as the Chong Kak, or Bell Kiosque, and behind wooden bars, hangs a famous old bronze bell, which is reported, with a modesty that I cannot think remarkable, since I have found it shared by at least half a dozen rival competitors in the course of my travels, to be the third largest in the world. It is in no respect an astonishing bell, being without ornament, save for an inscription, which relates that it was erected in A.D. 1468 by Taijo Tai Woang. But the Americans are said to have tried to get hold of it for Chicago; and it never allows its own presence to be forgotten by strangers, for it is banged with a swinging wooden beam every evening for some minutes between 7 and 9 P.M. before the gates are shut, and also before sunrise, between 3 and 5 A.M., as well as on other occasions, when there is a fire. The roads diverging from the Chong Kak are known as Chong Ro, or Bell Roads.

The Big Bell.

It was close to the Bell Kiosque that the stone was placed in 1866 by the old Regent, the Tai Wen Kun, who reigned before the present King had attained his majority, with an inscription calling upon the Koreans to kill all Christians; nor was it till 1883 that it was finally removed.

Shops. Adjoining the same site are the only two-storeyed shops, or warehouses, in Söul. They belong to the King, and are leased to the merchants of the six great trading guilds of Korea, who pay him a substantial price for the privilege of controlling the sale of Chinese and native silk, of cotton goods, of hemp and grass cloth, and of Korean paper. The shops open on to a narrow central court, but the goods there displayed, consisting of silk and cotton and figured gauze fabrics, Chinese shoes, native paper, and brass utensils,[1] do not greatly attract the foreigner. He is more likely to pick up something amid the old rubbish lying upon the open stalls in the main street outside.

In the back court of a mean hovel, at no great distance, stands a small and exquisite, though much defaced, white granite pagoda, whose ascending tiers are richly carved with images of the seated Buddha. The topmost tier has been broken off—it is said by the Japanese during their invasion 300 years ago—and is lying upon the ground hard by. This monument was variously reported to me as having been brought over from China by the Chinese wife of a Korean monarch some seven centuries ago, and as marking the site of what was once an important Buddhist monastery in the heart of the city. Not far away stands a Chinese *stele* or tall granite pillar, with wreathed dragons at the top, and an undecipherable inscription on the

Stone pagoda and pillar.

---

[1] Among these it is unfair to pass without notice the national implement of Korea, a circular brass pot, with a lid, but no handle, which is carried about by the attendant of every respectable citizen, and serves alternately as pillow, candlestick, ash-plate, spittoon, and *pot de chambre*.

face, reposing upon an immense granite tortoise.¹ There are a similar pillar and tortoise outside Söul, about 7½ miles from the east gate, with an inscription in Chinese and Manchu upon the opposite faces, commemorating the institution of the Korean king, who *kowtowed* at this spot to the Manchu conqueror, upon his second invasion of Korea in 1637, and renounced allegiance to the Mings in his favour. Under the philo-Japanese administration of the Korean ministers Pak and So, the Japanese attempted to destroy this monument in February 1895, with a body of police. But the villagers defended it so stoutly that the police had to retire *re infecta*. Between this pillar and the city is passed the Sen Kuang Kio, an old bridge of white stone slabs, resting upon twenty-one stone piers.

Religion at present has but few altars in or near to the capital. There is an altar to the Spirits of the Land (sometimes miscalled the Temple of Heaven), consisting of a bare open platform, upon which annual sacrifices are offered by the King, as on the She Chi Tan in China and in Annam. Temples. Inside the walls on the north-east is the Temple of Confucius, where there is the customary sanctuary containing the tablet of that philosopher, and a large building for students and *literati*. I also visited the Temple of the God of War, outside the southern gate, one of those semi-heroic additions to the Chinese pantheon (the god being reported to have been a real historical personage or distinguished general, who was canonised by Imperial edict) which are familar to the traveller in the Celestial Empire. The images in the temple are hideous beyond words, but in one of the courts is an interesting sun-dial in a basin; and two side galleries contain a curious collection of

---

¹ The tortoise in Chinese mythology is one of the nine offspring of the dragon, and is placed below memorial pillars and gravestones as an emblem of strength.

genuine old helmets and armour, exactly like those which I shall shortly describe in the Royal Procession, and a number of wall-paintings, representing battle-scenes by land and sea from the famous Chinese historical novel San Kuo Chih, or Record of the Three Kingdoms.

TEMPLE OF THE GOD OF WAR AT SÖUL.

One of the most conspicuous objects in Söul at the time of my visit was the Hong Sal Mun, or Red Arrow Gate, erected at some distance from the Palace. This was a lofty wooden arch, some 30 feet high, painted red—the royal colour—and consisting of two perpendicular posts, united at the top by two horizontal traverses, through which a number of red arrows were fixed with their points upwards. This archway, which was of Tartar origin, and somewhat resembled the *torii* (or so-called bird-rests) which precede both Shinto and Buddhist temples in Japan, as well as the commemorative arch or *pailow* in China, is a symbol of majesty and govern-

Red Arrow Gate.

ment in Korea, and is accordingly erected in front of royal palaces, Government buildings, and temples or monasteries (as at Sak Wang Sa) under royal patronage. In Sŏul it marked the approach to the Nam Piel Kung, or Palace of the Chinese Imperial Commissioners. A not dissimilar but far

ARCHWAY OF THE CHINESE COMMISSIONERS

more elegant and purely Chinese stone archway, called the Geo Mun, stood about a mile outside the western gate on the road to Peking, and marked the point to which the King went forth to meet the Imperial Envoys. Near to it was the Bokakan, or mansion in which he awaited their arrival.

Both the Hong Sal Mun, as symbolising Korean sovereignty, and the Geo Mun, as illustrating former Chinese suzerainty, have been destroyed by the Japanese since the termination of the war, in a spirit of iconoclasm as stupid as it is discreditable.

Continuing past this gate to a point about three miles from the city on the north-west, one arrives at a gigantic image of Buddha, 15 feet high, which has been painted upon the upright surface of a huge fallen granite boulder. The figure is all white, but the eyes, mouth, ears, and head-dress have been coloured; and a gaudily painted temple-roof has been erected as a shelter over the whole. One hand of the image is uplifted, the other reposes at his side.

The painted Buddha.

The place of execution used to be near the southern gate, where, after decapitation, the headless trunk and trunkless head of the criminal lay exposed for three days. The introduction of the foreign element, with its scruples, has removed the scene of operations to a site some miles from the city, where a friend of mine witnessed an execution of several culprits—the head never falling till after several slashes from a big sword—and even painted a picture of the gruesome scene.

Execution-place.

Among the other environs of Söul, the only ones worthy of mention are the two royal retreats or fortresses in the mountains of Pouk San and Sam Kok San, which are surrounded by walls and fortified, and are held by monkish garrisons.[1] To one or other of these, in times of invasion, revolution, or danger, the King escapes, provisions being stored there in anticipation of a long siege. The nearest of them is eleven miles distant, and is called Hokanzan, the walled enclosure being five miles in circuit. The larger is sixteen miles

Royal fortresses.

---

[1] This clerical militia is a legacy from the days when the Buddhist hierarchy was a great power in the land, and produced statesmen and warriors as well as devotees and students. The monasteries were then fortified buildings, and were garrisoned by their inmates. It was from one of these fortified monasteries that the French met with their disastrous repulse on Kanghwa Island in 1866.

distant, and its wall is seven miles round. It is called Nankanzan.[1]

I next turn to the Royal Palaces. Just as the capital is the centre of the kingdom, to which everybody and everything—society, officials, candidates, merchants, business, employment, relaxation—gravitate, so does the entire life of the capital revolve round the centre of the Palace and the King. The latter may be a small personage to the outer world—perhaps a large majority of mankind may be unaware even of his existence—but to his subjects he is something overwhelmingly great, while to these attributes is added, in the case of China and of its once dependent States, the prestige of a rank that is held divine, and entitles its wearer to be called the Son of Heaven. No celestial scion in the world in all probability exercises less influence upon its destinies than His Majesty the King of Korea; but that does not in the least detract from his titular eminence in the eyes of Koreans, which an ancient and inflexible etiquette maintains in a becoming atmosphere of mystery and isolation. Fortunately in the case of Korea, the hedge of royal dignity, still unimpaired in the case of the suzerain Power and of the Court at Peking, has been sufficiently broken through by the force of circumstances during the past twenty years, to admit of audiences being readily conceded by a monarch, whom close contact reveals as an amiable personage, not less human — perhaps in certain respects rather more so—than the bulk of his fellow-creatures.

Sovereignty in Korea.

There is quite a number of palaces in Söul. One of these, the Nam Kung, near the south gate, is employed for

[1] This must be the 'Fort of Numma Sansiang' of Hendrik Hamel, where the King retired in war, which was six to seven leagues, or three hours, from Sior, was stored with three years' provisions, and was garrisoned by 'religious.'

marriage ceremonies, and has sometimes been the residence of the Commander-in-Chief. Another, the Nam Piel Kung, near the west gate, was, until the war, reserved for the accommodation of the Imperial Envoys from Peking. A third, the Un Pyon Kung, in the northern quarter, was formerly occupied by the Tai Wen Kun, or Regent, the father of the reigning King, who practically usurped the throne during his son's minority, persecuted the Christians, tortured and killed the missionaries, and by his savage and reactionary policy forced upon foreign Powers the first opening of the country.

<small>Royal Palaces.</small>

The principal residence of royalty has usually been in one of two palaces of much greater size than those hitherto mentioned. Accounts vary as to the respective antiquity of the pair, the one that is temporarily occupied by the Sovereign being commonly denominated the New Palace, presumably because repairs have recently been required in order to render it habitable. The two together occupy an enormous space, surrounded by walls, and entered by great gates, in the northern part of the city; and in their precincts are included several hundreds of acres of enclosed but uncultivated ground, extending to the summit of the north hill, a conical elevation covered with low scrub, that rises to a sharp and lofty point just behind. As a matter of fact, the more easterly of the two palaces is the newer, having been erected for the Heir Apparent about 400 years ago. It has thirteen gates and covers an enormous space of ground, much of which is laid out in gardens and walks, and is adorned with lotus-ponds, bridges, and summer-houses. It was occupied by the King in the early years after his accession, was partly burned down in 1882, was rebuilt and re-occupied, but again deserted after the Rebellion of 1884, and, when

<small>East, or New Palace.</small>

THE CAPITAL AND COURT OF KOREA 143

I was in Söul in 1892, was without a tenant; though it was reported that the King was going back there, because a snake had fallen from the ceiling of the Crown Prince's room in the other palace. Shortness of supplies, however, interfered with the execution of this design; but the King had already connected the grounds of this palace by an

THE CITY AND NEW PALACE, SÖUL.

enclosed passage-way at the back with the other palace in which he was then residing.

The latter, which is the more westerly and now the principal, is also the older building, having been erected 500 years ago. It stands at the head of the broad thoroughfare known as Palace-street, the end of which is entirely filled by its massive stone gateway, surmounted by a heavy, double-roofed pavilion. Outside the gate are two grotesque stone lions

West, or Old Palace.

upon stone pedestals, and a ramp with eighteen low stone pillars on either side. In the base of the gate-tower are three arched doorways, closed with wooden doors, adorned with painted figures. Of these the middle door, or Thoi Hwa Mun, is only opened for the ingress or egress of the King, or of a Minister Plenipotentiary going to present his credentials from his Sovereign ; but the others are the

GATEWAY OF THE OLD PALACE

regular passage-way to the multitude of interior courts, which are crowded with officials, retainers, soldiers, ministers, secretaries, lackeys, runners, and hangers-on of every description. Five hundred guards protect the royal person, the remainder of the garrison of 4000 (which represents, under normal circumstances, the entire standing army of Korea) being stationed in barracks outside. There are further reported to be about 2000 retainers in the Palace enclosure.

THE CAPITAL AND COURT OF KOREA

First come two immense paved courts, surrounded by low buildings, and terminating in great gateways. The second of these conducts to a further quadrangle, also of great size, at the upper end of which, on a two-fold terrace or platform, surrounded by white granite balustrades, and ascended by triple flights of steps, the middlemost of which are reserved for the palanquin in

Great Hall of Audience.

GREAT HALL OF AUDIENCE

which is borne the royal person—stands the Great Hall of Audience, wherein is held the imposing pageantry of the annual *levées* on the King's birthday, on New Year's Day, and on other festive anniversaries. The building consists of a great twin-roofed hall, constructed entirely of wood, the richly carved and reticulated ceiling of which, painted red, blue, and green, is supported by immense circular pillars, coloured red above and white at the base. It is empty except for a lofty scarlet daïs facing the entrance, and

K

ascended by six steps, upon which, in front of a beautifully carved scarlet and black screen of pierced woodwork, is placed the chair of state of the King. From this position he looks down upon the matted floor of the hall, through the open doors on to the double terrace outside, and thence to the paved quadrangle, where twelve inscribed pillars on either hand indicate the various positions taken up by the different ranks of nobles and officials at the royal *levées*. The furthest of these is so distant as barely to render visible the august form of the Sovereign. The idea of this splendid Audience Hall, grandiose in its massive simplicity, is curiously analogous to the *talars*, or throne-rooms, of the Persian kings from the days of Darius to those of Nasr-ed-din Shah ; and the spectacle which it presents on the great days of audience, like that which I shall describe in my succeeding work at Hué, is one of the few surviving and intact pageants of the Far East.

In an adjoining court is the Summer Palace, a large hall or pavilion raised upon forty-eight pillars of stone, twelve feet high, in the middle of a lotus-pond. Hard by may also be seen the Chin Chang Hall, or Hall of Diligence, the Yun Hall, or Hall of Departed Spirits, which is used in the funeral celebrations of royalty, and the Chai Hall, or Hall of Fasting. The rear part of the building, where the King and his seraglio reside, consists of a number of smaller courts, kiosques, and pavilions, adorned with a good deal of bright painting, and possessing a certain fantastic elegance. The electric light was installed in this part of the Palace by order of the King, who has the Oriental's fondness for any new and expensive invention ; but it very soon came to grief. Another contract was given in 1893 to an American engineer, who imported the entire plant from the United States. It was in one of the smaller

Summer Palace.

edifices that I was admitted to an audience with His Majesty.

INTERIOR OF THE OLD PALACE

Li Hsi, King of Korea (whose original Korean name was Mong Pok-i), is the twenty-eighth sovereign of the reigning dynasty. He was the nephew of Li Hwan, the last king but one, who, having no children, had been succeeded by his uncle Li Ping, who also died childless in 1864. Thereupon the young boy, at that time twelve years of age, was selected as heir by the Royal Council, and was adopted by his great-grandmother, the Queen Dowager Chao, the widow of the Crown Prince Li Ying, who had never succeeded to the throne. This old lady died in 1890.

The King of Korea.

The young Sovereign being a minor, the royal authority was vested in a Council of Regency, one of whom, Li Cheng Ying, the father of the boy and a man of great strength of character, took advantage of his position to usurp the chief power. Nominally as Regent, with the title of Tai Wen Kun, Lord of the Great Court, he ruled the kingdom with great severity from 1864 to 1873.

<small>The Tai Wen Kun.</small>

He it was who was responsible for the furious persecution of the Christian missionaries that brought the unsuccessful French expedition of 1866 into Korea, and for the frantic anti-foreign crusade which eventually broke down under the combined pressure of the foreign Powers. He was once aptly described by a native writer as having 'bowels of iron and a heart of stone.' Upon the assumption by the King of full sovereignty in 1873, and the subsequent opening of the country, the Tai Wen Kun headed the Conservative or Reactionary party, against all treaties and all foreigners, while from time to time he 'kept his hand in' at conspiracy, for which he has a unique genius, by arranging plots to depose the King and Queen, and to replace the former by some more flexible member of his own family. One such attempt to plant another son upon the throne was detected in 1876, and the unhappy youth was invited to drink a cup of poison. Upon this the Tai Wen Kun, with an ability greatly in advance of his times, despatched some boxes of choice bonbons, concealing explosive bombs, to his successful adversaries, whom he thus triumphantly removed. After a short lull he is believed to have instigated the first outbreak against the Japanese Legation in 1882, when an attempt was made to kidnap the King and to kill the Queen,[1] and

---

[1] So universally were both the Queen and the Crown Prince believed to have been killed, that their death was printed as a fact in Mr. W. E. Griffis' *Hermit Nation*, which was published shortly afterwards. It being undesirable for a while to reveal the truth, national mourning for a year was even ordered, and was observed for the full period. It subsequently transpired that the Queen had been smuggled out in disguise as the wife of a soldier, and that one of the Court ladies had been killed in her place.

when the Japanese Minister, Hanabusa, and his following had to retreat fighting to Chemulpo, where they were picked up by a British man-of-war. Very shortly the Japanese Minister reappeared with demands for immediate and ample reparation; but, while the negotiations still lingered,

THE TAI WEN KUN

the sky was suddenly cleared by a thunderbolt launched by Li Hung Chang, the great Chinese Viceroy, who had seized the opportunity to reassert the compromised suzerainty of his Imperial master. The Tai Wen Kun was himself kidnapped and deported to China, where he was kept a prisoner at Paoting Fu.

During his absence in 1884, a second revolution, of somewhat similar character, broke out in the capital,[1] from which

[1] The leader of this revolution, Kim Ok Kiun, who escaped at the time and lived for some years as a refugee under Japanese protection at Kioto, having

the King only escaped by jumping on to the back of a
eunuch, in which not too dignified position he was carried
into the Chinese camp outside Söul. After matters had
been somewhat composed, the King began to think that the
abilities of the old Regent might perhaps after all be more
usefully employed at home; and accordingly he himself
applied to China for his restoration. It cannot be said that
the experiment was a success, so far as the relations of the
pair were concerned, for in the summer of 1892 a determined
attempt was made by the political opponents of the Tai Wen
Kun to blow him up with gunpowder, though the misdirection
of the explosive, which blew out the side of the room which
he occupied, instead of the floor, saved the old gentleman's
life. It could not fail to be remarked that the King evinced
no solicitude at the miraculous escape of his parent—a
callousness which was the more extraordinary in a country
where Confucianism has inculcated filial respect as the
highest duty. The Tai Wen Kun, now seventy-four years
of age, is still living, and continues to give proofs of a vitality
which neither age nor disappointment can impair. Just
before the commencement of hostilities between Japan
and China in July 1894, the Japanese appear to have contemplated making use of his influence in their own interest, and appointed him Commissioner or Regent for the
discussion of reforms. Very soon, however, the Tai Wen
Kun developed the most violent anti-Japanese inclinations,
and was accordingly shelved. He seems to have utilised his

incautiously proceeded to Shanghai, was murdered there in the spring of 1894
by a fellow-countryman, it is said at the direct instigation of the King. Anyhow, his remains, upon being taken back to Korea by order of the Government, were there subjected to mutilation and public exposure: the remaining
members of his family were put to death, and the murderer was loaded with
honours. Korea never so successfully vindicated her claim to exclusion from
the pale of civilisation. The murder of Kim Ok Kiun, however, was one of
the events that precipitated the late war.

liberty to embark in a fresh conspiracy against the King and Queen, for which, though he escaped scot-free himself, his grandson was arrested, tried, and sentenced in 1895 to ten years' banishment. The old man, after a short spell of retirement, has again, as these pages go to press in October 1895, asserted his indomitable spirits by a renewed plot, in which, after the King's Korean Guard, duly bribed in advance, and a number of Japanese, had penetrated into the Palace, and successfully atoned for the many previous failures on his part by killing the Queen outright, he once more usurped the supreme power, the King managing to escape with his life. This scandalous event, in which it is alleged that the Japanese were implicated, is not unlikely to mark a turning-point in Korean fortunes. To the remarkable experiences which I have related the Tai Wen Kun also adds the accomplishments of an artist; and I am the possessor of an excellent signed pen-and-ink drawing by his hand.

With the exception of the two above-mentioned revolts in 1882 and 1884, which were in both cases the result of political and Court intrigue, rather than of any popular movement, the King had until 1894 occupied the throne for twenty years without menace or peril. Upon both those occasions, though the external symptom of the outbreak was an attack upon the Japanese Legation, who invariably represent the least popular element of society in Söul, the real object of the conspirators was to capture, without injuring, the person of the King, whose seal and signature lent a much-coveted sanction to the successful faction.[1] It was not the life of the

The King's reign.

---

[1] The person of the Sovereign is held sacred and inviolable—his real safeguard against assassination ; but it is the royal seal that is the coveted object. Till recent years a change of party in Korean government (which there is no machinery for effecting by a general election) was invariably carried out as follows :—The conspirators gathered in sufficient numbers in the Palace,

Sovereign that was aimed at in either case, but the influence of those under whose control he was supposed to be. In February 1894 a plot was discovered for blowing up with gunpowder the King, Crown Prince, and chief Ministers of State while on a visit to the Royal Ancestral Temple; but what the exact object of this Korean Guy Fawkes may have been, or who were the real instigators of the design, did not transpire. It was generally supposed to have been the old Regent's reply to the attempt upon himself two years earlier. Then followed the second conspiracy before alluded to; and finally, the ignominy of the Japanese occupation, which, after subjecting the King to every variety of humiliation, has left him a monarch only in name, and, probably, the most disconsolate living occupant of a throne.

His Majesty is a man of much amiability of character; and many instances are related of his personal charm of disposition and bearing. If he does not share the bigotry, neither has he inherited the determination of his father; and placed as he has been in difficult circumstances, for which, by training and tradition, he was equally unprepared, there are many excuses to be made alike for volatility of purpose and irresolution of action. Until the Japanese came, he took a keen zest in any new discovery or invention, though he was not free from the superstition of his race and country. It will be accounted a remarkable fact in history that both Japan and Korea should have undergone in the second half of the present century the greatest revolution in their annals, under the sceptre of sovereigns whose personality struck in neither case a very definite or individual note.

<small>His character.</small>

---

seized and assassinated the leaders of the Government, laid hold of the King and of the seal of State, and compelled him to sign the warrants for the execution of the murdered officials, as well as their own commissions.

THE CAPITAL AND COURT OF KOREA   153

The most powerful influence in the Palace, and indeed in the country, has for long been that of the Queen, the members of whose family, known as Min, were, under the old *régime*, introduced into nearly every position of importance or emolument about the Court and in the Government, and thereby acquired an ascendency which

The Queen.

THE CROWN PRINCE

was the cause of great political jealousy and intrigue. The Queen's informants and spies were said to be everywhere, and nothing was done without her knowledge. It was against this omnipotent influence that the Tai Wen Kun directed all the forces at his disposal; and, though the Japanese could not depose her as long as they kept the

King, one of their first acts was to evict the entire Min faction, who have since been in disgrace, and have been replaced by more accommodating politicians. It is alleged that the Queen retaliated by making advances to Russia; in which, if true, we may perhaps find an explanation of the dramatic violence of her recent removal.

The King's eldest son by the Queen, Li Hsia by name, is the Heir Apparent, or Crown Prince, and was born in 1873. His abilities, however, are so much below the average, and there is so little chance of his founding a family, that his position in the State is less important than it might otherwise be. Attention has sometimes been directed to another and elder son of the King by a concubine, of whom more may be heard in the future; but in the meantime the Crown Prince continues to exist, an even more troubled phantom than his sire.

The Crown Prince.

The Korean monarchy is, in theory, absolute, hereditary, and divine. The King is master of the lives and property of his subjects and of the entire resources of the kingdom. All offices are held at his pleasure. His word is law. In his person is concentrated every attribute of Government. If in relation to China he was, till recently, a humble vassal, in his own dominions he was supreme. The opening of Korea to the world was, however, not accomplished without dealing many and inevitable blows at the peculiarly sacrosanct character of the royal authority, upon which stress has been laid by so many writers.[1] This

Theory of monarchy.

---

[1] Dallet, and Griffis, in the main copying from him, describe several features of Court ceremonial, and of the Korean theory of kingship, which were probably derived from the ancient statutes of the kingdom, but which have long been, or are now, obsolete. These fictions have attained a wide popularity, mainly owing to their repetition in works of comparative sociology such as *The Golden Bough*, by J. G. Frazer (2 vols. 1890). The latter, in vol. i. pp. 164, 172, says that the Kings of Korea are shut up in their palaces from the age of twelve or fifteen; that if a suitor wishes to obtain justice

THE CAPITAL AND COURT OF KOREA 155

had been effected beyond repair even before the experiences of the past year, and was already contracting into the more modest conception of kingship that has been evolved by Western experience.

Before proceeding to the royal audience, I enjoyed an interview with the President of the Korean Foreign Office,[1] an old gentleman with a faultless black hat, a benign and sleepy expression, plump cheeks, and a long thin grey moustache and beard. I remember some of his questions and answers. Having been particularly warned not to admit to him that I was only thirty-three years old, an age to which no respect attaches in

Audience with the Foreign Minister.

---

of the King he sometimes lights a great bonfire on a mountain facing the Palace; that when the King goes out of the Palace, all doors must be shut, and each householder must kneel before his threshold with a broom and a dust-pan in his hand, whilst all windows, especially the upper ones, must be sealed with strips of paper, lest some one should look down upon the King; that no one may touch the King; and that, if he deigns to touch a subject, the spot touched becomes sacred, and the person thus honoured must wear a visible mark (generally a cord of red silk) for the rest of his life. Not one of these observances is now maintained. Suitors wishing to obtain a hearing from the King do not light a bonfire, but sit outside the Palace-gate with their petition placed on a table in front of them, until the fact is reported to the King, and the petition is taken in and considered. When the King goes out of the Palace in procession, the shops along the route are closed, but no restriction is placed upon the spectators, who crowd the streets, and even the rooftops, coming in from the country in thousands to see the pageant; nor is any obeisance required from them. Red girdles, which are quite common, have also ceased to bear the alleged significance. Other statements popularly repeated (*e.g.* in the *Encyclopædia Britannica*), that it is sacrilege to utter the King's name, and high treason to touch him with iron, and that every horseman must dismount when passing the Palace, are equally erroneous. Only those officials dismount who propose to enter the Palace. Similarly, the oft-quoted rule forbidding any Korean subject to go out at night in Soul, except women, officials, and blind persons, has fallen into desuetude since the number of Chinese and Japanese in the city, and of servants in the employ of foreigners, has rendered its enforcement impossible.

[1] There were in 1892 three principal Ministers of State in Korea, denominated Councillors of the Middle, Left, and Right. There were also six Government Departments, namely, the Officers of (i) Civil Affairs or Public Employ; (ii) Finance, *i.e.* the Treasury; (iii) Rites or Ceremonies and Public Instruction; (iv) War; (v) Justice; (vi) Public Works. To these,

Korea, when he put to me the straight question (invariably the first in an Oriental dialogue), 'How old are you?' I unhesitatingly responded, 'Forty.' 'Dear me,' he said, 'you look very young for that. How do you account for it?' 'By the fact,' I replied, 'that I have been travelling for a month in the superb climate of His Majesty's dominions.' Hearing that I had been a Minister of the Crown in England, he inquired what had been my salary, and added, 'I suppose you found *that* by far the most agreeable feature of office. But no doubt the perquisites were very much larger.' Finally, conscious that in his own country it is not easy for any one to become a member of the Government, unless he is related to the family of the King or Queen, he said to me, 'I presume you are a near relative of Her Majesty the Queen of England.' 'No,' I replied, 'I am not.' But, observing the look of disgust that passed over his countenance, I was fain to add, 'I am, however, as yet an unmarried man,' with which unscrupulous suggestion I completely regained the old gentleman's favour.

In the Palace everything—dress, deportment, movement, gait—is regulated by a minute and uncompromising etiquette. Upon one occasion a British Consul was not admitted to audience with the King, because, having packed up his

since the opening of the country, had been added two new departments—the *Nai-mu-pu*, or Home Office, which had a President, two native Vice-Presidents, two foreign Vice-Presidents (namely, the Foreign Advisers), one Councillor, and a staff of twenty-five clerks, and which had virtually superseded the old six boards; and the *Oi-a-mun*, or Foreign Office, with a similar organisation, which was formerly under the Minister of Ceremonies, there having been in those days practically no Foreign Affairs. The entire hierarchy here mentioned has, however, been superseded since the war by the Japanese, who have set up the Cabinet system, as described in the chapter 'After the War,' and have instituted nine Ministries or Departments, with Ministers and Vice-Ministers at fixed salaries (so far unpaid), viz.: (i) Royal Household; (ii) Prime Minister's Department; (iii) Foreign Office; (iv) Home Office; (v) Law and Justice; (vi) War; (vii) Exchequer; (viii) Agriculture and Commerce; (ix) Education.

THE CAPITAL AND COURT OF KOREA

uniform, he came only in evening dress. The middle and lower officials wear brightly-coloured robes of scarlet, blue and yellow; but the ministers and chief notables affect a richer and more sober hue, usually dark blue or puce, the material being of figured silk.[1] On the bosom is fixed a plastron or panel of coarse embroidery, representing a tiger, or stalk, or some other symbolical

A KOREAN MINISTER

creature; while round the waist is worn a broad belt, variously adorned with gold, silver, jade, ivory, or horn, which projects several inches from the person, like the hoop

Court dress and etiquette.

[1] This has been superseded since the war by the Japanese, who have compelled the Korean officials to adopt a more sombre style of dress manufactured in Japan, in place of the particoloured silks of China.

of a beer-barrel that has started from its place. On the head reposes one of the winged tiaras which I have before described. There is also a peculiar strut, which is known as the '*yangban* walk,' and which all ministers or nobles affect when they appear in public. It is a slow and measured movement, with the feet planted rather wide apart, and an indescribable but unmistakable swing of the body that is most comic. The main attribute or manifestation of dignity in Korea seems, however, to be that its possessor is incapable of moving without support. Unsustained he would, I suppose, fall to the ground from the sheer weight of his own importance. Accordingly, a minister, if seen walking on the streets, is invariably supported by one, sometimes by two attendants, who deferentially prop him up under the arm or arms, as he slowly and consequentially struts along. If he be mounted, the same theory prescribes that he shall be held on to his saddle by retainers running on either side. Thus upheld, the Minister for Home Affairs and the President of the Foreign Office were solemnly escorting me to the presence of royalty, when I suddenly seemed to observe a vacuum. The supporters had disappeared, and the ministers had hurled themselves, forehead forward, on the ground. My old friend, who was far advanced in years, must have found it extremely trying.

The King was standing in a small, brightly-painted pavilion, which opened on to one of the minor courts of the Palace. His hands rested upon a table, on which a hideous Brussels table-cloth half concealed a gorgeous piece of Chinese embroidery. Behind and around him were clustered the Palace eunuchs in Court dresses. At the side stood the interpreter, with his shoulders and head bowed in attitude of the lowest reverence, repeating the words which the King whispered in his ear. On either

Audience with the King.

THE KING IN STATE PROCESSION

side stood the two sword-bearers of State, and at a little distance the two Ministers, who had resumed an erect position. Upon the royal brow was a double-tiered violet headpiece. His robe was of scarlet figured silk—the royal colour—with panels of gold embroidery upon the shoulders and breast, and a gold-studded projecting belt. Li Hsi is a man of small stature and sallow complexion, with hair drawn tightly up from the forehead beneath the Korean skull-cap, very slight eyebrows, small, vivacious black eyes, teeth discoloured from chewing the betel, a piece of which he continued to masticate throughout the interview, and a sparse black moustache and tuft below the chin. The King's countenance wears a singularly gentle and pleasing expression; and in the course of the audience, which lasted about twenty minutes, and was entirely conducted by His Majesty in person, he evinced the most lively interest in the friendship and consideration of Great Britain, and a personal regard for the services of Mr. W. C. Hillier, the capable officer by whom the Queen was at that time represented in Söul. After the audience with the King I was conducted to another pavilion, where I was similarly received by the Crown Prince. But his questions or remarks, which were dictated to him by his chief eunuch, were of no interest, and the interview was one of mere ceremony.

The true comicality, however, of the Korean Court can only be properly estimated upon one of the occasions, somewhat rare in occurrence, when the King goes in state through the city to visit some temple or tomb. Of one such function I was the interested witness. From an early hour in the morning the streets were guarded by military, of a species unique in the world. The infantry lined the roadway, and were for the most part lying asleep upon the ground. They had almost as many flags as

Royal procession.

men; and their muskets, which I examined as they stood piled together, were commonly destitute either of hammer, trigger, or plate, sometimes of all three, and were frequently only held together by string; while the bayonets were bent and rusty. Infinitely more remarkable, however, were the

A KOREAN COLONEL

cavalry. These were clad in uniforms probably some 300 years old, consisting of a battered helmet with a spikè, and of a cuirass of black leather studded with brass bosses, and worn over a heavy jerkin of moth-eaten brocade.[1] Enor-

[1] Compare the account of Hamel, 240 years ago:—'Their Horse wear Cuirasses, Headpieces, and Swords, as also Bows and Arrows, and Whips like ours, only that theirs have small iron Points. Their Foot as well as they wear a corselet, a Headpiece, a Sword, and Musket or Half-pike. The Officers carry nothing but Bows and Arrows.'

mous jack-boots completed the costume, and rendered it difficult for the men to mount their steeds, even although these were rarely more than eleven hands high. Banners of yellow, red, and green, with a tuft of pheasant-feathers at the top, and stacks of arrows, were carried in front of the officers, who were with difficulty supported by squires upon their pyramidal saddles. The middle of the roadway was supposed to be kept clear, and was strewn with a riband of sand, about a foot and a half in breadth; but this was trampled upon and scattered almost as soon as sprinkled.

Throughout the morning processions of ministers, courtiers, and officials passed along on their way to or from the Palace. The majority of these were borne by shouting retainers in open chairs, on the back of which rested a leopard-skin. In some cases the sedan was also supported by a single leg underneath, terminating in a wheel, which ran along the middle of the roadway, easing the burden and increasing the pace of the bearers in front and behind. Some of the officials wore gilt helmets of pasteboard, with Chinese characters upon the back. The Chinese Resident, the principal personage in the city, as representing the suzerain power, dashed past in a black velvet sedan, swiftly borne by stalwart Celestials with red tassels. Upon either side of the street the white-robed crowd were pressed back against the house-fronts, and were prodded by the soldiers with their muskets, or spanked by active runners, who laid about them liberally with long wooden paddles. On the occasion of the previous procession the mob had been suffered to approach too nearly to the person of royalty; and a notification had in consequence appeared in the *Official Gazette*, docking the Minister of War of three months' salary for his faulty arrangements.

At length, after hours of waiting, the Palace doors were

thrown open, and there issued forth the most motley procession ever seen outside of London on Lord Mayor's Day, or in the Christmas pantomime at Drury Lane. The soldiers snatched up their venerable muskets, or climbed on to their microscopic steeds. The banners were plucked up, and danced in lines of colour along the streets. First from the Palace gates emerged a company of men in red mitres, carrying scarlet lacquered chairs; then a similar band in blue. Presently appeared the Royal Standard, on which was emblazoned a mighty dragon upon a ground of yellow silk. The sound of drums succeeded; and there was a shout to keep silence. In the centre of a running crowd there followed upborne a single empty sedan, coloured the royal red. I heard two explanations given of this episode. One was that in former days, when etiquette had not been sufficiently relaxed to admit of any portion of the royal person being seen, two identical chairs were used in the processions, no one knowing which of the pair contained the King, much in the same way as an empty train frequently precedes or follows that containing the Russian Czar, with a view to frustrate the possible designs of conspirators. The other theory was that the first chair is kept intentionally empty, in order to hoodwink the evil spirits who would be likely to assault it in the idea that they had got hold of the royal person. I have also heard it suggested that the empty litter may contain the ancestral tablets of the royal family. Next came a long procession of the King's valets, in yellow robes and tiny straw hats, with worsted rosettes, perched sideways on their heads; the corps of royal drummers, beating with frantic flourish the royal drums; a medley of cavalry, shambling along without the least attempt at order; a small detachment of artillery, dragging after them two small Gatling guns; files of runners, in alternate blue and

KOREAN CAVALRY AND ROYAL STANDARD

green gauze, stretching across the street; a company of
flute-players, blowing a lusty monotone on a shrill note;
then a rush of feet and shouting of voices to make way, and
a phalanx of sturdy bearers, clad in red, with double mitres
on their heads, running swiftly, and supporting in a canopied
chair of state, with red silk screens and tassels, the uplifted
person of the King. As he passed along he looked to right
and left, and the movement of the bearers made him bob
up and down. At a little distance behind followed the
Crown Prince, in spectacles, in a similar scarlet palanquin,
carried by men in green mitres; and then came a heterogeneous jumble of courtiers, generals, colonels, matchlock-
men, and tottering cavaliers; the procession being closed by
the European-drilled troops, who made some attempt to
march in step, and whose commander, heralded by stentorian
cries, carried an immense banner on his own shoulder.
Later on, towards dusk, I met the same procession returning.
Everything and everybody had got thoroughly mixed up
in the narrower streets: soldiers and citizens, colonels and
chamberlains, were all wedged together in inextricable
confusion; but, above the heads of the crowd, ever oscil-
lated the scarlet palanquin of the King, lit up by lanterns
of blue and crimson silk, tossing at the pikeheads of the
infantry soldiers.

It will have been gathered from the above description
that the Korean Army was not the least rotten adjunct of
the unreformed Korean monarchy. Those infantry
regiments that had been taught by foreigners and Korean Army.
that constituted the garrison of the capital, 4000
strong, were said to show a capacity for drill and discipline.
Up till the rebellion of 1884 they were officered by Japanese;
but after that date they were placed in the hands of two
American drill-instructors, who possessed the high-flown

titles of Vice-President and Councillor of the Board of War, but who exercised no command, and did not accompany their men on to the field. This force was divided into three battalions, and was armed with rifles of a great variety of pattern. Its native officers were beneath contempt. There is an arsenal (Ki-ke-kuk) in Sŏul with foreign machinery; but it is only used for the repair of arms. As for the purely native regiments, they were and are not a standing army but a standing joke; while in Europe the cavalry would with difficulty secure an engagement as supers in the pantomime of a second-rate provincial stage.

Once every twenty or thirty years a review is held of the entire force on a parade-ground outside the city, the ex-

State review. periment being so costly that it cannot be more frequently repeated. As a spectacle it is more unique even than the royal procession. One such review was held during the summer of 1894. It was announced to begin at 9 A.M., but from that hour till 5 P.M. were the 30,000 spectators on the ground compelled to wait before the vanguard of the royal *cortège* appeared. This consisted of no fewer than 10,000 persons, in the midst of whom the King and Crown Prince rode on horseback. The troops, 7000 to 8000 in number, then marched past the saluting-point, saluting by bowing their bodies to the ground. So unsatisfactory, however, was the display held to have been that there was great fluttering in the military dove-cots, and the Commander-in-Chief was forthwith degraded from his post. It was then contemplated to hold a review of the troops drilled upon the modern system. But before this event could take place, the thunderbolt had fallen, and Korea, instead of providing a playground for the nursery-games of her own troops, had become a battle-field for the passions of others.

MODERN-DRILLED KOREAN INFANTRY

CHAPTER VI

POLITICAL AND COMMERCIAL SYMPTOMS IN KOREA

> Diogenes Alexandro roganti ut diceret si quid opus esset, 'Nunc quidem paullulum,' inquit, 'a sole.' CICERO: *Tusc. Disput.*

IF the people, the scenery, the capital, and the Court of Korea have each an individuality that distinguishes them from similar phenomena in other countries, there were yet in the Korean polity, viewed as a form of government, before the war, features inseparably associated with the Asiatic system and recognisable in every unreformed Oriental State from Teheran to Söul. A royal figurehead enveloped in the mystery of the palace and the harem, surrounded by concentric rings of eunuchs, Ministers, of State, officials, and retainers, and rendered almost intangible by the predominant atmosphere of intrigue; a hierarchy of office-holders and office-seekers, who were leeches in the thinnest disguise; a feeble and insignificant army, an impecunious exchequer, a debased currency, and an impoverished people—these are the invariable symptoms of the fast vanishing *régime* of the older and unredeemed Oriental type. Add to these the first swarming of the flock of foreign practitioners, who scent the enfeebled constitution from afar, and from the four winds of heaven come pressing their pharmacopœia of loans, concessions, banks, mints, factories, and all the recognised machinery for filling Western purses at the expense of Eastern pockets, and you have a fair picture of Korea as she stood after ten years

An Asiatic microcosm.

of emergence from her long seclusion and enjoyment of the intercourse of the nations. She was going to purchase her own experience, and to learn that, while civilisation is a mistress of rare and irresistible attractions, she requires to be paid for in coin of no small denomination.

Nominally, every Government post in Korea was given by competitive examination. In reality, the examinations —which were conducted in the open air in the Palace-grounds in the presence of the King, and consisted of little more than the composition of an essay (probably prepared in advance) upon some well-known sentence from the Chinese classics—were a farce; and the posts were given to those who paid for them, the successful candidate and the price paid by him being, as a general rule, matters of common knowledge beforehand.[1] This being so, it might be thought surprising that so many candidates should enter. The examination, however, was always an excuse for a visit to the capital and a pleasant holiday; and, a few posts being occasionally assigned, for form's sake, to merit, each competitor was firmly convinced that he would be the lucky man. The successful candidate has to undergo a sort of schoolboy 'bullyragging' at the hands of his comrades, which reminds one of the peculiar ceremonies formerly enacted on British ships when 'crossing the Line.' His face and clothes were smeared all over with ink, and were then bespattered by one of the examiners with white soap. Frequently, too, his hat was smashed in, and his clothes were torn of his back. Finally, after this ordeal was over, he was washed and dressed up and was taken round in state to receive the congratulations of his friends. All the higher posts were filled by the *yangbâns*, or gentry, and

Korean adminis- tration.

[1] The examination system, perhaps the most picturesque and fascinating of Korean abuses, has since been abolished by the Japanese.

the highest of all by the relatives of those in great positions at Court. The eight provinces and 332 prefectures of the kingdom absorbed an immense army of office-holders,[1] only the superior ranks among whom received any salary, and this usually in arrears, while the rest had to butter their own bread as best they could. All office was held for a period of three years, during which time the incumbent extracted from it whatever he could, the normal level of extortion being so mathematically ascertained by long practice, that while any excess was voted tyrannical, adherence to the average standard was regarded as a proof both of integrity and moderation. Under a form of government so organised it became easy enough to understand why the country languished and stagnation reigned supreme.

The Government itself—or, in other words, the King, who was the Government—was always in debt; and the financial assistance which in moments of embarrassment he was never loth to accept from interested parties, whilst it did not enable his exchequer to recover financial equilibrium, still further mortgaged the fast dwindling resources of national wealth and independence. The amount of the royal revenue could not be ascertained; but it was derived from the following sources:—(1) a Land-tax, principally paid in grain, and fluctuating according to the nature of the harvest; (2) a House-tax, very capriciously assessed and levied; (3) the Customs Revenue, which is levied upon imports and exports at the three Treaty Ports, and which in 1891, the high-water mark yet reached, amounted to over £90,000, but which, with a new tariff

Revenue and debt.

[1] This organisation was replaced, under Japanese auspices, in June 1895 by a redistribution into 23 counties (*fu*), with 337 prefectures (*chun*), the administration of each county being placed under a governor, deputy-governor, and a staff of secretaries or clerks, of whom there are not to be more than 330 for the whole kingdom.

classification, the opening of more Treaty Ports,[1] and a preventive service to stop the enormous amount of smuggling that prevails, might be very greatly increased; (4) the proceeds of the *ginseng* monopoly;[2] (5) the proceeds of other monopolies or Government licenses, such as gold-mining, and the various Trade guilds; (6) irregular taxation.

It is now nineteen years since the first Foreign Treaty was signed with Japan in 1876. Later conventions opened Gensan in 1879, and Chemulpo in 1880; and further Trade and Fishery Regulations were concluded between the two Governments in 1883 and

Foreign Treaties.

---

[1] The British and subsequent Foreign Treaties with Korea stipulated for the opening of a further Treaty Port, Yang-hwa-chin on the river Han, as a river-port for the capital. If the steam-traffic on the Han is developed, Yong-san or Ryong-san, which is only three miles from Sŏul, might be selected. Since the war two new Treaty Ports have been opened by the Japanese, viz. Chinnampo on the Ping-yang inlet or estuary of the Taidong River, and Mokpo, in the south-west, at the southern extremity of Chulla Province.

[2] *Ginseng* (*Panax quinquefolium*) is the plant, of the *Araliaceæ* or Ivywort tribe, whose root is so immensely valued for medicinal and recuperative purposes in China. One of its principal areas of production is Korea, where it both grows wild in the forests of the north (fabulous sums being sometimes paid for a single root), and is artificially cultivated under screens. A less valuable variety of the same plant is also produced in America, principally in Virginia. Red or clarified *ginseng*, which is prepared by steaming the root over boiling water, is a monopoly of the King in Korea. Its export, except by a single guild, is prohibited by Treaty, and is punishable by death. For years it has been farmed out to the *Chung In*, a body who used to accompany the Tribute Mission to Peking as interpreters, in which capacity they did a little trade on their own account. They are now a close corporation, and are said to pay the King from £80,000 to £100,000 a year. A tax is also levied upon the growth and export of ordinary *ginseng*, which is prepared by drying the root over a charcoal fire. As much again, however, is said to be smuggled out of the country as passes through the hands of the guild. *Ginseng* is consumed in China by cutting up the root into minute fragments and steeping them in wine. But it is usually mixed with other drugs. As long ago as 1617, Richard Cocks, Factor of the East India Company at Firando in Japan, sent home a piece of the root, of which he said that it was 'worth its weight in silver; all that can be got is taken by the Emperor; it is held in Japan the most precious thing in physic in the world, and sufficient to put life into any man if can but draw breath.' *State Papers, East Indies Series*, 1617-1621.

1889. The Chinese Trade Regulations and the American Treaty were signed in 1882. Great Britain and Germany followed in 1883, Russia and Italy in 1884, France in 1886. An Overland Trade Convention was also concluded with Russia in 1888; and finally Austria entered the list of Treaty Powers in 1893. For a full decade, therefore, excluding the special priority of Japan, Korea has had the experience of commerce and contact with the outer world. How had she benefited by it?

The sudden leavening of so archaic and stubborn a lump by the strenuous agency of civilisation had not been pursued without the familiar symptoms. Each foreign country had thought itself or its citizens the best qualified to act as guides to the trembling footsteps of the bewildered *ingénu*. Of these external aids to local embarrassment perhaps the most remarkable was the continuous maintenance of one or more so-called Foreign Advisers by the King. There were successively four of these gentlemen. The first was a German, who was appointed to the double post of Director of Korean Customs and Foreign Adviser by the Viceroy Li Hung Chang. He disappeared abruptly, in consequence, it is said, of having drawn up a secret treaty with Russia. The second was an American, who created quite a stir by issuing a pamphlet in defence of Korean independence, and in repudiation of the Chinese claims of suzerainty, and who spent his whole time in combating the Chinese Resident. There were two occupants of the post in 1892, both of whom were Americans. The function of these individuals was apparently to advise the Korean Government on any negotiation or complication that might arise with foreign Powers, and to assist them in the making of purchases from, or sale of concessions to, outside parties. With the policy

Foreign Advisers.

of the Government they had nothing to do; and the greater part of its administrative and executive action was performed behind their backs and without their cognisance. It was not surprising that a position so ambiguous should operate against any very lengthy tenure of the office in question. The historical sequence was, as a rule, the same in each case; great ambitions on the part of the newly appointed official; gradual disenchantment; salary in arrears; final *fracas* and departure, leaving behind unsatisfied claims, with futile threats of legal enforcement.

In other departments less official but equally officious auxiliaries proffered a not more disinterested assistance. A few years ago a German undertook to regenerate the country by introducing the silk industry; and the grounds of a deserted palace were handed over to the spade and the mulberry-tree. There were the trees; but the German and the silk-worms had disappeared. Somebody else was desirous of making matches and glass; others were unselfishly interested in the creation of an arsenal and the manufacture of gunpowder. A Post-office was started and stamps were printed, but the Postmaster-General lost his life in a political revolution, and the stamps are now only a joy to the philatelist. In 1893 a Government Postal and Telegraphic Service was announced in the *Official Gazette*; but up to the war very little had come of it. The Germans were willing to sell some steamers to the Korean Government in order to encourage the coasting trade. The Americans, as already observed, had taken in hand the Army. Nor was agriculture left out in the cold, for the King was persuaded to start a Model Farm for the growth of foreign cereals and the breeding of foreign stock. Almost all these ventures had failed; though a Foreign School, which was started in Söul to impart the elements

Projects and speculations.

of a modern education to young Koreans of good position, and in which the King takes or took such an interest that on one occasion he personally examined the pupils, and awarded rank or office to such as distinguished themselves, still continued, in spite of inadequate support, to exist. The average attendance of students was stated to be twenty-five.

The most interesting illustration, however, of the capacities of native ignorance in alliance with foreign speculation was supplied by the history of the Korean currency, to which the Japanese had turned an unremitting attention. Among the devices for replenishing its exchequer that was suggested to the Korean Government by one of its Foreign Advisers a few years ago was the issue of a new cash piece (the pierced coin of brass or copper and lead, which is the popular medium of exchange here as in China) that should be declared equal to five of the old cash then in circulation. The new cash being of very inferior quality (it was composed of copper and lead in the proportions of three to two, and its intrinsic value was less than two of the old cash), the Government looked to gain a tidy sum upon the transaction—a profit which they subsequently endeavoured to enhance by farming out the right to coin, or rather to cast (for the coins are moulded, not struck) this debased amalgam to native speculators. The results were threefold. The quality of the coin became steadily worse, brass being substituted for copper, and sand for lead; outside the capital and neighbourhood, where it was forced upon the people, traders absolutely declined to take it; and the depreciation advanced so rapidly that prices rose, trade was seriously affected, and the money market was paralysed. In 1892 the Japanese *yen*, or silver dollar (then equal to

The currency.

about 2s. 10d.), which, at the first institution of the *tangos*, or 5 cash pieces, represented 70 of the latter, or 350 old cash, was equivalent to as many as 650 new cash, or 3250 of the cash in common circulation. The drawbacks as well as the cumbersomeness of a currency so prostituted might easily be conceived.

In this emergency the Japanese saw their opportunity. In 1888 a Government Mint had been erected at Söul for the issue of a new silver currency on the European model, and a few specimen dollars had been coined but never circulated. An expensive annexe was now, in 1891, added to the disused mint, and heavy machinery was imported by a Japanese syndicate, who, in return for a loan to the King, obtained the concession to manufacture and issue a new silver and nickel currency of kindred denomination to the Japanese. No sooner, however, had the machinery arrived than it was found that the cost of putting it up in Söul and of importing the metal would render the speculation an unprofitable one. Accordingly it had to be carted back to Chemulpo, on the coast, where another mint, costing $20,000, was erected for its reception. Here a number of new coins were at last struck off, consisting of a silver 5 *ryo* piece or *yen*, equivalent to 500 cash, a silver *ryo* or 100 cash piece, a nickel 25 cash piece, a copper 5 cash piece, and a brass 1 cash piece, which, however, were found to be so unsatisfactory that it was rumoured they were all going to be melted down and minted again. They were finally issued, after the war, in 1894. Simultaneously it had been arranged so start a system of bank-notes, a few of which were printed in Tokio, but never issued. At this stage it seems to have struck all parties that the experiment of keeping open a State Mint in Korea, to which all the metal required must be imported at

<small>New Mint and silver coinage.</small>

ruinous cost, and where the machinery was not of first-rate quality, was absurd; having indeed nothing but the gratification of national vanity to recommend it. Accordingly the only possible refuge was at last adopted; and negotiations were entered into and a contract signed with the Japanese Government in 1893 to undertake the entire Korean currency in the excellent Imperial Mint at Osaka. Even so, the experiment was really superfluous and has since been abandoned; for since the Japanese *yen* and the Mexican dollar are made by treaty legal tender for customs dues, and are everywhere freely accepted (except perhaps in the remote interior) in Korea, all that is really wanted is the issue of a stable cash coinage, the old debased currency being called in and melted down or destroyed. This tale of currency woe fills, however, a most characteristic page of Korean history.

Among other commercial ventures in Korea, the Japanese had also started branches of Japanese banks at Chemulpo and Sŏul, into one of which *inter alia* the Customs revenue was paid, and whereat the Government account was permanently overdrawn; and were said also to have contemplated, in connection with their new currency, the institution of exchange offices, or banks in disguise, where the new coinage should be procurable in exchange for the old copper cash, which it was fondly but foolishly expected would thereby disappear from popular use. In the meantime, with the view of placing Korean finance in more experienced hands, it was suggested that a branch of the Hongkong and Shanghai Banking Corporation should be opened in Korea—a venture by which, if carried out, no one would have profited more than the Korean Government.

Banks.

By an administration so sorely embarrassed and in such

habitual financial straits as the Korean, one might expect that, instead of embarking upon risky if not unsound financial transactions with adventurous outsiders, a resolute attempt would have been made to develop the internal resources of the country, which a consensus of opinion admits to be considerable. My journeys in the interior, restricted as they were, convinced me that there might be a great future for Korean agriculture; and this view was borne out by those who had travelled over a wider range. Indeed, in the possession of an excellent climate, a soil of more than ordinary fertility, vast tracts of still virgin country, and a robust rural population, Korea possesses the four conditions of agricultural prosperity. Already as a rice and bean-producing country she was rising before the war into commercial importance, and provided a valuable feeder for the neighbouring islands of Japan. Among the self-created obstacles that intervene between her and a full enjoyment of these advantages one has long stood out in discreditable prominence—viz. the scandalous poverty of means of communication between the producing and the consuming areas, and between the interior and the coast. There are no roads in the country in any sense in which the word would be understood in Europe. The pack-roads are mere bridle-tracks, which frequently degenerate into rocky torrent-beds, or precarious footpaths across inundated swamps. No one looks after them; they are never repaired. Transport upon them is very costly, and on some occasions absolutely prohibitive. No means for conveying the surplus produce of any area to an available market in time of dearth are forthcoming; and one district may be smitten with sore famine, while its neighbour, at no great distance, cannot get rid of its superfluous grain. Better roads would be followed at

Obstacles to commercial development. Means of communication. Roads.

once by a better organised system of transport and by a rapid increase in the volume of exports.

The same remarks apply to river and coast communications. On two only of the five great navigable rivers of Korea [1] do steamboats attempt to ply. Small native steamers run between Fusan and the mouth of the Nak- tong River, seven miles distant, and even ascend the stream for fifty miles as far as Miriang. On the Han River, which, if properly navigated, would almost convert the capital into a seaport, two small steamers started running from Chemulpo in 1880; one was wrecked, the other was usually aground. Vessels of lighter draught and special build were required for the shifting and shallow channel. By the energy of the Chinese Resident a Chinese company was at length organised in 1892 to undertake this venture. Two new steamers were placed upon the river, running the fifty-four miles from Chemulpo to Ryong-san, three miles from Söul (which it was proposed to connect by tramway with the landing-place); and by one of these Sir N. O'Conor, the British Minister to Korea, ascended to the capital, to present his letters of credence in 1893.

River navigation.

Similarly upon the coasts the supersession of the Korean junk, which is one of the least seaworthy of crafts, by a line of small schooners running from port to port, would develop the provincial trade to an enormous extent, and would cheapen the cost of the necessaries of life. A Korean steamship company which charters foreign vessels has for some little time been in existence, and has lately extended its voyages to Chefoo on the one side and Vladivostok on the other. Enjoying the monopoly of the transport of tribute rice from the non-treaty ports to

Coast navigation.

---

[1] The Yalu in the north, the Taidong or Ping-yang River, the Han, and its tributary the Im-jin-gang, and the Naktong.

Chemulpo, it might easily become a most lucrative concern; though in competition with the two keenest mercantile nationalities of the East, it can hardly be expected that either monopolies or bounties will ever galvanise an undertaking owned and worked by such a people as the Koreans into permanent vitality.

A concession was at one time applied for by some American financiers for a short railway between Chemulpo and Söul; and it is believed that the contract was about to be signed when it was vetoed by the Chinese Resident. This railway is one of the first of the boons with which Japan has undertaken since the war to endow her *protégé*; and there can be little doubt that it will be carried into execution before long. Wild schemes for a network of railways throughout Korea are said to have been formulated in the brains of those who anticipate an early Russian seizure of the entire peninsula, or who believe that Japan will speedily convert control into possession. But it will be worth while to wait till the Russians or the Japanese are finally installed before discussing what they will do.

Railways.

The drawbacks which I have enumerated—viz. a debased currency; dearth of communications by land and water; the consequent cost of transport; the incubus of native monopolists who control the prices and evade the Treaties by fresh local *likin* or *octroi*-dues in the interior; the apathy of the Korean producer, the poverty of the Korean consumer, and the lack of enterprise of the Korean merchant; above all, the inexperience and misjudgment of the Korean Government—are obstacles to any such heroic expansion of trade as was once predicted by the optimists. Nevertheless, both in volume and value, Korean trade has pursued, with occasional relapses, an upward career. In 1891, which was the best year yet realised, the

Growth of trade.

net value of the foreign trade was nearly £1,400,000, and the total trade during the ten years since the opening of the Treaty ports is stated to have been $50,000,000, a figure which, if the enormous amount of smuggling that goes on be taken into account, does not probably represent more than two-thirds of the real value. The trade before the war was practically shared by the Chinese and Japanese, between whom the most acute competition prevailed. The former, had almost entirely monopolised the retail business, both in native produce and foreign imports. They penetrated everywhere, and everywhere their stores and shops were to be found. The Japanese, on the other hand, had acquired the virtual command of the export trade, over ninety per cent. of which was to Japan. The two great staples of Korean produce are rice and beans, which are increasingly demanded by her southern neighbour, as the population of Japan increases and more soil is surrendered to the cultivation of silk. Hence the intense Japanese irritation when, for reasons of internal policy, the Korean Government saw fit to place even a temporary embargo upon the export of native grain. As regards imports, though there were no British, but only German and American merchants in the country—the system of Chinese or Japanese brokers operating with sufficient success—over sixty per cent. of the sum total, and practically the whole of her trade in piece goods, hailed from Great Britain, who might claim, even in remote Korea, to have discovered one more market for Manchester.[1]

[1] It is nearly 300 years since, in 1604, the first Royal Licence 'to discover the countries of Cathaia, China, Japan, Corea, and Cambaia, and to trade with the people there,' was issued by James I. to Sir Edward Michelborne, for the East India Company. In 1614 E. Sayer was sent to Tushma (i.e. Tsushima), but reported that 'there was no hope of any good to be done there or in Corea.' In 1618 Richard Cocks, the head of the Factory at Firando in Japan, on the occasion of one of the Tribute Missions from Korea, 'endeavoured to gain speech with the Ambassador, but was un-

Evidence of commercial expansion is also provided by the increasing number of steamships that have found it profitable to include the Korean ports in their published sailing lists. The well-known Japanese steamship company known as the Nippon Yusen Kaisha keeps up a service of three mail steamers fortnightly between Kobe and the Korean ports, besides sending outside steamers for the carrying trade direct from Osaka. Another Japanese company, the Osaka Shosen Kaisha, has lately appeared upon the scene, and runs boats at unstated intervals from the former port.[1] The year 1891 also witnessed the introduction of a liberally subsidised fortnightly Russian packet service between Shanghai and Vladivostok, touching at the harbours of Fusan and Gensan on the way. Though this venture cannot as yet conceivably be attended with profit, it is characteristic of the energy with which the Russians advance their flag in Eastern waters, and make an experimental and even expensive commerce subserve larger political ends. It is not for mercantile gain that the Russian subsidies are given, but for the avowed object of providing a useful auxiliary marine, with well-organised complement, in time of war.

In the nurture of Korean commerce too much credit cannot be given to members of the Chinese Imperial Customs Service, into whose hands the predominant influence of the suzerain power insured that the collection of Korean

---

successful, the King of Tushma being the cause, he fearing that the English might procure trade if Cocks got acquainted with the ambassadors. The Japan Lords asked why he sought acquaintance with such barbarous people.'
—*State Papers, East Indies Series*, vol. i. (1513-1616), Nos. 336, 699; vol. ii. (1617-1621), No. 273. From that day till the British Treaty in 1883 there was no direct Anglo-Korean trade, although in 1702 the idea of a Korean Factory was reconsidered by the Directors of the East India Company (Bruce's *Annals*, vol. iii. p. 483).

[1] The Japanese have acquired such a command of the shipping that out of a total tonnage of 391,000 in the Treaty Ports in 1892, 328,000 were Japanese, as against 25,000 Russian, 15,000 Chinese, and 8000 Korean.

Customs should be committed when the Treaty Ports were first opened in 1883. A number of European officials were subsequently lent for the purpose from the admirably organised Chinese service under Sir Robert Hart. Their salaries in Korea were only in part paid by the Korean Government, for they continued to remain on the Chinese list and to receive Chinese pay. It was rumoured that the Viceroy Li Hung Chang would have liked to supersede Sir Robert Hart's service, which he was said to regard with a jealous eye, by a privately organised Chinese service of his own. In the interests of Korea this would have been a most unfortunate step, since it would have meant the substitution of universal jobbery and smuggling for a pure and efficient administration. Since the war the Japanese have done their best to oust the former employees of China. But the Korean Government has managed so far to retain them in its own service—almost the sole case in respect of which it has successfully vindicated its so-called independence.

Customs Service.

Were steps taken by the Korean Government to check the systematic smuggling that even now prevails all along the coast between the Treaty Ports (to which the jurisdiction of the European Customs officers is confined), much more business would pass through their hands. Opium, which is prohibited in the Foreign Treaties, is smuggled into the country, and *ginseng* out of it in great quantities. Of the enormous surreptitious traffic in gold-dust I shall speak presently. Under the terms of the Fishery Convention between Japan and Korea, the fishermen of the former country have hitherto been permitted to land and sell their fish wherever they please on the Southern Korean coast. Each man does a little contraband business as well. It is the same with the Chinese junkmen on the west coast.

Smuggling.

In 1894 the King was persuaded to organise a small cruiser service, which should deal with this abuse, and might further in time develop into the nucleus of a small but effective Korean navy. For this purpose he applied for the loan of two English officers, to give the requisite start to the undertaking. The war, however, put a stop to all further proceedings.

Though the symptoms of commercial development in Korea are thus encouraging, it is not believed that the trade has hitherto been profitable to those engaged in it, mainly owing to the difficulties arising from a debased and fluctuating medium of exchange; whilst the natural apathy of the Koreans, which renders them irresponsive to any appeal that places an unaccustomed strain upon their energies or prepossessions, has so far found an undeniable stimulus in the fact that the advent of the foreigner cannot be said as yet to have brought much profit to them. The prices of everything in Korea have, since the opening of the country, shown a tendency to assimilate themselves to those of surrounding markets, with the result that the necessaries of life have become dearer, and the cost of food-stuffs in particular has been greatly augmented. None of the Customs revenue derived from increased trade goes into the pocket of the Korean peasant, and he probably has moments of acute though stolid disgust at the boasted regeneration of his country.

Native standpoint.

Among the resources to which the attention of foreigners has long been drawn, either as unrealised assets of national wealth or as a source of possible lucre to themselves, are the minerals of Korea. It is known that gold, lead, and silver (galena), copper, and iron ores are found in some abundance, although hitherto worked in the most spasmodic and clumsy of fashions. Some years

Mines and minerals.

ago the most roseate anticipations were indulged in of impending mineral production; and a financial authority was even found to assert that the currency problem of the world would be solved by the phenomenal output of the precious metals from Korea. Latterly there has been a corresponding recoil of opinion, which has led people to declare that the Korean mines are a fraud, and that the wealth-producing capacity of the peninsula will never be demonstrated in this direction. Those, however, who have the most intimate knowledge of the interior agree in thinking that the minerals are there and are capable of being worked by European hands at an assured profit. Should the Government consent to a concession on at all a liberal scale, and personally assist instead of obstructing its operations, the money would be forthcoming to-morrow from more than one quarter, and it is inconceivable, vain though the Koreans are about treasures of which they know nothing, but which, because a few foreigners are running after them, they conceive must be unique in the world, that many more years can elapse before a serious attempt is made to open them up. Excellent coal, a soft anthracite, burning brightly and leaving little ash, is already procured by the most primitive methods from a mine near Pyong-yang, which is said to contain unlimited quantities. Nearly all the iron that is used in the country for agricultural and domestic purposes is also of native production, the ore being scratched out of shallow holes in the ground and smelted in charcoal furnaces. The Koreans have no conconception either of ventilation, drainage, blasting, or lighting. There is or was a Mining Board among the Government Departments at Söul; but of its activity no evidence has ever been forthcoming.

The mineral, however, that has excited most interest abroad is gold, which, in the form of dust from river washings, has formed a notable item in the exports of Korea for many years. During the last decade £8,000,000 of gold and gold-dust have passed through the hands of the Customs in export. But this does not in all probability represent more than twenty per cent. of the real export, few Japanese or Chinese leaving the country without smuggling out a little of the precious dust upon their persons; while the fluctuations in the annual returns may be explained by the higher rate of wages procurable from agriculture during years of good harvests, whereby labour is diverted from the more precarious essay of the goldfields. Placer mining is probably best suited to Korean conditions; but the introduction of quartz crushing and of scientific appliances might be expected to add largely to the annual production. Five years ago the Government did purchase foreign machinery, and engaged foreign miners to work the gold-mines in the Pyong-yang district, but the enterprise was abandoned before it had had a fair trial.

Gold.

Anyhow, with mineral resources of undoubted value, even if of uncertain quantity, with grain-producing capacities that are susceptible of indefinite multiplication, with ready markets and willing customers close at hand, Korea will only have to thank herself if she prefers to remain plunged in poverty and squalor. The initiative must, of course, come from the Government. Hitherto in Korea, unhappily, as in Persia, *quicquid delirant reges plectuntur Achivi*. Perhaps the Japanese *régime* may bring about an improvement. The first thing that the Government has to do is to abandon the idea that Korea is an Amalthea's horn, into which foreigners will pay enormous prices (in the shape of royalties or commission) for the privilege of dipping their fingers. The next step is to realise that without foreign capital little can be done, and under

Future prospects.

native management nothing. At the same time a wary eye must be directed upon the not too dispassionate offers of financial assistance which are pressed upon the interesting *débutante* with such suspicious emulation by her astute neighbours.

Owing to the so recent opening of the country and to the savage persecution by which Christianity had been practically exterminated a short time before, the missionary question in Korea is in a far less advanced state of development than it is in either of the neighbouring countries of Japan and China. Not that the record of Christian missionary effort in the peninsula has been either slender or abortive. It is now a little more than a hundred years since the intercourse with Peking (where there was a flourishing Roman Catholic Church), originating from the journeys to and fro of the annual Tribute Missions, was responsible for the first Korean convert to the faith of Christ. Since that date the infant Korean Church has shown a heroism, has endured sufferings, and has produced a martyr-roll that will compare favourably with the missionary annals of less obscure countries and more forward peoples. From the start it was proscribed, hunted down, and delivered over to occasional spasms of fierce persecution. It was not till after half-a-century of disturbed and precarious existence, in which the flame was only kept alive by the devotion of native or of Chinese converts, that in 1836 M. Maubant, the second Papal nominee to the post of Vicar Apostolic of Korea, succeeded in getting across the frontier, the first European priest who had set foot in Korea since 1594. In 1837 the first Catholic bishop of Korea, Msgr. Imbert, followed, only to lose his life in a violent persecution that immediately ensued. In spite of continued and relentless hostility on the part of the Government, the native

Missionary work in Korea.
1. Persecution.

Christians are said in 1859 to have numbered 17,000. After the usurpation, however, of the Tai Wen Kun in 1864, the man with 'the bowels of iron and the heart of stone' was content with no half-measures. A merciless war of extirpation was waged against the heretical sect; the French expedition of 1866 that was sent to avenge these murders beat an inglorious retreat; and by 1870, 8000 native Christians were said to have paid the penalty with their lives.

The end, however, was near at hand. The reign of the bloodthirsty Regent was now over; more liberal ideas animated the young Sovereign; and the warning clamour of the nations was heard sounding at the gates. The earlier Treaties, it is true, demanded nothing more than the free exercise of their religion in the Treaty Ports for the subjects of the signatory Powers; nor to this day does any article, expressly sanctioning missionary enterprise, appear in any of the Treaties. The French are said to have held out long for such a concession; but the only substitute for it which their Treaty, concluded in 1886, contains, is a clause permitting of the employment of natives as *literati*, interpreters, or servants, or in any other lawful capacity, by the French, and promising the latter every assistance in their study of the native language and institutions.[1] Whatever may have been the ulterior meaning of these words, the Korean Government, with representatives of all the great Powers of Europe stationed in its capital, and with the gunboats of their squadrons floating upon the neighbouring seas, is no longer in a position, even if it had the

2. Toleration.

---

[1] Article ix. runs as follows: 'Les autorités Françaises et les Français en Corée pourront engager des sujets Coréens à titre de lettré, d'interprète, de serviteur, ou à tout autre titre licite, sans que les autorités Coréennes puissent y mettre obstacle. . . . Les Français qui se rendraient en Corée pour y étudier ou y professer la langue écrite ou parlée, les sciences, les lois et les arts, devront, en témoignage de sentiments de bonne amitié dont sont animées les Hautes Parties Contractantes, recevoir toujours aide et assistance.'

desire, to assume a hostile attitude; and missionaries are at liberty to come and go as they please, and to make converts where they can. There are said to be many thousand native Christians, Roman Catholics, in the country. In a letter dated May 1894, Monsignor Mutel, Vicar Apostolic of the Roman Catholic Church in Korea, stated that whereas the number of Korean Christians in 1886 was 14,000, in 1894 it was 208,423. Their priests, many of whom are Koreans, live in their midst; and every member of the flock, however remote his residence, is visited once in each year by his spiritual father. The French Catholic Church and Establishment, occupying a natural elevation, are one of the most prominent objects in Söul, and their earlier start has given them an advantage which the Protestants will not easily retrieve.

In 1890 an English Protestant Bishop (whose diocese is Korea and Shing-king, i.e. Manchuria) first appeared upon the scene, and when I was in Söul, the Mission establishment consisted, in addition, of several clergy, some lay-helpers, a doctor, and some sisters of St. Paul's, Kilburn. Churches had been built in Söul and Chemulpo, hospitals had been opened in both places, a printing-press had been established at Söul, and the missionaries were still engaged in acquiring the language before turning their energies either to evangelisation or to the translation of the Prayer-book into Korean.[1] There was as yet neither Korean congregation nor Korean convert. Simultaneously, and even earlier, American, Canadian, and Australian Societies or Churches had deputed bands of ardent workers to enter the field; and, all told, there were

English Protestant Mission.

---

[1] The New Testament was translated into Korean over twelve years ago by Rev. J. Ross of Newchwang; and in 1882 the Religious Tract Society published an introduction to it, and a catechism of the chief Biblical doctrines, in Korean.

between thirty and forty Protestant ministers at work in Korea.

What may be the future that lies before them it would be hazardous at this stage to predict. The Korean wolf has not been converted straight away, by the exigencies of national weakness or outside pressure, into a lamb; and a people at once so incurious, and so firmly wedded to Chinese ethics and ancestor-worship, may be expected in some places to oppose a stubborn front of resistance, in others to indulge in occasional outbursts of frantic antagonism. A few such cases have occurred even since the Treaties. In 1888 an outbreak took place in the streets of Sōul, the ridiculous rumour (not unlike that which preceded the famous Tientsin massacres in 1870, as well as later outrages in China) having been spread that the American missionaries had been stealing and boiling Korean babies in order to manufacture chemicals for use in photography. Nine native officials who were alleged to have been concerned in the transaction were seized and decapitated by the mob; and the crews of the foreign gunboats at Chemulpo were marched up to the capital to protect the subjects of their several nationalities. More recently there has been a recrudescence of the same feeling. In 1892 a Catholic missionary was attacked and beaten at a town in the interior, and a threatening proclamation was posted on the missionary doors in Sōul. Early in 1893 a politico-religious party, calling itself the Tokaguto or Tonghak, *i.e.* the Party of Oriental Learning, and appealing to the Conservative instinct of the people, started into being and attained menacing proportions, both in the capital and in the provinces. Its leaders presented a petition to the Throne demanding the prohibition of all foreign religions and the expulsion of the merchants— in other words, the abrogation of the Treaties. Nor was it

Native sentiment.

till after the ringleaders had been arrested, and foreign men-of-war had hurried from all quarters of the China Seas to Chemulpo—while the Japanese community in Söul, who are always the first victims of attack, had organised a militia in their own defence—that the peril subsided.

In the following year, in the disturbances again organised by the Tonghaks, which preceded and furnished the main Japanese plea for the declaration of war, the native Christians suffered severely. A French missionary, Père Jozeau, was brutally murdered in July. Christian villages were pillaged and burned, many native Christians were killed, and, before the war had half run its course, there were less than half a dozen Catholic missionaries left in Korea, and those at or near to the Treaty Ports. The Tonghaks have now been suppressed, and almost all spirit has been crushed out of the Koreans. Nevertheless the outlook is not reassuring. Because the Korean is ordinarily friendly to foreigners, it does not follow that he has any genuine fondness for us, still less for our creed. Instinctive in him is the Conservatism of a hide-bound stolidity ; and to suppose that the walls of the Korean Jericho are going to fall flat down at the first blast of the missionary trumpet is to cherish a belief from which the future will in all likelihood provide some more sharp awakenings. On the other hand, since, in the dramatic history of Korean Christianity, there is much cause for admiration, there is consequently good ground for hope.

CHAPTER VII

THE POLITICAL FUTURE OF KOREA

> Behold, a people shall come from the north, and a great nation, and many kings shall be raised up from the coasts of the earth. They shall hold the bow and the lance: they are cruel, and will not show mercy: their voice shall roar like the sea, and they shall ride upon horses, every one put in array, like a man to the battle, against thee. — *Jeremiah* l. 41-42.

BEFORE leaving Korea I must devote a final chapter to a discussion of the subject to which all other Korean questions are subsidiary, and to find a clue to which I was attracted thither from afar—viz. the political future that awaits this shuttlecock among the nations. I use the phrase as accurately descriptive of the relation in which Korea stood in 1892 to the various Powers who were represented at her capital, who treated her from entirely different and wholly irreconcilable standpoints, according to their own interests or prejudices, and at whose hands she was alternately—nay, even simultaneously—patronised, cajoled, bullied, and caressed. A more anomalous political condition certainly did not exist in the world than that of a country which itself claimed to be both independent and dependent, and could produce powerful evidence in support of either hypothesis; and as to which outside Powers advanced pretensions of suzerainty, control, protectorate, alliance, most-favoured-nation treatment, or technical equality, for all of which there was considerable show of justification. This curious state of affairs had arisen, in the first place, out of the peculiar

Margin note: Anomalous political status of Korea.

THE POLITICAL FUTURE OF KOREA

geographical situation of Korea as a sort of political Tom Tiddler's ground between China, Russia, and Japan; and, secondly, out of the contradictory policy pursued by the first-named of these Powers in moments of calculation or of alarm at the attitude or encroachments of the others. By a survey of the respective positions occupied or claimed by this trio, who were the protagonists in the international play for which Korea provided an involuntary stage, while the remaining nations were either cast for minor parts in the same piece, or sat as interested spectators in the auditorium, we may succeed in elucidating the earlier history of the drama that assumed such sanguinary developments in 1894.

Though Korea has been ruled by successive dynasties of monarchs for centuries, there has scarcely been a time since the commencement of the Christian era when it has not acknowledged a greater or less dependence upon either China or Japan. The claims of *Connection with Japan.* the latter Power, which in the declining years of the Shogunate were allowed to shrink into the background— to the great regret of Japanese patriots—were both the earlier in origin and have been exercised over the longer space of time. It was as early as the third century A.D. that a masculine Empress-Regent of Japan, bearing the appropriate name of Jingo or Zingu, herself led an expedition against Korea and received the submission of that State. From that time down to the end of the fourteenth century the relations between the two countries, though frequently disturbed, were, as a rule, those of Japanese ascendency and Korean allegiance. Tribute Missions constantly sailed from Fusan to the Court of Mikado or Shogun; and there grew up in Japanese minds the conviction, which has never been extirpated, that to surrender

Korea would be as indelible a stain upon the national honour as Mary of England felt it to lose Calais. After 1392, however, when the Mings assisted the Ni dynasty to establish itself on the Korean throne, the influence of China became paramount, and the marks of deference to Japan dwindled, until in 1460 the last Korean Embassy started for the Shogun's Court at Kamakura. It was accordingly as much to punish a refractory vassal as it was to prosecute loftier schemes of conquest against China herself that Hideyoshi designed his famous Korean expeditions. This invasion, by which the peninsula was desolated from end to end for six years (1592-98), had, even before the recent war broke out, permanently affected the relations between the two countries. It had left a heritage of wounded pride and national antipathy in the breast of the Koreans which three centuries had not availed to erase; while it heightened the exasperation felt by Japan that the vassal whom she crushed so utterly should for so long have managed to elude her clutch.

The retreat of the Japanese for a time suspended communications between the two States; but in 1618 occurred the Korean Mission, to which I have already alluded in a footnote; and in 1623 Iyemitsu demanded the revival of the tribute; and from that date, in spite of the absolute submission of the Korean Throne to the Manchus from 1637 onwards, Missions continued to make their annual excursion to Tokio, entirely at the expense of the Japanese, and with no advantage to the latter beyond the barren compliment to their pride. Owing to the exorbitant cost of entertainment a change was effected in 1790, when the envoys, instead of crossing to the Japanese mainland, were invited to proceed as far as Tsushima only; with which change the so-called tribute

Tribute Missions.

shrank still more into an annual exchange of presents with little or no admission of political subordination. This incongruous condition of affairs lasted till 1832, when the last complimentary mission upon a Shogun's accession was despatched from Korea to the Japanese Court.

A new era now opened, in which Japan, by dint of her own political resuscitation, was to re-establish a powerful influence in Korea, although at the cost of the feudatory relationship which for so many centuries it had been her boastful pretension to maintain. *Friction and rupture.*
When the Korean Government was threatened by the French invasion in 1866, it is said to have remembered its old connection, and to have solicited the advice and aid of Japan. No reply being returned to this request it was not surprising that when in 1868 a Japanese embassy arrived in Sŏul to convey the formal announcement of the political revolution in Japan, and the resumption by the Mikado of full sovereignty, and to invite from the Koreans a renewal of ancient friendship and vassalage, an insolent refusal was returned by the Tai Wen Kun. In Japan the Samurai party were furious; but the country was too poor and too much hampered by other complications to go to war; although the Chauvinist spirit found angry vent in rebellion in Saga, and in an attempt upon the life of the Japanese statesman Iwakura, who, on his return from Europe with Okubo in 1873, stoutly resisted a policy of stronger measures. To satisfy these ardent spirits, two successive but bootless Japanese missions, conducted by Hanabusa and Moriyama, were sent to Korea in 1873 and 1874, to re-establish Japanese authority by peaceful means, while the filibustering Formosan expedition was undertaken to keep the war-party employed in 1874. Nevertheless, when in 1875 a Japanese man-of-war, the *Unyokan*, had been fired

upon by the Koreans from the island of Kanghwa on the Han, and after an appeal to Peking and the receipt of an assurance from the Chinese Government that all responsibility was disowned by them, the first Japanese Treaty of 1876 was presented as an ultimatum and signed, the military party again broke forth into stormy discontent, and the great Saigo of Satsuma, splitting irrevocably with the Government, retired to his patrimony to plot the terrible civil war that commenced in the following year.

The self-restraint and caution of the then race of Japanese statesmen were, however, amply rewarded. They wisely recognised that the time for an aggressive policy was not then, and that Japanese influence in Korea could best be recovered, not by sustained invasion or conquest, but by the subtler movements of diplomatic *finesse* and commercial control. In this sagacious policy they were assisted by the weakness and indecision of China. When the above-mentioned Treaty was concluded, in 1876, with Korea, the opening words in Article 1 contained the remarkable statement that 'Chosen, being an independent State, enjoys the same sovereign rights as does Japan'—an admission which was foolishly winked at by China from the mistaken notion that, by disavowing her connection with Korea, she could escape the unpleasantness of being called to account for the delinquencies of her vassal.

Recovery of influence. Treaty of 1876.

This preliminary advantage was more than doubled in value to Japan when, after the revolution in Sŏul in 1882, by which her diplomatic representative was compelled to flee from the Korean capital, she concluded a Convention with Korea, containing a stipulation that she should have the right to station troops for the protection of her own nationals in that country. It was quadrupled when, after the second

Convention of Tientsin in 1885.

revolution in 1884, and the second Hegira to Chemulpo. Japan at once sent troops to avenge the insult and declined to remove them until China had made a similar concession with regard to the Chinese garrison, which had been maintained since the previous outbreak in 1882 in that city. By the Convention of Tientsin, which was negotiated in April 1885 by Count Ito with the Viceroy Li Hung Chang, both parties agreed to withdraw their troops and not to send an armed force to Korea at any future date to suppress rebellion or disturbance without giving previous intimation to the other.[1] This document was a second diplomatic triumph for Japan; for, whilst it was safe to aver that neither Power would ever be seriously deterred thereby from hostile action, it yet involved the very admission of substantial equality of rights as regards Korea which Japan had all along been labouring to reassert, and which China, except in the moments when she had been caught napping, had as consistently repudiated. Japan, therefore, if she had not recovered her former position, had at least re-established her credit. It was, in my judgment, greatly to be regretted that in the summer of 1894 her Government, anxious to escape from domestic tangles by a spirited foreign policy, abandoned this statesmanlike attitude, and embarked upon a course of aggression in Korea, for which there appeared to be no sufficient provocation, and the ulterior consequences of which, even after the brilliant issue of the campaign, it is still too early to forecast.

So much for the political revindication of Japan prior to

[1] This stipulation was contained in the concluding article of the Convention, which ran as follows:—'In case of any disturbance of a serious character occurring in Korea rendering it necessary for the respective countries (Japan and China) or either of them to send troops to Korea, it is hereby understood that they shall give, each to the other, previous notice in writing of their intention so to do, and after the matter is settled, they shall withdraw their troops immediately and not further station them there.'

the war. Simultaneously she pursued with unflagging energy the policy of commercial and fiscal ascendency in Korea.

Commercial ascendency. Active and business-like as compared with the indolent Koreans, possessed of capital, and understanding how to make others pay through the nose for the loan of it, her colonists and merchants had gradually fastened a grip on the weaker country which it would in any case have been exceedingly difficult to shake off. The Japanese had got the mint and banks already. The Government was largely in their debt. They were daily pressing for concessions of every description. Their eye had long been fixed upon the Customs, then in the hands of their rivals, the Chinese, and in a few years' time they hoped to have obtained so commanding a hold upon the national resources of Korea as to render her political dependence upon China a constitutional fiction which the wisdom born of accomplished facts might ultimately allow to expire. This policy was, of course, one of selfishness. But its success was not thereby so much imperilled as it was by the national race-hatred between Koreans and Japanese, that was and is one of the most striking phenomena in contemporary Chosen. Civil and obliging in their own country, the Japanese even before the war had developed in Korea a faculty for bullying and bluster that was the result partly of national vanity, partly of the memories of the past. The lower orders illtreated the Koreans on every possible opportunity, and were cordially detested by them in return. Indeed, it was very amusing to contrast the extreme sensitiveness of Japan towards the Treaty Powers in her own territories and her indignant protest against the severity of the Treaties, with the domineering callousness with which she, the first of the Treaty Powers in Korea, treated the latter unfortunate country because of its weakness, and exacted every ounce

THE POLITICAL FUTURE OF KOREA 195

of flesh permitted by the Treaties between them.[1] Such a relationship, which was in marked contrast with the amicable terms on which the Koreans and Chinese subsisted side by side, did not assist Japan in the war, during which the Koreans lent every possible aid to China, and, aggravated as it has been by the issue of the conflict, will not facilitate the issue which Japanese ambition has in view.

A striking instance of this attitude was afforded just before the outbreak of hostilities. In the course of 1889 the Korean Government, finding that the native-grown beans were being bought up in great quantity by Japanese merchants for exportation to Japan, issued a temporary prohibition of export in two provinces. *Political bluster.* By this decree the purchasers, who had already made advances to the cultivators, alleged that they were the losers by nearly $220,000, owing to their inability to recover their loans and to the non-delivery of the grain. Now by the Trade Regulations agreed upon between Korea and Japan in 1883, the former country had the right to prohibit the export of cereals in time of scarcity or emergency.[2] The Japanese, however, alleged that the emergency had not arisen in this case, and also that the stipulated month's notice had not been given in advance. The claim was pressed with greater or less insistence for four years, the Korean Government admitting a certain liability, but expressing its incapacity, owing to continued impoverishment, to pay more than $60,000 in compensation. At length the Radical and Jingo party in Japan became very much excited at this insulting

---

[1] When Japan dictated the first Korean Treaty in 1876, she copied the extra-territorial clauses almost *verbatim* from Articles IV. and V. of the Anglo-Japanese Treaty of 1858; and has never shown any reluctance to set in operation against Korea the provisions of which she complains so bitterly when applied to herself.

[2] Regulation xxxvii.

procrastination. As a sop to them the Japanese Minister to Söul was recalled, and a young Radical firebrand, who had recently published a book on Korea on the strength of a short visit there, was sent out to pursue a policy of brag. This individual, by presenting an ultimatum at the throat of the Korean Court, eventually compounded the dispute for $110,000; but, being totally destitute either of manners or of official training, he affronted the King and his Ministers to such an extent by his unseemly violation of all diplomatic etiquette in his interviews with them, that he was summarily recalled by the Japanese Government, returning to Tokio to be made the recipient of a popular ovation.

At that time Count Ito and his colleagues were not believed to have any sympathy with this intemperate and swaggering attitude towards the weaker State. They appeared to recognise that Japanese policy in Korea could only attain its ends by a friendly understanding with China; that the effort to recover purely political ascendency in Söul was incompatible with such an understanding; and that every attempt to humiliate or terrorise over Korea was to play China's game, and to tighten the bonds that united the vassal with the suzerain. At the same time no Japanese minister could afford altogether to abandon the immemorial claims of his country over the petty adjacent kingdom; while every Japanese minister has now to deal with a people—namely, his own countrymen—who, when their so-called patriotic instincts are appealed to, are apt to respond by going stark mad.

True policy of Japan.

It is the latter phenomenon, and the skilful but not too scrupulous use that was made of it, coupled with a justifiable confidence on the part of the Japanese in the superiority of their naval and military armaments, that prompted the rupture with China and the sustained invasion of Korea in the summer of 1894. Taking advantage of disturbances in the peninsula, which demonstrated with renewed clearness the impotence of the native Government to provide either a decent administration for its own subjects, or adequate protection to the interests of foreigners, and ingeniously profiting by the loophole left for future interference in the Tientsin Agreement of 1885, Japan in July 1894 responded to the despatch by China of a body of 2000 men, at the request of the Korean King, to assist him in putting down the Tonghak rebellion, by herself landing a much larger military force, estimated at 10,000 men, in Korea, and by seizing the capital. Li Hung Chang retaliated by the despatch of the Chinese fleet and of an expeditionary force, marching overland into the northern provinces. Both parties declined to retire: China relying upon her genuine authority and influence, but feeling that she had been somewhat outwitted; Japan being resolved to atone for previous blunders, and to reap a full advantage from her crafty but scarcely defensible diplomacy. After preliminary engagements, the result of which was entirely in favour of Japan, war was declared by the latter; and its subsequent progress, which on her side almost amounted to a procession, and on that of China to a stampede, is sufficiently recalled by the names of Ping-yang, Yalu River, Port Arthur, and Wei Hai Wei. With its consequences I shall deal in a later chapter.

Outbreak of war.

I turn next to the position of China. Her ascendency in Korea, which had far more natural conditions in the shape of common language, customs, religion, and philosophy, as well as territorial connection, to recommend it than could be advanced by Japan, practically dated from the foundation of the present reigning dynasty of Korea 500 years ago. It was under the patronage of the Ming

Connection with China.

Emperors that Ni Taijo, a soldier of fortune, raised himself to the Korean throne, and established a Court and capital at Söul, which till 1894 faithfully reproduced the Chinese characteristics of that epoch. When the Japanese invaded the peninsula from 1592 to 1598, the Chinese defended it with as much energy as though it were part of their own territories, and ultimately expelled the intruders. Subsequently, on their way to China, the Manchu conquerors devastated and exacted an even more humiliating submission from Korea, which till recent events was never surrendered, and was punctiliously enforced by the suzerain Power. While Hamel was in Korea, 1653-1666, he testifies to the constant visits of the representative of the 'Great Cham,' and to the complete humility of the Korean Government. Annually a Tribute Mission wended its way by land from Söul to Peking, conveying the specified tribute,[1] and receiving in return the Calendar, which it was the imperial prerogative to prepare, and the mark of vassalage to receive. In the succeeding century the tribute was gradually reduced, and the embassy appeared at times to dwindle into a ceremonial function, carrying presents in return for the permission to trade at the frontier, rather than tokens of political submission. Nevertheless, during this epoch a violent disturbance took place if there was the slightest omission of prescribed deference; and one Korean monarch was smartly fined for his omission of some punctilio. From the time of the Manchu invasion to the present day every King and Queen of Korea have received their patent of royalty from the Court at Peking;[2] and the historical

[1] Its ingredients are stated by Dallet (vol. i. p. 15); but it is long since they were scrupulously exacted.
[2] M. Scherzer has translated into French and published in *Recueil d'Itinéraires et de Voyages dans l'Asie Centrale et l'extrême Orient* (1878) the diary of the principal Chinese Envoy who was sent from Peking to invest the present Queen of Korea in 1866.

tutelary position of China continued up till the war to be vindicated in the following manner.

In addition to the Imperial investiture, and to the annual despatch of the Tribute Mission from Sŏul, which was still maintained—although a practical and mercantile aspect was lent to the proceeding by its being utilised for the export to China by the Chung In of the King's red *ginseng*—the name of the reigning monarch of Korea was also given to him by China, and the era specified in Korean Treaties was that of the accession, not of the King, but of his Suzerain the Emperor. The King of Korea was not allowed to wear the Imperial yellow. When the Imperial Commissioners arrived from Peking, he was required to proceed outside of his capital in order to receive them, the chief Commissioner being of higher rank in the Chinese official hierarchy than himself; and I have previously spoken of the now destroyed ornamental archway outside the west gate of Sŏul, at which the vassal prince received the envoys of his Suzerain. When any notable events occurred in the Court at Peking they were communicated to the vassal Court, and were the cause of a respectful message either of condolence or of congratulation from the latter. Similarly, if any death occurred among the leading members of the Royal Family at Sŏul, an official intimation of the fact was sent to Peking.

<small>Existing evidences of Korean vassalage.</small>

When the late Queen Dowager of Korea died in 1890, the King deputed a mission at once to report the fact to the Emperor; and, in petitioning the latter to dispense with the ordinary ceremonial of a return mission to convey the condolences of the Suzerain, because of the difficulty that would be experienced by Korea in consequence of her financial embarrassment in carrying out all the prescribed ceremonies—he

<small>Death of the Queen Dowager in 1890.</small>

made the following statement of his position *vis-à-vis* with China:—

'Our country is a small kingdom and a vassal State of China, to which the Emperor has shown his graciousness from time immemorial. Our Government was enabled to survive the political troubles of 1882 and 1884 through the assistance received from the Throne, which secured for our country peace and tranquillity. Since His Majesty has been good enough to confer these favours upon us, we should make known to him whatever we desire; and whatever we wish we trust that he may allow, as to an infant confiding in the tender mercies of its parents.'

These compliments, however, did not induce the Suzerain to forgo one tittle of his traditional rights; although he so far yielded to the Korean plea of poverty as to permit his Commissioners to travel by sea to Chemulpo, instead of overland, thereby greatly reducing the cost of their entertainment. An account of the minute and elaborate ceremonies observed on both sides was afterwards published with evident design by the Secretary to the Imperial Commissioners.[1] The latter, it appears, among other marks of condescension, suggested the omission from the programme of the state banquets, music, and jugglery, with which it was usual to entertain them. 'Their motive for this suggestion was to show their consideration for Korean impecuniosity.' They also declined to receive parting presents from the King, at which the latter 'felt very grateful, and at the same time regretted the fact.' When all was over the King sent a memorial to the Emperor, thanking him for his graciousness. 'The sentiments of this memorial—in their sincerity and importance—are beyond expression in words, demonstrating that China's manifold graciousness towards her dependencies is increasing with the times. The Emperor's consideration

[1] *Notes on the Imperial Chinese Mission to Corea in* 1890. Shanghai, 1892.

for his vassal State, as evinced by his thoughtfulness in matters pertaining to the Mission, is fathomless. How admirable and satisfactory! And how glorious!'

Such is the technical and official expression of the suzerainty of China that was observed until July 1894, and such were the evidences of the indisputable reality of that relationship. Of even greater importance is it to trace the extent to which in recent years it had been accompanied by practical domination of Korean statecraft—a subject which brings us into immediate acquaintance with the diplomatic indecision of China, as well as with her great latent strength.

Up to the time of the massacre of the French missionaries in Korea in 1866 the claim of Korean independence had never seriously been made. At that date it was advanced, of all people in the world, by the Chinese themselves. Anxious to escape responsibility for the act, as well as the irksome duty of either paying an indemnity themselves or extorting it from their vassal, when M. de Bellonet, the French *Chargé d'Affaires*, inquired of the Tsungli Yamen what he was to do, the latter disowned Korea altogether, and left the Frenchman to publish a ridiculous manifesto to Prince Kung, in which he took upon himself to announce in advance the deposition of the Korean Sovereign. Similarly when, in 1871, the American Expedition, under Admiral Rodgers, proposed to sail against Korea to demand reparation for the loss of the *General Sherman* and the murder of its crew on Korean shores in 1866, and to force a treaty upon the Korean Court, it was again with the connivance of the Chinese Government that the project was undertaken. Finally, when in 1876 the Japanese, before sending an expedition to Korea with a similar object, applied for in-

Thread of Chinese policy.
1. Repudiation.

formation to Peking in advance, a third time came the disclaimer of China, which is said on this occasion to have even been committed to paper. This was a policy of Repudiation, and was China's first inconsistency.

Discovering her mistake, and realising that the foreigner, having once been allowed to meddle with Korea *proprio motu*, could not be permanently excluded from closer relations, she then tried to repair her error by encouraging the various Powers to enter into Treaty relations with Korea on an independent basis, hoping, apparently, that the mutual jealousies of all would preclude the ascendency of any one. Commodore Shufeldt, an American naval officer, who in 1867 had been sent upon a futile mission to Korea after the loss of the *General Sherman*, being in Tientsin in 1881, was utilised by Li Hung Chang as the first instrument of this new policy. The American Treaty, intended to serve as a pattern for its successors, is said to have been drafted by the Viceroy himself; and it was with the escort of a Chinese squadron that the Commodore presented himself at the mouth of the Han. Simultaneously the Viceroy wrote a letter to the Tai Wen Kun, strongly urging upon the Korean Government the signature of treaties with the foreign Powers as the sole means of continued security and independence for the threatened kingdom. Under these conditions the American Treaty was signed in 1882, and the Treaties with Great Britain and Germany in 1883; the first British draft Treaty, which was framed by Admiral Willes in 1882 on the model of the American, being superseded by the more liberal instrument negotiated with great ability and concluded by Sir Harry Parkes in the following year.

2. Neutralisation.

Now the first article of the Japanese Treaty of 1876 had opened with these words:—'Chosen, being an independent State, enjoys the same sovereign rights as does Japan.' Conscious of the serious significance of this admission, China, in recommending the additional foreign Treaties, now sought to guard herself by a statement of her own position. The American Treaty, when first drafted, contained a clause which ran as follows:—' Korea has always been tributary to China, and this is admitted by the President of the United States'; but 'The Treaty shall be permanently regarded as having nothing to do therewith.' This absurd contradiction was of course expunged by the Washington Government, who, being invited to conclude a treaty with Korea, naturally insisted upon treating Korea as an independent State. Accordingly in the American, as in the British and subsequent foreign Treaties, the King of Korea is throughout regarded (though not actually described) as an independent Sovereign; and provisions are made for the customary diplomatic representation, familiar in the case of Powers negotiating upon an equal basis, of each of the High Contracting Parties at the Court of the other. Not to be circumvented, however, China insisted upon the King of Korea sending the following despatch to the President of the United States, prior to the actual conclusion of the treaty; and facsimiles of the same have since been transmitted to the Sovereigns of each of the remaining Treaty Powers at the corresponding juncture :—

Terms of the Treatise.

'The King of Korea acknowledges that Korea is a tributary of China; but in regard to both internal administration and foreign intercourse it enjoys complete independence. Now, being about to establish Treaty relations between Korea and the United States of America on terms of equality, the King of Korea, as an independent monarch, distinctly undertakes to carry out the articles contained in the Treaty, irrespective of any matters affecting the tributary relations subsisting between Korea and China, with which the United States of America have no concern. Having appointed officials to deliberate upon and settle the Treaty, the King of Korea considers it his duty to address this despatch to the President of the United States.'

It will, I think, be conceded that a more strictly illogical State-paper than the above was never penned, and that a more incongruous or contradictory position was never taken up. The King of Korea acknowledges his vassalage to China; but in the same breath pronounces his complete independence both in the administration of his own country and in foreign relations. In what, then, we may ask, does his vassalage consist? He describes himself simultaneously as a tributary and as an independent monarch. So double-faced a portent, so complex a phenomenon, has neither parallel nor precedent in international law. If he is a vassal, he has no business to be making treaties, or to be sending and receiving envoys on a footing of equality. If he is independent, why does he declare himself a feudatory?

Such was the irrational position in which China, by her policy of an attempted neutralisation of Korea, landed both herself and the vassal State. The full consequences of her attitude were clearly manifested when, a few years later, Korea proposed to carry out her initial prerogative of sending duly accredited envoys to the foreign Courts who were already represented at Söul. The Viceroy Li, who had in the meantime sensibly tightened the reins, was consulted; and once more seeking to recover the ground which had been technically abandoned, he attached conditions to the proposed appointments which, strictly regarded, were, if possible, even more anomalous than the original paradox. The Korean Envoy, on arrival at his destination, was to report himself to the Chinese Representative there, and to be introduced by him to the Foreign Minister of the State. On all public occasions he was to yield precedence to the Chinese Minister, and he was invariably to consult and take the advice of the latter. Here was the same contradiction in terms in a more pronounced shape. If the King of Korea was a vassal, he had no business to be sending representatives at all; if he was an independent monarch, China had no business to interfere with him. Either his envoys were private individuals or they were diplomatic representatives. If they were the former, no question of precedence could arise; if they were the latter, they were subject to the normal regulations of diplomatic etiquette. For some weeks the President of the United States, naturally somewhat bewildered, kept the Korean Envoy at Washington waiting for his audience; but when the common-sense view of the question prevailed against the quibbles concocted in self-defence by the Chinese Government, and the Envoy was received, without any reference to the Chinese Minister, as the representative of an independent Sovereign, Li Hung Chang was very wroth with His Majesty of Korea, who for his part returned the stereotyped reply that the offending envoy had exceeded his instructions. However this might be, his brother-minister, who had been accredited to the Courts of Petersburg, Berlin, Paris, and London, never got beyond Hongkong; so that the European Foreign Offices were saved from a repetition of the same inconvenient wrangle.

Before the dispute about the envoys arose, China, not yet alive to the initial error that had led her to authorise the Treaties, had been tempted into a repetition of the same weakness, on an even larger scale, by the Convention, already referred to as concluded at Tientsin in 1885 between herself and Japan. If China was the suzerain Power, she had the same right to march troops into Söul, in the event of disturbance, as the Indian Government has, for instance, to order British regiments in a similar emergency to Hyderabad — whilst Japan had no corresponding right whatsoever; and any agreement by

Question of troops at Söul.

China with a second Power involving a surrender of that right was to derogate from her own pretensions. If China was not the suzerain Power, how could she claim any right, but that which war confers upon any belligerent strong enough to exercise it, to send troops to Korea at all?

If, however, on the field of diplomacy, where she is ordinarily supposed to be so clever, but where I think I have shown that in the case of Korea she has always been tacking to and fro between opposite extremes, China had been more timid or less far-sighted than Japan, she had to a great extent atoned for her discordant policy by a very practical assertion of sovereignty in Sŏul itself. When the rebellion broke out there in 1882 and the King appealed to Li Hung Chang for help, the latter responded by at once sending a number of ironclads, and 4000 troops, the bulk of whom remained in a permanent camp outside the city for nearly three years. He compelled the Korean Government to accept the Japanese demands with a quite unusual alacrity; and effectively nipped all antagonism in the bud by instructing the Chinese commander, Ma Kien Chung, to invite the Tai Wen Kun to dinner, to pop him into a sedan-chair, and carry him down to the coast, whence he was deported straight to China and interned for three years. Again it was Li Hung Chang whom the disconsolate King was obliged to petition for the restoration of his troublesome parent, and who allowed the old intriguer to go back. When the Treaty Ports were opened, the same statesman took good care to reserve the Customs service for Chinese hands; and in the summer of 1892 the Bean question with Japan was only settled by his intervention and by a Chinese loan to Korea, the security for which was to be the Customs Revenue—an ingenious frustration of one of the pet projects of Japan. When in 1885 negotiations were

3. Practical sovereignty.

opened with Great Britain about the evacuation of Port Hamilton, it was China, and not Korea, who took up the pen. Until 1893 the only overland telegraphic connection which the Viceroy allowed to Korea outside of her own dominions was a junction with the Chinese wire to Peking, and when the Russian demand for a connection with Vladivostok could no longer be refused, he wisely backed it up by offering to construct and to officer the line with Chinese material and men.

Finally, in Sōul itself every one of the Foreign Diplomatic Corps, though he gaily proclaimed himself the representative of his sovereign at an allied and equal Court, knew perfectly well who was the real master. *The Chinese Resident.* The Chinese Resident, who was a man of great energy and ability, named Yuan Shih Kai, was in the position of a Mayor of the Palace, without whose knowledge nothing, and without whose consent little was done. Alone among the foreign representatives, he was entitled to sit when received in audience by the King. His establishment and guard and display in the streets were among the sights of Sōul. The various champions of the academic theory of Korean independence have one by one disappeared from the stage, but the Chinese Resident remained. Time after time he had been reappointed, as was the Marquis Tseng in Europe; and even after his promotion to the Taotaiship of Wenchow in China had been formally gazetted in 1893, it was still felt that he could not be spared from Sōul, and he stayed on, until the war had irretrievably shattered the structure to the building of which he had devoted such pains. He is one of the few Chinese I have met who impressed me with frankness as well as with power.

Judged, therefore, by its results prior to the war, it might be said that the policy of Li Hung Chang, however little shaped by the canons either of logic or of international custom, was not unsuccessful. Each logical *faux pas* was in Justification of Li Hung Chang. the end retrieved by some practical advantage. If he declined to punish Korea in the first place for her attacks upon missionaries and foreigners, he thereby escaped responsibility for her cruelties. If he allowed Korea, a vassal State of China, to make Treaties with foreign Powers, he at the same time vindicated his right to appear as go-between—a capacity in which Japan was most anxious to figure. By these means he might claim to have enlisted the interest of foreign Powers as a set-off to the only two rivals whom China seriously fears in Korea, viz. Japan and Russia. Finally, having surrendered some of the technical symbols of suzerainty, he offered a very practical demonstration of the remainder at all moments of crisis; and by judicious advances of money obtained a firm hold upon Korean administration. How futile, however, such a policy was destined to be, when, in the face of a serious emergency, it had nothing to lean upon save the incredible rottenness of Chinese administration, the events of the past year were required to expose.

Upon this scene Russia, having been brought by the Chinese concessions of 1858-1860[1] down to the River Connection with Russia. Tiumen, and having thereby become coterminous with Korean territory on the north, appeared for the first time as an actor about thirty years ago. At her maritime harbour and base of Vladivostok she is but

[1] Mouravieff, the Russian Governor-General of Siberia, taking advantage of the absorption of China in her impending war with Great Britain, and of the gross ignorance of the Manchu frontier officials, persuaded the latter to sign the Treaty of Aigun in 1858, ceding to Russia the Amur province. In 1860, before the war was concluded and while the Emperor was still a fugitive, Ignatieff went to Peking, and by a further Treaty from the terrified Government got the Primorsk province (i.e. all the territory lying to the east of the Ussuri, and 600 miles of sea-coast) as well. Never was a fine dominion so cheaply or more cleverly won.

little removed from the Korean frontier, across which her
officers and agents have pursued their surveys far and wide
(the only decent map of Korea, before the war, being one
that emanated from Russian sources), while the Koreans
have been encouraged to develop a corresponding familiarity
by invitations to come and settle in Russian villages across
the border. Here they were utilised at first as squatters
and colonists in the practically uninhabited country, later
on as farmers and graziers and woodcutters. In the towns
labour was found for them and schools were opened for their
children, in which the latter were brought up in the Russian
faith, supplying, as they grew to manhood, a native pasto-
rate to evangelise their fellow-countrymen. In 1885 there
were said to be 20,000 Koreans in Russian territory, and
the figures are probably now much higher, there having
been a steady exodus across the frontier ever since the war.
It was through the agency of these volunteer emigrants and
naturalised citizens that Russia first opened her campaign of
political intrigue in the peninsula.

The general territorial acquisitiveness of Russia at the
expense of weaker neighbours, her admitted desire for a
naval marine in the Pacific, and the superior advantages possessed by Korean harbours over the *Aggressive designs.*
more northerly port of Vladivostok, which is ice-
bound for four months in the year, as well as the diplomatic
tactics adopted by her representatives, have given universal
credence in the East to the belief that Korea is regarded by
Russia with a more than covetous eye. There is considerable evidence in support of this hypothesis. It was during
the Kulja dispute with China in 1880 that her unconcealed
affection for the sheltered recesses of Port Lazareff[1] (the

---

[1] At the outbreak of the recent war a Russian engineer who had been sent in 1886 to survey and report upon Port Lazareff, wrote to the *Novoe Vremya*

plans for the seizure and fortification of which are said to have been long prepared) was first made use of as a diplomatic menace, and is believed in consequence to have still further inclined the mind of Li Hung Chang towards the policy of the Korean Treaties. In 1884, while France was at war with China and was anxious to enlist the sympathy and alliance of Japan, the question of the price to be paid to the latter soon brought matters to a deadlock, when it was discovered that Russia would not let the opportunity slip of also doing a stroke of business in Korean waters. In 1884 the Russians were said by many to have been at the bottom of the conspiracy and outbreak in Sŏul; but I am not aware of the evidence upon which this is based. About the same time rumours, not without solid foundation, were circulated of a secret agreement between Russia and Korea, negotiated by the German Adviser of the King, by which Russia was to reorganise the Korean army and to support the Korean claims to Tsushima,[1] while Korea in return was to cede Port Hamilton; and it was something more than rumour of the latter intention that induced the British Government to anticipate an impending Muscovite seizure by hoisting the

that Port Lazareff itself was unsuited either for a commercial harbour or for a naval base; but that sixty miles further north was a harbour named Port Shestakoff, formed by the island of Gontcharoff and the mainland, which could easily be defended and was admirably adapted to either purpose. The Russian Minister of Marine, who had himself visited the spot, reported in the same sense to his Government.

[1] Others said that Russia was to occupy Tsushima herself—a course which the *Novoe Vremya* urged upon the Government in a most unblushing article, and which possessed the charm of an historical precedent. For in 1861 the main island was actually occupied for six months by the crew of the Russian frigate *Possadnik*, who hoisted the Russian flag, formed a small settlement ashore, and cultivated the soil. Sir R. Alcock, who was British Minister in Japan, sent Mr. Laurence Oliphant, then a member of the Legation, to find out what was going on. The latter reported to Admiral Sir J. Hope, who was in command of the neighbouring squadron, and who represented to the Russian Admiral that he should be compelled to go to Tsushima himself and to stay there as long as did the Russians. The result was immediate evacuation. (*Vide* an article by Laurence Oliphant in *Blackwood's Magazine*, Dec. 1885, and also *Rolling Stone*.)

British flag upon those islands. In 1886 a further plot for placing Korea under Russian protection was detected by the Chinese Resident. Four leading Korean officials were arrested and imprisoned, and subsequently admitted their complicity by flight. In 1886, however, China, furnished with a golden opportunity by the willingness of Great Britain to evacuate Port Hamilton, provided she could obtain guarantees that no other foreign Power would occupy it, scored her first genuine diplomatic triumph as regards Korea by extorting a distinct and official pledge from the Russian Government that under no circumstances would Russia occupy Korean territory. This pledge was alluded to with some pride in the conversation which I enjoyed at Tientsin with the Viceroy Li Hung Chang. But an Englishman who remembers the official pledges as to Samarkand, and Khiva, and Merv, might be pardoned for preferring an attitude of more sceptical reserve. This, however, was, for the time being, the cue to Russian official argument touching Korea, and has been followed more recently by the *Novoe Vremya*, which acts as a sort of *ballon d'essai* for the schemes of the Russian General Staff, and which has gone so far as to reason against Russian annexation of Korea on the ground that the country is too thickly populated to admit of easy conquest, too different from Russia to render assimilation possible, and too poor to make the experiment remunerative. There is much to be said for this view; and undoubtedly it cannot for some time be to the interest of Russia, with her Siberian Railway still unfinished, and with her military resources on the Manchurian border in no very forward condition, either of numbers or equipment, to involve herself in a warlike adventure at so great a distance from her base. On the other hand, she can hardly desire to have as her permanent neighbour, within a few hours' sail of Vladivostok, so pugnacious and aspiring a Power as Young Japan.

would be seriously jeopardised, if not absolutely overturned, by such a development; and England is prohibited alike by her imperial objects and her commercial needs from lending her sanction to any such issue.

Occupation of Port Hamilton in 1885.

The temporary occupation of Port Hamilton, an almost uninhabited group of islets forty miles from the southern coast of Korea, by the British fleet in 1885, was dictated by the political necessities of that time, being undertaken in order to anticipate a Russian seizure, and as an answer to the Russian aggression at Penjdeh, but was not subsequently persisted in—a retirement which, less for its own sake than for the possible use of continued occupation as a plea by others, was gladly welcomed both by China and Korea, and cemented the friendly relations between Great Britain and those States.[1]

[1] Port Hamilton is formed by two large and one small island, called respectively Sodo, Sunodo, and Chuwen, or Observatory Island, belonging to the Nanhow group, thirty-eight miles from the north-east end of Quelpart. When occupied by the British they were found to contain a few villages and Korean officials. Lord Granville, in announcing the temporary occupation to China, expressed his readiness to come to an agreement with her on the matter, and to pay yearly to Korea any revenues derived from the islands. The Tsungli Yamen, who in the meantime had been threatened with corresponding movements both by Russia and Japan, declined, and instructed the Korean Government to protest—an action which Lord Granville endeavoured to meet by offering a yearly rent of £5000. In the meantime three British admirals successively reported that the port could not be safely held unless great expense were incurred in fortification, and that in war a protecting squadron would be required to prevent its being shelled from without. After much correspondence, Lord Rosebery, in April 1886, offered to retire upon a guarantee being given by China against the occupation of Port Hamilton by any other Power, or upon the conclusion of an international agreement guaranteeing the integrity of Korea. A combination of these suggestions was ultimately adopted; and the Russian representative at Peking having given 'a most explicit guarantee' that if the British evacuated Port Hamilton ' Russia would not occupy Korean territory under any circumstances whatsoever,' the British flag was hauled down in February 1887. (*Vide* China, No. 1, 1887.) This engagement has not been affected by the recent war, and was pronounced in the House of Commons in June 1894 to be in the opinion of the British Government still valid. The Korean Government in 1894 reasserted its authority over the islands by sending there as Governor an official of some distinction.

In the negotiations that passed between the respective
Governments it was obvious, indeed, that what China shrank
from, and what Korea dreaded, was not the establishment
of a British naval or coaling station, or even of a British
maritime fortress in the mouth of the Sea of Japan, but
the chance of a corresponding Russian movement in some
neighbouring quarter; and both Powers were grateful for
a step which forced the hand of Russia, and compelled her
to give a guarantee, which lent a renewed lease of life to
the phantom of Korean integrity, and has so far saved the
little kingdom from sudden or surreptitious deglutition at
the hands of her formidable neighbour. The evacuation
of Port Hamilton also showed that, while Great Britain is
interested in keeping out others from this Naboth's vine-
yard of the Far East, she has no reversionary desire for
its possession herself, and is about as likely to seize or to
annex Korea as she is to invade Belgium—a demonstration
which was not merely grateful to China, but was also useful
in allaying the phenomenal sensitiveness of Japan.

The remaining Powers in Korea before the war, according
to their political predilections or objects, were disposed
to range themselves partly on the side of those
who proclaimed, partly with those who dis-   *The other Powers.*
couraged, the pretensions of Korean autonomy;
their attitude being generally ascertainable from the
character and title of the diplomatic representation which
they maintain at the Korean Court. France, of course,
adopted the former line and deputed a Consul and
Commissaire, claiming precedence of the British and
German Consuls. Russia, her ally, was represented by
a *Chargé d'Affaires*. America appointed a Minister and
vigorously encouraged the dream of Korean independence,
as best qualified to provide employment for American

dollars and brains. Germany sent a Consul and Commissioner. Great Britain was and is technically represented by a Minister Plenipotentiary, the Minister at Peking being simultaneously accredited, in virtue of the Treaty of 1883, to the King of Korea. Till 1893, however, when Sir N. O'Conor went up to Söul and presented his letters of credence to the King, no visit of a British Minister had taken place since that date; and the Queen is ordinarily represented in Söul by a Consul-General, whose relatively subordinate position is the source of not unnatural vexation on the part of the Korean Government, as well as of misunderstanding among the Diplomatic Body. These absurd anomalies and disputes were a further but inevitable consequence of the illogical policy of the Treaties.

Such was the position occupied by Korea in the summer of 1894 *vis-à-vis* with the more powerful nations with whom the march of events had brought her into direct contact. She was confronted with the ill-suppressed cupidity of Russia, the mysterious latent force of China, the jealous and vainglorious interest of Japan. By herself she was quite incapable of successful resistance to any one of these three, though her statesmen were not deficient in the skill required to play off each against the other. Her intrinsic weakness was in reality her sole strength; for had she been powerful enough to render her own alliance an appreciable weight in the scale, she might have been tempted to adopt a course of action that would have precipitated final absorption. Unfortunately for her, the conflict for which she supplied a convenient battle-ground, rather than a legitimate provocation, was forced upon her by the tempers of her Asiatic neighbours, too highly charged to postpone any longer the

The carcase and the eagles.

inevitable explosion. My own conviction, expressed in my first edition, that the only hope of continued national existence for Korea lay in the maintenance of her connection with China has not, in my opinion, been falsified by the issue of the campaign, since the independence, which was the nominal pretext of the latter, and is now claimed as its result, is a phantom which not even the interested auspices of Japan have so far persuaded to materialise, and which will assuredly be the source of further trouble in the future.

CHINA

'And so he passed with his folk, and wan the Lond of Cathay, that is the Grettest Kyngdom of the World'

SIR JOHN MAUNDEVILLE: *Travels*

CHAPTER VIII

THE COUNTRY AND CAPITAL OF CHINA

Mimcque
Murorum ingentes, aequataque machina cœlo.
VIRGIL: *Æneid* iv. 88, 89.

A MORE singular contrast can scarcely be found than is presented by the transition from Korea to China. From romantic mountain-scenery the traveller passes, at least on his way up to Peking, to flat and featureless plains. He exchanges the miniature Korean stallion, which rarely advances beyond a walk, for the sturdy China pony, upon which he will with ease cover seven miles an hour, or a day's march of forty miles. In place of the confined and filthy Korean hostelry, he will sleep with comparative comfort in the ample surroundings of a Chinese inn. He has left behind the most supine and spiritless of the peoples of the Far East, and sees about him the frugal, hard-limbed, indomitable, ungracious race, who oppose to all overtures from the outside the sullen resistance of a national character self-confident and stolid, a religious and moral code of incredible and all-absorbing rigour, and a governing system that has not varied for ages, and is still wrapped in the mantle of a superb and paralysing conceit. Most travellers deplore the transition from Japan to China as one from sweetness to squalor, from beauty to ugliness, from civilisation to barbarism, from warmth of welcome to cheerless repulsion. And yet I am

Transition to China.

not sure that a truer estimate is not formed of the prodigious strength of Chinese character and custom by the ability to contrast them with the captivating external attributes of Japan; whilst a check is placed upon the too indiscriminate laudation of the latest recruit to civilisation by the spectacle of a people who have lived and would be content, if we permitted them, to go on living without any contact with the West at all, and who think what we call truth error, our progress weakness, and our fondest ideals an abomination. Perhaps as a stepping-stone between the two, akin to yet also profoundly dissimilar from either, Korea supplies a link that may at once break and lend point to the abruptness of the contrast.

The journey from the coast of the Gulf of Pechili up to the capital seems to have won an undeserved reputation for painfulness in travellers' writings. It is true that the visitor may lie tossing for one, two, or more days on the mud-bar outside the Taku forts at the mouth of the Peiho—in which position he may picture the plight of the British gunboats, which, on that fatal day in 1859, rolled helplessly in precisely the same plight under the pitiless pounding of the enemy's guns. But, once landed, he may now avoid the further delays of the serpentine river-course to Tientsin by taking the railway train that runs thrice daily to that city; while the sights of Tientsin itself are, to any but those who have never before seen a great Chinese centre of population, very rapidly exhausted. To the ordinary European traveller almost its sole interest lies in the fact that it was the scene of the famous massacre of 1870, an eloquent testimony to which still survives in the ruined towers and façade of the French Catholic Cathedral on the right bank of the Peiho.

Tientsin.

To all who have followed the course of Chinese history during the last quarter of a century, Tientsin will present the additional interest of being the residence of the foremost living Chinese statesman, the Vice-roy Li Hung Chang. First made famous by his conduct and generalship during the Taiping Rebellion, his connection in which with the late General Gordon is well known, he succeeded Tseng Kwo Fan (the elder of the two Tsengs, and father of the ambassador) as Governor-General of Kiangsu in 1862, and became Viceroy of Kukuang in 1867. In 1870 he settled at Tientsin, where he succeeded the same eminent statesman as Viceroy of the metropolitan province of Chihli, and was entrusted with the delicate negotiations with England, arising out of the Margary murder, that resulted in the Chefoo Convention of 1876. Now for nearly twenty years the Senior Grand Secretary of State, the first Chinese subject who has ever been promoted to that dignity,[1] he also combines in his

The Viceroy Li Hung Chang.

[1] The Grand Secretariat, or Nei Ko, which was the Supreme Council, or Cabinet, of the Chinese Empire under the Ming dynasty, is the senior of the two bodies which intervene between the Sovereign and the Administrative Departments in the Chinese *régime*, and consists theoretically of two Manchu and two Chinese Grand Secretaries, with their assistants and staffs. It now forms the Imperial Chancery, or Court of Archives, and admission to one of its superior posts confers the highest distinction attainable by a Chinese official, although entailing little more than nominal duties. For purposes of actual administration it has been superseded by the second body, viz. the Chun Chi Chu, or Grand Council, which is the acting Privy Council of the Sovereign, in whose presence its members daily transact the business of State, in a hall of the Imperial Palace at Peking, at the inconceivable hour of four o'clock in the morning. It is a Cabinet composed of Ministers in the capital holding other substantive offices. Their number is undetermined, but for many years past did not exceed five. During the war with Japan it was raised to seven. Its Presidential chair, which was successively occupied by Prince Kung and Prince Chun, and is now again filled by the former, is practically equivalent to the post of Prime Minister. Two or three members of the Tsungli Yamen, or Foreign Board, generally hold seats in this Council, and all its members enjoy the technical right of audience with the Emperor. For a more minute account of the theoretical organisation and functions of the two Councils, *vide* Professor R. K. Douglas's excellent recently published work, *Society in China*.

person the viceregal functions above mentioned, as well as those of Senior Tutor to the Heir Apparent (who is not yet

LI HUNG CHANG

in existence), Earl of the First Rank, Superintendent of the Northern Ports, and Imperial Commissioner for Foreign Trade. As such he not merely divides with the late

Marquis Tseng the distinction of being the most remarkable figure whom his country has produced during the last thirty years, but he has for long filled the part of a sort of unofficial Foreign Minister and confidential adviser to his Sovereign, without whose knowledge nothing, however unimportant, takes place, and without whose advice nothing important is done. His Chinese extraction and his commanding position have sometimes suggested to others the hypothesis of a rising against the Manchu occupants of the throne, and of a new Chinese dynasty, founded by Li Hung Chang himself; and it is even said that he has at different times, in troublesome crises, been sounded upon the matter both by England and by France. There has never, however, been any reason to suspect his loyalty, which, if tempted, has not been seriously impugned; and he has long remained the strongest pillar of the Imperial throne. Many times has the Viceroy, who is now seventy-two years of age, petitioned to be relieved from the responsibilities, official and supernumerary, of his great position, but on each occasion has appeared an Imperial Rescript, commanding him in complimentary terms to continue the discharge of duties from which he could not be spared. During the recent war, after the shameful collapse of the Chinese naval and land forces, for which he was held to be largely responsible, he was temporarily disgraced; and the various phases of his official degradation and reinstatement followed each other with a kaleidoscopic rapidity that must, except to any one versed in the ways of Chinese officialdom, have been sufficiently bewildering. As soon, however, as it became necessary to send an Imperial Plenipotentiary to Japan to negotiate the terms of peace, it was once more found that the veteran was the only man; and, though he emerges from the terrible ordeal of the war, to use a colloquial phrase, as only 'the best of a bad lot,' he has, ostensibly at any rate, recovered his former position, and continues to offer to the foreigner the interesting spectacle of the one Chinaman who with the ingrained characteristics of his countrymen combines a diplomatic astuteness, and a respect for the externals of reform that are variously described as admirable and deceiving. According to the latest news, he has been relieved of his Viceroyalty of Chihli and his Imperial Commissionership, and has been ordered to Peking to take up the functions of Head of the Imperial Chancery. Whether this is intended as a compliment or the reverse, no one outside the Palace at Peking can as yet say.

At Tientsin I was honoured by the Viceroy with an interview, to which I look back with the greatest pleasure. The Viceroyal Yamen is a building in the official quarters of which, at any rate, there is neither distinction nor beauty. Carried in green palanquins to the gate, we there descended and passed through one or more dingy anterior courts, small, squalid, and coarsely painted, to an inner room, where seats had been placed round a long table. The Viceroy entered, a tall and commanding figure, considerably over six feet in height, dressed in a long grey silk robe, with a black silk cape over his shoulders. Taking his seat at the head of the table, the Viceroy, with the aid of a competent interpreter, commenced a discussion, mainly upon contemporary politics, which lasted for over an hour. He continually put the most searching and ingenious questions; being renowned, indeed, for his faculty of 'pumping' others about what he desires to ascertain, without emitting the least corresponding drop of moisture himself. While speaking or listening his small, black, restless eyes follow keenly every movement of the features. A big moustache overhangs and partially conceals his mouth,

Interview.

and a sparse Chinese beard adorns his chin. His hair is quite grey and is turning white. Speaking of England, he wished particularly to know whether the recent change of Government involved a change in foreign policy, or whether Mr. Gladstone might be expected to pursue the same line as Lord Salisbury. Upon this point the nomination of Lord Rosebery as Foreign Secretary enabled me to give the Viceroy consolatory assurances. Discussing the tortuous policy which had been followed in relation to the Chinese vassal State which I had just left, he admitted that Korea had been ill-advised, and even allowed that 'there had been ill-advisers in China also.' The Pamirs and Lhasa were the remaining subjects of our conversation, and the Viceroy produced one of the Royal Geographical Society's small maps of the former region. He has subsequently sent to me the photograph with an autograph inscription that accompanies the text.

From Tientsin the traveller has the choice of covering the distance that separates him from Peking either by an agreeable two days' ride of eighty miles,[1] or by a house-boat on the river, which, by alternate sailing, poling, rowing, and tracking, should convey him to his destination in something between two and three days.[2]

Journey to Peking.

The scenery, consisting as it does of a vast expanse of alluvial mud, not uncommonly under water, and relieved only by mud villages of greater or less size, may strike the new-comer as repulsive. But a little deeper insight will

[1] First day—three hours' ride to Yangtsun (inn) 20 miles; ditto to Hoh-Hsi-wu (inn), 20 miles. Second day—three hours' ride to half-way village, Hsin-ho (inn), 20 miles; ditto to Peking, 20 miles. Total, 80 miles.

[2] It is best, of course, to ride up and sail down; since the upward journey by river sometimes, with an unfavourable wind, occupies from four to five days. The return journey can be shortened by riding from Peking as far as Matou, 28 miles, and picking up the house-boat there.

show him in these self-same villages, and in the wide-tilled plains about them—countless replicas of which I have seen during both my visits to China—the evidences of an agricultural contentment and prosperity that contrast favourably with the more picturesque surroundings of village life in neighbouring countries. The main street of each village is frequently sunk considerably below the level of the houses, and is apt to be filled with the ebb of an unexhausted inundation. The houses are humble, but neither small nor poverty-stricken. Artificial privies, made of reeds, are frequently erected outside, with a view to economise all available manure. The village threshing-floor, rolled to a compact and level hardness, lies near by. The shops exhibit at least as many commodities as in an English village of corresponding size. Women and children abound, the former neatly dressed and coiffured, the latter dirty but cheerful. Upon a wage of less than five shillings a month the men can find adequate subsistence. A great variety of animals in good condition—mules, donkeys, ponies, and oxen—are employed either for tillage or burden. The eating-houses and tea-shops are filled with noisy crowds, and the inns are frequent and commodious. The people inhabiting such a locality are liable to occasional and appalling visitations of flood, pestilence, or famine. But, these risks excepted, their lives are probably as happy, their condition as prosperous, and their contentment as well assured as those of the rural population in any European country. The taxation imposed upon them is only nominal. The obligations which they stupidly incur to pawnshops or usurers, in pursuit either of the national vice of gambling or of other forms of extravagance, are a greater burden upon them than is the hand of the State. So little fear is there of disturbance that the force behind the provincial government is in

Chinese rural life.

most cases ridiculously small. In China there are no police except the unpaid hangers-on of the *yamens*, assisted, in the event of a riot, by any soldiery in the neighbourhood. Life may be uneventful; but so it is to the peasant in every land. He usually demands little beyond the means of livelihood, freedom from exaction, and the peaceful enjoyment of his modest wage.

From such surroundings, which, however respectable, are too unlovely to be idyllic, the stranger rides into the din and dust, the filth and foulness, the venerable and measureless bewilderment of Peking.[1] Unique, and of its kind unequalled, is the impression produced by this great city of over three-quarters of a million souls[2] upon even the seasoned traveller. He may have seen the drab squalor of Bokhara and Damascus, have tasted the odours of Canton and Söul, and heard the babel uproar of Baghdad and Isfahan; but he has never seen dirt, piled in mountains of dust in the summer, spread in oozing quagmires of mud after the rains, like that of Peking; his nostrils have never been assailed by such myriad and assorted effluvia; and the drums of his ears have never cracked beneath such a remorseless and dissonant concussion of sound. These are the first impressions of the stranger; they appear, in a great many cases, to be the abiding association of the resident. If, however, a man can succeed in detaching himself from the sensuous medium upon which such constant and violent attacks are made from without, he will find in Peking much both to excite his astonishment and to arrest his concern. In the mighty walls, in some parts fifty feet

Entrance to Peking.

---

[1] Peking is written and pronounced by the Chinese Pei-chang, and signifies Northern Capital, just as Nan-king signifies Southern Capital.

[2] This seems to be the most reasonable estimate, the population having greatly dwindled in modern times. In the seventeenth century the Jesuit Grimaldi estimated the total at 16,000,000! Du Halde reckoned 3,000,000, which numbers were also given to Lord Macartney in 1793. Klaproth named 1,300,000.

high and well-nigh as broad, covering a rectangular circumference of twenty-one miles,[1] and rising skywards with colossal symmetry of outline, save where their vertical profile is broken by huge projecting bastions, or their horizontal edge is interrupted by enormous castellated keeps or gate-towers, he observes a sight without parallel in the modern world—one which, more than any relic of the past that I have ever seen, recalls that Babylon whose stupendous battlements were the wonder of antiquity, the mystery of our childhood, and the battleground of our academic days. Shrouded behind these monumental defences, the gates of which are still opened and closed with the sun, just as they were in the Cambaluc of Marco Polo, of which this modern Peking is both the lineal heir and the faithful reproduction,[2]

[1] The walls of the Manchu or Tartar city (called by the Chinese Nei-cheng, *i.e.* Inner City) in their present condition date from the time of the Ming Emperors, *i.e.* from the beginning of the fifteenth century onwards. They are from forty to fifty feet in height, and sixty feet wide at the base, consisting of a stone foundation and two walls of immense bricks, the space between which is filled in with mud and paved with bricks at the top. The Tartar city is over fourteen miles in circumference and is entered by nine gates, six in the outer wall and three in the inner or south wall, which is also the north wall of the Chinese city. The latter, or Outer City, Wai-cheng, is nine miles in circumference, excluding the northern or common wall, and its walls are from twenty-five to thirty feet high, and twenty-five feet wide at the base. They are entered by seven outer and three inner gates (the latter being identical with those already named). The grand total of gates is therefore sixteen, of which thirteen are in the outer wall. In the embrasures of the gate-towers are fixed boards upon which are painted the nozzles of imaginary cannon—an innocent device which is supposed both to terrify the advancing enemy and to deceive the war god Kuan-ti, who, as he looks down from heaven, is overjoyed to see the city in a state of such splendid defence. In deference to the misogynist prejudices of the same deity, women are not allowed upon the walls.

[2] Yen-king, the capital of the Kin Tartars, which was situated a little to the south of the present Peking, was captured by Jinghiz Khan in 1215. His grandson Kublai Khan (the patron of Marco Polo) rebuilt the capital on a rather more northerly site in 1264-67, and called it in Chinese Tatu or Taidu, *i.e.* Great Court. It was also called Khan-baligh, *i.e.* City of the Khan, the Cambaluc of Marco Polo, and covered approximately the same site as the modern Tartar city, beyond which, however, its wall, which still exists, extended about two miles on the north.

the fourtold city—Chinese, Tartar, Imperial, and Forbidden—is at once an historical monument, carrying us back to the age of Kublai Khan; a vast stationary camp of nomads, pouring down from Mongolian deserts and Tartar steppes; the capital of an empire that is to Eastern Asia what Byzantium was to Eastern Europe; the sanctuary of a religion that is more manifold than that of Athens and more ob-

WALLS AND GATES OF PEKING

stinate than that of Rome; and the residence of a monarch who is still the Son of Heaven to 350,000,000 of human beings, whom a bare score of living foreigners have ever seen, and who at the end of the nineteenth century continues to lead an existence that might better befit either the Veiled Prophet of Khorasan or the Dalai Lama of Tibet.

The ground-plan of Peking, which dates directly from the time of the Mongol Kublai Khan, and was practically a reproduction in brick and mortar of a military camp, is exceedingly simple; and its principal landmarks are so prominently placed, that in spite of its vast size and the sameness of its disgusting streets, a stranger very soon learns his way about. The walls of the Tartar city frame an immense quadrangle, almost a square, facing the points of the compass, and on the southern side subtended and slightly overlapped by the more elongated parallelogram of the Chinese city. It should be added that this ethnographical distinction of inhabitants, which was enforced for expediency's sake at the time of the Manchu conquest in 1644, has since been almost entirely effaced, the Tartar element having been in the main absorbed, and the Chinese having overflowed into the quarters that were at first reserved for the conquering race. Within the walls of the Tartar city is a second walled quadrangle, constituting the Huang-cheng, or Imperial city, about seven miles in circuit, containing the public offices, barracks, and many temples and residences of princes, nobles, and officials; and in the centre of the Imperial city is the final and innermost walled enclosure of the Tzu-chin-cheng, or Pink Forbidden city, a succession of magnificent yellow-tiled halls, of palaces, kiosques, lakes, and gardens, where, behind the protection of pale pink rampart and wide moat, the Lord of this great domain, the master of 350,000,000 human beings, and the Vicegerent of Heaven, himself all but a god, lives a prisoner's life. On the northern side of the Palace rises the Ching-shan, or Prospect Hill, whose wooded sides and five summits, crowned with kiosques or temples, are the most conspicuous object in the city as seen from the Tartar wall. Tradition relates that this elevation is made of coal, and was artificially raised by the Ming Emperors as a provision against the hardships of a prolonged siege; it is

Ground-plan.

therefore also called Mei-shan, or Coal Hill. But I am not aware that this hypothesis has ever been tested by driving a shaft into the interior; and the hill, which seems to be absolutely identical with the one described by Marco Polo as having been thrown up by the Mongols, is more likely to have been raised as a screen to the Imperial dwelling on its northern side, in deference to the popular superstition of the *fengshui*. There is something imposing and hieratic in the mysterious symbolism of the ground-plan of Peking, in the conception of these concentric defences successively protecting and shielding from mundane contact the central sanctuary, the ὀμφαλος γῆς, where the representative of Heaven, as it were in a Holy of Holies, resides.

From another point of view there may be said to be three Pekings—the exterior Peking as seen from the city walls, which is a delicious wilderness of green trees, in the depths of which the dust and nastiness are submerged, and from whose leafy surface rise only the curled roofs of yellow-tiled palaces and temples, an occasional pagoda, a distant tower; the interior Peking, or the Peking of the streets, tumultuous, kaleidoscopic, pestilential, shrill; and the innermost Peking, or the mysteries hidden behind the pink and yellow walls that conceal so hermetically from the alien eye the *penetralia* both of secular and spiritual adoration. The first of these is the only aspect in which the charm is unshattered by jarring associations; although, when we descend into it we wonder where the shade and the verdure have gone to, so completely do they seem to have disappeared. To the second, however, a few more words may be devoted, inasmuch as it is the Peking of every-day life.

<small>The three Pekings.</small>

As we go forth into it for every excursion, either of duty or pleasure, we have to settle our means of locomotion.

Shall they be ponies, whose least movement will envelop us in an acrid whirlwind of dust, or the Peking cart, that

<small>Panorama of the streets.</small> strange and springless wooden vehicle of which it is doubtful whether it was first invented to resist the chasms and crevasses and moraines of the streets of Peking, or whether they were devised to harmonise with its primitive and barbaric structure? Or, rejecting the two

STREET IN PEKING

sole means of assisted locomotion—for no other animal and no other vehicle are available, chairs being reserved for very high officials in the capital, and Europeans preferring for etiquette's sake not to use them—shall we proceed on foot, and pick our way cautiously from peak to peak amid the archipelago of universal ordure? Presently we emerge on to a main street. Its great breadth is successfully concealed by the two lines of booths that have sprung up in the kind of ditch that extends on either side of the elevated central roadway; but through the dust we may discern a long vista, the parallel walls of which present a line of fantastic poles, gilded signboards, carved woodwork, and waving streamers and lanterns—the insignia and advertisement of the shops that open below. Down this avenue streams and jostles a perpetual crowd of blue-clad, long-queued, close-shaven, brazen-lunged men; Chinese women hobbling feebly on their mutilated stumps; thickly-rouged Tartar wives, blushing (artificially) beneath a headdress of smooth black hair, parted in several places on the crown, and plastered tightly over a projecting comb that stands out like a long paper-cutter at right angles to the head; a sparsely-bearded mandarin seen nodding behind his saucer-like spectacles in a screened sedan; long strings of splendid two-humped camels, parading a magnificent winter coat, and blinking a supercilious eye as they stalk along to the heavy cadence of the leader's bell, laden with sacks of lime or coal from the hills; Mongolians in shaggy caps bestriding shaggier ponies; half-naked coolies wheeling casks of oil or buckets of manure on creaking barrows; boys perched on the tails of minute donkeys; ramshackle wagons drawn by mixed teams of mules, asses, ponies, and oxen yoked together by a complicated entanglement of rope traces passing through an iron ring; abominable and hairy black pigs running in and out of the animals' legs; good-looking but cowardly dogs that bark and skedaddle; and above all the crush and roar of the ubiquitous Peking cart, thundering with its studded wheels over the stone bridges and crashing into the deep ruts, drawn by the most majestic mules in Asia, cruelly bitted with a wire across the upper gum.

This is the panorama of the central aisle. In the side aisles or alleys all the more stationary purveyors of the amusements or necessities of life are jammed up together; barbers shaving without soap the foreheads of stolid customers seated upon stools, dentists and chiropodists proclaiming their extraordinary skill, auctioneers screaming the glories of second-hand blouses and pantaloons, cobblers puncturing the thick sole of the native shoe, gamblers shaking spills or playing dominoes, or backing against all comers a well-nurtured fighting cricket, pedlars and hucksters with their wares extended on improvised stalls or outspread upon the ground, curio-dealers offering carved jade snuff-bottles or porcelain bowls, vendors of the opium-pipe and the water-pipe, charm-sellers and quacks with trays of strange powders and nauseating drugs, acrobats performing feats of agility, sword-players slashing the air with huge naked blades, story-tellers enchaining an open-mouthed crowd, itinerant musicians tweaking a single-stringed guitar, country folk vending immense white cabbages or ruddy red persimmons, soldiers with bows and arrows behind their backs going out to practise, coolies drawing water from the deeply-grooved marble coping of immemorial wells, and men and boys of every age carrying birds in cages or a singing chaffinch attached by a string to a stick. A more than ordinary shouting will herald the approach, though it will hardly clear a way, for a bridal procession, in which the bride, tightly locked in an embroidered red palanquin,[1] follows after a train of boys

_{Native practitioners.}

[1] Red is the festive colour in China. The bridal chair is first carried to the bride's home, accompanied by music, lanterns, and trays of sweatmeats. There she enters, and, preceded by her lady's maids and followed by one of her brothers, is conveyed to the bridegroom's house, being so hermetically shut up in the sedan that sometimes in the hot summer weather she is taken out fainting, and occasionally even dead.

THE COUNTRY AND CAPITAL OF CHINA 237

bearing lanterns and men blowing portentous trumpets or tapping Gargantuan drums; or of a funeral *cortège*, in which the corpse, preceded by umbrellas and tablets, rests upon a gigantic red catafalque or bier, with difficulty borne upon the shoulders of several score of men.[1] In curious contrast with the cacophonous roar of this many-tongued crowd a melodious whirring sings in the air, and is produced by whistles attached to the tails of domestic pigeons.

Such is the street life of Peking, a phantasmagoria of excruciating incident, too bewildering to grasp, too aggressive to acquiesce in, too absorbing to escape. If we turn from it to the Peking of sanctuaries, palaces, and shrines, we are in a very different atmosphere at once. For just as everything in the other Peking is public and indecent, so here everything is clandestine, veiled, and sealed. The keynote to the remainder is struck by the enclosure within enclosure, the Forbidden city inside the Imperial city, where the Lord of countless millions, so well described as the 'solitary man,' resides. In former days, indeed as late as 1887, parts of the Palace-grounds, the lakes and gardens and marble bridges, were accessible to foreigners; photographs can be purchased that reveal their features, and the majority of resident Europeans can speak from recollection of the site. Now all is closed; and from the exterior nothing can be seen but the yellow roofs of the great halls and the elegant pavilions that crown the higher elevations. To the innermost *enceinte* or Palace no man is admitted. There the Imperial person and harem are surrounded by a vast body of eunuchs, estimated at from

The Imperial Palace.

---

[1] The number of bearers ranges from 16 to 128 according to the rank of the deceased, 64 being a not uncommon and respectable number.

8000 to 10,000. When the Emperor goes out to worship at any of the temples, or to visit his palaces in the vicinity, no one is allowed in the streets, which are swept clear of all stalls and booths, and are very likely paved for the occasion, while the houses are barricaded or closed with mats. Only in the country, where such precautions are impossible, can the Imperial person be seen, borne swiftly by uniformed retainers in a magnificent sedan.[1]

Of the disposition and tastes of a monarch thus shrouded from human gaze but little can be known. His imperial Majesty, whose ruling title is Kuang Hsu, is now twenty-four years of age, and succeeded his cousin, the Emperor Tung Chih, twenty years ago, under circumstances that throw an interesting light upon the inner mysteries of Court existence in Peking. Tung Chih also was a child when he succeeded his father, Hsien Feng, the fugitive of the Anglo-French campaign, in August 1861. During his minority the Government was virtually in the hands of two ladies, one of whom, the Empress of the Eastern Palace, named Tsi An, had been the principal wife and Empress of Hsien Feng, while the other, who, though the mother of Tung Chih, had not been Empress, was in consideration of the accession of her son named Empress-Mother and Empress of the Western Palace. She was only twenty-seven years of age at the time. Seizing the reigns of government by a bold *coup d'état*,[2] in which they were assisted by one of Hsien Feng's brothers, well-known to Europeans as Prince Kung, these ladies ad-

The Emperor Tung Chih.

[1] The Imperial palanquin is usually carried upon the shoulders of eight bearers, clad in green coats spotted with red and white, and running in the midst of several hundred horsemen.

[2] They arrested the entire Council of Regency, as they were returning to Peking with the body of the deceased Emperor, and sentenced them, one to public execution, two to compulsory suicide, and the remainder to deprivation of all office and rank.

ministered the State as Regents, with Prince Kung as
Chief Minister, until in 1873 Tung Chih attained his
majority and shortly afterwards married. The young
wife then became Empress, and the two elder ladies
retired nominally into the background.

Tung Chih, however, was addicted to dissipation, and very
soon gave signs of a failing constitution. During his illness
a decree was issued, no doubt at their initiative,
in which the Emperor, passing over his own wife,
invited them to resume their former functions
until his restoration to health. By this clever step the two
ladies, who foresaw a second and not less agreeable lease of
power during the minority of a second infant, found themselves in the highest place, when, in January 1875, the
Emperor Tung Chih died childless, but leaving a widow who
expected before long to become a mother. They were now
in a position to manipulate the succession according to their
own desires. The natural course, following the ordinary
practice of Imperial succession, would have been to wait for
the birth of the deceased Emperor's posthumous child, and
in the event of its being stillborn, or a girl, to select from
among the members of the Imperial family a child who
should be adopted as his son, and during whose minority the
widowed Empress should rule as Regent. This, however,
was not at all to the taste of the two ex-Empresses Regent.
Of these the one who was mother to the late Emperor had a
sister married to Prince Chun, the younger brother of Prince
Kung, the child of which union was therefore twice over a
nephew of the Emperor Hsien Feng and cousin of Tung
Chih. Ignoring the pregnancy of the Empress Ah-lu-ta, and
passing over the sons of Prince Chun's elder brothers,[1] they

The two Empresses Regent.

---

[1] Prince Kung was willing to submit to this, because it assured him a
renewed lease of power as First Minister, which, according to Chinese

selected this infant, whose name was Tsaitien, and who, having only been born in August 1871, would ensure them a second long spell of Regency. The Empress-Mother went in person to the house of her brother-in-law, and brought out the intended claimant. He was adopted as a son to Hsien Feng, thus ensuring to the two ladies a continuation of their functions as dowagers, and was elevated with the ruling title of Kuang Hsu (Glorious Continuity) to the Dragon Throne; the Regents further producing what purported to be a nomination of the child by the late Tung Chih as his heir. The only step that remained to complete the success of the arrangement was the disappearance of the young widowed Empress of Tung Chih before the birth of her child could upset the plot; and Chinese opinion can have been little surprised when the early announcement of her death was made, the catastrophe being generally explained by the popular Chinese practice of suicide, though whispers were not lacking of a more sinister doom. It will be seen from the above account that there was quite a cluster of irregularities, to use no stronger term, in the nomination of the reigning Sovereign. But, according to Chinese ideas, the main flaw in his title consists in his belonging to the same generation as the Emperor Tung Chih, and in his consequent disqualification from performing the sacrifices that are due from a descendant to his Imperial predecessor, whose legal successor therefore he cannot be. It was this injury done to the memory of Tung Chih that formed the protest of the censor Wu-ko-tu, who committed

views of parental dignity, would not have been possible had his own son become Emperor. The latter, moreover, had already passed by adoption into the family of a younger brother of the Emperor Hsien Feng. Prince Chun, however, violated all precedent later on by serving his own son, the reigning Emperor, in the same capacity until his death in 1891.

suicide during one of the Imperial visits to the ancestral tombs, in order to attract public attention to the scandal.

The second Regency lasted for fourteen years, until in 1889 the young Emperor assumed the reins of power and married his cousin Yeh-ho-na-la. Providence has not yet favoured him with an heir, although, according to the Chinese practice, several appointments have already been made to the titular office of Guardian to the Heir-Apparent. The senior of the two Regents, the Empress Dowager of Hsien Teng, had died in 1881, but the second, or mother of Tung Chih, the Empress Tzu Hsi, continued and continues to survive, and, in spite of her nominal withdrawal from public life, still wields a predominant influence in the government of the Empire. In the opinion of every European who has lived long in Peking, and of all the Chinese statesmen with whom they have conversed, the Empress is a woman of remarkable abilities. In November 1894 she attained her sixtieth year (the 'cycle of Cathay'), and the celebrations and rejoicings in honour of this auspicious event, for which a compulsory subscription had been imposed upon the various provinces, and which were to have assumed unequalled dimensions, involving an expenditure of £5,000,000, were interrupted only by the calamitous sequence of the war. The Emperor paid her the supreme compliment of adding two more ideographs to her already elongated title, which now runs as follows: 'Tzu-hsi-tuan-yu-kang-i-chao-yu-chuang-cheng-shou-kung-chin-hsien-chung-hsi.' An issue of the *Peking Gazette* also contained the following eminently filial announcement :—

'The superlative goodness of the most August Empress Dowager is brightly manifest, and Her comprehensive foresight benefits the whole race. By ceaseless diligence within Her palace she secures the peace of the entire realm. Since Our accession to the Throne We have in respectful attendance constantly received Her admirable instructions. With great gladness We perceive Her Gracious Majesty in robust health and cheerful spirits. In the year 1894 Her Majesty will happily attain the illustrious age of sixty years, and it will be Our duty at the head of the officials and people of the whole Empire to testify our delight and to pray for blessings.'

It is a curious coincidence—in contradiction of the popular theories concerning the Eastern subjection of women—that both in China and Korea I should have found the *de facto* sovereign belonging to the female sex.

Upon no bed of roses, however, can the Emperor of China lie. The ceremonial functions of his life, whether as Supreme Ruler or as Pontifex Maximus of his people, are manifold and engrossing. His education, both in the native classics and in such departments of foreign learning as may be thought desirable, is not neglected; and the present Emperor, who is known to take a deep interest in everything English, receives daily English lessons, at a very early hour in the morning, before giving audience to his ministers, from two Chinese students of the Tung Wen Kuan, or Foreign College at Peking, who, unlike the Ministers, are allowed to sit in the Imperial presence. As an instance of the young ruler's keen concern in his English studies, I may mention that when he received a copy of the *Life of the Prince Consort* as a present from Her Majesty the Queen, he sent it down at once to the Tung Wen Kuan to be translated, and was impatient until he had received it back.[1] In the still hours of the night,

The Emperor Kuang Hsu.

---

[1] The following description of his personal appearance was given by an eye-witness of the Audience of 1891:—'His air is one of exceeding intelligence and gentleness, somewhat frightened, and melancholy looking. His face is pale, and though it is distinguished by refinement and quiet dignity, it has none of the force of his martial ancestors, nothing commanding or

when no sound but the watchman's rhythmical tap intrudes upon the silence, palanquins may be seen wending their way to the Palace-gates; and there, at 3 and 4 A.M., long before sunrise, custom prescribes that the young monarch shall give audience to such of his Ministers as have access to his person, and shall give or refuse to the documents which they present the crowning sanction of the vermilion seal.

What with the necessary but dolorous routine of his official existence on the one hand, rigidly prescribed by an adamantine and punctilious etiquette, and with the temptations of the harem on the other, it is rarely that an Emperor of China — usually an infant, and selected because of his infancy in the first place, and exposed through the tender years of his youth to these twofold preoccupations—can develop any force of character, or learn the rudimentary lessons of statecraft. The safety of the dynasty and the sanctity of the Imperial title are supposed to be summed up in the unswerving maintenance of this colossal Imperial nightmare at Peking. Were it to be dissipated or shattered by the appearance of a strong Sovereign, who to the ascendency of personal authority added an emancipation from the petrified traditions of the Palace, the phantom of Imperial power would, it is commonly said, suffer irretrievable collapse. But at least the spectacle, or the experiment, would be one of surpassing interest; nor do I see any very clear reason why a present or a future Emperor should not take that more public part

<small>Palace routine.</small>

<small>imperious, but is altogether mild, delicate, sad, and kind. He is essentially Manchu in features; his skin is strangely pallid in hue; his face is oval-shaped with a very long narrow chin, and a sensitive mouth with thin nervous lips; his nose is well-shaped and straight, his eyebrows regular and very arched, while the eyes are unusually large and sorrowful in expression. The forehead is well-shaped and road, and the head is large beyond the average.'</small>

which was filled only a century ago by the Emperor Kieng Lung, and a century earlier by the Emperor Kang Hsi.

Profound, however, as is the obscurity attaching to the Palace life, a scarcely less, and a far more exasperating, mystery has in the last few years been allowed to gather about the various sacred enclosures within the city, which are the goal to which the traveller's gaze has been turned from afar. Till within the last fifteen years most of these were easily accessible, and old residents record how they have played at cricket in the park of the Temple of Heaven, and explored the Temples of Agriculture, the Sun, and Moon. In proportion, however, as the memory of the war of 1860 has receded, and the power for menace of the foreigner been diminished, so has the arrogance of the Chinese grown ; and nothing now gives them greater pleasure than the sullen and sometimes insolent rejection of the 'foreign devil' from the doors to which he once gained undisturbed entry. In the case of the Imperial temples or enclosures there is the further excuse, that whereas during the long minorities of the present and the preceding Emperor, they were not used for worship, and were consequently neglected, their sanctity has now been vindicated and revived. I know of no foreigner, accordingly, who has been admitted to the Temple of Heaven for ten years; although, having climbed, not without judicious bribery, the southern wall of the Chinese city, which immediately overlooks the sacred enclosure, I could with ease observe from thence the vast roofless altar, three stages high, of glittering white marble, whereupon, at the summer and winter solstice, at two hours before sunrise, the Emperor makes burnt-offerings and sacrifice on behalf of his people to the Supreme Lord of Heaven ; could recognise the Hall of Fasting, where he remains in solitary meditation during

The Temple of Heaven.

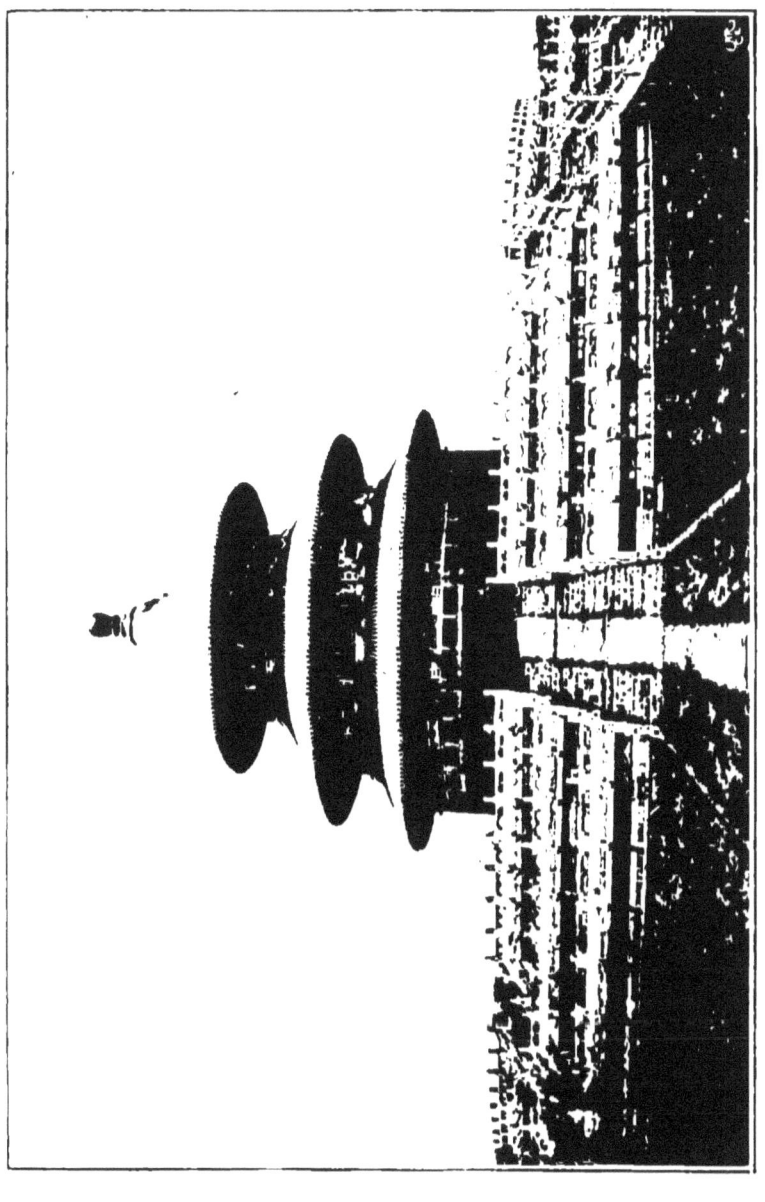

TEMPLE AND ALTAR OF HEAVEN

the night ; the southern circular Temple of the Tablets ; the three great red poles, from which are hung lanterns to illumine the ceremony ; and the scaffolding surrounding the site of the renowned triple-roofed, blue-tiled temple above the northern altar, the chief glory of the entire enclosure, which was burned to the ground a few years ago, and is now in course of a snail's-pace reconstruction.[1]

It is still quite possible to pass the outer wall of the entire enclosure, which is a parallelogram about three miles in circumference, for the dust has blown up against it in a manner which renders it easy to clamber on to the coping and then to drop down the other side. Here, however, the visitor merely finds himself in the wooded park where the sacrificial animals are kept ; and though he may succeed in taking the guards by surprise and in rushing one of the doorways that lead into the inner enclosures, he is hardly likely to repeat the success sufficiently often to conduct him to the innermost *enceinte* where are the altars. In former days nothing but a little dash to start with, and a subsequent *douceur*, were required to overcome the scruples of the custodians ; but such a venture, it is generally thought, might in the present state of native feeling be provocative of violence. *Difficulty of admission.*

Fascinating, indeed, would be the experience of the man who, by whatever device, succeeded in witnessing the great annual observance of December 21 ; when, in the glimmer of the breaking dawn, the Emperor, who has passed the night in solitary prayer in the Hall of Fasting, comes forth and dons the sacrificial robe of blue ; *The Annual Sacrifice.*

[1] It was struck by lightning in 1890. The contract for its reconstruction was 1,000,000 taels (about £210,000), and the new building is to be complete in 1898. At the time that I was in Peking (November 1892) the workmen had struck for higher pay, although receiving 2s. a day, an enormous wage in China. One half of the time-limit for reconstruction expired in 1895.

when he leaves on his left hand the northern altar and the circular temple upon it, with its curving azure roof, like unto a threefold outspread parasol; when he moves along the marble causeway between the cypress groves, and beneath the *pailows* or arches of sculptured marble; when he passes the single-peaked Circular Hall of the Tablets, whence the tablets of Shang-ti, the Supreme Lord, and of the eight deified Manchu Emperors have already been transferred to

SOUTHERN ALTAR OF HEAVEN

their temporary resting-places on the roofless southern altar; when to the music of over 200 musicians, and to the mystic movements of a company of dancers, he approaches the marble mount, and ascends the triple flight of nine steps each, from the ground to the lower, and from the lower to the central tier, whereon are disposed the tablets of the Sun, Moon, and Stars, and of the Spirits of the Air and Water; when, finally, from the central he mounts to the uppermost terrace, where, under the open vault, a pavilion of yellow silk overshadows the tablets of the deified Emperors and of Shang-ti, the Supreme Lord. There arrived, he kneels; there he burns incense and offers libations on behalf of his people before the sacred tablets; there, nine times, he bows and strikes the marble platform with his Imperial forehead, in obeisance to the God of Heaven.

While in Peking I saw the sights or buildings which are still accessible to the foreigner, though in some cases not without difficulty, and in few without long parleying at the wicket, and the gift of an exorbitant bribe. Of these, perhaps, the best known is the Kuan-Hsiang-tai, or Observatory, originally founded in 1279 by Kublai Khan, to contain the instruments of his famous Astronomer-Royal, Ko-chow-tsing. Four hundred years later the Mongol instruments were pronounced out of date by Ferdinando Verbiest, the Jesuit father, who was President of the Board of Works at the Court of the Manchu Emperor Kang Hsi, and were superseded by a new set of instruments, manufactured under Verbiest's directions at Peking, or (as in the case of the azimuth dial, presented by Louis XIV. to the Chinese sovereign) imported from Europe. The Ming instruments, all of bronze, and polished to a glassy smoothness by long exposure to the dust-charged air of Peking, are placed under the open sky, on an elevated bastion rising above the summit of the east Tartar wall, which, however, is only accessible through a wicket and courtyard at the base. Of far greater interest, to my mind, than these objects, which consist of a sextant, a quadrant, an armillary sphere, a great celestial globe adorned with gilt constellations, and other instruments, are the older and discarded fabrications of the Mongols, which repose under the shadow of trees in the grassy courtyard below. Here are

The Observatory.

two armillary spheres, great intertwined circles or hoops of bronze, on stands supported by chiselled dragons rampant. Here also, shut up in two dusty compartments of an adjoining building, are two objects which no modern traveller, whose writings I have seen, appears to have noticed, although one of them is mentioned by Sir H. Yule in his edition of *Marco Polo*.[1] One is a *clepsydra*, or water-clock, probably dating from the Mongol era, and composed of three great bronze jars, placed in tiers one above the other, so that a measured quantity of the water overflowed within a given space of time. Attached to them in former times was a figure holding an arrow, on which the hours were marked, and which rested on a vessel floating in one of the cisterns, and changing its elevation as the water rose or fell. This I think, must be the disused water-clock, which the early Jesuit missionaries describe as having formerly been placed in the Ku-lou, or Drum Tower. The remaining instrument is a gnomon, or long table of bronze, along which, down the middle, is marked a meridian of fifteen feet, divided by transverse lines. Upon this the sun's rays struck, passing by an aperture in the wall, the horizon being formed of two pieces of copper suspended in the air. The instrument has now fallen to pieces, and no one seems ever to notice it.

Among other places which are usually visited within the Tartar city is the Kao Chang, or Examination Building, which lies below and is easily visible from the Observatory Platform. It consists, like the corresponding structures in the provincial capitals of China, of long parallel rows of many thousand cells or pens, in which, once every three years, the candidates for the second and third degrees of literary promotion are immured for several days and nights, while they are composing the

Examination Building.

[1] Vol. i. p. 366.

jejune though flowery disquisitions that are to turn the successful competitors into the higher class of mandarins. It is the apotheosis—or shall I not rather say the *reductio ad absurdum*?—of the system, from whose premonitory symptoms our own country, a tardy convert to Celestial ideas, is already beginning to suffer.

In the northern part of the city beyond Prospect Hill are the Ku-lou, or Drum Tower, containing an immense drum, which is beaten to announce the watches of the night, and the Chung-lou, or Bell Tower, erected by the Emperor Kien Lung in 1740 to shelter one of the five great bells that were cast by the Emperor Yung Lo at the beginning of the fifteenth century. Both these towers are immensely lofty structures, quite 100 feet high, pierced below by a wide arch. Drum and Bell Towers.

Every one also goes to see the Temple of Confucius, a vast and dusty hall, of the familiar Chinese pattern, raised upon a stone terrace, and containing nothing inside but the dull red pillars that support the lofty timbered roof, the tablet of the sage standing in the centre in a wooden shrine, with the tablets of the four next most eminent sages, two on either side, and those of another dozen a little lower down. The Emperor is supposed to visit and worship at this temple twice in every year; but at the time of my visit the reigning monarch was reported not yet to have been at all. In an adjoining court are the so-called stone drums, black cheese-shaped blocks of granite inscribed with stanzas in an ancient character, that are supposed to refer to a hunting expedition of the Emperor Siuen in the eighth century B.C. On the opposite side of the same gateway are the replicas that were made of them by the Emperor Kien Lung. A neighbouring enclosure contains the commemorative tablets, like the carved Temple of Confucius.

letters in the Upper School at Eton, that display the names of all the learned doctors who have taken the highest literary degree, or Chin-shih, since the days of the Mongol.

Adjoining again is the Kuo-tzu-chien, or Imperial Academy of Learning, an educational establishment which exists only in respect of habitation and of name; and in the centre of this enclosure stands the Pi-yung-kung, or Hall of the Classics, where, upon a raised throne, the Emperor is supposed to, but, I believe, does not read an address to the *literati*. On the sides of a court in the Kuo-tzu-chien are also placed under cover the 200 tablets containing the graven text of the Confucian classics. About all these fabrics, and their silent and deserted courts, there is an air of academic and supreme repose.

<small>Hall of the Classics.</small>

No such impression is derived from a visit to the Yung-ho-kung, or great Lama temple, which stands close to the last-mentioned enclosure in the north-east corner of the city. Its 1200 Mongolian inmates, presided over by a Gegen, or Living Buddha, are celebrated for their vicious habits and offensive manners. It was considered a stroke of rare good fortune that, with the aid of an experienced Chinese scholar, I obtained entrance to the monastery; although our small party did not escape from the clutch of its filthy and insolent inhabitants without being heavily mulcted at the gate of each court and sanctuary, which were barred against us one after the other, and being subjected at intervals to rough usage as well. Subsequent visitors to Peking have been unable to gain admittance at all. I retain a vivid recollection of the main temple, with its three seated Buddhas and two standing figures, one on either side of the central image; with the eighteen Lohans, or disciples, along the sides; and with a

<small>Great Lama Temple.</small>

unique collection of old *cloisonné* and gilt bronze vessels, censers, and utensils, the gifts of emperors, on the various altars. The furniture of this temple is the finest that I have seen in China, and reflects a sumptuous antiquity befitting a sanctuary of such high repute. Behind the main temple is the Prayer Hall, filled with rows of low forms or stools, facing east and west and divided by mats. As the hour for evensong was approaching we were unceremoniously hustled out of this building by the assembling monks. Beyond again is a temple containing a huge gilt wooden image of Maitreya, the Buddha To Come, not seated but standing, and with his head touching the roof seventy feet above. It is possible to climb up to the top by wooden stairs leading to two upper stories, where are innumerable small brass Buddhas disposed in shrines and niches. The Lamas declined to part with any of these except at an exorbitant price; but I have one in my possession which was subsequently brought to the Embassy by a monk, less pious or more pliable than his fellows. At the back is another altar with a number of porcelain Buddhas, resembling Luca della Robbia ware. We next saw a dilapidated building containing the terraced structure or throne, on the top of which the Emperor Kien Lung is said to have fasted for a night prior to his initiation into the Church. In another part is the temple of Kuan-ti, the God of War, crowded with hideous painted and grinning images, and with figures of warriors in helmets and armour. Here also are the wooden models of two hippopotami with their young, which are said to have been killed by Kien Lung while hunting at Kirin in Manchuria. On our way out we saw the monks and their pupils, many hundreds in number, engaged at evensong in the various chapels. Loud rang the deep, base monotone of their voices, shouting with irreverent iteration the responses of the Tibetan liturgy. All wore yellow mantles, and in front of each upon the bench was his yellow tufted felt helmet, exactly like the headpiece of a Hellenic or Roman warrior. The Lamas of higher grade, in purple and crimson mantles, wore these upon their heads as they walked to and fro between the benches, conducting the service. The appearance of a group of Europeans excited indignant protests from these individuals; and we had a long wait, in hope of a crowning bribe, before we were permitted to leave the final gate and quit this nest of profligate scoundrels. However, the experience was well worthy of the time and trial to temper involved, and is thought by the best resident authorities to be the most singular of the now available sights of Peking.

Very gratifying is it to turn one's back upon this city, where all that is worth seeing is so difficult, and where such savage inroads are made upon equanimity, patience, and every human sense, and to make a trip to some of the well-known sites that lie within a range of from forty to sixty miles of the northern gates. Here, outside the Tartar wall, but within the mud rampart of the Mongolian Kambalu, is the Huang-ssu, another Lama monastery, commonly called the Yellow Temple. It consists of a series of great enclosures with tranquil courts, old trees, shrines covering memorial tablets, and vast temple-halls. The largest of these possesses one of the most impressive interiors that I have ever seen. Three great solemn seated Buddhas are raised aloft, and peer down with the inscrutable serenity of the familiar features and the ruddy glimmer of burnished gold. The adjacent figures of Lohans, the coloured fresco of Buddhistic scenes, the lofty timbered roof, the splendid altars and censers, are all features seen elsewhere; but the majestic stature of the images, the

Outside the walls.

sumptuous though faded colouring of the pillars and walls, and the deep gloom in which the hall is plunged, compel a reverence which is almost without alloy. In a neighbouring court is the *dagoba*, or white marble tomb, erected by the Emperor Kien Lung to the Teshu Lama of Tibet,[1] who, while on a visit to Peking, died there of smallpox in 1780. The shape of the monument is ugly, but the sculptures on its eight sides, which represent scenes in the history of the deceased Lama, are fine and humorous in their fidelity to life.

At a short distance to the north-west, the largest of the five bells of Yung-Lo, which was cast about the year 1406, is suspended in a temple that was erected 170 years later. The dimensions ordinarily given are 14 feet in height, 34 feet in circumference at the brim, 9 inches in thickness, 120,000 lbs. in weight. More remarkable is the fact that the surface of the monster, both inside and outside, is covered with thousands of Chinese characters, representing extracts from two of the Buddhist classics. *The Great Bell.*

One of the bitterest of the many disappointments of modern Peking is the inability, also of recent origin, to see the grounds or ruins of the celebrated Summer Palace that was demolished by the Allies in 1860. Of this act I observe that it has become in recent years the fashion among travellers, who have probably never read a line of the history of the war itself, to say that it was a thoughtless or intemperate act of vandalism appropriately committed by the son of that Lord Elgin who had perpetrated a corresponding deed of violence by wresting from the rock of the Acropolis the marble treasures of Athens. Both criticisms are equally ignorant and empty. For though *The Summer Palace.*

---

[1] The Teshu Lama, or Banjin Prembutcha, is the second dignitary in the Buddhist hierarchy of Tibet, and resides at Shigatze.

we may regret that the modern Acropolis, now for the first time tended and cared for, does not contain the sculptures that once formed its chief glory, and though we may deplore the loss to the world of architecture and art of the splendid fabrics and the priceless treasures of the Chinese Versailles; yet in the one case it must be remembered that, but for the first Lord Elgin's intervention, the marbles which bear his name would probably not now be existing at all; and in the other, that the second Lord Elgin's act was a deliberate and righteous measure of retribution for the barbarous cruelties and torture that had been practised for days and nights in the courts of that very Palace upon British prisoners of war; that more than any other possible step, short of the sack of the Imperial Palace at Peking, it signified the humiliation and discomfiture of a throne claiming a prerogative almost divine; and that the reason for which the suburban instead of the urban residence of the Emperor was selected for destruction was the merciful desire to save the inhabitants of the capital from a retribution which was felt to have been specially, if not solely, provoked by the insolency and treachery of the Court. Twenty-seven years later the Marquis Tseng, writing in the pages of an English magazine,[1] admitted that it was this step, or 'singeing of the eyebrows of China,' as he called it, that first caused her to awake from her long sleep, and to realise that she was not invulnerable. So far from cherishing an undying grudge against the French or English for the act, as is also commonly represented by travellers, the Chinese themselves, who have a wonderful faculty for oblivion, have invented the fiction that the Summer Palace was looted by robbers; and this is now the popular belief.

[1] *Asiatic Quarterly Review*, January 1887.

The term Summer Palace is strictly applied to the Yuan-ming-yuan, *i.e.* Garden of Perfect Clearness, a large enclosure surrounded by a high wall four and a half miles in circuit, about seven miles to the north-west of Peking. Here the Emperor Yung Ching in the first half of the eighteenth century first built a palace and laid out the grounds—a work of twenty years; and here it was that a series of magnificent buildings, designed upon the model of Versailles, and framed in a landscape garden-ing that was a similar reminiscence of France, were raised for the Emperor Kien Lung by the Jesuit missionaries in his service. Of these, Père Benoist undertook the hydraulics in 1747-50; and the descriptions by Père Attiret, who was the Emperor's Court Painter, and by Père Bourgeois, which are to be found in the *Lettres Édifiantes*, give a most interest-ing account of the manner and success of their undertaking. To the average European sitting at home it is probably news to learn that the Summer Palace, of which he has heard so much, was a series not of fantastic porcelain pagodas or Chinese pavilions, but of semi-European halls and palaces adorned with the florid splendour of the Court of the Grand Monarque. The greater part of these were wrecked in 1860, but for the last twenty years the work of restoration has been slowly proceeded with, and no foreigner can now gain access to the interior.

<small>Yuan-ming-yuan.</small>

Till lately this prohibition did not apply to the Wan-shou-shan, *i.e.* Hill of Ten Thousand Ages, a similar Imperial Pleasaunce about three-quarters of a mile to the south-east; and many are the Europeans who have visited and described its beautiful lake and island connected with the shore by a white marble balus-traded bridge with sixty marble lions on the parapet; the marble boat that lies in the water; the bronze cow reposing

<small>Wan-shou-shan.</small>

on a stone pedestal; and the great hill rising from the lake's edge, ascended by a lofty staircase upon both sides of a colossal terrace of stone, and crowned by elegant temples and pavilions. The bulk of these too succumbed to the bayonet and the torch; but on attempting to enter the great gates, where are the bronze lions, I found the whole place alive with movement. Thousands of masons and coolies were at work, rebuilding the ruins as a palace for the Empress Dowager. Entrance was strictly prohibited, and only from one of the neighbouring mounds was it possible to obtain a view of the interior. The work of reparation has been suspended since the war.

No visit to Peking is accounted complete without an expedition to the Great Wall and the Tombs of the Ming Emperors; and though I shall refrain from describing an excursion that is so well known, I may remark that neither section of it should be omitted by the traveller. The Wall is most easily and commonly visited at one of two places, either at Pataling, the far exit of the Nankow Pass, forty miles from Peking, or at Ku-pei-kow, nearly double that distance on the road to the Emperor's Mongolian hunting-lodge at Jehol. The first-named point is in the Inner Wall, the second in the Outer.[1]

The Great Wall.

[1] As most persons know, there are two Great Walls of China, the main or Outer Wall, called Wan-li-chang-cheng, i.e. the Ten Thousand *Li* Wall, which runs from Shan-hai-kuan on the Gulf of Pechili, in a westerly direction along the northern frontier of China Proper for 1500 miles; and the Inner Wall, which branches off from the first, to the west of Ku-pei-kow, and describes the arc of a circle round the north-west extremity of the province of Chihli, dividing it from Shansi, for a total distance of 500 miles. The Outer Wall is attributed to the Emperor Tsin-shi-huang-ti in 214-204 B.C.; but of the original structure it is supposed that very little now remains. Near the sea it is made of unhewn stones; in the greater part of its course it is faced with large bricks resting upon a stone foundation, and is from 15 to 30 feet in height and 15 to 25 feet in thickness; in its western part it is commonly only a mud or gravel mound, over which horsemen can ride without dismounting. In parts it has entirely disappeared. The Inner Wall is

GREAT WALL OF CHINA

This great monument of human labour, that still, with some interruptions, pursues its aerial climb over 2000 miles of peak and ravine, almost invariably excites the enlightened abuse of the foreigner, who can see in it nothing but a blindfold conception and misdirected human power.[1] To me, I confess, it appears as a work not merely amazing in plan, but of great practical wisdom (in its day) in execution. To this date the Mongol tribes regard the Great Wall as the natural limit of their pastures; and though it could not have been expected at any time to render the Empire or the capital absolutely secure from invasion, yet in days when men fought only with bows and arrows, and indulged in guerilla raids of irregular horse, times without number its sullen barrier arrested the passage of predatory bands, caused the examination of passports, and prevented the illicit entry of goods. Because we do not now, in days of artillery, encircle an empire any more than a city with a wall, it by no means follows that such a defence may not once have been as useful to a kingdom as it was to a town.

Of the Shih-san-ling, or Thirteen Tombs of the Ming Emperors, which at unequal distances, each in its own wooded enclosure, surround a wide bay or amphitheatre in the hills, thirty miles nearly due north of Peking, I will merely observe that the famous avenue of stone animals through which one enters the valley from the south is to my mind grotesque without

<small>The Ming Tombs.</small>

<small>attributed to the Wei dynasty in A.D. 542; but in its present state it is almost entirely the work of the Ming Emperors. Their part of the wall is built of stone, and is from 25 to 50 feet in height, including the outer parapet, and has a paved walk along the summit 14 feet in width, passing through frequent and more elevated towers with embrasured stone walls 9 feet in thickness. At the Pataling Gate it is a very imposing structure.</small>

<small>[1] Dr. Williams, for instance, in his *Middle Kingdom*, speaks of it as an 'evidence of the energy, industry, and perseverance of its builders, as well as of their *unwisdom and waste*.'</small>

being impressive, the images being low, stunted, and without pedestals; that the Great Hall of Yung Lo, which contains his tablet, is in design, dimensions, and extreme simplicity, one of the most imposing of Chinese sacred structures; that, like the Egyptian kings in the Pyramids of Ghizeh and in the subterranean galleries of Thebes, and the Persian kings in the rock-sepulchres of Persepolis, the object of the Chinese Sovereigns appears to have been either to conceal the exact spot in which the royal corpse was deposited, or at least to render it impossible of access; and that a visitor should be recommended to compare the Ming Tombs with the Mausolea of the reigning dynasty, which are situated in two localities known as the Tung-ling and Hsi-ling, to the east and west of Peking (while the ancestors of the Imperial family were interred in Southern Manchuria), and are reported to be of great beauty and splendour; though no European would stand a chance of being admitted to their inner temples or halls.

These and similar excursions to the delightful monastic retreats in the western hills, or rides in the Nan-hai-tzu,[1] a great Imperial park three miles to the south of the Chinese city, surrounded by a wall and containing some very peculiar deer,[2] are an agreeable relief to the visitor, who soon tires of the dirt and confusion of Peking. Even such relaxations, however, are found to pall upon the resident; and he is apt to turn from the surfeit of *désagréments* in the streets to the repose of the

British Legation.

[1] In a fit of belated economy, the Empress Dowager, since the war, is said to have closed her palace in the Nan-hai-tzu.

[2] This is the Ssu-pu-hsiang (*lit.* Four-Parts-Unlike, because the various parts of the body resemble those of different animals), or Tail-deer, called after its first discoverer *Cervus Davidianus*. It has an immense tail, over a foot in length, and gigantic antlers, somewhat resembling those of a reindeer. The species has never been found wild, and is not known to exist anywhere in the world except in this park.

walled compounds within which the various Foreign Legations reside, and where life, though confined, is at least cleanly and free. Of these by far the most imposing is the British Legation, an enclosure of three acres inside the Tartar city, once the palace of an Imperial prince, whose entrance-archways and halls have been skilfully adapted to the needs of European life, where the members of the staff are accommodated in separate bungalows, where the means of study and recreation alike exist,[1] and where a generous and uniform hospitality prevails.

[1] The premises of the British Legation include the Minister's reception-rooms and residence in the *quondam* palace, separate houses for the First and Second Secretaries, houses of Chinese Secretaries, Physician, and Accountant, the Chancellery, Library, Student Interpreter's quarters and mess, Dispensary, Fire Engine, Armoury, Lawn Tennis and Fives Courts, and Bowling Alley, with a body-guard of two constables.

CHAPTER IX

CHINA AND THE POWERS

Lasciate ogni speranza, voi ch' entrate.
DANTE: *Inferno*, Canto ii.

AT no capital in the world are relations between the Government of the country and the representatives of Foreign Powers conducted under circumstances so profoundly dissatisfactory as at Peking. There is absolutely no intercourse between the native officials and foreigners. Few of the latter have ever been, except for a purely ceremonious visit, inside a Chinese Minister's house. No official of any standing would spontaneously associate with a European. Even the Chinese *employés* of the various Legations would lose 'face' if observed speaking with their masters in the streets. Superior force has installed the alien in the Celestial capital; but he is made to feel very clearly that he is a stranger and a sojourner in the land; that admission does not signify intercourse; and that no approaches, however friendly, will ever be rewarded with intimacy. This attitude is more particularly reflected in the official relations that subsist between the Diplomatic Corps and the Foreign Office at Peking.

That office, if it can be said so much as to exist, is an office without either recognised chief or departmental organisation. After the war of 1860, a board named the Tsungli Yamen was invented in 1861 by Prince Kung, who

[marginal note: Relations between Chinese and Europeans.]

became its first President—a titular post which he held till his fall in 1884—in order to take the place of a Foreign Office, and to conduct dealings with the Ministers of the Powers who insisted on forcing their unwelcome presence upon Peking. Up till that time all foreign affairs had been conducted by the Li Yan Yuen, or Colonial Office, a department of the Ministry of Rites, which dealt with the dependent and tributary nations, and therefore—since, according to the Chinese theory, the whole exterior universe fell into that category—with all foreign peoples. The war, however, showed conclusively that Europe did not appreciate this sort of logic; and some deference required to be paid to scruples that had just been so inconveniently enforced. The new Board consisted at the start of three members only: Prince Kung; Kuei Liang, senior Grand Secretary; and Wen Hsiang, Vice-President of the Board of War. In the following year, 1862, four additional members were appointed, and by 1869 successive additions had brought the number up to ten. In recent years the total has ranged from eight to twelve, with a preponderance, as a rule, of Chinese. But it possessed, from the start, this remarkable idiosyncrasy, that its members did not constitute a separate department in any legitimate sense of the term, being mainly selected from the other Ministries,[1] without any special aptitudes for or knowledge of foreign affairs. For many years past it has been closely identified with the Grand Council, a majority of the members of the latter Board being also members of the Yamen. It is much as though the Board of Admiralty at Whitehall were

The Tsungli Yamen.

[1] These are the Ministries of (1) Civil Affairs and Appointments, or Treasury; (2) Revenue and Finance, or Exchequer; (3) Rites and Ceremonies; (4) War; (5) Public Works; (6) Criminal Jurisdiction or Punishments. — *Vide* Professor R. K. Douglas's *Society in China*, pp. 44-57.

composed of the Home, Indian, and Colonial Secretaries, with perhaps the President of the Board of Trade and the Chancellor of the Duchy of Lancaster thrown in. This is the scratch body that takes the place of a Foreign Minister, and acts as an intermediary between the foreign representatives and the Imperial Government in Peking. A number of its members, ranging, maybe, from three to a dozen, sit round a table covered with sweetmeats to receive the diplomat and listen to his representations. No privacy is possible, since the conversation must in any case be conducted through interpreters, and there are plenty of hangers-on standing about as well.[1] While Prince Kung was President, all correspondence was carried on in his own name. But during the *régime* of Prince Ching from 1884 to 1894 official communications were drawn up in the names of himself and his colleagues conjointly. The Prince, though unknown in Europe, is a typical specimen of the Manchu gentleman, and a statesman of great ability, with a wide grasp of foreign questions. At the end of September 1894, after the double defeat of China by Japan in the naval battle of the Yalu, and in the land fight at Ping-yang, he was dismissed by the Emperor, and Prince Kung, then sixty-two years of age, was recalled from his long exile (dating from the Franco-Chinese war of 1884) and was reappointed President both of the Tsungli Yamen and of the Chun Chi Chu or Grand Council, with powers almost amounting to a Dictatorship. Prince Ching

---

[1] In the excellent recently-published *Life of Sir Harry Parkes*, by Mr. S. Lane-Poole, there are several extracts from his correspondence, describing with characteristic candour his impressions of the Tsungli Yamen. He speaks of 'going to the Yamen and having a discussion with eight or ten men, who all like to speak at once, and who, when refuted, just repeat all they have said before. In some respects it is a question of physical endurance; and, if you are not in good condition, the struggle is trying.'—Vol. ii. p. 389; compare pp. 386, 394.

has since been readmitted to favour and now acts as junior colleague to Prince Kung.

It may be imagined that, whatever the knowledge or the ability of the President, business can with difficulty be conducted with a body so constituted. Their lack of individual experience ensures irresolution; their freedom from all responsibility, ineptitude; and their excessive numbers, paralysis. With whom the decision ultimately rests no one appears to know. The Board is in reality a Board of Delay. Its object is to palaver, and gloze, and promise, and do nothing—an attitude which has been in great favour ever since its notable success after the Tientsin massacres of 1870, when the Chinese, by dint of shilly-shallying for several months, till the French were hard pressed in the Franco-German war, escaped very much more lightly than they would otherwise have done. Sir Harry Parkes said that to get a decision from the Tsungli Yamen was like trying to draw water from a well with a bottomless bucket. So long as the result is procrastination, and China is not compelled to act, except as she herself may desire, the Tsungli Yamen has served its purpose. As a matter of fact, any important business between the British Minister and the Chinese Government is far more likely to be successfully concluded in London, where, although no Chinese representative, with the exception of the Marquis Tseng, has so far had any knowledge of English, the assistance of Sir Halliday Macartney, the accomplished Councillor and English Secretary of the Chinese Legation, gives to his chief an advantage which is not enjoyed by the official superiors of the latter in Peking.

This dilatory attitude on the part of the Tsungli Yamen is encouraged by the discovery, which the Chinese have

A Board of Delay.

made long since, that the Powers, whose joint action would still be almost irresistible, are sundered by irremediable differences, and can be played off one against the other. They know that an allied French and British army is in the last degree unlikely ever again to march up to Peking and sack another Summer Palace. Other hostile combinations are almost equally improbable. When, as in the recent co-operation of France and Russia, any two of the Powers do combine, they carry all before them. In this conflict of interests lies the opportunity of the Chinese. Past masters in every trick of diplomacy, they picture it in the light of a balance-sheet, with credit and debit account, in which no expenditure must be entered without a more than compensating receipt. China never voluntarily makes a concession without securing a substantial *quid pro quo*; and the tactics that recovered Kulja would have done credit to Cavour. With equal ability have they recently pressed upon the British Government their somewhat shadowy pretensions on the confines of Kashmir, Burma, and Siam. The Tibetan negotiations, that, after going on for years, reached an apparent conclusion in 1894, were conducted in precisely the same spirit. With such a people the only system to adopt is to borrow a leaf from their own book, to act remorselessly upon the *Do ut des* principle, to pursue a waiting game, and to demand a concession, not solely when it is wanted, but rather when they want something else. In this way will the transaction present the aspect of a mercantile bargain so dear to the Oriental mind.

<small>Chinese diplomacy.</small>

The one question of foreign politics at Peking which equally affects the representatives of every foreign Power, is the Right of Audience; of which, as it fills a most important and a thoroughly characteristic page of Sino-

European history, I will give some account. The Emperors of China do not appear at any time to have taken up the position that their own person was so supremely sacred as to render audience with a foreigner an indignity. On the contrary, in olden days, when the Imperial state and prestige were immeasurably greater than they now are, audience was freely granted, and the person of the Sovereign was less hermetically concealed than is now the fashion. Two questions, however, have successively been made uppermost in the settlement of the matter, viz. the character of obeisance made by the foreigner admitted to the interview, and the nature and locality of the building in which it took place. As regards the former, the favoured individual was expected to comply with the Chinese usage by performing the *kowtow*, *i.e.* kneeling thrice and knocking his forehead nine times upon the ground. The theory of Chinese sovereignty being that the Emperor is the *de jure* monarch of the whole earth, of which China is the 'Middle Kingdom,' all other nations, therefore, must be either his tributaries or his subjects; whence the exaction of this mark of deference from their envoys. As regards the site of audience, the practice of emphasising the lowliness of the stranger in presence of the Son of Heaven by fixing the audience in a building that carries with it some implication of inferiority, appears to have been the growth only of the last fifty years, if not more recently.

The Right of Audience.

As early as 713 A.D. an Arab Embassy from Kutaiba, arriving at the Court of the Chinese Emperor, Hwen Thsang, found themselves called upon to perform the *kowtow*. This they declined to do, and were accordingly tried and sentenced to death by the Chinese, but were graciously pardoned by the Emperor.[1] Conversely,

History.

[1] *Nouveaux Mélanges Asiatiques*, by J. P. Rémusat, vol. i. p. 441, 442.

ten Chinese envoys were themselves put to death by the Burmese in 1286 A.D., because they insisted on appearing before the king of that country with their boots on—the Burmese equivalent in insult to the refusal of the *kowtow* in China.[1] In the seventeenth and eighteenth centuries both the Jesuit Fathers who were in the service of the Emperor and the envoys of European Courts or companies, who came to Peking for complimentary purposes or to secure facilities for trade, performed the *kowtow* without apparent compunction. One Russian official, however, who arrived at Peking in the reign of the first Manchu Emperor Shun Chih (1644-1661) was refused an audience because he declined to *kowtow*. In those days the audience commonly took place in one or other of the great Ceremonial Halls of the Imperial Palace in the heart of the Forbidden City, where no European is now permitted to enter. Here stands the Tai Ho Tien, or Hall of Supreme Harmony, a magnificent structure, 110 feet in height, erected upon a terrace of marble 20 feet high, with projecting wings, ascended from the outer court by flights of steps. The Great Audience Hall on the summit of the platform is a vast pavilion, in design not unlike the Memorial Temple of Yung Lo at the Ming Tombs, 200 feet in length by 90 feet in depth, sustained by 72 immense columns of painted teak. In this Hall the Emperor held and still holds the splendid annual Levees at the Winter Solstice, at the New Year, and on his own birthday. As in the Audience Hall, which I have previously described at Söul, and as in that which I shall afterwards describe at Hué—both of which, being erected for the Levees of tributary sovereigns, were exactly modelled upon the Chinese pattern—so here in the Tai Ho Tien the Emperor takes his seat upon a raised throne in the centre.

[1] *Narrative of Mission to the Court of Ava*, by Sir H. Yule, p. 79.

A few Manchus of exalted rank alone are admitted to the building. Outside and below the marble balustrades are ranged the nobility and officials in eighteen double rows, the civil officers on the east side, and the military officers on the west, their respective ranks and positions being marked by low columns. Here at the given signal they kneel, and nine times strike their foreheads upon the ground in homage to the Son of Heaven, dimly seen, if at all, through clouds of incense, in the solemn gloom of the pillared hall. The earliest picture published in Europe of an Imperial Audience, which was granted to a Dutch Embassy in 1656, represents it as having taken place in the Tai Ho Tien.[1] The second Hall beyond this in the series of successive pavilions, of which the ceremonial portion of the Palace consists, is the Pao Ho Tien, or Hall of Precious Harmony, also raised upon a marble terrace, wherein the Emperor confers the highest triennial degrees, and in former days gave official banquets to foreign guests (notably to the Mongol princes and to the Korean and Liuchiu envoys if in Peking) on the day preceding the New Year. Here also we read of a Dutch ambassador, one Van Braam, as having been received by the Emperor Kien Lung in 1795.[2] Both these ambassadors kowtowed. So also had done a Russian envoy in 1719, in whose company travelled John Bell of Antermony, a Scotch doctor;[3] and a Portuguese Envoy, Metello de Sousa Menezes, in 1727.

[1] *Relation de l'Ambassade de la Compagnie Hollandaise vers l'Empereur de la Chine.* Paris, 1663.

[2] *Voyage de l'Ambassade de la Compagnie des Indes Orientales Hollandaise vers l'Empereur de la Chine.* 2 vols. Philadelphia, 1797.

[3] *Journey from St. Petersburg to Divers Parts of Asia, with an Embassy from H.I.M. Peter I.*, by John Bell. 2 vols. Glasgow, 1763. The excellent Scotchman did not at all like having to go through this servile operation. But at the audience he says: 'The masters of the ceremonies then ordered all the company to kneel and make obeisance nine times to the Emperor. At every third time we stood up and kneeled again. Great pains were taken to avoid this piece of homage, but without success.'

The first English Plenipotentiary admitted to an audience with a Chinese Emperor was Lord Macartney in 1793. He was twice received by the aged Kien Lung; first in a pavilion in the grounds of the Emperor's hunting-retreat at Jehol, in Mongolia, and afterwards at the great Birthday Levee in Peking.

<small>English embassies. Lord Macartney in 1793.</small>

There were long disputes beforehand as to the exact nature of the obeisance which the Plenipotentiary should perform; and in his desire to be agreeable, the latter carried complacency so far as to offer to *kowtow* on condition that a Chinese official of corresponding rank did the same before a picture of George III., which he had brought with him. This offer was refused, and Lord Macartney is said to have only knelt upon one knee on the steps of the Imperial throne as he presented his credentials.[1] Whatever he actually did, the Chinese ever afterwards insisted that he had *kowtowed*; and furthermore took advantage of the British nobleman's ignorance of the Chinese language to fix above the boat that brought him up the Peiho River, and on the vehicle that took him to Jehol, a flag bearing the inscription, 'Ambassador bearing tribute from the Country of England'—an incident which is in itself a highly condensed epitome of the national character.

The next British Envoy, Lord Amherst, in 1816 escaped, it is true, the *kowtow*, but he never saw the Sovereign at all. While at Tientsin and during his journey up the river, prolonged daily conferences took place between himself and the Chinese officials, who insisted that Lord Macartney had *kowtowed*, and demanded

<small>Lord Amherst in 1816.</small>

---

[1] *Authentic Account of the Embassy from the King of Great Britain to the Emperor of China.* Taken from the papers of the Earl of Macartney by Sir G. Staunton. 2 vols. London, 1798. Among the presents taken by Lord Macartney to the Emperor of China from the British Government was a watch that cost £500. During the sack of the Summer Palace by the allied armies in 1860, it was found by a French soldier, who sold it to an Englishman for $20.

the same deference from him. Lord Amherst not merely repeated his predecessor's first offer, with equal lack of success, but he even consented to *kowtow*, if the next Chinese Ambassador to England would do the same to the Prince Regent. This proposal also was scouted; and Lord Amherst finally proceeded upon the understanding that instead of *kowtowing, i.e.* kneeling on both knees three times, and knocking the ground nine times, he should kneel on one knee three times, and make a low bow nine times. Upon his arrival, however, at the Summer Palace, where the Emperor Chia Ching was then staying, he was bidden by the latter, who was either devoured with curiosity or was bent upon a rupture, to an immediate audience, before his baggage had arrived, and consequently before he could either cleanse himself after the journey, or don his uniform, or prepare his presents. Lord Amherst, suspecting in this inordinate haste some intentional slur upon the Sovereign whom he represented, begged to be excused the honour of the interview, and was bundled unceremoniously out of the Palace the same evening. Thus abruptly ended his mission.[1]

No other British representative was admitted to the Imperial presence up till the war in 1860; and the right of audience upon the terms that prevail in every other foreign Court was one of the first advantages exacted by the conquerors. Article III. of the English Treaty of 1860, without actually claiming the right, inferred it by stipulating that the British representative 'shall not be called upon to perform any ceremony derogatory to him as representing the Sovereign of an independent nation on a footing of equality with that of China.' After the conclusion of the war no audience was

Interval.

---

[1] *Journal of Proceedings of the late Embassy to China*, by Henry Ellis, Third Commissioner. London, 1817.

possible in the reign of Hsien Feng, because he was a fugitive and an exile from his capital till his death in 1861; nor, during the minority of Tung Chih, in which interval the Duke of Edinburgh visited Peking in 1869 without the question being raised, could the demand be put forward. As soon, however, as Tung Chih assumed the reins of government in 1873, the foreign Ministers in Peking addressed to him a collective note, in which they asked to be permitted to present their congratulations in person.

The days had long passed when the Chinese authorities could insist upon the *kowtow*. June 29, 1873, at a very early hour of the morning (Lord Macartney had been received at daybreak) was fixed for the collective audience. Compelled to evacuate their original redoubt, however, the Chinese, with characteristic strategy, fell back upon an inner and unsuspected line of defence, endeavouring to safeguard the dignity of their own Sovereign and to humiliate the foreigner by selecting for the site of audience a building in the outskirts of the Palace enclosure known as the Tzu Kuang Ko, which stands on the western shore of the big lake. In this Hall, which is hung with pictures of combats and of eminent Chinese generals, many of them painted by the Jesuits, it is the habit to entertain the envoys from tributary or dependent States, such as Mongolia and Korea—and in former days also the Liuchiu Islands, Nepal, and Annam—at the festival of the New Year; and the object which was directly served by the flag upon Lord Macartney's boat in 1793 could, it struck the crafty Chinaman, be now indirectly secured by admitting the foreigners to audience in a building that possessed to Chinese minds a tributary significance. The audience, at which Great Britain was represented by Sir Thomas Wade, took place; but considerable

Audiences with Tung Chih in 1873 and 1874.

irritation was caused by the official announcement of the event in the *Peking Gazette*, which described the foreign Ministers by an incorrect and inferior title, and represented them as having 'supplicated' for an interview. The objections, however, to the building were, it is said, not shared in their entirety by some eminent authorities, including Dr. Williams, who was present at the audience, and Sir Thomas Wade himself.

In the succeeding year, the precedent of 1873 was so far improved upon that audience was given to several newly arrived Ministers separately in the same hall as on the previous occasion.

In 1875 the Emperor Tung Chih died, and was succeeded by a minor. It was not, therefore, till after the assumption of government by the Emperor Kuang Hsu, in 1889, that the question again rose. This time, however, the Emperor (or rather the Empress Dowager, inspiring him) himself took the initiative by issuing on December 12, 1890, the following Proclamation, which testified to a common-sense or a conversion on the part of the Government, which was in either case remarkable :— *[Audience with Kuang Hsu in 1891.]*

'I have now been in charge of the Government for two years. The Ministers of Foreign Powers ought to be received by me at an audience ; and I hereby decree that the audience to be held be in accordance with that of the twelfth year of Tung Chih (1873). It is also hereby decreed that a day be fixed every year for an audience, in order to show my desire to treat with honour all the Ministers of the Foreign Powers resident in Peking.'

These sentiments were eminently laudable, but by reviving the precedent of Tung Chih, they offered no solace to the spirits that had been outraged by the reception in the Tzu Kuang Ko. Here finally, in spite of a good deal of preliminary grumbling, the audience again took place on March 5, 1891.[1] Six Ministers and their staffs were received by the Emperor, who sat cross-legged upon a daïs with a table draped in yellow silk in front of him; the Ministers being first received separately, in the order of their length of residence in Peking; and the united staffs being subsequently introduced *en masse*. The Emperor and his suite wore long blue silk coats lined with white fur, and embroidered on the back and front with the insignia of their different ranks. On their heads were winter hats of black felt with red silk tassels and coloured buttons on the crown. Each Minister, upon entering, marched up the hall, bowing at stated intervals, and paused at the Dragon Pillar, where, after reading his letter of credence, and hearing it translated by the interpreter, he handed the document to the President of the Tsungli Yamen. The latter placed it on the yellow table in front of the Emperor, and subsequently knelt to receive the Imperial reply, written in Manchu, which, after descending the daïs, he repeated in Chinese to the Minister through his interpreter. Some of the representatives are said to have been dissatisfied with the arrangements, and the foreign press re-echoed and magnified the cry. It was perhaps not surprising after this that the Cesarevitch, in his tour round the world in the same year, should have been successfully kept away from Peking, both by the Chinese, who dreaded a compulsory surrender, and by the Tsar, who could hardly have brooked anything approximating to an indignity.

---

[1] Herr von Brandt, the German Representative on this occasion, mentions in his book, *Aus dem Lande des Zopfes*, that beside the road which the diplomats had to follow in order to reach the Audience Hall, runs the track of a small Décauville Railway, upon which the Emperor is pushed along in a light car by the Palace eunuchs.

After the audience of 1891, the Doyen of the Diplomatic Corps gave becoming expression to the dissatisfaction of his colleagues, among whom the French and Russians have always taken the lead, by applying to the Tsungli Yamen for reception on a future occasion, not outside the Palace, and in a tributary building, but, as in old days, inside the actual precincts of the Imperial residence. A sort of half compliance with this request was made, first by the promise to erect a new building for the ceremony, and afterwards by the offer of another hall. This is the Chang Kuang Tien, a building dating from Mongol times, which appears to have no peculiar significance or application, and stands on the eastern side of the marble bridge across the ornamental lake. It is not one of the ceremonial halls of the Palace proper, but, on the other hand, its use conveys no slur. Acting upon this opinion, the Austro-Hungarian Minister was the first of the Foreign Diplomatic Corps to be received here in 1891; and here also Sir N. O'Conor, Her Majesty's recent representative in Peking, was granted an audience upon his arrival in December 1892, and Herr von Brandt, the retiring German Minister, upon his departure in 1893; a more honorific character having in these latter cases been lent to the reception of the envoy by his introduction through the main or Porcelain Gate, instead of a side gate of the Palace.

[margin: Subsequent audiences.]

A still further advantage was gained, under the stress of the war then proceeding with Japan, in November 1894. The Chang Kuang Tien was exchanged for the Wen Hua Tien, a hall adjoining the Palace (though not, it appears, actually inside it), where the Emperor sits to hear the Confucian classics expounded. There, on November 12, the Foreign Representatives, who had been admitted by the Central Gate, were received by the Emperor Kuang

Hsu to present their congratulations on the sixtieth anniversary of the Empress Dowager. The latter was present, though concealed from view by a silk-curtain adorned with peacocks' feathers, that was hung behind the throne. Upon leaving, the Ministers were conducted out of the grounds through the Eastern Gate. In the present year (on June 7, 1895) the Ministers of France and Russia, who have always adopted a more uncompromising attitude than the remainder of their colleagues, were granted a special audience, arranged somewhat theatrically on their behalf, in order to present new letters of credence from the heads of their respective States. They are reported to have secured the privilege of having the missives carried up the central flight of steps to the Imperial throne — a technical admission of the titular equality of their rulers with the Son of Heaven.

It will be observed from this historical summary that, since Lord Macartney's audience at Jehol just one hundred years ago, the following points have been gained.

Summary of achievement. Not merely does a Special Plenipotentiary enjoy the right to an audience with the Sovereign, but to every foreign Minister accredited to the Chinese Court is this prerogative now conceded, both upon his arrival and departure, or when presenting any communication from his Sovereign; and, if the terms of the Imperial Proclamation of 1890 be carried out, once every year in addition. The *kowtow* has disappeared, not merely from foreign practice, but even from discussion. Its place has been taken by a ceremonial not essentially different from that with which a new Member of Parliament is introduced to the British House of Commons. These are considerable forward moves. On the other hand, the diplomats, though advancing by steady degrees, have not yet quite won their way back to one of the great Audience Halls in the main body of the Palace, to which it appears to me that precedent and equity alike entitle them to advance a claim. Perhaps the recovery of the Tai Ho Tien is one of the triumphs that is reserved for the diplomacy of the ensuing century.

Englishmen, living freely in a democratic country, where the Fountain of Honour is inaccessible to few, and where humility has never been confounded with humiliation, may not be able to comprehend all this pother about the nature of a bow and the significance of a building. To the Chinese they are all-important; and just as the Greek Timagoras was condemned to death by the liberty-loving Athenians 2260 years ago, because he had *kowtowed* at Susa to Artaxerxes Mnemon, the Great King, so have British representatives —instructed to maintain the equal prerogative of their Sovereign, in face of the inadmissible pretensions of a majesty that was supremely ignorant of its own limitations—been justified in fighting strenuously for what to Europe may seem a shadow, but in Asia is the substance. When Lord Macartney took out a beautiful coach with glass panels as a present from George III. to the Emperor Kien Lung, the Chinese officials were horrified at a structure which would place the coachman on a higher level than the monarch, and promptly cut away the box-seat.

True significance of the dispute.

Such and so imperfect being the status of foreign diplomats, and the methods of diplomatic intercourse at Peking, we may next inquire what are the main objects for which their intervention is required? In other words, what is the foreign policy of China, in so far at least as concerns our own country? We have not here, at any rate for the present,

Foreign policy of China.

any demand similar to that which we have noticed in Japan, for the revision or abrogation of the Treaties under which Europeans are admitted to trade or residence in certain ports on the sea-coast, and in cities in the interior.[1] China has not, like her neighbours, any judicial system, nominally based upon a European model, to offer in substitution for the consular courts of the foreigner. She is far more dependent upon the latter for her wealth, particularly as derived from the Imperial Customs, which, under the extremely capable management of an Englishman, Sir Robert Hart—who enjoys the unique distinction of having resigned the appointment of British Minister in order to remain Inspector-General, a post which he has now held for thirty years—have poured a large and annually increasing revenue into her exchequer.[2] The foreign element itself is both much more numerous and more powerful than it is in Japan.[3] Moreover, the Chinese temperament is naturally disposed to acquiesce in established facts, and is wrapped in a complacency too absorbing to feel the perpetual smart of foreign intrusion. Such a movement may rise into view later on; but at present it is below the horizon.

The foreign policy of China chiefly concerns Englishmen in its relation to St. Petersburg and to Downing Street. The successive advances made by Russia, largely at China's own expense, have taught her to regard that Power as

[1] A single exception must be noted in the person of the present Chinese Minister in England, who, when Taotai at Ning-po, some years ago, wrote a series of essays on this and kindred subjects, which have appeared in book form.

[2] The Customs' Revenue derived from the Foreign Trade of China in 1892 was £4,500,000.

[3] In 1892 the number of foreigners residing in the twenty-four Treaty Ports, including Japanese, was close upon 10,000. Of these nearly 4000 were British; America came next with 1300; then France with less than 900 and Germany with 750.

her real enemy, whom, however, she fears far more than she abhors. It is Russia who threatens her frontiers in Chinese Turkestan and on the Pamirs; Russia who is always nibbling, in scientific disguise, at Tibet; Russia who has designs on Manchuria; Russia whose shadow overhangs Korea; Russia who is building a great Trans-continental railway that will enable her to pour troops into China at any point along 3500 miles of contiguous border. All this she knows well enough, and when the Cesarevitch passed through Asia he was, as I have pointed out, neither invited to nor himself proposed to visit Peking; but the knowledge, so far from instigating China to any definite policy of self-defence, except in the isolated case of the proposed Manchurian Railway, fills her with an alarm that is only equalled by her suspicion of the counsels of any other Power.

Attitude towards Russia

China pretends, for instance, to be interested in the Pamirs, but she cannot be reckoned upon to move a single battalion in their defence, particularly if it is whispered in her ear that she is thereby helping to pull somebody else's chestnuts out of the fire. We read in the newspapers mysterious paragraphs about the activity of Chinese diplomats at St. Petersburg, and of Russian diplomats at Peking; and the world is invited to believe that China is as solicitous of her Turkestan frontier as Great Britain is, for instance, about the Hindu Kush. We hear of garrisons being reinforced in Kashgaria, and of the telegraph wires being pushed westwards over the Mongolian desert. All this is intended to give, and perhaps succeeds in giving, a general impression of abounding activity; and so far as mere diplomacy is concerned, China will no doubt fight as stubbornly to retain her precarious foothold on the Roof of the World as she did to recover

China and the Pamirs.

Kulja. But no greater mistake, in my judgment, can be committed than to suppose that this mixture of diplomatic finesse and bravado masks either any intention to fight seriously for the territories in question or the possession of any materials to fight with. During the fracas on the Pamirs in 1892, when small detachments of Russians marched about filibustering and annexing whatever they could, the Chinese outposts at Soma Tash and Ak Tash skedaddled with headlong rapidity at the first glimpse of a Cossack; and an English traveller found the Chinese authority, which claims to be paramount over the entire eastern half of the Pamirs, represented by less than a dozen soldiers. And yet there exists a large corps of writers who never cease to press upon the public acceptance an implicit belief in the strength and resolution of China in Central Asia. I prefer to accept the opinion of General Prjevalski, Colonel Bell, Captain Younghusband, Mr. Carey, and every authority (so far as I know) who has visited the Chinese frontier dominions, that, however long Russia may find it politic to postpone a forward move, her advance, when finally made across the outlying western portions of the Chinese Empire, inhabited as they are by a Mussulman population who have no loyalty towards their present masters, will be a military promenade, attended by little fighting and by no risk. Meanwhile, the golden hour in which China might make herself strong if she either had the will or could resolve upon the way, is allowed to slip by; and a frontier which might, with certain modifications, be rendered almost invulnerable, continues by its ostentatious helplessness to invite the enemy's assault.

The experiences of the present year (1895), which might by some be thought to testify to the friendly feeling of Russia, since it is the latter Power that has stepped in to check the impetuous advance of Japan, to recover for China the Liao-tung Peninsula, and to supply her with the cash wherewith to discharge her indemnity obligations, are in reality only a further illustration of my proposition. Russia does not render this assistance from a superfluity of unselfishness, or for no end. She has her price, and she will receive her reward. That reward will involve the still further enfeeblement of the victim for whose inheritance she is waiting, and to whose invalid gasps she prescribes with tender hand the dose that imparts a transient spasm of vitality, to be followed presently by an even more profound collapse.

Russia in 1895.

The very conditions that render Russia the natural enemy of China would appear to constitute Great Britain her natural friend. China desires, or should desire, to keep the Russian army out of Korea and the Russian navy away from the Yellow Sea. We are similarly interested in both objects. China wants, or should want, to retain Yarkund and Kashgar, and therefore requires a defensible and defended frontier on the Pamirs. We also are anxious to avoid Russian contiguity with ourselves at the Hindu Kush or the Karakoram. China attaches or should attach a high value to her suzerainty over Tibet, which Russia notoriously covets. England does not quarrel with the former, but could hardly welcome the latter status. If the Trans-Siberian railway will be a menace to Chinese territorial integrity, it will also generate a sharp competition with British Asiatic trade. Farther to the south the recent apparition of France as an aggressive factor upon the confines of Siam and Burma has been a source of no slight annoyance to China, already exasperated by the theft of Tongking. It is not more acceptable to ourselves, who have no desire for France as a next-door

Attitude towards Great Britain.

neighbour on the borders of our Indian Empire. There are therefore the strongest *a priori* reasons in favour of a close and sympathetic understanding between China and Great Britain in the Far East. Nor, though Chinese armaments are, in the present state, a delusion and China's military strength a farce, and though the full extent of the imposture has been relentlessly exposed during the recent war, can any one deny that the prodigious numbers of China, her vast extent, her obstinate and tenacious character, and her calculating diplomacy, render her a coadjutor in Central and Eastern Asia of no mean value; just as it would appear that the prestige and power of Great Britain in the same regions might be of corresponding and even greater service to her. A fuller confidence in the honesty of Great Britain than in that of her rivals has for long existed in the breast of Chinese statesmen, and has been largely due to the integrity of our commercial relations, and to belief in the straightness of British character; whilst no efforts have been spared to conciliate Chinese scruples in every point where the concession could be made without sacrifice of principle. The ascendency of British influence thus acquired at Peking appears to have been temporarily shaken by the negative and cautious attitude assumed by the British Government during and after the war with Japan, and by the skilful though interested interference of Russia and France. But the passage of time may be trusted to reveal to China the more than Platonic limitations of the affections of her new friends, and to remind her of the less suspicious amenities of older allies.

Unfortunately the relations of Great Britain and China are liable from time to time to be imperilled by outside circumstances, which play a large part in determining the character of their official intercourse. I do not allude to the question of Trade, which is the principal ground of meeting between the two countries, because a commerce which enriches both is unlikely to be seriously risked by either, and because the wider the sphere of mercantile relations between them (and it must expand instead of shrinking) the less rather than the greater are the sources of friction likely to become. Already Anglo-Chinese Trade has attained dimensions that, at the time of the first war, fifty years ago, would have been laughed at as an idle dream. At that time China sent to England less than half a million sterling of goods in the year. In 1892 the total foreign trade of the Empire amounted to £47,550,000, of which £27,050,000 were imports and £20,500,000 exports; and of this enormous total Great Britain and her Colonies (including Hongkong) claimed 60 per cent., or £28,500,000; and Great Britain alone £8,000,000, over three-fourths of which were expended by China in imports from this country. If we take the returns of shipping, the British preponderance was even more clearly marked; for out of a total of 29,500,000 tons that entered and cleared from the Treaty Ports in 1892, 65 per cent., or nearly 19,500,000 tons, were British vessels; Germany, the next European competitor, having only 1,500,000.[1] Taught by us, the Chinese themselves now absorb no inconsiderable part of the Treaty Port trade; but the vessels which Chinese merchants own and run are commanded by British officers, and are guided into the rivers and harbours by British pilots.

Nor is this trade, immense though it seems to be in relation to the time within which it has been developed,

Anglo-Chinese Trade.

[1] The Returns for 1893 showed that the total value of Chinese Foreign Trade had increased by £6,000,000. The British share of the total was 56 per cent., and of the shipping 65 per cent. In 1894, in spite of the war, there was a continued rise, and the British share, both in trade and in shipping, amounted to 69 per cent., and in the carrying trade to 61 per cent., or out of the carrying trade under a foreign flag, to 83 per cent.

more than a fraction of what, under more favourable conditions, may be expected in the future. When we reflect that to supply the needs of a population of 350,000,000 there are only twenty-four ports at which foreign commerce is allowed in the first place to enter;[1] that river navigation by steam, except upon the Yangtse, can scarcely be said to exist; that vast markets are hidden away in the far interior which are practically under prevailing conditions inaccessible; that the paucity and misery of communications are a by-word; that every form of native enterprise is strangled unless powerful officials have a personal interest at stake; that officialism operates everywhere by a mathematical progression of squeezes; that the multiplication of inland *likin* or *octroi* stations swells the cost of foreign commodities to famine prices before they are offered for sale in the inland markets; that China is deliberately throwing away her staple source of wealth, the tea-trade, by failure to adapt it to the altered requirements of consumers; that in the same period in which she has doubled her trade Japan has trebled hers; and that with 60,000,000 more mouths to feed and bodies to clothe, her total commerce is yet £80,000,000 less per annum than that of India: when all these facts are remembered, it cannot be doubted that, compared with what might be, and some day will be done, we are only standing on the threshold of Chinese commercial expansion.

[1] The Treaty Ports, opened by various Treaties or Conventions with Great Britain, France, and Germany, since the Nanking Treaty in 1842, are as follows: Canton (with Customs stations at Kowloon and Lappa), Amoy, Foochow, Ningpo, Shanghai, Nanking, Tientsin, Newchwang, Chefoo, Swatow, Kiungchow (in Hainan), Tamsui and Tainan, with their dependencies Kelung, Takow, and Anping in Formosa, Chinkiang, Kiukiang, Hankow, Ichang, Wuhu, Wenchow, Pakhoi, Chungking. The French, by a Trade Convention in 1887, also trade overland with Lungchow, Mengtse, and Manghao. By the Treaty of Shimonoseki with Japan (April 1895) the following additional ports have been opened: Shashih, Suchow, and Hangchow. By the Franco-Chinese Treaty of June 1895 Hokeow has been substituted for Manghao, and Ssumao has become a Treaty Port, with rights of residence for a French Consul and French subjects.

Neither, in speaking of the occasional sources of friction between China and ourselves, do I allude to the Opium Question, which in the hands of enthusiastic or prejudiced ignorance in London has been pre-sented to English audiences in a guise that excites a smile in every Treaty Port in China. There, at least, everybody knows that the helpless Celestial is neither being forced nor befooled by an insidious and immoral Government at Calcutta; that if not an ounce of Indian opium ever again passed through a Chinese custom-house, Chinamen would go on smoking their own inferior drug as keenly as ever;[1] and that the pretence that China is hostile to the British people or to Christian missions because we introduced to her the opium habit (which she had already practised for centuries), is about as rational as to say that the national soreness that sometimes arises between England and France is due to our resentment at having to cross the Channel for our best brandy. In any case, long before our domestic Puritans have purged the national conscience of what they style this great sin, the Opium Question will have settled itself by the rapid decline of the Indian import and the acceptance by China herself of the undivided responsi-bility for her own moral welfare.

<small>Opium Question.</small>

There remains the Missionary movement in China, which, next to, perhaps even more than, the merchants, compels the attention of the British Foreign Office, and will here be treated only in so far as it affects the international relations between the two countries. The missionary himself resolutely declines to regard it from this standpoint. He conceives himself to be there in obedi-ence to a divine summons, and to be pursuing the noblest

<small>Missionary Questions.</small>

---

[1] As it is, Indian opium is only smoked by about 2 in every 1000 of the population.

of human callings. A friend of my own, an eminent divine in the English Church, speaking at Exeter Hall in answer to some observations which I had made in the columns of the *Times* upon Christian Missions in China, thus stated the case from the Church's point of view :—

'The gain or loss to civilisation from Christian missions is not the question for the missionary. He is subject to a Master higher than any statesman or diplomatist of this world. It is not the missionary who has to reckon with the diplomatist, but the diplomatist with the missionary.'

A variation of the same reply is that which I have in many lands received from the lips of missionaries, and which in their judgment appears to cut the ground away from all criticism, and to render argument superfluous. This is a repetition of the divine injunction which closes the Gospel of St. Matthew: 'Go ye therefore, and teach all nations, baptizing them in the name of the Father, and of the Son, and of the Holy Ghost.'[1] Obedience to this supreme command is the sole final test to which the missionary is willing to submit his action. He is the unworthy but chosen instrument of God himself. It is useless, as I have experienced, to point out to him that the selection of a single passage from the preaching of the founder of one faith, as the sanction of a movement against all other faiths, is a dangerous experiment. If, for instance, the disciple of Confucius were to quote an aphorism of that philosopher that justified the persecution of Christian missionaries as the sponsors of a mischievous innovation, what value would the Christian missionary attach to such a form of Chinese exculpation ? Equally useless is it to remind him that Christ Himself seems to have contemplated the likelihood of an unsuccessful or inopportune propaganda when He said :

[1] Matt. xxviii. 19.

'When they persecute you in this city, flee ye into another';[1] and again: 'Whosoever shall not receive you nor hear you, when ye depart thence, shake off the dust under your feet for a testimony against them.'[2] The authority which the missionary enthusiast is willing to attach to the ukase that accredits his enthusiasm, he ignores or deprecates when it appears to qualify its sanction. To him the course is clear, and has been mapped out in advance by a higher hand. That governments should fight, or that international relations should be imperilled over his wrecked house or insulted person, would strike him as but a feather's weight in the scale compared with the great final issue at stake—viz. the spiritual regeneration of a vast country and a mighty population plunged in heathenism and sin. Just, however, as the statesman is frequently called upon to correct the fighting general's plan of campaign in the light of diplomatic possibilities, so the impartial observer must submit even the impassioned *apologia* of the Christian evangelist to the cold test of political and practical analysis.

In endeavouring to arrive at an opinion upon so vexed a question, the risks, even after a careful study upon two separate occasions on the spot, of involuntary ignorance or unconscious bias, are so great that it will perhaps be wisest to state the case *pro* and *con* with as much fulness as space will permit, leaving the reader to form his own conclusion. The facts are these. Whilst the Jesuit missionaries have been in China for centuries, and in many cases have done splendid work, the Protestant missions (of whom, principally, I desire to speak) in the main date their institution from the Treaties that closed the first China war fifty years ago,[3] and the second in

Protestant missions.

---

[1] Matt. x. 23.   [2] Mark vi. 11.
[3] The first Protestant missionary in China was the Rev. R. Morrison, who

1858-60. Whereas in 1844 there were but thirty Protestant missionaries in China, their numerical strength in 1890 was 1300 (including women), and in 1894 was said to be 1511. The total strength of all Christian missionaries in China is said to be 2000. Every year America, Canada, Australia, Sweden, and in a not inferior degree England, pour fresh recruits into the field, and the money that is subscribed for their support and that of their propaganda excels the revenue of many States. The question is, How do the soldiers of this costly crusade acquit themselves?

The points that will universally be conceded in their favour are as follows: The devotion and self-sacrifice of many of their lives (particularly of those who in Their good native dress visit or inhabit the far interior), and service. the example of pious fortitude set to those among whom they labour; the influence of the education and culture thus diffused in kindling the softer virtues and in ameliorating the conditions of life; the slow but certain spread of Western knowledge; the visible products of organised philanthropy in the shape of hospitals, medical dispensaries, orphanages, relief distribution, and schools; the occasional winning of genuine and noble-hearted converts from the enemy's fold;[1] the exalted character of the spiritual sanction claimed by the missionaries; the plausibility of the analogy drawn by them from the tardy inception of Christian labour in other countries and earlier times; the excellent work done by missionaries in writing learned,

came to Canton in 1807, and published his famous dictionary and translation of the Bible in 1823. But this was all the more remarkable for being an isolated effort.

[1] A hostile critic might retort that the leader of the Taiping Rebellion, who was a Christian convert, and as such was hailed by many of the missionaries as the herald of a new dispensation, succeeded in nothing better than in devastating thirteen out of the eighteen provinces of China, and in sacrificing the lives (at the lowest computation) of 20,000,000 men.

though often unreadable, essays about the country and people.

I should be the last person to claim that even this tabulated statement contained a complete record of the good work done by the missionaries. Much of their labour is necessarily devoid of immediate result, and is incapable of being scientifically registered in a memorandum. They sow the seed; and if it does not fructify in their day or before our eyes, it may well be germinating for a future eartime. No fair critic would withhold from the Christian missions in China the credit of any prospective harvest that may be reaped by their successors when they have gone. *Sowing the seed.*

On the other hand, it would be foolish to deny that in China their operations evoke a criticism, even at the hands of their own countrymen, of which Exeter Hall very likely has no inkling, but which in China itself, where Exeter Hall has never been heard of, is not to be despised; and that there are features in their conduct of the campaign which may be said, not altogether unwarrantably, to furnish the enemy with cause to blaspheme. The alleged drawbacks to the work, or at least to the *modus operandi* of the missionaries, fall under three heads: (1) religious and doctrinal; (2) political; and (3) practical; with each of which I will deal in turn. *Objections and drawbacks.*

With rare exceptions, more liberal-minded than their fellows, the missionaries adopt an attitude of implacable hostility to all native religions and ethics, ignoring alike their virtuous aspects and influence, the all-powerful hold which they have acquired upon Chinese character, and the sanction lent to them by a venerable antiquity. Particularly is this the case with regard to ancestor-worship, with which they decline all parley; although a rare retort would appear to *1. Religious and doctrinal. Hostility to Chinese ethics.*

be open to a Chinaman in England who accidentally found his way into Westminster Abbey or St. Paul's. In 1790 the young Christian Church in Korea, very much exercised about this question, sent to the Roman Catholic bishop at Peking to inquire what its members ought to do. The response came that ancestor-worship of any kind or in any degree was incompatible with Christianity, and that no Korean could be a Christian who worshipped or burned incense before the family tablets. What the French bishop then answered, his coreligionists have always answered; and the same reply was from the earliest period returned by the Protestant missions also. I am not here concerned with the doctrinal justice of this decision, which is a matter for theologians rather than for the lay mind. I am interested only in pointing out the inevitable consequences of such an attitude. The Chinaman, who is entirely content with his own religion, and only asks to be left alone, is assailed by a propaganda that commences with an attack upon all that he holds most dear. To him the ethics of Confucius sum up the whole duty of man to the family and the State; while the payment of homage to the higher powers is provided for by the polytheistic conceptions of the Buddhist cult. He hears the former disparaged, the latter derided. He is invited to become a convert at the cost of ceasing to be a citizen; to tear up the sheet-anchor of all morality as the first condition of moral regeneration. Small wonder that a propaganda, which thus lays the axe to the very root of the tree, should encounter the stubborn resistance of all those who have been accustomed to seek shelter under its branches.[1]

[1] It is equally beginning at the wrong end to adopt the needless subservience to native superstitions that is in vogue at some of the Catholic establishments; e.g. in the Lazarist Orphanage at Kiukiang, where the feet of girls are deformed in order to conciliate native opinion.

If the evangelists of some new faith were to appear in England, drawn from a race whom we hated and despised, and were to commence their preaching by denouncing the Bible, and crying Anathema upon the Apostles' Creed, what sort of reception would they meet with? Moreover, this attitude on the part of the missionaries incurs the risk of defeating its own object; for such iconoclasm, in the eyes of many critics, could only, even if successful, lead to two results, both equally to be deplored—the complete disintegration of the Chinese social fabric, and the collapse of Chinese morality.

While thus warring with the most cherished beliefs of their hoped-for converts, the missionaries have not agreed among themselves as to the Chinese word to express the single Deity whom they preach, and for whom the Jesuits, the Americans, and the English have at different times employed different titles, with the result of complete bewilderment to the native understanding, ill able to cope with the subtleties of theological logomachy. The first-named adopt the title Tien Chu, *i.e.* Lord of Heaven. The Americans and some English prefer the more impalpable Chen Shen, *i.e.* True Spirit. The English Protestants and American Methodists adopt the Chinese Shang-ti, or Supreme Lord, the Deity whose worship (a survival of the primitive nature worship) I have described upon the Altar of Heaven at Peking. Indeed, I have heard of an English missionary who, in the old days when the latter enclosure was accessible to foreigners, is said to have conducted a service of the Church of England on the summit of the marble altar.

Disputes as to name of the Deity.

Still less do the foreign teachers coincide upon the form of religion itself, which is promulgated by the divines of a score of different schools, each claiming the accredited custody of the oracles of God. To Chinamen a separate

<small>As to the form of religion.</small> sect is not always distinguishable from a separate creed; and between Jesuits, Lazarists, Trappists, Russian Greeks, Protestants, Churches of England, Scotland, Canada, and America, Baptists, Presbyterians, Methodists, Congregationalists, Episcopalians, Free Christians, and all the self-accredited polyonymous missionary societies, he finds it hard to determine who are the true and who the false prophets, or whether any are true at all. Again, conceive the parallel case in our own country. Suppose the apostles of some new manifestation to reach our shores with a creed in their pockets that claimed a supernatural origin and a divine authority; and suppose these pioneers to be presently succeeded by others, not in one batch only, or in half a dozen, or in a dozen, but in a score of detachments, each proclaiming the fallibility or spuriousness of the others, and its own superior authentication—what should we say to these bearers of the heavenly message, who could not even agree together upon its terms?

Another cause for stumbling has been supplied by the circulation of imperfectly revised translations of the Bible through the country. The missionary societies do

<small>Unrevised translations of the Scriptures.</small> not seem to have sufficiently realised that the Holy Scriptures, which require in places some explanation, if not some expurgation, for ourselves, may stand in still greater need of editing for a community who care nothing about the customs or prepossessions of the ancient Jews, but who are invited to accept the entire volume as a revelation from on high. I am aware of a so-called English missionary who rampages about Central Asia with the funds supplied by societies at

home, and who, taking with him a portmanteau full of
Bibles, thinks that by dropping its contents here and there,
he is winning recruits to the fold of Christ. What is the
educated Chinaman likely to think, for instance, of Samuel
hewing Agag in pieces before the Lord, or of David setting
Uriah in the forefront of the battle, and commissioning
Solomon to slay Shimei, whose life he had himself sworn
to spare, or of Solomon exchanging love-lyrics with the
Shulamite woman? Even in the New Testament the
bidding to forsake father and mother for the sake of Christ
must to the Chinaman's eyes be the height of profanity,
whilst if he can follow the logic of St. Paul, he accomplishes
that which is beyond the power of many educated Christians.
To the Chinese people, who have great faith but little hope
in their own creeds, a simple statement of the teaching of
Christ might be a glorious and welcome revelation. But
the text of the Scriptures, unsoftened and unexplained, has
no such necessary effect, and is capable, in ingenious hands
(as the Hunan publications sufficiently showed), of being
converted into an argument against that which it is intended
to support.

If the text of the Bible is thus wrested into a cause of
offence, neither is the intrinsic abstruseness of the dogma
which it inculcates easy of interpretation in a
manner that conveys enlightenment to the Chinese Christian dogma.
intellect. The mysteries, for instance, attaching
to the Christian theogony, and to the doctrine of the Trinity,
whilst to the believer they only supply welcome material
for faith, are to the unbeliever excellent ground for
suspicion.

Finally, the religion whose vehicles of diffusion I have
discussed is disseminated in many cases by a number of
irresponsible itinerants, each of whom is a law unto himself,

many of whom disown communion with any Church, and whose single-minded fervour is dearly purchased at the cost of the doctrinal confusion entailed. Some of my own schoolfellows had felt the call, and had spontaneously given to China what was meant for mankind. Upon inquiry as to their whereabouts and doings, I learned that more than one had severed his connection with any denomination, and was proceeding against the infidel upon his own plan of campaign. This may be magnificent, but it is not scientific warfare.

Irresponsible itinerancy.

The political drawbacks to the missionaries' work are less exclusively matters of their own creation. China can never forget that, unlike the Christians in early Rome, in early Gaul, or in early Britain, they owe their admission here to no tacit acquiescence on her own part, much less to any expressed desire; but solely to the coercion of a superior and victorious strength. Each station is a sardonic reminder to them that they have been made to pass under the Caudine Forks. Nay, it is more; for it is a reminder of the duplicity as well as of the power of the conqueror; seeing that the right of residence in the interior of China is only enjoyed by the British and other missionaries in virtue of the most favoured nation clause in our own Treaty, taking advantage of a spurious paragraph introduced by a French missionary into the Chinese text of the French Treaty of 1860, and either not discovered by the Chinese, or not repudiated by them until it was too late. Let me briefly recapitulate the history of this curious and not altogether creditable page of history.

2. Political.

The only passage in Lord Elgin's Treaty of Tientsin in 1858, relating directly to the missionaries, is that commonly known as the Toleration Clause, which was copied without substantial alteration from

History of the Treaties.

the treaties already concluded by China with Russia and the United States. Article VIII. of the English Treaty runs as follows:—

'The Christian religion, as professed by Protestants and Roman Catholics, inculcates the practice of virtue, and teaches man to do as he would be done by. Persons teaching or professing it, therefore, shall alike be entitled to the protection of the Chinese authorities; nor shall any such, peaceably pursuing their calling, and not offending against the law, be persecuted or interfered with.'

A later clause in the same treaty (Article XII.) was subsequently appealed to as giving English missionaries the right to rent or own land and buildings in the interior:—

'British subjects, whether at the ports *or at other places*, desiring to build or open houses, warehouses, churches, hospitals, or burial-grounds, shall make their agreement for the land or buildings they require at the rates prevailing among the people, equitably and without exactions on either side.'

But it was then explained, and has always been held by the British Government, that the words, '*at other places*,' upon which alone the pretension rested, had never been intended to confer, and could not be construed as conferring, such a right, Lord Elgin having only introduced them in order to cover the case of places such as Whampoa, Woosung, and Taku, which are situated respectively at the distance of a few miles below Canton, Shanghai, and Tientsin, and where it might be found desirable, instead of or in addition to the Treaty Ports, to establish foreign settlements. Indeed, if the words had meant places in the interior promiscuously, there would obviously have been no necessity for subsequent treaties opening fresh Treaty Ports, which concessions have only been procured as a compensation for outrage, or with immense difficulty.

The British Treaties, accordingly, while they secure to

the missionary full protection everywhere in the pursuit of his calling, and in the possession of house and church property in the Treaty Ports, do not give him the right either of residence or of ownership in the interior. It was reserved for the French to supply the deficiency.

Already, in the French Treaty of 1858, the privileges above mentioned had been definitely guaranteed. Article XIII. says, in terms not unlike those of the English Treaty:—

> 'The Christian religion having for its essential object the leading of men to virtue, the members of all Christian communities shall enjoy entire security for their persons and property, and the free exercise of their religion; and efficient protection shall be given to missionaries who travel peaceably in the interior, furnished with passports as provided for in Article VIII. No hindrance shall be offered by the authorities of the Chinese Empire to the recognised right of every individual in China to embrace, if he so please, Christianity, and to follow its practices without being liable to any punishment therefor.'

Two years later, after the capture of Peking and the sacking of the Summer Palace by the allied forces, both England and France exacted supplementary Conventions, which were signed at Peking in 1860. Article VI. of the French Convention stipulated for the restoration to them of the religious and philanthropic establishments, the cemeteries, and other dependencies which had been confiscated during the persecutions. At this juncture and in this section of the treaty it was, that a French missionary, acting as interpreter for the French mission, introduced the following clause into the Chinese text, while the document was being transcribed:—

> 'It is, in addition, permitted to French missionaries to rent and purchase land in all the provinces and to erect buildings thereon at pleasure.'

Now by Article III. of the previous Treaty of Tienstin (1858) it had already been agreed that the French text should be considered the authoritative version; and therefore this clause, thus surreptitiously interpolated into the Chinese text only, and not to be found in the French text, was invalid *ab initio*. The Chinese, however, did not at once detect the fraud; and when they did, were either too proud or too fearful of the consequences to contest the point. The British Government professed its readiness to retire from a position which had no solid or legitimate foundation. But as the claim was consistently vindicated by the French, without serious protest from the Chinese, so the British tacitly acquired the right also; and to it is owing the privileged status which the missionaries now enjoy, and which is not shared by a single other class of their countrymen.

Though the Chinese did not repudiate the interpolated clause, there was nevertheless some dispute and correspondence thereupon; which culminated, in 1865, in an understanding between the Tsungli Yamen and the then French Minister as to the exact interpretation that was to be placed upon it. Among other things, it was agreed that property acquired by French missionaries in the interior should be registered in the name, not of individual missionaries or converts, but of the parent society. Other stipulations provided for due notice to the local authorities of the intention to acquire property, etc., in the interior.[1] As a matter of fact, these conditions are not always observed by the Protestant missionaries, much of the property acquired by them being

Subsequent understanding.

[1] In December 1894, M. Gérard, the French Minister at Peking, taking advantage of the recovered influence of France, hunted up the Berthemy Convention of 1865, and procured its formal ratification by the Tsungli Yamen, and its official circulation to the Provincial Governors.

registered and held in the name of converts, and made over by private agreement to the foreign missionary.

In the diplomatic complications arising out of the missionary massacres at Wuhu and Wuhsueh in 1891, the combined pressure of the foreign representatives, reinforced by gunboats, availed to extract from the Chinese Government an Imperial Edict, which was published in the *Peking Gazette* of June 13, 1891, and was ordered to be posted in the principal cities of the Empire— an order which, it is needless to add, the Provincial Governors, wherever they conveniently could, disobeyed. To this decree the Christian missionaries are now disposed to look as the charter of their liberties, confirming and to some extent superseding the text of the Treaties. After directing the civil and military authorities in the disturbed provinces to arrest and try the principal criminals, and to condemn the guilty to death, the Emperor proceeded with this general statement of the missionaries' rights :—

Imperial Edict of 1891.

'The right of foreign missionaries to promulgate their religions in China is provided for by Treaty and by Edicts which were previously issued; the authorities of all the provinces were commanded to afford them protection as circumstances required. . . . The religions of the West have for their object the inculcation of virtue, and though people become converts they still remain Chinese subjects, and continue to be amenable to the jurisdiction of the local authorities. There is no reason why there should not be harmony between the ordinary people and the adherents of foreign religions; and the whole trouble arises from lawless ruffians fabricating baseless stories and making an opportunity for creating disturbance. These bad characters exist everywhere. We command the Manchu Generals-in-Chief, the Viceroys and Governors in all the provinces, to issue proclamations clearly explaining to the people that they must on no account give a ready ear to such idle tales and wantonly cause trouble. Let all who post anonymous placards and spread false rumours, inflaming the minds of the people, be at once arrested and severely punished.

The local authorities are bound to afford due protection at all times to the persons and property of foreign merchants and foreign missionaries, and must not allow them to be injured or molested by evil characters. Should the precautionary measures be lacking in stringency, and trouble be the result, we command that the local authorities be severely denounced.'[1]

This decree may perhaps be said to cover and condone any previously existing flaw in the missionaries' position, and to lend a direct Imperial sanction to their presence and propaganda in the interior. Extracted as it was, however, by sheer compulsion from the Chinese Government, and in the main dictated by the foreign Ministers, it represents no spontaneous change of attitude on the part of the former; whilst it is to be feared that its practical influence will be very small.

Such is the history of the circumstances under which the Christian missionaries have gained a foothold in the interior of the Chinese Empire. If the Chinese, with their ingrained disposition to accept facts, have forgotten alike the duplicity of the foreigner and their own humiliation, nevertheless the presence of the missionaries is a testimony to the continued ascendency of an alien Power, still maintained, as it was originally introduced, by force. As such the Chinese, who dislike all foreigners, regard the missionaries in particular with an intense aversion, considering them the agents of a policy which has been and is forced upon them in opposition both to the interests of the Government, the sentiments of the *literati*, and the convictions of the people. A converse illustration, minus the stimulus of the *odium theologicum*, is supplied by the detestation with which the Chinese immigrant is himself elsewhere regarded by the white man, by the Australian in Sydney, or the American in San Francisco.

Chinese sentiments.

[1] *Parliamentary Blue Book*, China, No. 1, 1892.

Nor is this impression diminished by the attitude of the missionaries themselves, many of whom, though they buckle on their armour as the soldiers of Christ, remember only in times of peril that they are citizens of this or that empire or republic, and clamour for a gunboat with which to insure respect for the Gospel. To this too ready appeal to the physical sanction of a national flag there are many honourable exceptions—men who carry their lives in their hands, and uncomplainingly submit to indignities which they have undertaken to endure in a higher cause than that of their nationality. Nevertheless the presence of the missionary bodies as a whole in the country is a constant anxiety to the Legations, by whom in the last resort their interests, resting as they do upon treaties, must be defended; and is equally distasteful to the Chinese Government, which frequently finds itself called upon to reprimand a native official or to punish a local community at the cost of great odium to itself. This is the explanation of the extreme reluctance exhibited, as a rule, by the central authority in bringing to justice the notorious authors of calumny or outrage. The secret sympathies of the people are behind the malefactor; and the Government feels that it may be straining a bond of allegiance, which already, in the case of many of the outlying provinces, is stretched almost to the point of rupture.

The appeal for gun-boats.

In some districts the unpopularity of the missionaries has been increased by the special privileges which they are disposed to claim on behalf of native converts engaged in litigation or other disputes; and by their interference in the civil affairs of the neighbourhood in which they reside. Just as in Southern India many a native becomes a Christian in order to get

Privileges claimed for converts.

a situation as a servant or a clerk, so in China it not infrequently happens that a shady character will suddenly find salvation for the sake of the material advantages or protection which it may be expected to confer upon him.

But to the thoughtful Chinaman's eye, penetrating a little below the surface, the real political danger is more deeply rooted than any such superficial symptoms might appear to suggest. He sees in missionary enterprise the existence of an insidious *imperium in imperio*, of a secret society hostile to the commonwealth, of damage and detriment to the State. *An imperium in imperio.* He remembers that the most frightful visitation which China has suffered in modern times, the Taiping rebellion, by which over 20,000,000 of her people perished, was in its inception a Christian movement, led by an alleged Christian convert, and projected to Christianise his countrymen; and with these experiences before him he may well feel qualms at any signs of increasing missionary influence. In the case of the French missions, with whom as Roman Catholics I have not here been dealing, there is an additional ground for mistrust; for the Chinese see that the French Government is here engaged in forcing upon them the very men and the selfsame religion whom it has sought to expel from its own land—an act of duplicity which in their minds can only mask some dark political cabal.

It is sometimes said by missionary champions, that of the recurring outbreaks against them, the missionaries, though the victims, are commonly not the cause; the movement being in reality a deep-seated plot concocted by political malcontents to embroil either the provincial with the Imperial Government, or the latter with foreign Powers. *Plea of political agitation.* How far this is the case there exist few means of accurately determining. But the plea is believed, by those who know best, to be destitute of validity; though there are obvious reasons for its encouragement by the Tsungli Yamen, who can thereby plead internal disorder as an excuse for their own responsibility.

Finally, there are the practical charges brought against the work, arising partly from the missionaries' own conduct, partly from the gross superstitions of the people. Of the former character are the allegations that are so frequently made, not without apparent justification, about the *personnel* and surroundings of the missions, particularly in the Treaty Ports; about the lack of personal aptitudes, inseparable from a career that has already in some cases, especially in that of the American missionaries, come to be regarded as a profession; and about the well-appointed houses, the comfortable manner of living, the summer exodus to the hills, the domestic engrossments and large families, which, strange to say, are encouraged by a liberal subsidy from the parent society for each new arrival in the missionary nursery.

3. Practical. Mission life.

Another source of misunderstanding is the constantly increasing employment of women, and particularly of unmarried women, by the missionary bodies. A steamer rarely sails from the American shores for Yokohama without carrying a bevy of young girls, fresh from the schoolroom or the seminary, who, with the impulsive innocence of youth, are about to devote their young lives and energies to what they conceive to be the noblest of purposes in Japan or China. A scarcely inferior stream of female recruitment flows in from the United Kingdom and the Colonies.[1] Now I do not say that the

Employment of women.

---

[1] Of the 1300 Protestant missionaries in China in 1890, as many as 700, or more than half, were women; and of these 316 were unmarried women.

work of the female missionary is thrown away, or that there may not be cases in which her devotion reaps an ample harvest. Neither do I presume for one moment to question the honest self-sacrifice of the act; but I do say that in a country like China—where, on the one hand, very different notions of the emancipation of women prevail from those to which we are accustomed, and on the other hand an element of almost brutal coarseness enters largely into the composition of the native character—the institution of sisterhoods, planted alongside of male establishments, the spectacle of unmarried persons of both sexes residing and working together, both in public and in private, and of girls making long journeys into the interior without responsible escort, are sources of a misunderstanding at which the pure-minded may afford to scoff, but which in many cases has more to do with anti-missionary feeling in China than any amount of national hostility or doctrinal antagonism. In 1893, at the remote inland town of Kuei-hwa-cheng, a friend of mine encountered a missionary community consisting of one male and of twenty Swedish girls. The propaganda of the latter consisted in parading the streets and singing hymns to the strumming of tambourines and guitars. The society that that had committed the outrage of sending out these innocent girls only allowed them $200, or £27, 10s. a year apiece, for board, lodging, and clothing. As a consequence they were destitute of the smallest comforts of life, and could not even perform their toilette without the impertinent eyes of Chinamen being directed upon them through the paper screens. Can anything more futile than such an enterprise be conceived, or more culpable? The popular feeling against female missionaries was illustrated in the recent massacres at Kutien (August 1895), where out of ten persons that perished, eight were women.

To the same class of preventible sources of mischief belong the charges of arrogance and tactlessness that are sometimes levelled against the missionaries in their selections of sites for Churches or private dwellings. To the European an elevation or commanding site is always, both for picturesque and sanitary reasons, preferable to a lower position; while for purposes of privacy or protection, a high enclosure wall is superior to a low one. But to the Chinaman, with his extraordinary ideas about the *fengshui*, or Spirits of Air and Water, and his geomantic superstitions, a building in an elevated situation appears to have an effect like the ' evil eye,' and is a source of genuine suspicion and alarm; while anything appertaining to secrecy suggests to his depraved imagination the ambiguous character of Eleusinian mysteries. It is strange that missionaries of all sects and creeds seem to be quite unable to resist these easily surmounted temptations. At Tokio, in Japan, the most commanding edifice in the entire city is the Russian Cathedral that crowns one of its timbered heights. At Canton the twin towers of the French Gothic Cathedral, erected under circumstances that should bring a blush to every Christian's cheek, may be seen for miles across the level country. At Peking, one of the French Cathedrals, the Peitang, actually overlooked the sacrosanct enclosure of the Forbidden City; until at length, after prolonged negotiations, and the gift of a superior site elsewhere, the French authorities were persuaded, in 1885, to acquiesce in its removal.

Situation of buildings.

Another source of friction between the missionaries and the Chinese is the refusal of the native converts made by the former to contribute to the expenses of the numerous semi-religious festivals that form such an important factor in the social life of China. A certain quota is demanded from every Chinese family to-

Refusal of converts to subscribe.

wards these periodical ceremonies; and the more converts there are in the town or locality, the more the unconverted have to pay. The exemption of the Christian proselytes from claims of this kind has been more or less recognised by the Chinese Government; but no official sanction can avert the social ostracism that is the local penalty of refusal. The name of the defaulter is removed from the family register, and he is debarred from participating in all the advantages conferred by the institution of clan life in China.

Furthermore, the missionaries are universally credited by the people with a power of witchcraft, essentially similar in kind to the beliefs that used to prevail widely in England, and are still not altogether extirpated, Belief in witchcraft. as to the magical powers of individual persons, commonly old women, supposed to be in intimate alliance with the devil himself. If there is a drought, or a flood, or any sudden visitation in China, it is frequently attributed to missionary incantations. If sickness or death assails a house contiguous to the missionary's abode, it is equally ascribed to the malevolent influence of the foreigner.

More fantastic in appearance, but also more sinister in operation, are the abominable and disgusting charges that are freely brought against the missionaries by the *literati*—charges of gross personal immorality and Horrible charges. of kidnapping and mutilation of children, which, however monstrous and malevolent, are not the less, but the more serious, because they are firmly believed by the ignorant audiences to whom they are addressed. The mystery of the Feast of the Holy Sacrament, the privacy of the Confessional, may be to the Christian among the most idolised and sacred of his religious associations. The foul-minded Chinese critic sees in them only a hypocritical mask for indecency and wrong-doing. The hospitals and orphanages of the Christian societies have sometimes been recruited for with a not too judicious avidity by their philanthropic patrons; while they receive many miserable inmates whom an early death overtakes in the natural course of things. It is firmly believed by the masses in China that foundlings are taken in, and that sick women and children are enticed to these institutions to be murdered by the missionaries for the sake of the therapeutic or chemical properties attaching to their viscera, or eyes, or brains.

It must be remembered that in the Chinese pharmacopœia anthropophagous remedies are held in the highest esteem; and that particular parts of the human body, administered in powders or decoctions, are recommended as a sovereign remedy. A son who thus sacrifices some portion of his flesh for a sick parent, or a wife for an invalid husband, is regarded as having performed the most meritorious of acts, and is sometimes rewarded by the provincial Government with a *pailow*, or commemorative arch. The medicines distributed in the mission dispensary, the chemicals employed in the scientific processes, such as photography, to which the foreign magician is prone, have undoubtedly, in the eyes of the ignorant masses, been obtained by these methods. It was to such a belief that the famous Tientsin massacres in 1870, the Wuhsueh murders in 1891, and the Cheng-tu outrages in 1895, were mainly due; and when these horrible charges are reinforced by every variety of pamphlet and leaflet and filthy caricature and obscene lampoon, issued with the secret connivance of the local authority, as in the publications of the notorious Chow Han in 1891, in the province of Hunan, it may readily be conceived what a terrible and almost insurmountable weight of prejudice is excited. To intelligent persons all this may sound senseless and irrational enough; but again I am compelled to remind my readers that to this day there are many parts of Europe where precisely analogous superstitions prevail among the ignorant peasantry, against the Jews in particular; and that the last decade alone has witnessed a longer list of murders and outrages in Christian Europe, due to an almost identical cause, than has been contributed in the same period by the whole of pagan China.

Such, briefly summarised, is a list of the main drawbacks, or in some cases failings, by which the Protestant missionary movement in China is retarded. I refrain from indicating any personal acceptance of their truth, since it may be said that my opportunities for forming a trustworthy judgment have not, in spite of two visits to the country, been sufficient; but I state them as I have derived them orally from numerous resident authorities, as well as from the study of newspapers published in China, of official reports, and of the writings and speeches of the missionaries themselves.[1] I have no other desire than to enable my readers, firstly, to see that there are two sides to the missionary question, and secondly, before making up their own minds upon it, to form some idea of what those sides are.

Summing up.

Whatever the proportion of truth or falsehood in this presentment of the case, there seems, at least to my mind, to be small doubt that the cause of Christianity is not advancing in China with a rapidity in the least commensurate to the prodigious outlay of money, self-

Results.

[1] For the study of the question may be recommended, *The Anti-Foreign Riots in China in 1891*, republished from the *North China Herald* at Shanghai; The *Parliamentary Blue Books*, China No. 1, 1891; No. 2, 1892; a recent pamphlet by Mr. C. T. Gardner, of the British Consular Service in China; and above all, two excellent brochures entitled *Missionaries in China*, and *China and Christianity*, by Mr. A. Michie of Tientsin, an authority whose writings on all subjects connected with China are distinguished both by remarkable insight and great literary ability.

U

sacrifice, and human power. To many it appears to be receding. Such, of course, is not the impression that will be derived from missionary publications. But, if we accept their own figures, which in the year 1890 showed a total of 1300 Protestant missionaries (women included) and only 37,300 native converts,[1] or a fold of less than 30 to each shepherd, and a proportion of only one in every 10,000 of the Chinese population, it must be admitted that the surviving harvest after half a century's labour is not large.[2] Meanwhile the temper of the native peoples may be gathered from the incidents of contemporary history. During the short time that I was in the China Seas in 1892, three fresh cases were recorded of aggravated assault upon missionaries and their wives. Since then two unoffending Swedish missionaries have been brutally murdered at Sungpu. In the spring of 1895 occured the Szechuan riots at Cheng-tu and other places; and then in August ensued the ghastly atrocities, involving the murder of ten persons, at Kutien. This does not look as though the reign of peace had yet dawned.

Here, however, I am only concerned with the danger that a movement exposed, whether justly or unjustly, to these attacks must entail upon the general interests of foreign Powers in China. Those interests are not solely co-extensive

[1] The missionaries have explained that these are 'the inner circle of communicants' only. They claim that if 'the whole number of adherents be reckoned, including baptized persons who are not communicants, and bona fide candidates for baptism,' the total must be multiplied by at least three, perhaps by four. To a layman, however, these grades of proselytism are a little puzzling.

[2] A few years ago the Roman Catholics published the figures of their missions in China, which were as follows: Bishops 41, European priests 664, Native priests 559, Colleges 34, Convents 34, Native converts 1,092,818. Thus, for one-half the number of European missionaries, they have thirty times the number of disciples. On the other hand, they have the advantage of a much older establishment.

with the work of evangelisation. They embrace the entire field of international relationship upon which peoples meet and hold intercourse; and it should be the first object of diplomacy to remove from this arena, or at least to minimise upon its surface, all possible sources of complication. The Christian missions are in China; they were introduced there by ourselves; they were accepted or at least submitted to by the Chinese Government; there we have hitherto maintained them; there undoubtedly they will remain. However much the unfriendly critic might welcome their wholesale deportation, no such solution is practicable. So long as the Treaties are not rescinded, their obligation can neither be evaded by foreign Governments nor trampled on with impunity by the Chinese. Whether it was wise or not to introduce missionaries in the first place, China, having undertaken to protect their persons and to tolerate their faith, must fulfil her pledge, and cannot be permitted to combine a mere lip respect for the engagement with secret connivance at its violation. Still less must the idea be allowed to prevail that a mere money compensation will suffice to expiate any or every outrage. The exaction of blood-money is at the best but a poor form of diplomatic amends; but blood-money in return for the lives of innocent men, whose protection has been guaranteed by treaty, and who have been brutally done to death, is almost an aggravation of the offence. The Chinese themselves will be the last to feel surprise at an attitude of resolution on the part of the foreigner. Firmness is the only policy for which they entertain any respect. It would of course be best if, in all cases of outrage or crime, whether happening to an Englishman, a Frenchman, or an American, joint action were taken by all the Powers. Such united pressure it

The right policy. Respect for the Treaties.

would be almost impossible to resist. Unfortunately, international jealousies or differences render such a co-operation difficult of attainment; and the steps in that direction which were taken, at Lord Salisbury's initiative, after the murders of 1891, and which assumed the form of a collective note addressed by the Powers to the Tsungli Yamen, failed in their object, owing to the withdrawal of the United States from the concert. That the action of a single Power, if taken with sufficient evidence of earnestness, is capable of bringing the Chinese Government to its knees, has been shown by the rapidity with which, as these pages go to print (October 1895) Lord Salisbury's ultimatum in regard to the degradation of the late Viceroy of Szechuan, the proven author of the Cheng-tu riots, has been accepted, when backed up by the appearance of a British squadron in the Yangtse.

Nevertheless, while the primary canon of political action should be the adequate fulfilment of admitted obligations, statesmanship has other and supplementary duties to perform. It should aim at a cautious tightening of the reins, whereby the causes of offence may be abridged, the vagaries of indiscreet enthusiasm kept in check, and the political aspects of missionary enterprise contracted within the smallest possible dimensions. There are some who recommend that the missionaries should dispense with foreign protection altogether, and, proceeding without passports, should live as Chinese subjects under Chinese laws. Such a solution is probably more Quixotic than feasible, and might lead to worse disaster. A very strict revision, however, of the conditions of travel and residence in the interior is much to be desired. Some limitation ought to be placed upon the irresponsible vagrancy of European subjects over remote and fanatical parts of the

Stricter precautions.

Chinese dominions. Passports should be absolutely refused at the discretion of the Minister, exercised with regard to the character both of the locality and the applicant. When granted, they might specify the name of the province, district, or town to which, and to which only, the bearer is accredited. Already they give a general sketch of the route which he proposes to follow. Upon his arrival he might be compelled to report himself to the local magistracy, and to notify his future movements to the latter. Such a demand has, I believe, more than once been made by the Chinese Government, but has been steadily refused. The relations between the civil authorities and the Christians in matters pertaining to the acquisition and tenure of land should be clearly defined and assimilated as far as possible to native custom. The opening of all mission establishments to the inspection of Government officials is recommended by some as an antidote to the horrible prevalent superstitions. Of more avail would it be to curtail within the narrowest limits the institutions, such as orphanages and sisterhoods, that give currency to these odious beliefs. The employment of hundreds of young unmarried foreign girls in various branches of missionary work, though the most popular current phase of the movement, is greatly to be deprecated, as giving rise to the very pardonable misinterpretations of which I have spoken; and ought to be curtailed by educated opinion at home.

In the last resort more will depend upon the character and conduct of the missionaries themselves than upon the checks devised by even a friendly diplomacy. Impulsive virtue and raw enthusiasm are not necessarily the best credentials for a missionary career. The sensational appeal from the platform of Exeter Hall, and the despatch of the heterogeneous company that

Choice of material.

respond to the summons, like a draft of young volunteer recruits to the theatre of war, are fraught with infinite danger. It behoves the parent societies, both in Great Britain and America, by a more careful choice of the men whom they send forth, and the emissaries themselves, by an anxious regulation of their own conduct, to anticipate and, if it may be, to avert the danger which, under existing conditions, confronts alike the interests of the country under whose flag they march, and the sublime cause to which they have devoted their lives.

CHAPTER X

THE SO-CALLED AWAKENING OF CHINA

Idem semper erit, quoniam semper fuit idem.
Non alium videre patres aliumve nepotes
Aspicient. Deus est qui non mutatur in ævo.
MANILIUS: *Astron*. i. 528-530.

SEVEN years ago the Western, and I dare say the Eastern world also, in so far as it was made aware of the fact, was startled by the appearance in the pages of an English magazine of an article purporting to have been written by the foremost Chinaman then living, a tried statesman and a successful ambassador, in which, with a skilfulness that was to be expected of his abilities, and with an emancipation of sentiment that was surprising in his nationality, he advanced the propositions that China had at length been aroused from her age-long sleep, and, with the same energy with which she had for so many centuries pursued and idealised the immobile, was about to enter into the turbulent competition of modern progress.[1] Possibly the Marquis Tseng, assuming that he wrote the article —which I believe that there is good reason for doubting—may have believed in his own assurances; unquestionably they proved palatable to the large class of European readers who cannot conceive of any standard of life, either for an individual or a nation, except that which prevails in the country of which they themselves are citizens, who bisect mankind into two

Is China awake?

[1] 'China, the Sleep and the Awakening,' by the Marquis Tseng. *Asiatic Quarterly Review*, January 1887.

camps, the civilised and the barbarian, and hold it to be both the destiny and the duty of the latter to wear the former's gyves. Had China at last, the most arrogant of the rebels, the most formidable of the barbarians, been driven to capitulate? Was the Celestial about to sit, a chastened convert, at the feet of Western doctors? So blessed a proclamation had not for long been spread abroad upon the earth; and loud were the Hosannas that went up from chapel and conventicle, from platform and pulpit and press, at these glad tidings of great joy. It may be worth our while, who are neither, like the Marquis Tseng, diplomats whose interest it is to conciliate, nor prophets who are ahead of our times, to examine how far it is true that China has really awakened from her ancestral sleep, or whether she may not merely have risen to stop the rattling of a window-sash, or the creaking of a shutter, that interferes with her quietude, with the fixed intention of settling down once more to the enjoyment of an unabashed repose.

For now more than fifty years has the combined force of the Western nations, exercised commonly by diplomacy, frequently by threats, and sometimes by open war, been directed against that immense and solid wall of conservative resistance, like the city walls of their own capital, which the Chinese oppose to any pressure from the outside. In parts an opening has been effected by the superior strength of the foreigner, backed up by gunboats or cannon. Of such a character are the concessions as regards missionaries and trade, which fall more properly under the heading of China's external than of her internal relations, and, as such, have been dealt with in the previous chapter. In what respects, however, may she be said to have yielded, or to be even now abating her stubborn opposition, in deference to no exterior compulsion,

A tactical surrender.

but of her own free will? The answer, whether we look at the introduction of the electric telegraph and railways, at the adoption of foreign mechanical appliances in arsenals, dockyards, and workshops, at the institution of a native press, at the development of internal resources, or at the encouragement of domestic enterprise — the familiar first lessons of the West to the East—will teach us that it is with no lighthearted or spontaneous step, but from the keenest instincts of self-preservation alone, that China has descended from her pinnacle of supercilious self-sufficiency, and has consented to graduate in Western academies. One might think that in the contemplation of the magnificent wharves and streets and buildings of Shanghai, which worthily claims to be the Calcutta of the Far East; of the spacious and orderly foreign settlement of Tientsin, contrasted with the filth of the native city adjoining; or of the crowded dockyards and shipping of Hongkong—the Chinese would have found at once a reproach to their own backwardness and a stimulus to competition. It is doubtful whether any such impression has ever been produced upon the Celestial mind. What suits the foreigner's taste is not necessarily required by his. If the foreigner prefers to be comfortable, he is content to be squalid. If space and grandeur are essential to the one, they have for centuries been dispensed with, and are, therefore, not necessary to the other. Were it not that experience has shown beyond possibility of cavil that, in the struggle with the foreigner to which the march of events has committed her, China is herself handicapped by the absence of those appliances which have rendered her antagonists so formidable, she would not have made the smallest concession to a pressure which she still despises, even while yielding to it. In a word, her surrender is the offspring, not of admiration, but of fear. It is based upon expediency, not upon conviction.

No more striking illustration of this thesis can be furnished than the enterprise which will seem to the superficial observer the evidence of its very opposite, viz. the introduction of railways into China. When I first visited the Chinese Empire in 1887, there was not a mile of railroad in the country. The little abortive railway from Woosung to Shanghai, which had been constructed in 1876 by English merchants, and had been compulsorily acquired and torn up by the provincial authorities in 1877, was only a memory and a warning. Now, however, the stranger can travel in an English-built carriage upon English steel rails from the station of Tongku, near the Taku forts at the mouth of the Peiho River, over the 27 miles that separate him from Tientsin; while from Tongku the main line is already prolonged for 67 miles to the Tungshan and Kaiping coalfields, and thence as far as Shan-hai-kuan, at the seaward terminus of the Great Wall, in the direction of Manchuria beyond.

Railways in China.

The reason of these several extensions has been as follows: Of the first (which was begun in 1887), the alarm produced by the French war in 1884; of the second, the necessity, in the event of a future campaign, of possessing native coalfields, instead of being dependent upon foreign supply—as well as the interests of a speculation in which the Viceroy Li Hung Chang is personally concerned; of the third, the fear of Russian aggression on the north;—self-interest or apprehension having been, therefore, in each case the motive power. In other words, the introduction of these railways has been a compulsory operation, not undertaken of free will or inclination, but forced from the outside. At one period the works were stopped by

Manchurian Railway.

the resurgence of old-fashioned and superstitious ideas,[1] and by the weight of Palace intrigue. But the influence of Li Hung Chang has triumphed; and the line, though nominally mercantile in its inception, has now become in reality a strategical railway, which before the war was being steadily pushed forward in the direction of Kirin. Its total length will then be just short of 650 miles. The first 94 miles were constructed by a company, the China Railway Company; the remainder is a State railway. But inasmuch as both undertakings are controlled by the Viceroy, and as the former is in no sense a commercial speculation, the shareholders being all officials, and no accounts being published, the entire project may be considered as one scheme. At the rate of advance before the war, 40 or 50 miles were being laid yearly, a sum of £400,000 being allocated for the purpose. This left a gap of several years before Kirin was expected to be reached; but it was calculated that, owing to the paucity of physical obstacles, and the ability of the Chinese navvies in throwing up earthworks, the whole line could, at a pinch, be completed in two years. In 1894, however, progress was for a while suspended, in order that the funds so released might be devoted to the celebrations of the sixtieth birthday of the Empress-Dowager—a proceeding profoundly Chinese. Before these could take place the war-cloud burst upon China; and railroad-construction went the way of every other Chinese undertaking. Had the line been pushed forward without interruption before the outbreak of hostilities, it is conceivable that Port Arthur might

[1] When it was announced that a branch line was to be constructed from Moukden to Newchwang, the Tartar General of the former place, who did not want it at all, consulted the geomancers, who reported that the vertebræ of the dragon encircling the holy city of Moukden would infallibly be sundered by driving the long nails of the railway sleepers into them. Accordingly, he advocated the removal of the line from Moukden. The spinal cord of the dragon was ultimately secured by shifting the rails a few hundred yards.

have been saved. Branch lines were contemplated in the original scheme from Moukden to the Treaty Port of Newchwang, a distance of 110 miles; and from Newchwang to the naval dockyard of Port Arthur, both strategical in design. The entire scheme, in fact, was China's reply to the Trans-Siberian Railway of Russia to Vladivostok—the prodigious effect of which upon the future of Asia, at present but scantily realised in this country, was clearly appreciated by a few Chinese statesmen—and was a warning to the Tsar that China does not mean to let Manchuria and the Sungari River slip from her grasp quite as easily as she did the Amur and Ussuri channels, and the provinces upon their northern and eastern banks. The circumstances have been changed by the clever and resolute diplomacy of Russia since the war; and few persons would be surprised if the price that China is now called upon to pay included some concession affecting the alignment or completion of that very Siberian railway, which will ultimately seal her doom.

It was originally contemplated to run a line from Tientsin to Tungchow, the river port thirteen miles distant from Peking—a project which would have been of great service both to the Chinese inhabitants of the capital, who find the prices of the necessaries of life swollen to exorbitant figures by the difficulty of communications in winter, and to the Europeans who, by the same conditions, are cut off for months every year from the outer world. But Chinese conservatism could not stomach any such affront to the footstool of Royalty, while the argument that a railroad to the capital would only avail to transport an invader all the more quickly is one that possessed peculiar fascination for Celestial ears. Accordingly, the direct connection of Peking with the coast will probably be postponed for some time longer, although I entertain no

Line to Peking.

doubt that it will ultimately be accomplished. Many more foreigners will then visit the Chinese capital, hotels will spring up, and the curio-dealers will rejoice. In practice the familiar objection to railways in China that they will offend the *fengshui*, or Spirit Powers, and disturb the repose of the dead, is found to be less serious than the contention, which there is no school of political economy in China to controvert, that the displacement of labour caused thereby will throw so many hundreds or thousands of coolies or junkmen or cartmen out of employment. This is a line of reasoning that has already been successfully employed for years to resist the opening of the Upper Yangtse to steam navigation, and that will be repeated *ad nauseam* against every proposal for railway extension for many years to come.

There are of course statesmen in China who, like Li Hung Chang, are superior to the fallacies or the superstitions of their countrymen. It will be remembered that a few years ago the Emperor, or rather the Empress-Dowager, who was still Regent, issued an interrogation to the principal provincial Governors and Governors-General, inviting their counsel upon the subject of railway extension in the Empire. Their replies, which were published, contained several expressions of very sensible opinion. One Governor recommended not merely the Manchurian Railway, but a second line in a north-westerly direction through Shansi and Kansu to Ili, and a third as far as remote Kashgar, assigning these reasons :—

Great Trunk Line.

'We shall thereby be able to send troops, money, etc., anywhere in our Empire within ten days ; and morover, we shall be able to found prosperous colonies in those outlying regions of people who in China proper are only a starving proletariat, and a source of trouble to the Government, but who, once transplanted thither, will be able to find a fruitful field for their now unemployed labour, and will turn the desert into a garden.'

But the most stalwart of these advocates was the celebrated Chang Chih Tung, Viceroy of the Two Kuangs,[1] who pressed for the construction of a great Trunk Railway connecting Peking with Hankow, to be commenced simultaneously at both ends. Not the most conservative of Chinamen could deny that such a line at least was sufficiently removed from the coast to be of little assistance to an invader. In 1889 appeared an Imperial Proclamation authorising the execution of this only half-considered scheme, and Chang Chih Tung was sent as Viceroy to Hankow to carry it out. Subsequent reflection appears to have convinced him that it must not be undertaken except with Chinese capital, and with steel rails manufactured in Chinese furnaces from Chinese metal—a decision which looks very much like a postponement to the Greek Kalends. Until the Chinese have realised that they are incapable of constructing a great line except by foreign assistance, and (unless they are prepared to pledge the Imperial Exchequer to the undertaking) to some extent by foreign capital, it is safe to predict that the great Hankow-Peking egg will never be hatched at all.

In the meantime the Viceroy, until his recent promotion to Nanking, continued energetically to pursue the first part of his curtailed scheme by erecting iron and steel works and a great rolling-mill (in addition to already existing cotton, brick, and tile factories in the neighbourhood) at Hanyang, near Hankow, while he could flatter himself that he had a railway all his own in the shape of a short line of the standard gauge, seventeen

Hankow Line and factories.

---

[1] In the course of the war with Japan, Chang Chih Tung was made Viceroy of the Hu Provinces, and afterwards of Nanking.

miles long, which he had constructed from Shih-hin-yao on the banks of the Yangtse, seventy miles below Hankow, to the iron mines of Tienshan-pu, whence the ore was to be derived. Branch lines were also contemplated to the neighbouring collieries of Wang-san-shih and Ma-an-shan. In Wuchang a laboratory was established in 1891 for the analysis of the various local minerals. Additional ironworks are now being constructed by the indefatigable Viceroy at his new seat of Government, to assist those of Hanyang in carrying out his pet scheme and supplying material for the Great Trunk Railway of the future. Simultaneously, but even more leisurely, the second part of the scheme is being advanced by the despatch of a number of Chinese to Europe, to acquire the necessary mechanical and engineering experience. These are the resorts, cumbersome, dilatory, and infinitely costly, to which China is impelled by an imperishable confidence in herself and a corresponding dislike of external assistance.

The only other railway in the Chinese dominions in 1892 was a line in the north of the island of Formosa, originally commenced with the torn-up Woosung rails, by one of the most enterprising of Chinese statesmen, Liu Ming Chuan, who, having gained great credit for his skilful defence of Kelung against the French fleet, under Admiral Courbet, in 1884, was reported in 1894, in consequence of scares upon the Pamirs, to be about to proceed as military commander to Chinese Turkestan. The idea of the Formosa Railway was to connect the port of Kelung, on the north-east coast of the island, with that of Tainan on the west. About fifty miles of this railroad have been laid by the Chinese; and it now remains for the victors in the recent war to enter into the fruition of their predecessors' labours.

Formosa Railway.

Since the conclusion of peace, railways have been, so to speak, 'in the air'; and all manner of schemes have been reported as having been sanctioned by the Emperor and as being on the brink of execution. Of these the line from Tientsin to Peking is said to be the first that will be undertaken. Railroad extension is indeed the single respect in which China seems at all likely to show that the rhinoceros-hide of her complacency has been so much as pricked by the goad of recent calamity.

<small>New schemes.</small>

This short sketch of the inception of railroad enterprise in China will, however, have proved that whilst the advice of a prominent statesman here, or the influence of an energetic governor there, or the momentary warning of military disaster, may result in the commencement of isolated undertakings, which are recommended by particular exigencies of policy or speculation, the Chinese Government is far from having realised the overwhelming importance, not merely to the economic and industrial development, but to the continued national existence of the Empire, of a wide-reaching and promptly executed system of railways. The prediction may safely be hazarded that, without railroads, Manchuria, Chinese Turkestan, and Western Mongolia, as well as other outlying parts of the Empire, cannot be permanently held. There is not the slightest good in manufacturing Krupp, and Hotchkiss, and Gatling, and Winchester, and Martini-Henry implements of war by the thousand, if there exist no means of conveying the troops who are to use them to the scene of action. In railroads and telegraphs (the latter were stoutly resisted at the start by the provincial governors because of the restraints which would thereby be placed upon their independence) lies the sole hope that China still possesses of retaining her territorial integrity. And yet, so

<small>Other communications.</small>

THE SO-CALLED AWAKENING OF CHINA 321

perversely ignorant has the Government always been of this elementary axiom, that communications of any kind have been treated by it with undeviating neglect. The military reliefs have been compelled to trudge to their stations over thousands of miles of execrable track. Even the few military roads that have been constructed near the coast have been allowed to fall out of repair. Simultaneously, with the most magnificent rivers in Asia running through her territories, and inviting cheap and rapid communication with the populous cities of the interior, it is only, so to speak, at the bayonet's point that assent can be gained to the extension of river navigation by steam; and whole populations must be starved in order that small communities of boatmen or raftmen may live.

Similar reflections are suggested by an examination of the military equipment and resources of China, which, until the pitiless exposure of the war, formed the subject of much premature congratulation. It is true that, particularly since the French war in 1884-85, which, in spite of the comparative failure of the French, and the pretensions to victory that have since been advanced by the Chinese, yet taught the latter a great many well-needed lessons, millions have been spent in providing the Empire with the mechanical appliances that shall enable it successfully to resist the foreigner. At Kirin, Tientsin, Shanghai, Nanking, Foochow, and Canton, are factories or arsenals, capable of turning out gunpowder, cartridges, repeating rifles, field and mountain artillery, projectiles, and machine guns of the most approved and recent pattern. The majority, if not all of these, were established in the first place, and for a long time supervised, by foreigners. It is true also that a military school for officers has been founded at Peking, and schools of gunnery,

Military reform.

musketry, and engineering, under the patronage of Li Hung
Chang, at Tientsin. Simultaneously, a large number of
foreign officers or instructors, principally Germans, have been
engaged to instruct the Chinese in the manufacture or use
of these scientific appliances. Thus equipped, the Chinese
Army is on paper a force not merely numerically strong, but
mechanically powerful. A more minute and searching
scrutiny, however, is needed before we can accept these
exterior symptoms as irrefutable evidence of a reformed
military system. Let me briefly examine both the constitution of the Army as a whole, and the opinions that
have been entertained of its efficiency by competent
observers.[1]

The military organisation of China is little less antique
and no less rigid than its civil counterpart. It has not
varied since the Manchu invasion 250 years ago.

The Man-
chu and
National
Armies.

The descendants of the conquerors, with a certain
admixture of Mongolians and Chinese, still form
the Army of the Eight Banners,[2] from which the
garrisons of Peking and other great provincial capitals are
drawn; constituting a sort of hereditary profession or caste
maintained at the expense of the Crown, and, like the
Roman legionaries in the outlying provinces of the Empire,
owning military lands. The nominal strength of the Eight
Banners is variously returned as from 230,000 to 330,000
men; but of these considerably less than 100,000, perhaps
not 80,000, are in any sense of the term upon a war footing.

[1] I am indebted for some portions of the following information to the
courtesy of Baron Speck von Sternburg, Secretary to the German Legation
at Peking, who has made a close personal study of the military resources of
China.

[2] Strictly speaking, the Eight Banners are subdivided, ethnologically, into
three groups of eight corps each—Manchus, Mongols, and Chinese, the two
latter being descendants of the troops which took part in or assisted the
Manchu invasion. Intermarriage is compulsory among the twenty-four
Banner Corps.

THE SO-CALLED AWAKENING OF CHINA 323

The best of them, amounting to an army corps 37,000 strong, are stationed in Manchuria itself, where, face to face with the dreaded enemy, Russia, large garrisons are maintained at Moukden, Kirin, and along the Ussuri. The Imperial Guard in Peking, which is drawn from the Banner Army, consists of eight regiments, or 4000 to 6000 men. Side by side with them is the Ying Ping, or national Army, called in contradistinction the Green Flags, or Five Camps (five being the unit of subdivision), and constituting a territorial army, frequently designated as 'Braves.' Of this army there are eighteen corps, one for each province of the Empire, under the orders of the local Governor or Governor-General. Their nominal strength is given by different authorities as between 540,000 and 660,000 men,[1] of whom from 170,000 to 250,000 are variously reported to be available for war. The National Army is in fact better described as a militia, about one-third of whom are usually called out, and the whole of whom are never organised, and are probably incapable of being organised, for war. To this force must be added the mercenary troops, raised in emergencies, and dating from the time of the Taiping Rebellion; and some irregulars, consisting of Mongolian and other cavalry, nominally 200,000 in number, in reality less than 20,000, and of no military value. The only serious or formidable contingent of the National Army is the Tientsin army corps, called Lien Chun, or drilled troops, which was first started with European officers after the war of 1860, and acquired its cohesion in the suppression of the Taiping Rebellion, since which it has been maintained in a state of comparative efficiency by the Viceroy Li Hung Chang, its organisation and instruction being based on the Prussian model. Nominally this division is 100,000 strong, but its mobilised

[1] The Chinese Army List gives 651,667 men and 7157 officers.

strength is not more than 35,000, or a full army corps, which is employed to garrison the Taku and Peitang Forts, the city of Tientsin, and Port Arthur. It is sometimes called the Black Flag Army, and is equipped with modern firearms, breech-loading Krupp guns, and Snider, Hotchkiss, Remington, and Mauser rifles. The pay is also superior to that of the Banner Army; for whereas in the latter a cavalry soldier receives only 10s. a month and forage allowance, and the foot soldier 7s. a month and rations, the Tientsin private receives 15s. a month. If any real business requires to be done in the metropolitan province or neighbourhood, it is to the Tientsin contingent that recourse is made. This is the total land army of China—on a peace footing not more than 300,000, on a war footing about 1,000,000 men—that is called upon to garrison and defend an Empire whose area is one-third of the whole of Asia and half as large again as Europe, and whose population is half of the total of Asia and equivalent to the whole of Europe.

So much for the men, numerically considered. It is when we approach the question of their discipline, training,

Discipline. and *personnel*, still more when we examine their officers and leading, that the true value of the Chinese army emerges. The Chinaman has many excellent qualities as a soldier, viz. a splendid physique, natural docility and sobriety, considerable intelligence, and great powers of endurance. The sum total of these acquirements does not, however, necessarily make a first-rate fighting-machine. Indifference to death is by no means identical with real bravery; animal ferocity is a very different thing from moral courage. Of discipline in the highest sense the Chinese have none; and no arms in the world, shuffled out from the arsenal upon the declaration of war, like cards from a pack, and placed in untrained hands, can make them follow leaders who are nincompoops, or resist an enemy whose tactics, except when it comes to getting behind a mud rampart themselves (and not always then, as was shown by the experience of Asan [or Yashan] and Ping-yang in September 1894), they do not understand. They have no idea of marching or skirmishing, or of bayonet or musketry practice. The only recruiting test is the lifting to the full stretch of the arms above the head of an iron bar, from the ends of which are hung two stones, weighing 9½ stone the pair. Their drill is a sort of gymnastic performance, and their ordinary weapons are tufted lances, spears, battle-axes, tridents, and bows and arrows, with an ample accompaniment of banners and gongs. Rifles of obsolete pattern, bought second-hand or third-hand in Europe, are dealt out to those who are on active service. These and their ammunition are mostly worthless from age. The weapon of the majority is, however, an ancient matchlock, of which the most familiar pattern is the *jingal*, which requires two men to fire it. On almost any day in Peking the Manchu garrison may be seen engaged in archery practice under the walls, or shooting with the same weapon, while at full gallop, at a straw doll stuck up in a ditch. In war there is no unity, either of administration or armament. There is no organised transport service or commissariat column. A medical or ambulance service is also unknown. In the fighting against the French in Tongking the men of the same regiment had different rifles, and an even larger confusion of cartridges. To a Chinaman all cartridges are alike; and what with those that were too large and those that were too small, and those that jammed and could not be extracted, it may be judged what amount of success attended the firing. In the recent war with Japan it was the provision of faulty, or obsolete, or worthless ammunition, and in some cases the total lack of it altogether, that decided the fate of the majority of the combats, almost before they had begun.

All these drawbacks or delinquencies, however, shrink into nothingness when compared with the crowning handicap of the native officer. In many parts of Asia I have had occasion to observe and to comment upon the strange theory of the science of war (confined apparently to the East), which regard the *personnel* of an army as wholly independent of its leading. In China there is a special reason for this phenomenon. There, where all distinction is identified with familiarity with the classics, and depends upon success in a competitive examination, the military profession, which requires no such training, is looked upon with contempt, and attracts only inferior men. In the bulk of the army (I except the Tientsin army corps) an officer still only requires to qualify by passing a standard in archery, in fencing with swords, and in certain gymnastic exercises. To the same deeply embedded fallacy must be attributed the collateral opinion that a civilian must be much better fitted to command a battalion than a military man, because he is supposed in the course of his studies to have read something of the art of war. And when we examine what this art, in its literary presentation, is, we find that the standard military works in China are some 3000 years old; and that the authority in highest repute, Sun-tse by name, solemnly recommends such manœuvres as these: 'Spread in the camp of the enemy voluptuous musical airs, so as to soften his heart'—a dictum which might have commended itself to Plato, but would hardly satisfy Von Moltke. The British army could not be worse, nay, it would be far better led, were the Commander-in-Chief compelled to be a Senior Wrangler, and the Generals of division drawn from Senior Classics.

It cannot be considered surprising that the Chinese officers, so recruited and thus taught, destitute of the slenderest elements, either of military knowledge or scientific training, should earn the contempt of their followers. Their posts are usually acquired either by favouritism or purchase. When it is added that they are also, as a rule, both corrupt and cowardly; that they stint the men's rations and pilfer their pay; and that when an engagement takes place they commonly misdirect it from a sedan-chair in the rear, we have the best of reasons for expecting uniform and systematic disaster. The General officer is seldom (there have, of course, been remarkable exceptions) any better than his subordinate; in warfare there is no single moving spirit or plan of campaign; and on the field of battle each commander acts with irresponsible light-heartedness for himself, and yearns for the inglorious security of the rear.

It may, however, be thought that in the occasional employment of European officers some sort of guarantee is provided against the universal prevalence of this huge scandal. It is with no such intention that China hires the brain or the experience of the foreigner. She is ready enough to enlist and to pay for them, perhaps at a high rate, in the initial stages of a policy of military or naval reconstruction; but she is too jealous to give him the power or the chance to which he is entitled; and, like a sucked orange, she throws him away as soon as she has drained him dry. In such a manner has she treated both the English officer, Captain Lang, who provided her with the nucleus of a powerful reorganised fleet, and the German officer, Captain von Hanneken, who has for years been engaged in fortifying her coasts and reconstituting her arsenals. She *kowtows* to the foreigner as long as she has something to gain from him; but her inordinate conceit presently reasserts itself, and a Chinaman is appointed to continue, one might rather say to take to pieces, the laborious efforts of his predecessor. In the recent war, while the Chinese Government looked askance upon any European assistance in the opening stages, a point was soon reached at which they were willing to pay exorbitant sums for any such aid, and to appoint to important posts almost any foreigner who could train a gun, or help to handle a ship.

To these details must be added the fact that the annual military expenditure, or perhaps I should rather say waste, of China, is estimated at between £15,000,000 and £20,000,000.

Cost.

But it may be said, is it not the case that on several occasions during the last thirty years, *e.g.* in the suppression of the Mohammedan revolt in Yunnan, in the recovery of Kashgar, and in the Franco-Chinese war, China showed a military capacity which would render her anywhere a formidable adversary? Such, not unnaturally, is her own conclusion. But there are qualifying considerations that must be borne in mind. The Mussulman uprising, it is true, was quelled, but this was mainly due to the deplorable tactics of the insurgents. Eastern Turkestan was won back; but only because, after Yakub Beg had been got rid of by treachery and poison, the life and soul of the rebellion were extinct. In the French war, which is claimed as a victory by both parties, the Chinese pride themselves greatly on having successfully resisted the ridiculous French demands for an indemnity of £10,000,000, on having repulsed the attack on Formosa, and on having made peace after Langson, *i.e.* in the hour of temporary triumph. Every one knows, however, that had China been able to continue the struggle, she would

Alleged successes.

have done so; and that she eagerly seized the opportunity
for coming to terms. The French committed every conceivable blunder. Instead of striking at Peking, which is
the only way to bring the Chinese Government quickly to
its knees (a fact which was very early apprehended by
Japan), they conducted a foolish campaign in Tongking,
under a deadly climate, with a vastly inferior force, and in
a country utterly unsuited to European warfare, namely,
rice-fields intersected with canals, or hills covered with
dense covert. The campaign afforded little or no criterion
of the newly equipped and foreign-drilled armaments of
China; for these can hardly be said to have been engaged.
Had the Chinese Army really been worth what is claimed
for it, the French would scarcely now be comfortably
installed in the Red River delta.

Let me fortify my opinion, however—which must in
itself be valueless—of the Chinese army, by citing the
verdict of three European officers, probably better
qualified from their peculiar experience to judge
than any three other men during the last quarter
of a century. I do not know that even their opinion is
necessary at this date, ratified as it has been by the
overwhelming testimony of the war with Japan. But
inasmuch as these pages were originally written before
that war had broken out, it may not be inopportune to
reproduce the various grounds upon which I had been led
to the conclusion that in any conflict with a considerable
Power, China must inevitably suffer defeat. When war
was on the eve of breaking out between Russia and China
in 1880, over the affair of Kulja, the late General Gordon
was invited to Peking to give his advice to the Imperial
Government. In a characteristic and outspoken memorandum to his old fellow-officer, the Viceroy Li, he exposed

General Gordon's opinion.

the utter rottenness of the Chinese military organisation, and strongly advised them to give up playing the game of scientific warfare with foreigners, in which they were sure to be beaten, and to adhere to the traditional irregular warfare for which their aptitudes especially fitted them. Skirmishes as against battles, breech-loading rifles as against big guns, this was his motto of advice.[1]

The late General Prjevalski, the famous Russian explorer, who spent many years of his life on the confines of the Chinese Empire, and made a profound study of its military resources, thus summed up, only six years ago, a long and interesting essay upon the Celestial Army :—

General Prjevalski.

'China, under its present conditions, and for many a long day, cannot possibly hope to create an army at all similar to those of European States. She lacks both the material and the spirit. Let Europeans supply the Chinese with as many arms as they please, let them strive to train the Chinese soldiers, let them even supply leaders—and the Chinese army will nevertheless never be more than an artificially created, mechanically united, unstable organism. Subject it but once to the serious trial of war, and speedy dissolution will overtake it.'

Thirdly, I quote the opinion of Colonel Mark Bell, V.C., one of the greatest, though the most modest, of living English travellers, who, after covering the prodigious journey, 3500 miles in length, from Peking to Kashgar, thus summed up his impressions of the Chinese army :—

Colonel Bell.

'A study of China's interests, position, and material strength, all along her Russian border, whether in Kashgaria, or Mongolia, or Manchuria, has led me to conclude that she has no military strength, and must be valueless to us as a military ally during the next several decades.'

[1] This Memorandum is reproduced in A. G. Hake's *Story of Chinese Gordon*, p. 379. London, 1884.

Statistics differed as to the exact strength of the Chinese Navy before the war, and were hardly required afterwards in consequence of its almost complete obliteration; but its history and equipment afford an almost precise parallel to those of the Army. Just as the disasters of the war of 1860 heralded the summons of European officers to Peking, and a complete scheme of military reorganisation, so does the modern Chinese Navy date from the same epoch and events. In 1862, Mr. H. N. Lay, who had been appointed Inspector of the Imperial Customs at Shanghai before the war, was entrusted with the commission to purchase a fleet of small gunboats in England. Nominally these vessels were to be employed for the protection of the Treaty Ports and the suppression of piracy. They were really intended for use against the rebels who had not yet been subdued. Seven gunboats and one storeship were bought in England and taken out. But upon their arrival a dispute arose between Mr. Lay and Captain Sherard Osborn (who had been offered the command) on the one hand, and the Chinese authorities on the other, as to the appointment of a Chinese colleague, and as to the source whether provincial or Imperial, from which orders were to be received. So long was the squabble protracted that the ships were never used at all, and were finally sent back to Bombay, where they were sold at a loss of half a million sterling, Mr. Lay having in the meantime left the Chinese service. This unfortunate misunderstanding greatly retarded the naval advance of China, and was thus alluded to, twenty-five years later, by the Marquis Tseng :—

The Chinese Navy.

'Twice since 1860 China has had to lament this as a national misfortune, for twice since then she has had to submit to occupations of her territory, which the development of that fleet would have rendered difficult, if not impossible.'

Since those days, however, and more particularly since the war with France, China has bestirred herself in the matter of naval equipment. The first result of the French war was the addition, in 1885, of a Ministry for the Navy, or Board of Admiralty, to the seven existing administrative departments. At Foochow, Port Li, Tientsin, Wei Hai Wei, Canton, Shanghai, and Port Arthur (Lu Shun Kou),[1] have been established powerful arsenals or dockyards, the last-named place being the naval base of defence for Peking. Four naval colleges for the education of cadets have been started at Wei Hai Wei, Tientsin, Whampoa, and Nanking. There is a torpedo-school under a German at Canton. Sir W. Armstrong at Elswick has built for them fast cruisers; Herr Krupp at Essen has turned out the best ironclads. The total Chinese fleet, divided into four squadrons, the Pei-yang, or north coast squadron, and the fleets of Foochow, Shanghai (called the Nanyang squadron), and Canton, comprised at the outbreak of hostilities about 65 vessels of war, mostly built abroad, and including 4 ironclads, 16 cruisers, and 17 gun-boats, as well as over 30 torpedo-boats, and 6 floating batteries. The tonnage of the combined fleets was about 65,000 tons, the armament 490 guns, and the complement of men 7000. The usual experiment of a European commander had been tried, with the usual result, expulsion. The

[1] The dockyard at Port Arthur, now the principal naval station of the Empire, was only commenced in 1887, the French, in virtue of a clause in their Treaty of 1885, having secured the contract. It was completed in 1890, and defended by heavily armed forts, with a garrison of 7000 men and 13 torpedo boats. When the Japanese took it by storm in November 1894, the Chinese seem to have practically ignored the land defences, which should have been impregnable, and to have allowed themselves to be caught in a trap. After the war Port Arthur remained in the occupation of the Japanese, who proposed to retain it along with the Liao-tung Peninsula, on which it is situated. It formed, however, that portion of the plunder which they were compelled by the new Triple Alliance, France, Russia, and Germany, to disgorge.

fleet was officered and manned by Chinese, foreigners being retained only for instruction in gunnery, electricity, torpedo-practice, etc. No doubt this fleet, like the army, was, on paper, a fighting force of no mean capacity. But, as I wrote in my first edition, with an anticipation that, substituting only the word Japanese for European, was strictly prophetic, the question was, whether under native commanders it was not likely to prove a greater source of weakness than of strength, and by falling a prey to the first European force that seriously engaged it, to lend no inconsiderable increment of strength to the latter. A further element of weakness in the Chinese Navy is the total lack of administrative centralisation. The Navy is not properly an Imperial or even a National force. The four fleets are Provincial squadrons, raised, equipped, and maintained by the viceroys or governors of the maritime provinces to which they are attached. Each acts independently in its own area, though they are mobilised for common evolutions every autumn. For instance, when in 1885 the French blockaded Formosa, they were not opposed by the combined Chinese fleet, but only by the Foochow squadron; and when this had been annihilated, by the Nanyang squadron, which took its place, no idea of concerted action being entertained. The same thing occurred in the recent war, where the Canton squadron never left the Canton River. There is, finally, in the Navy, as in the Army, a total want of a competent staff.

Two reflections are suggested by this review of the military and naval reforms of modern China. The first is this. Unaware that her main danger continues to lie upon her land frontiers, she thinks only of gunboats and maritime defences, and spends millions in fortifying her coasts. Because England and France once landed their troops at Canton and Tientsin, she appears to think

The false and the real danger.

that no European enemy can ever attack her except in ships. Because the great Powers of Europe are represented in the Far East by naval flotillas, she must have an equivalent or superior flotilla, in order to simulate the idea of being a great maritime Power also. Meanwhile, on the one hand, no steps are taken to combat or excise the canker of official corruption that preys upon the vitals of both services. On the other hand, in full view of the bewitched prey, the toils are being spread, and from the Pamirs and Turkestan and the Trans-Amur[1] will flow into Kashgaria, Mongolia, Sungaria, and Manchuria the tide that will overwhelm her outlying provinces, and may possibly not be arrested till it has attained the capital itself. Truly *Quem Deus vult perdere, prius dementat.*

Nevertheless, disrespectful to purely Chinese susceptibilities as these remarks may appear to have been, it must not be forgotten that in her vast empire China, however ill she may utilise it, possesses an inexhaustible supply of the very finest raw material, so far as mere manhood is concerned, in the East; and that what she is too blind or too obstinate to do for herself, others, with a superior foresight and strength, may insist upon doing for themselves. In other words, the Chinaman, who now fights for the Tartar just as he once fought for the Mongol, may one day be persuaded to fight for the Russian also. If the mandarin with spectacles on his nose and a cane in his hand cannot make a soldier of him, perhaps the European drill-sergeant will. Under good leadership he can fight sufficiently well, as was shown by Gordon's men. Valueless, therefore as, under existing conditions and management, we

The mercenaries of Europe.

---

[1] China has by Treaty an equal right to navigate the Amur with the Russians. But she has not placed a single gunboat on the river, though its right bank is still mainly Chinese.

may believe Chinese armaments to be, their potential value in the hands of another Power must not be lost sight of. It is conceivable that, so organised and directed, the Chinese Army and Navy may yet have a good deal to say in determining the destinies of the Far East.

Some writers have pointed to the tentative institution of a native Press in China as evidence of an internal fermentation synonymous with reform. No such inference can with justice be drawn. Outside of Peking, where the *Peking Gazette* is a strictly edited Court journal and Government record and nothing more,[1] the native journals are only or mostly to be found in the Treaty Ports. They are utterly unlike the native Press as it is rapidly becoming developed in Japan, as it has already been developed in India. Free criticism, the formation or reflection of public opinion, an independent attitude—for these it is vain to search them, and hazardous in China would be the experiment. Politically, their editors

The Press in China.

---

[1] The *Peking Gazette*, which is the oldest newspaper in the world, its origin being attributed to the Sung dynasty, which ended in 1366 A.D., is not actually an official publication, like the *London Gazette*, but is a sort of ministerial or Government organ, the issue of which is authorised by the Government, who also supply the greater part of the material. As such it is indirectly official and is absolutely authentic. Therein are contained all the Imperial acts, promotions, decrees and sentences, petitions from provincial governors, proclamations of the censors, etc., without any editorial comments or leading article. It is published daily in a manuscript and in a printed form, the former containing more matter, and is read and discussed with avidity by educated Chinese in every part of the Empire. In the provinces thousands of persons are employed in copying and abridging its contents for those who cannot afford to purchase the complete edition. It is printed by means of wooden movable types of willow or poplar wood. An average *Gazette* consists of ten to twelve leaves of thin brownish paper, measuring $7\frac{1}{2}$ by $3\frac{1}{4}$ inches, and enclosed between leaves, front and back, of bright yellow paper, to form a species of binding. The whole is roughly attached or stitched together. The inside leaves, being folded double in the usual Chinese fashion, give some twenty or more small pages of matter, each page being divided by red lines into seven columns. Each column contains fourteen characters from top to bottom, with a blank space at the top.

are sufficiently wise to tender a general support to the Government, while the advantages of public encomium are sufficiently recognised by the local officials to induce in some cases a liberal payment for complimentary mention. Outside of this harmless diversion, they serve a useful purpose in acquiring telegraphic information, in circulating general news, and in calling attention to visitations such as floods, etc., which might otherwise be ignored by the official eye.[1] The total absence of party politics in China is itself a discouragement to the existence of an organised Press. On the other hand, the absence of such a Press is a welcome preventive to the dissemination of novel or revolutionary ideas, or to the spread of any propaganda at which the Government would look askance.

China is a country of immense, probably of unequalled, natural resources. Her mineral wealth is believed to be greater than that of any other country in Asia. Her ports receive or diffuse a trade that employs thousands of keels, and pours wealth into the pockets of half the nations of Europe. Her people are gifted with infinite perseverance, industry, and sobriety. Under these circumstances, one might expect to find native enterprise everywhere active and triumphant, and to see the

Native enterprise.

[1] The first native newspaper appeared at Shanghai a little over thirty years ago, and was followed by two others at Tientsin and Canton, which were nominally started by Europeans, in order to escape Government inquisition, but were really owned and conducted by Chinese mandarins. There are now several Chinese newspapers at Hongkong; three at Canton, with a daily circulation of 5000 each; and one has recently been started at Hankow. The best native organ is the *Shanghai News*, a daily paper (with a weekly illustrated supplement), claiming a circulation of over 12,000. It usually contains a leading article, one or two political and social reviews, copies of official decrees and reports, police news, the telegrams of European agencies, local intelligence, and advertisements. On the other hand, the Tientsin paper has proved a failure. The people like gossip and scandal, which are unsafe, and their own classics, which are unsuited for publication; but in general news they take little interest.

resources of the country profitably exploited by her own
citizens. The very reverse is the spectacle before us. Of
the many well-stocked mines, only the coal-mines near
Tientsin are successfully worked by a native company
(under foreign management). Among the hundreds of
merchant steamers carrying loaded bottoms from port to
port, only thirty (and those officered and engineered by
foreigners) fly the flag of a native company worth men-
tioning, that of the China Merchants. And in both these
cases the exception is merely due to the fact that official
patronage is concerned in promoting the venture, and that
the money of eminent mandarins is at stake. The Viceroy
Li Hung Chang is reported to be behind the Kaiping Coal
Mining Company. He it was who secured for the China
merchants an Imperial subsidy and an assured revenue in
the freight of the tribute rice. Quite lately a fresh bounty
was given to them in the shape of a remission of import
duties to native merchants shipping by their vessels, and
of customs examination to native officials travelling in them;
but the discovery being made that these exemptions constituted a breach of Article III. of the Commercial Treaty
concluded between China and the United States in 1880,
they were rescinded as the result of a protest from the
British Minister. Yet in the cases of both these companies
I have heard that the profits are not what they might be,
and that shareholders complain of scant accounts and of
infrequent and arbitrary dividends. In fact, as a commercial
speculation, the China Merchants' Company is said to be a
failure.[1] What, then, is the secret of this paralysis that
would seem to have overcome the energies of China just

[1] It is very different with the China merchants of Hongkong, who, free to
invest and develop their capital without the peril of Government interference
or squeeze, run large ships to Manila and Batavia, to Saigon, Singapore, and
Bangkok.

at the very moment and in the very direction where they might be employed to such obvious advantage? The answer lies in the immemorial curse of Oriental countries, the trail of the serpent that is found everywhere from Stamboul to Peking—the vicious incubus of officialism, paramount, selfish, domineering, and corrupt. Distrust of private enterprise is rooted in the mind trained up to believe that the Government is everything and the individual nothing. The bough may rot and its fruit may never be garnered sooner than that the spoil should fall into any but official hands. So it has always been, and so it must continue to be. Were all Viceroys far-sighted and all mandarins liberal-minded, there would be less cause for reproach. But a system that has prevailed for twenty centuries does not easily relax the rigour of its bonds or admit of converts from its own ranks; and those who have been bred and nurtured in a satisfied twilight do not relish the sensation of a sudden introduction to the noontide blaze. Let me give an illustration of the manner in which this system affects the development of the national resources. Near to Kelung in Formosa are some coal-mines. They were opened in the first place and worked by private individuals. Then the Provincial Government marched in, shut up all the private mines, and thus procured for itself a monopoly, which it proceeded to develop by sending for European plant and European engineers. The next step was to appoint a Chinese superintendent as colleague to the foreign engineer; with the normal result of (1) friction, (2) dismissal of the foreigner, (3) resumption of the mine by the natives, (4) complete collapse and closure of the pits. Later on, a foreign financial syndicate offered to take over the mines on favourable terms. Taught by adversity, the

The curse of official-ism.

Provincial Government gladly accepted; but this time the Central Government refused. So the mines lay idle until the opportunity of ever developing them in Chinese hands has now itself disappeared; and this is the way in which things are done in China.

In reality, therefore, the institution of which China is most proud, viz. a lettered bureaucracy, is the source of her greatest weakness. Educated upon a system which has not varied for ages, stuffed with sense- *The Mandarinate.* less and impracticable precepts, discharging the ceremonial duties of his office with a mechanical and servile accuracy, the victim of incredible superstitions and sorceries, but arrogant with a pride beyond human conception, furnished with an insufficient salary, and therefore compelled to peculate and plunder, the Chinese mandarin is China's worst enemy. All private enterprise is killed by official strangulation, all public spirit is extinguished by official greed. Nor, as it is the ambition and is within the scope of everybody, whatever his class, to become an official himself, is there any order to which we can look for successful protest. The entire governing class, itself recruited from the mass of the people, is interested in the preservation of the *status quo*. The forces ordinarily enlisted on the side of change, those of the *literati* or student class, are more reactionary in China than any other, seeing that, unlike Russia—where they are trampled upon and ignored—and unlike India—where they complain of inadequate range for their ambition—they already, by virtue of their degrees, hold the keys of power. Neither can it be supposed that, with a people so obstinate and so vain, there is the smallest inclination among the lower strata of society to move where their leaders decline to advance. Both find an equal charm in stagnation.

What the foreigner realises only dimly and by slow degrees is that the Chinaman has not the slightest desire to be reformed by him; that he disputes *in toto* that reform is reform; and that no demonstration in the world will convince him of the existence of a flaw in his own theory of national perfection. He points to a Government infinitely more stable than that of any European State, to order observed, and to justice effectively, if roughly, administered (the fact that rebellion simmers in some provinces, where official embezzlement in times of hardship reduces the people to semi-starvation, not being of sufficiently wide application to disturb the general proposition); he claims a civilisation that was already at a high pitch when Britons were wandering painted in the woods; he boasts of a code of ethics equal in wisdom and amplitude to our own; he observes a religion which, while it touches the extremes of purity in doctrine and of degradation in practice, is yet accommodated to every situation in life, and enables him, subject only to the test of dutiful observance, to pass with confidence into a future world. And he turns round to us, and, with a pardonable self-confidence, asks what we have to give him compared with these.

<small>The Chinese standpoint.</small>

This is one aspect of the question—namely, the convinced and embittered resistance of all classes to reform, and the fear that reform, if forced upon them, may dislodge some of the foundation-stones of that fabric of which they are so exorbitantly proud. On the other hand, must not some weight be attached to the consideration—which to the European mind appears so irresistible—that the first tentative steps have been taken in a forward direction, that the awakening trumpet has sounded in China's ears, and that, once embarked on the path of progress she is already launched upon an inclined plane where

<small>The picture of progress.</small>

THE SO-CALLED AWAKENING OF CHINA

it will be impossible for her to stop? This is a plausible and
a pretty picture, and even its approximate realisation might
enable the Chinese—a nation superbly gifted and possessing
unique advantages of character, country, and clime—once
again to repeat the history of the ages and to overrun the
world. Is this the future that awaits them? Is this the
fate that threatens us?

I must have argued feebly if I have not already shown
that in my judgment this consummation is not either to
be expected or to be feared. Reform, it is true, The reality
cannot altogether be hustled out of the door. of stand-
Its force is like the wind, that bloweth where still.
it listeth, and can penetrate even through the chinks and
crannies. Doubtless in time, as from different quarters
foreign railways touch the confines of China, native railways
will be made to meet them. A day will come when mines
will be exploited, a decent currency adopted, and rivers will be
navigated by steam. Neither, though China may be overrun,
and may even, as she has often done before, accept a change
of masters, is she likely to be submerged. She is for ever
proof against such a fate by reason of her moral character,
her swarming millions, and her territorial extent. The continued national existence of the Yellow Race may be regarded
as assured. But that the Empire which in the last fifty
years has lost Siam, Burma, Annam, Tongking, part of
Manchuria, Formosa, and Korea, which has already seen a
foreign army in Peking, and the maritime approaches to
whose capital have been for a year in the armed occupation
of a victorious enemy; whose standard of civil and political
perfection is summed up in the stationary idea; which, after
half a century of intercourse with ministers, missionaries, and
merchants, regards all these as intolerable nuisances, and one
of the number with peculiar aversion; which only adopts

the lessons that they have taught her when the surrender is dictated by her necessities or her fears; and which, after a twenty years' observation of the neighbouring example of Japan, looks with increasing contempt upon a frailty so feeble and impetuous—that this Empire is likely to falsify the whole course of its history and to wrench round the bent of its own deep-seated inclinations, simply because the shriek of the steam-whistle or the roar of cannon is heard at its gates—is a hypothesis that ignores the accumulated lessons of political science and postulates a revival of the age of miracles. I have narrated the stages of China's tardy advance, and I have shown how far she has condescended to reform. But it remains a mechanical and not a moral advance; it is an artificial and not an organic reform. She may still continue to play an important part in the development of the Asiatic world. Her hardy colonists may sail to every quarter of the Eastern hemisphere, and by their frugal toil may enrich themselves, while they fail to aggrandise her. But, politically speaking, her star is a waning and not a rising orb. *Sedet æternumque sedebit* is the limit of China's own aspirations. It may even turn out to be beyond the limit of her powers.[1]

[1] This problem is further discussed in Chapter xiii.

CHAPTER XI

MONASTICISM IN CHINA

Tantum relligio potuit suadere malorum.
  LUCRETIUS: *De Rerum Natura*, Lib. i. 101.

IN a previous chapter I have said something about Buddhism in Korea, where it is the discredited but not wholly disavowed survival of a once dominant creed. I propose in this chapter to deal with Buddhism in China, where, though decadent, it is still dominant, and where the explanation of its influence provides a clue to many of the dark riddles of the national character. Buddhism in China is indeed a curious mixture of perishing rites and popular superstitions. There is probably no country where there are fewer evidences of faith or devotion, or where, on the other hand, an apparently doomed system dies so hard. From the squalid and dilapidated condition of the temples, from the indifference and irreverence with which the worshippers enact their artificial parts, and from the miserable status of the priesthood, it might be inferred that the days of Buddhism were numbered, and that a rival system was driving it from dishonoured shrines. Such, however, would be a most superficial view of the case. This mysterious religion, which has survived the varied competition of Rationalism, Confucianism, and Ceremonialism, and which has an antiquity not far short of two thousand years in China, is yet the favourite creed of a community numbering 350,000,000 ; and despised and de-

Chinese Buddhism.

generate though it be, it will still lift its head and smile its serene Buddha-smile long after its purer and prouder and more splendid counterpart in Japan has crumbled into the dust.

The explanation of this strange anomaly is that the popular faith has with rare discretion intertwined itself with the popular superstitions. Partly creating and partly accommodating itself to them, Buddhism, involved in the sacred ties of Ancestor-Worship, and claiming to dispense the portions of another life, has wrapped itself in a covering of triple brass, and can afford to laugh at its enemies. It has found the key to the inner being of this inscrutable people, and, in secure command of the lock, takes good care that none other shall tamper with the wards. It may safely be contended that, were it not for the uneasy anxieties of the Chinese about their souls, and the universal and cherished cult of the Family Tree, and for the part played in relation to both by the Buddhist priesthood, Chinese Buddhism would long ere now have languished and disappeared.[1] Dogmas, tenets, ritual, and liturgy in themselves are of small import to the Celestials. The stately ceremonial of the official creed, the intellectual axioms of Confucius, the painted image-worship of the Buddhist temple, the mysticism of the Rationalists, or sect of Lao-tzu, produce little permanent

Its super-stitious sanction.

---

[1] In an interesting letter, the late Sir T. Wade, formerly British Minister in Peking, wrote to me on this subject as follows: 'The original capture of the lettered classes of China by the apostles of Buddhism was largely due to the fact that the period of their greatest activity as writers or translators (viz. the Tang Dynasty, A.D. 600-900) was at the same time eminently remarkable for the elegance of its prose and its poetry. It was, as we should say, the Augustan age of Chinese composition. It has also been due to the support which it received with tolerable steadiness from the Central Government, notably under the two last dynasties. And yet, almost universal as is the thraldom of its puerile superstitions, it has never supplanted Confucianism as the national code of ethics, nor has its literature ever been able to maintain a footing in the national education.'

effect upon their stolid imaginations. The beautiful teaching enshrined in the sacred writings as they came from India, the precepts that made white lives and brought tearless deaths, that almost Christianised idolatry and might have redeemed a world, have long ago died down into frigid calculations, tabulating in opposite columns with mathematical nicety the credit and debit accounts of the orthodox disciple. Thus, on the one hand, the people are plunged in gloomy dread of a hereafter, determined by the exact laws of moral retribution; on the other, deeply embedded in the springs of their nature, is a fanatical attachment to their Lares and Penates, and to the worship of the dead; and hence it comes about that the religion which, whatever its shortcomings and disqualifications, ministers to their requirements in both these respects, is simultaneously derided and advocated, neglected and espoused.

No better illustration of this anomalous state of affairs can be given than the condition and public estimation of the Buddhist monks. A stranger will at first be puzzled by the opposite verdicts which he hears passed upon this class of men. He will hear them denounced as contemptible outcasts, *Contradictory opinion of monks.* as pariahs from society, who have forfeited all the sympathies of humanity by cutting themselves adrift from all human ties. And this is a sentence which to some extent finds its corroboration in their forlorn and decrepit appearance, in their cheerless mode of life, and in their divorce from the haunts and homes of men. On the other hand, he will find these despised exiles supported by popular contributions, recruited by voluntary adherents, and engaged in the discharge of essential rites at the most solemn moments of life and death, and in the service to the dead. A grosser seeming contradiction can scarcely be imagined.

And yet it is an identical feeling which is partly responsible for both attitudes, and which prepares for these unhappy creatures this opposite mixture of toleration and contempt. The peculiar sanctity of the family relations is one cause both of their ostracism and of their employment. They are needed to discharge on behalf of others the very obligations which they have renounced themselves. Expelled from the world because they have ignored the family, they are brought back into it to testify that the family is the first of all earthly ties. Can anything more strange be conceived? It is a creed whose apostates are enlisted as its prophets, and whose perverts become its priests.

Its explanation.

When Sakyamuni first instituted the monastic order, like St. Anthony he did not contemplate the creation of a priestly office, or the rise of a hierarchy. The clerical profession had no special connection in his mind with monkish life. The first Buddhist monks, like those of Egypt, were pious men who, in pursuit of their master's teaching that worldly and carnal ties were the source of all evil, and the main obstacle to that serene altitude of contemplation by which absorption into the higher life at length became possible, severed themselves from their fellow-creatures, and sought remote and unfriended retreats for purposes of spiritual exercise and self-mortification. They were primarily recluses and secondarily preachers, but in no resort priests. It was only in later times, as the first pattern was forgotten, and accretions developed by other countries and circumstances grew up, that the manifold accessories of sacerdotalism, particularly among the peoples of the north, environed and obscured the original ideal.

Original conception of monasticism.

The logical carrying out of Buddha's precepts, however,

brought the anchorite into early collision with the most idolised beliefs of Chinese life. The essence of monasticism, viz. the repudiation of all earthly connections, the lifelong abandonment of father, mother, brothers, and sisters, the surrender of the covenant of wedlock and the hopes of paternity—above all, the utter severance of the limb from the ancestral trunk, is the very antipodes of the highest conception of duty that a Chinese can entertain. Hence arose the dishonour in which the monkish order has long been held, and from which it has only rescued its existence by abandoning its traditions. The monastery has, in fact, become the very converse of what Buddha ever intended that it should be. The secular has put on the religious, and the monk has saved himself by turning priest.

Its inversion.

We have seen how indispensable are his ministrations in the worship of the dead, and in expediting the happy transmigration of the departed soul. There the mummeries of the temple are enlisted to fill up the incomplete credentials of the deceased, and to visé his passport, so to speak, to another world. To the more pious or superstitious (there is no distinction between the two classes in China) they are not less obligatory as a policy of spiritual insurance, to be taken out with precautionary object during lifetime. The Chinaman is a firm believer in the doctrine of justification by works; he expects a return in the next life exactly proportionate to the labour and money he has spent or caused to be spent in deserving it in this. Every mumbled prayer, every tap of the drum or clash of the cymbal by the paid hierophant whom he has engaged, will be rewarded by so much tangible gain in the next stage of existence. Metempsychosis may bring him a worse or a better lot; he may groan in poverty or loll in

A spiritual insurance.

wealth; he may sink to hell or rise to the acme of paradisal felicity in a future state. The Buddhist monks are the established mediums through whom his merits may be demonstrated and made known in heaven; and from whose hands he looks to receive his official diploma of celestial promotion.

The isolation of the novice from all the ties and consolations of life may well conflict with Chinese prejudices; for it is ghastly in its completeness. Not only, as has been said, does he renounce all relationships and take vows of celibacy, but he casts aside even the ultimate symbol of identity, his own name. From the hour that he passes the convent threshold, he is known only by a religious appellation, in the very grandiloquence of which there is something pitiful and absurd. Henceforward he must shave his head, eat no animal food, drink no strong drink, and wear no skin or woollen garment, but only the prescribed vestments of his order. His life is mapped out before him in a sterile and dolorous routine. And not only has he ceased to be a member of domestic society, but as a unit in the civil community he can scarcely be said to exist. For he acknowledges no real allegiance to the Emperor, albeit the latter is of the family of the gods; yielding a discretionary obedience to the civil authorities, with whom he rarely comes in contact, but concentrating all capacity for duty in a slavish obedience to the jurisdiction of his abbot or religious superior.

Ostracism of the cloister.

The terrible exclusiveness of this discipline, repellent though it is to Chinese ideas, would not be sufficient to account for the odium in which the monastery is held, were it not for the suspicion that its stringency is a sham, and that the cowl is often either assumed as an escape from justice or worn as a cloak of

Popular odium.

hypocrisy. It is difficult, for obvious reasons, to discover how far the charge that fugitives from the clutch of the law shelter themselves within the monastery walls is a true one, though it is certain that when once admitted the culprit is safe from the bloodhounds of official retribution. I have even heard it argued, by way of repudiation of this charge, that it is only the most abandoned characters, fleeing from the penalties of a capital offence, who will take advantage of a refuge so discredited as the cloister; though to contend that a society is not criminally recruited because only criminals of the deepest dye can be persuaded to attach themselves to it, does not seem to me a very happy method of exculpation. I am reminded by it of an incident which I came across while travelling in Greece some years ago. The public executioner in that country was a character held in such general detestation that he was forced to live apart, strictly guarded, on a little island in the harbour of Nauplia. And not only that; but such difficulty was experienced in filling the place, that the selected candidate was, as a rule, taken from the criminal class itself—a bandit being pardoned in order that he might be utilised to cut off the heads of other bandits. At the time of my visit one of these worthies had just completed the term of his office, but whether owing to the unpopularity he had contracted by its discharge, or to the distrust he had inspired by his previous habits of life, he considered himself in so much danger that he solved the problem of his future mode of existence by entering a monastery and assuming the cowl. In China he would presumably have taken this step at an earlier stage in his career.

Whatever be the truth about the Buddhist monasteries in China as Cities of Refuge, and whether the slur cast upon them by that suspicion be just or not, there is less room for doubt that the pattern of ascetic life to which the monk is understood to aspire is one to which he most infrequently conforms. His celibacy and his vegetarianism are freely impugned. It is perhaps only natural that the theory that drinking-water and vegetables are teeming with animalculæ or with the germs of animal life should be one which he indignantly rejects, seeing that were he to accept it he would be hard put to subsist at all, with any regard at least to the precepts of the Buddhistic canon. But, alas! he is the victim of more substantial charges. It is whispered that the odour of meat and fish, and the tell-tale fragrance of the opium-pipe are no strangers to the recluse's cell. With greater certainty he is accused of being dirty, degraded, and ignorant, subsisting on alms which he does nothing to merit, and of prostituting his worship into a mummery which he does not himself comprehend. If even a fraction of these charges be true, there can be small surprise that the monastic profession is held in so little repute among a people who are by no means deficient in their standards of the sober moral virtues.

Common imposture.

It may be wondered how a society held in such slight esteem, and offering so few advantages, save to the stupid or indolent, can continually replenish its ranks. The means of doing so are, however, many and varied, even if we reject the criminal hypothesis to which I have alluded.[1] In some cases the children are bought at an early age from their parents; though so strong is the family feeling in China that it is only under pressure of

Different classes of recruits.

[1] It is scarcely possible to do so, in the face of the evidence of such an authority and eye-witness as the late Archdeacon Gray, who, in his work on *China*, embodying the experience of a long life, said (vol. i. chap. iv.) that he himself saw at different times in Buddhist monasteries an escaped murderer, a brothel-house keeper, and a condemned rebel, who had been gratefully admitted because he possessed a little money, which went to swell the corporate funds.

the direst necessity that the average *paterfamilias* will consent, even for a price, to part with his offspring, particularly of the male sex. Sometimes the young children are kidnapped and sold to the priests; this profession being, however, a dangerous one, as, if detected, it is punishable by death. More commonly young lads are voluntarily dedicated by their parents in fulfilment of some vow, or for the sake of spiritual gain, the transfer being effected with all the formalities of a mercantile transaction. It is forbidden, however, by law to surrender the entire male stock of a family to the cloister; and in the event of there being two sons, the younger only may be sacrificed. A second class of adherents will be those who, from satiety of the world, or pecuniary collapse, or official failure, or material disappointment in some form or other, have decided to abandon the thorny paths of life, and to seek a safe retreat from its multitudinous cares. Lastly, there will be some, even in China and in the nineteenth century, to whom a life of joyless penance and austerity will appeal with irresistible force as an expiation for the sins of the flesh, and a plank of passage into the world to come—sad, sorrowful wretches, after the pattern of St. Simeon, who live apart in isolated cells, performing acts of cruel self-torture, and mumbling in solitude the accents of an unintelligible ritual.

Their means of subsistence are as varied as the ranks from which their disciples are drawn. The large monasteries possess endowments of property, principally in land, from which they derive an income, either in rent or in the profits of the cultivation of their own hands. Voluntary donations are also made to their funds by those who, while despising the monastery, cannot dispense with the services of the monk. The sale of joss-sticks and incense, of gilt paper and tapers, and the fees for

Means of subsistence.

services, ceremonies, and prayers, are also a considerable source of emolument. And when all these fail, there is always begging to fall back upon, the ultimate resort of all creeds in all ages. The Buddhist priests are no amateurs in the art of mendicancy. Sometimes large bands of them may be seen patrolling the streets, and by the discordant clamour of a gong calling attention to the unmistakable character of the errand which has brought them down into the thoroughfares of men. By these different methods they manage to scrape along; their buildings and temples just saved from dilapidation; their persons and costumes in the last stage of seediness and decay; their piety an illusion, their pretensions a fraud; themselves at once the saviours and the outcasts of society, its courted and its despised.

I have visited many Buddhist monasteries and temples in China; and have usually found that they correspond to the following description. Three buildings are ranged one behind the other on terraces, and approached by a series of paved courts and rows of granite steps. There is something solemn and imposing in this succession of structures, each one properly exceeding its predecessor in magnificence, and leading on the imagination from what it has already seen to what is yet to come. It is an architectural device that we know was familiar to the Jews and Egyptians, and that appears to be common to all Oriental religions. It is nowhere employed with greater effect than in the splendid Buddhist sanctuaries and royal mausoleums of Japan.

Monastic temples.

The entrance gateway, which is of the nature of an open temple, sometimes contains a colossal gilt idol in the centre, representing Maitreya Buddha (in Chinese Mili Fo), or Buddha To Come; and on either side are the four diabolical-looking monsters, with painted faces and flaming eyeballs, who represent the deified warriors appointed to keep guard over the shrines of Buddha, and who symbolise an absolute command over all the forces of earth and heaven. They are identical with the Maharajahs, or Great Kings, of Hindu mythology, who, attended by a host of spiritual beings, march hither and thither to the protection of devout disciples and the execution of Buddha's will over the four quarters of the universe. In China they are known as the Tien Wong. One of them, with a white face, holds an umbrella, the circumference of which, when opened, overshadows the whole earth, and is lord of the forces of thunder and rain. Another, with a red face, controls the elements of fire, water, and air, and plays a species of stringed instrument, the vibrations of whose chords shake the foundations of the world. The third, with a green face, brandishing a sword, and the fourth with a blue face, clasping a serpent, are typical of supreme dominion over nature and man. In these figures, which are common throughout China, and are uniform in design and monstrosity, the artist has combined the hideous and the grotesque in very equal proportions. But little skill seems ever to have been expended upon their construction.

Entrance gateway.

This gateway leads into a spacious paved court, at the upper end of which, on a granite platform, rises the fabric of the main temple. A huge high-pitched tile roof almost eclipses the front and side walls, which are commonly destitute of ornamentation. The interior consists of a big parallelogram, divided by circular painted columns into three main and two side aisles. Fronting the principal avenues are the three familiar figures called the Sang Po, or Precious Ones, which are always found in the churches of Buddhist monasteries, and which are incarnations respectively of the past, the present, and the

Main temple.

z

future Buddha; or, to give them their correct titles, of Sakyamuni, Kwanyin, and Maitreya.[1] These idols are made of clay, thickly gilt, and highly burnished. Their faces wear that expression of ineffable self-complacency which is common to the Buddha all over the East, but which, while in Japan it is always sublime, in China is apt to overslip the razor's edge into the ridiculous. The bodies are seated, and rise from the calyx of a lotus-flower. Below the images are altars laden with weighty bronzes, with big candelabra, and with censers, a thin smoke curling upwards from the slow combustion of blocks of sandalwood, or from sheaves of smouldering joss-sticks standing in a vase. On either side of the lateral aisles are ranged along a recess in the wall the smaller gilt figures of the Eighteen Lohans or Disciples of Buddha, whose features exaggerate the silliness, while they altogether miss the serenity depicted in the countenance of their illustrious master. The prevailing colours in the surface decorations of the columns and rafters, which are rudely painted, are everywhere red and green.

When service is going on, the aisles are laid out with rows of long, low, sloping stools, upon which at intervals rest circular straw hassocks. Behind these stand the monks intoning the words of the prescribed liturgy. The service is led by one of their number, who officiates at an isolated mat before the great altar. Their dresses are cut after one pattern, and are dingy in the extreme, consisting of loose cotton robes of two colours—yellow and an ashen-grey—with turn-down collars, and a

Service.

[1] Sometimes in the main hall of Buddhist temples in China this trinity represents Sakyamuni in the centre, with two of his most famous disciples, Kashiapa, the first patriarch, represented as an old man, on one side, and Ananda, the second patriarch, as a young man, on the other. Sometimes the two supporters are Bodhisattwas, or prospective Buddhas, who, in the evolution of their salvation, have reached the penultimate stage; and of whom the best known is the jovial image of Maitreya, the Buddha To Come.

clasp in front. No monk is allowed, according to the strict regulation of the canon, to possess more than one set of garments, and this he is compelled to wear both day and night. Their heads are clean-shaven, a ceremonial which is performed about twice a month. Here and there on the bald craniums one may note small disc-like cicatrices, or scars, burnt in by the hand of the abbot alone, as a badge of their sacred calling, or in fulfilment of some particular vow. Their hands are piously folded in front of them, and the nails have been suffered to grow to inordinate dimensions.

The expression of their features is usually one of blank and idiotic absorption; which is, perhaps, not surprising, considering that of the words which they intone scarcely one syllable do they themselves under- *Vox et prætrea nihil.* stand. The mass-book is a dead letter to them, for it is written in Sanskrit or Pali, which they can no more decipher than fly. The words that they chant are merely the equivalent in sound of the original sentences, rendered into Chinese characters, and are therefore totally devoid of sense. To this stale shibboleth, or ignorant repetition of unmeaning sounds, they attribute a vital importance.[1] It is, they point out, the sacred language of Fan (the birthplace of Buddha), and is therefore of divine origin and efficacy. The ‘blessed word Mesopotamia’ was not more fraught with consolation to the incurious Christian than is this stupid jargon to the Chinese bonze. Or let me give a more practical illustration. The case would be a similar one if the responses in an English church were to be uttered in the Greek tongue, transcribed into English spelling and gabbled out by illiterate rustics—an absurdity of which, as a matter of fact, our chant-

[1] Compare Matthew vi. 7: ‘But when ye pray, use not vain repetitions, as the heathen do; for they think that they shall be heard for their much speaking.’

books are not altogether guiltless, seeing that the responses to the Commandments in the Communion Service are always described in their pages as Kyrie Eleison, a phrase which must be gibberish to nine out of every ten choristers who read it. The effect upon a service so conducted, and still more upon the ministrants, is obvious. No sincerity can be expected of a purely phonetic devotion. It is *vox et praeterea nihil*.

And yet we must not be too severe upon these benighted disciples of Buddha in the uplands of the Celestial Empire. Other churches and other creeds have been guilty of the same pretence, and have found a saving virtue in the use of an unknown tongue. Jew and Gentile, Christian and heretic, Catholic and Moslem have all acted upon the principle that the more restricted the understanding the more implicit the acceptance, and have imparted the secrets of salvation in accents that kept them secrets still, to be interpreted not by the ear of sense, but by that of faith. To this day how many of the singers in the choir of a Catholic church understand even a fraction of the Latin litany which they intone?

<small>Tenants of glass houses.</small>

The murmur of the chant is accompanied by intermittent music from such instruments as the Oriental loves. An acolyte from time to time strikes a drum, the framework of which is of wood, carved and painted to represent a huge pot-bellied fish. Another tinkles a bell in the background, and now and then breaks in the dissonant clangour of a gong. After a while a fresh note is struck; and at the signal the priests separate into two companies, and proceed for a long time to wind in and out of the lines of stools in a slow and solemn procession. Backwards and forwards, in

<small>Procession.</small>

and out, with measured tread and even steps they pace along, their hands clasped, their heads bowed, their lips still murmuring the same unintelligible refrain, in which may be distinguished the sounds Omito Fo (Amitabha Buddha), the repetition of which many thousands of times is pregnant with salvation.

Behind and beyond the Main Temple extends a second paved quadrangle, a further temple at the upper end of which very frequently contains a marble *dagoba*, or sculptured reliquary, with altars and shrines. Reliquary. Here is concealed some peculiarly sacred object, very possibly a tooth of the great Buddha himself. Even devotees have been somewhat staggered by the number of these well-authenticated relics that are scattered throughout the Eastern world; and an early Chinese geographer, visiting Ceylon, and being everywhere shown tooth after tooth, ended by solemnly remarking of his master, 'He was born with an excessive number of teeth.'

At the rear and sides of the temples are the domestic premises of the monks; the kitchen, where the daily rice is boiled in a huge earthenware vat; the refectory, where on hard tables and harder benches it is Domestic premises. consumed in silence under the supervision of the abbot; the guest-chambers reserved for the not too enervating entertainment of guests; and the sleeping apartments beyond these, which can rarely, save by a euphemism, be so leniently described.

The bodies of the monks themselves are in the greater part of China burned and not buried after death; although in the north this is a privilege that is reserved for the Fang-chang, or head-priests. Contrary Cremation. to the custom in Japan, where cremation is universal among the common people, in China it is only the prerogative or the peculiarity of the religious order. Each monastery contains its *crematorium*, and its *campo santo*, where are deposited the ashes of the dead. The body is placed in a sitting position in an open plank coffin, and is carried out to the furnace, which is of the simplest description, consisting merely of a small brick chamber or tower, standing by itself in a detached situation. There the corpse is placed upon the ground, surrounded and supported by faggots; the attendant monks intone a chant; and the mortal remains of their departed brother are speedily reduced to ashes, while the smoke from the pyre escapes through a single orifice in the roof. Thus, unpretentiously and with scant attempt at decorum, the mortal coil is shuffled off, and its discharged inmate goes on his way to solve the great mystery.

THE PROSPECT

'Tu regere imperio populos, Romane, memento!
Hæ tibi erunt artes, pacisque imponere morem,
Parcere subjectis, et debellare superbos.'

VIRGIL: *Æneid*, vi. 851-853.

CHAPTER XII

AFTER THE WAR

μετὰ τὸν πόλεμον ἡ συμμαχία.
Paroemiographi Graeci: MACARIUS, v. 85.

IN the earlier chapters of this book I have narrated the sequence of events that preceded and culminated in the outbreak of hostilities between Japan and China in the summer of 1894. I have no desire here to give a history of the war, which might indeed be recorded in a few sentences, but which, in the hands of one who was not upon the spot, could only be a compilation. The question, however, of the partition of responsibility between the two combatants is one that has naturally excited much attention, and has elicited the most opposite verdicts. On the one hand have been those, the majority in numbers, who have attributed the entire provocation and initiative to Japan. On the other hand a small but devoted band of adherents has consistently represented the struggle as one between Civilisation and Barbarism, to which the former was impelled by a challenge which it could not honourably resist.

Responsibility for the War.

In one sense it is true that the war was inevitable. It was the historical corollary of the events of 1592-8. Japan had never forgiven the humiliation which she then sustained at the hands of China, upon Korean soil, and for three centuries *La Revanche* had been as fixed an idea in the bosom of Japanese patriots as it has been

An Eastern vendetta.

for the last quarter of a century in a not dissimilar case in Europe. Sooner or later an appeal to arms was almost certain for the settlement of this traditional feud; and the long and strenuous military and naval preparations of Japan since her apparition on the international stage as an organised modern Power were not obscurely directed to such an issue, and might have been interpreted as a warning by any nation less arrogant and blind than China. For her part, the latter did nothing whatever either to avoid or to postpone the rupture; and her policy of obstructive and dilatory conservatism in Korea, though based upon a suzerainty which I hold to have been technically indisputable, must have been intensely exasperating to the already wounded susceptibilities of Japan. To this extent, therefore, may it be said that China, by her tactics and her temper, brought upon herself the retribution that was to come.

Nevertheless, it cannot be denied that, in the chain of events immediately preceding the war, Japan, having long before made up her mind to fight at the first convenient opportunity, 'forced the pace'—if such a metaphor may be permitted—in order to suit the exigencies of the moment; and that in the actual outbreak of hostilities she was pointedly the aggressor. A variety of circumstances contributed to render the juncture favourable, in her opinion, for an appeal to arms. After long preparation, her armaments on land and sea had reached a pitch of efficiency which her experts assured her could leave no doubt of the issue of a conflict with China, but which it was at the same time desirable and convenient to test upon the *corpus vile* of a second-rate Power. The Parliamentary situation in Japan was fraught with so many difficulties, owing to the undisciplined development of party feeling and to cabals against the Government, that some appeal to a larger

Secondary motives.

patriotism seemed essential in order to save the new Constitution from premature shipwreck. A forward policy would be acceptable to the Radical or Opposition party, with whom the recovery of Japanese influence in Korea had always been a favourite cry. Simultaneously, there was among the leading Japanese statesmen an anxious and far-sighted desire, imperfectly realised by European observers or critics, to anticipate the completion of the Trans-Siberian Railway by Russia, and to vindicate, before it was too late, the pretensions of Japan to a leading voice in the impending reconstruction of the balance of power in the Far East. Among the secondary motives here mentioned, I say nothing of the unselfish desire to endow Korea with the beauties of civilisation; since that plea, after figuring for a short time in the magazine-apologies of enthusiasts, was less and less heard of as the war proceeded, and it was found that Korea was the principal sufferer by the venture, and has subsequently disappeared altogether from view in the complete breakdown of the attempt to force upon her the unwelcome luxury, expressly imported for the purpose from Japan.

War having once been declared, it was evident that the national spirit was intensely and unanimously enlisted in the enterprise. It was felt that Japan was playing for a high stake, and that there must be no bickering or jealousy at the table. No country, in all probability, ever went to war, sustained by *Japanese patriotism and preparations.* a higher or more unfaltering fervour of patriotism than did Japan. Then, too, it was discovered how ubiquitous and exhaustive, and almost Machiavellian in their patient secrecy, had been her preparations. Skilled topographers in disguise had mapped the high-roads of China, and had plotted their angles over the interior of Korea. Hydrographical surveys, unostentatiously pursued for years, had acquainted the Japanese with every inlet in the Korean coast, and had furnished the chart-room of every vessel in her Navy with hitherto unpublished maps. Her mobilisation proceeded with a smoothness and rapidity that excited the admiration of the European military *attachés*; her organisation and equipment were wonderful in their completeness. The Japanese Intelligence Department might have been engaged upon, just as it had certainly been preparing for, a campaign for years. Its spies were everywhere, in the offices and arsenals, in the council-chambers and amid the ranks, of the enemy. The Press was manipulated and controlled with a masterly despotism that would have been impossible in Europe. Finally, the strategy of the Japanese generals, if not brilliant, was deliberate, scientific, and successful.

If, however, we turn from the contemplation and admission of these excellent merits to the actual fighting on the battlefield, it by no means follows, as has been too generally supposed, that Japan either showed or had the opportunity of showing, the capacities of a first-rate military Power. During the seven months of active operations, she never encountered an enemy, and hardly fought a battle, worthy of the name. There confronted her, in the majority of cases, not a disciplined army but a rabble of tramps; she was opposed, not by fire, but by fireworks. The Chinese resistance was in nine instances out of ten a farce that would have been laughable had it not been piteous. It was generally known in advance when and where the Japanese attack would be delivered; and after a preliminary volley from the Celestial rank-and-file in order to 'save their face,' a general stampede followed in order to save their lives. It is even said that many of the Chinese commanders were in the pay of Japan. That this criticism, which is based upon the observations of actual spectators of

[marginal note: Japan on the battlefield.]

the war, is correct, might also be inferred from the figures of the death-roll as officially published by the Japanese themselves. Though they lost 3284 men in the entire war, 2489 of these perished from cholera or other diseases, while 795 only were killed or died of their wounds, over half of this total being claimed by the storming of Port Arthur. *Per contra*, the Japanese claim to have killed 27,917 of the enemy. So prodigious a disparity between the two death-lists is quite irreconcilable with severe fighting. The Japanese artillery is said to have been well served and to have wrought great execution; but the infantry fire is reported to have been uniformly bad. The fact that Japan was confronted by an enemy who had not the courage to stand up to her, is of course no proof that she would not have vanquished an enemy who had. Nor does it detract from the valour and discipline which her troops seem, as a rule, to have displayed. But it does fail to justify the conclusion, which has been very widely drawn from the issue of the conflict, that the Japanese proved themselves thereby to be a military Power of the first order, capable of being arrayed against the best troops of European States. The lessons of the naval battle of the Yalu, where the Japanese, in spite of their victory, could not prevent the enemy's ships from escaping, were not dissimilar from those of the more numerous land fights. From the later incidents of the struggle the truth became even more apparent. For it was owing solely to the exhaustion entailed by what had been, after all, but a brief campaign, that Japan was obliged to abandon the fondly-cherished idea of a march upon Peking, and, at a still more recent date, to give back, under European pressure, Port Arthur and the Liao-tung Peninsula.

No detraction however from the credit legitimately due to Japan, which, in any case, stands sufficiently high to suffer little from the loss, will avail anything to redeem the stupendous and unimaginable ineptitude of China. To those who have read this book, the reasons of that collapse, which is without a parallel in history, will have been manifest on almost every page; and it is surprising to me that they should have been so long and obstinately ignored, not by Englishmen in China, to the majority of whom they were well known, but by Englishmen at home, for whom the Celestial imposture has always possessed irresistible attractions. Journalists and writers have ever since been engaged upon the attempt to find out why it was that China was so disastrously beaten. The reasons, in their broader aspect, were twofold; although when we come to sub-headings it is difficult to find a point at which to stop. Most of the causes may, however, be classified under the title either of civil corruption, permeating every stratum of society, or of military imbecility, with a particular asterisk to the names of those enjoying high commands.

Causes of Chinese disaster.

From the Palace downwards there was no centralisation of authority or responsibility, no unity of counsel, no agreement as to action, no plan of campaign. Stupefied bewilderment, helpless inertia, or arrogant contempt for the invader, prevailed alternately, sometimes simultaneously, in every *yamen*. Each man was absorbed in the effort to get the better of somebody else, and to make something for his own pocket out of so paying a concern as a campaign. Viceroys swindled governors, governors swindled generals, and generals swindled subalterns. There were infinite and delicately-shaded grades of peculation. Of patriotism, or enthusiasm for the war, or loyalty to the dynasty, or self-respect for the race, there was not a sign. Chinese telegraph-clerks sold important information to the Japanese; Chinese

Civil corruption.

officers accepted bribes to retreat or to surrender. Nobody thought of China. In the first resort a man cared only to 'save his own face'; in the last, as I have before said, to save his skin. For years had China succeeded in baffling the distant European Powers by the poet's Riddling of the Bards:

'Confusion, and illusion, and relation,
Elusion, and occasion, and evasion';

and the same policy she thought would equally suffice for an exasperated and revengeful neighbour, with three army corps landed upon her soil. One brave sailor, the Admiral Ting, who committed suicide after the fall of Wei Hai Wei, and a few of his officers stand out as having endeavoured with single-hearted courage to do their duty. The remainder of the civil and military hierarchy were like a frightened herd of cattle cowering beneath a tree during a storm, and each trying to squeeze itself furthest away from the lightning and the rain.

Not less deplorable were the disorganisation and dishonesty that permeated every branch of the military and naval services, and predestined the campaign to ignominious failure, even before it had begun. I have already explained in this book that military *Military incapacity.* efficiency, in the modern acceptation of the term, is incompatible with the blind dominion of a system that regards warfare as a degradation of manhood, and inculcates the despicability of military service. The best men in China will not join the army; and the officers are of little superior origin to the untutored coolies whom, from a safe distance, they order to destruction. China was supposed for years to have been preparing herself, after the European example and with European mechanism, for war with any foreign Power sufficiently rash to attack her. But, as I pointed out at an earlier date, these preparations had been limited to the defence of such spots upon her coast-line as an enemy depending upon sea power would be likely to assault. No idea of an overland march by an invader had entered her head; whilst, though she has since been accused of having herself contemplated an attack upon Japan, not a thought had ever been turned to the requirements of a foreign expedition. When the war broke out, neither War Office, Horse Guards, nor General Staff existed to formulate or to direct the campaign. There was no Chinese Commander-in-Chief. Each commanding officer acted with the cheerful irresponsibility of combined jealousy and ignorance. Commissariat, transport, and ambulance can scarcely be said to have broken down, for they had never even been artificially bolstered up. The army was an unwieldy and disjointed mass, without unity, without cohesion, without a brain, without strength, with no mark of an organism save a ravenous stomach for the rations that were only procurable by plunder, and for the retrograde movement that grew to be so alluring.

Man for man, the Chinese rank-and-file were reported by observers to be physically superior to the Japanese. In any test, either of strength or endurance, they ought, apart from armament, to have swept their little opponents off the field. But under-fed, ill-equipped, unpaid, and disgracefully led—driven, in fact, like sheep to the shambles—who could expect them to fight for a cause in which they took no interest, and against an enemy with whom they had no passionate quarrel? Spears, tridents, cutlasses, gingals, pikes, old muzzle-loaders stuffed with stones and nails, which were the common weapons of the Chinese infantry, did not in themselves suggest at all an equal combat against repeating rifles, however clumsily

The Chinese soldier.

handled. But even so, the mere human instinct might somewhere have provoked a manly response, had it not been for the paralysing incubus of the native officer. The latter sustained a reputation already unique in the world. He stole the men's pay; he sold their warm clothing; he provided them with bad ammunition; and he took to his heels with a celerity that the most insubordinate of subordinates found irresistibly catching. Had the petty officers only developed the additional aptitude for suicide, which prescription dictated to the failures of a higher grade in the service, it might have fared better with the Chinese fortunes. At Wei Hai Wei, where almost alone there was decent leading, there was also, among the sailors, decent fighting.

Such were some at least of the main causes that were accountable for the ignominious defeat of China, and for the easy victory of Japan. I pass on to consider the effect that has been produced by the issue of the war upon the temper and policy of both nations, as well as upon the position of the unhappy little country whose misfortune it was to provoke the contest.
 Effects of the war.

It might have been thought, after the appalling thoroughness of the Chinese exposure, that that Power, though she could hardly feel grateful to Japan for the service so remorselessly rendered, would at least have shown some inclination to profit by its lessons. *1. Upon China.* Some symptoms of recovered initiative in the Palace, of a belated admission of convicted fiascoes on the part of the ruling junta, or of reformatory zeal among the more intelligent mandarins, might have been looked for. China having escaped, owing to the interested intervention of foreign Powers, with no worse penalty than the surrender of an island which she had never been able either to conquer or to administer, and the payment of an indemnity, for the loan of which she was willing to mortgage a security whose value she owed to the foreigner, not to herself—had a rare opportunity, as soon as peace was concluded, and she had satisfied the natural claims of her saviours, of putting her own house in order and of fortifying her still prodigious resources against another day. No such reflection, however, seems to have presented itself to the Chinese mind. She appears to have learned nothing, and, what is worse, to have unlearned nothing, from the war. She is content to remain the same old China, untaught and unteachable. Satisfied at having emerged from the struggle with no very serious interruption of internal order (the frail thread of connection by which the inert and heterogeneous mass of the Empire continues to be held together is one of the most remarkable of Chinese phenomena), without detriment to the dynasty, and without the dreaded profanation of Peking, she has settled down once more into the enjoyment of her traditional repose. Her complacency is stimulated by the consciousness that rival jealousies may be counted upon to retard, if not to prohibit, her disruption; and is flattered by the international competition for a share in her financial spoils. Some tentative steps in the direction of so-called Reform she may take, rather with the view of appeasing others than of benefiting herself. A railroad here, an arsenal there, an order in one country for ships, an appeal to another for officers—these may be duly anticipated. But to the idea of any radical change in the system, or of any voluntary effort at national recuperation, the answer returned will prove to be the eternal and contemptuous 'No.'

To those who are interested in China for her sake rather than for their own, and who are conscious of the wonderful and admirable capacities of her people, this cannot fail to be a most heartrending response. Whatever solution the

AFTER THE WAR 371

jealousy of rival Powers may suggest to the prepossessions of each, there are few dispassionate persons who would not welcome the spectacle of a resuscitated China, seriously grappling with the hard facts of her position, and addressing herself to the earnest utilisation of her magnificent resources, and of the virtues of a richly endowed race.. She might undertake the reconstruction of a National Army, in the true sense of the word, for which the most splendid material is spoiling to be employed. A fresh Navy might be created, not by the mere order of ironclads, but by engaging an entire foreign staff, and by the institution of genuine scientific training in Government Colleges. The construction and the custody of the national defences should be taken out of the hands of provincial governors and viceroys, and should be subordinated to a single plan of Imperial defence. A genuine policy of railroad construction, of the improvement of river navigation, and of public works and communications generally, would not merely add greatly to the wealth of the country, but would strengthen the central authority and retard the chances of rebellion. The success of the Imperial Customs, under European management, furnishes a model which might be applied to almost every branch of the public service. Trained financiers could be hired to reorganise the obsolete and cumbrous system of revenue and taxation. A complete reorganisation of the Civil Service and of salaries would in time ensue. Above all the Upas-tree of the Mandarinate should be attacked and cut down.

The possible.

If China were, even now, at the eleventh hour, to undertake this task ; if, in fact, she were to borrow a leaf from the school-book of her recent adversary and conqueror, not merely would she extort universal sympathy in place of contempt; but in twenty

The probable.

years' time she might place herself on the level of her own lofty conceit, and might hold her own even against a combination of those who are now individually too powerful for her. If she deliberately refrains from doing so, the tutelage which she will not voluntarily engage for herself will some day be forcibly applied to her by others; her industrial exploitation, once taken seriously in hand, will pour wealth into other coffers, not into her own: in her refusal to employ foreign servants she will discover that she has invited foreign masters; and where procrastination has been the sole policy, she may find, when it is too late, that partition is the inevitable result.

From China I pass to her recent vassal and faithful disciple, Korea, who has suffered even more than herself in the overthrow of Chinese fortunes, and who now, in sackcloth and ashes, bewails the independence of which she has been the forced recipient. In my original edition I described Korea as she appeared on the eve of the struggle. It was not a happy or a creditable spectacle; but such as it was, the Koreans, so far as they took any part in the contest, fought for its maintenance and not for its overthrow, and are now engaged in the effort to set up again a duplicate of the system, to relieve them from which the war was ostensibly undertaken. I wrote in my first edition: 'A country that is too weak to stand alone gains nothing by an affected indifference to external support. If Korea is not to collapse irretrievably, she must lean upon a stronger Power; and every consideration of policy points towards maintaining China in the position of protector which she has hitherto filled.' Let me now describe how the experiment has fared, not of substituting the protectorate of Japan for that of China—for independence, and not a mere exchange of suzerainty,

2. Upon Korea.

AFTER THE WAR

was the avowed object of the campaign—but of replacing an accepted vassalage by an independence which the petty little kingdom is far too corrupt to profit by, and too decrepit to retain. I know of no more interesting page in modern history than the attempt to dragoon Korea into a civilisation that is abhorrent both to her tastes and to her traditions.

Let it be admitted to start with that few countries in the world have ever stood in greater need of reform than Korea, and that the Japanese anxiety to apply the purge, though only a secondary motive of the war, has been of no make-believe character, but has been pushed with the professional earnestness of the physician enforcing a disagreeable medicine upon some refractory patient. This book will have shown the accumulated mass of abuses in Korea—the fearful extortion and misgovernment of the ruling classes, the sale of offices, the confusion of the Court with the administration, the judicial oppression and negation of civil rights, the scandalous state of the currency, of communications, and of native industry—with which it should not have been outside the scope of cautious statesmanship to grapple; but for the successful eradication of which were required, not the canons of abstract perfection, nor the servile standards of the class-room and the copy-book, but a conciliatory temper, inexhaustible patience, and a resolute though gentle hand. It has been in too headlong a spirit that the Japanese have addressed themselves to a task that would have frightened any less eager or more experienced people; and the fruit of their hasty sowing is now manifest in the deplorable failure of the harvest. If this is disparaging to Japan, it is equally disappointing to those who would have liked to see the Korean house swept and garnished, but had no particular desire that it should be turned inside out or upside down.

Need for reform.

The Japanese were well acquainted with the manifold evils that called for redress in Korea, and long before the war broke out, they were prepared, in the pigeon-holes of Tokio bureaux, with a cut-and-dried scheme of reforms as precise as their military plan of campaign. The first revelation of these was contained in the demand addressed by Viscount Mutsu to China in June 1894, to join with Japan in enforcing upon Korea the reorganisation of her finances, a reform of the civil service, and the institution of a national army. These suggestions, in the hands of Mr. Otori, the Japanese minister at Sŏul, presently assumed a larger shape, as the Chinese refusal to join Japan in this gratuitous programme of purification became more obstinate; and were found to include educational and judicial reform, as well as the compulsory development of Korean resources by mining, railway, and commercial concessions, in which an opening would be found for the profitable outlay of Japanese capital. Before July was over, Mr. Otori had abandoned all idea of co-operating with China, and had appointed on his own account a sort of Royal Commission, which sat daily in the Palace, and excogitated fresh revolutionary plans, for the due execution of which the old Tai Wen Kun was brought out from his retirement and temporarily invested with a kind of Regency. In this third edition of the Korean Charter, which extended to twenty-five articles, were further included the abolition of slavery and of the mourning-laws, the prohibition of imprisonment without trial, the disappearance of the Foreign Advisers, the establishment of an independent Korean era—or, in other words, the repudiation of Chinese suzerainty, and the despatch of duly accredited plenipotentiaries to Foreign Courts. The war then followed; and for a time the reforming

Japanese efforts.

fever burned with a more subdued flame. With the early victories of Japan, however, it broke out with renewed activity, and before the close of the autumn a brand new constitution, printed and bound, and embodying several of the aforesaid changes, had been promulgated, and Count Inouye had been sent to Korea as Imperial Commissioner, or practical Dictator, to carry it out.

In the first month of the new year (1895) the King went in solemn procession (escorted by blue-coated Japanese policemen) to the Ancestral Temple, and there, before the 'Holy Spirits of the Imperial Ancestors,' declared the independence of Korea, and swore to the following fourteen articles of the amended constitution:

Proclamation of Korean independence.

1. Our dependence on China shall now be severed, and the foundations of our independence firmly established.
2. We will complete and make perfect the laws of the State.
3. The King alone being the true ruler, must acquaint himself with all the affairs of the government, consulting with the various Ministers before deciding. The Queen and her relatives must not oppose these.
4. The affairs of the Palace and the affairs of the Government must each be separated from the other.
5. The powers and limits of the Council of State and of the various Boards must be defined.
6. Taxes must all be collected according to fixed laws, and these must not be exceeded.
7. The expenses incurred in collecting taxes must all be reckoned and regulated by the proper *yamen*.
8. The expenses of the Palace and of the various magistracies throughout the country must be diminished.
9. The expenses of the Palace, as well as of the various magistracies throughout the country, must be calculated for one year, and these shall form the basis for future expenditures.
10. The regulations of the various magistrates must be reformed and perfected, and their limits and powers defined.
11. Those students who possess ability must be sent abroad to study the arts and sciences.

12. Military science must be properly studied, so as to make the foundations of the State secure.

13. Laws for the punishment of crimes must be clearly defined and not exceeded, so that life and property will be afforded security.

14. Those possessing ability must be appointed to office without regard to social station.

A rain of reforms.
If there was a considerable suspicion of vagueness about these high-sounding phrases, there was no corresponding dearth of precision in the steps simultaneously taken by Count Inouye to provide the machinery for running the new *régime*. The Min faction was degraded and exiled; the existing Ministerial Departments were overhauled or abolished; and government by Cabinet was introduced. For the proper manipulation of this system suitable instruments were required. One Pak Yong Hio, who had been conspicuous among the conspirators and assassins in the revolution of 1884, and who had since lived in retirement, under the name of Boku Eiko, in Japan, was invited back and appointed Minister of Home Affairs. A scarcely less notorious partisan, named So Kwang Pem, was made Minister of Justice. These agents loyally performed their part of the bargain. Three times a week the Cabinet met, under the titular presidency of the King, but in the presence of Count Inouye, to pass resolutions, nominally proposed by Pak and So, but in reality dictated by the Dictator. Fresh Proclamations, Decrees, Constitutions, and Reforms, continued to rain like hailstones from heaven upon the devoted kingdom. Japanese advisers and instructors overflowed in the Court, the Army, the Law Courts, the Treasury and the Civil Service; and the work of reconstruction proceeded with a rapidity that almost equalled the six days' wonder of the Mosaic Creation.

In April 1895 appeared an order, under the signature of Pak, whose zeal for regeneration knew no bounds, containing no fewer than eighty-eight new rules of reform. I will not here recapitulate the entire number, the majority of which were still-born, but the principal fell under the following heads:—(1) Regulations against the abolished suzerainty of China, and in vindication of the national independence of Korea.—The honours paid to the Ming and Ching dynasties of China were to be discontinued. The era of Kuang Hsu was no longer to be employed in documents, but was to be replaced by the adoption of a Korean Calendar. Particulars of the service rendered by Japan in the recovery of the national independence were to be circulated broadcast throughout the country. Chinese literature was to be discouraged in the educational curriculum; and Koreans were to be taught the *eunmun* or native alphabetic script. (2) Regulations against social inequality and against the aristocracy.—There was to be no distinction between the *yiu-im* (including the *nyang-pan*) and the *nyang-im* or middle class. Laws were promulgated against extravagance, and against land robbery for graveyards. A number of rules dealt with the rank, etiquette, and commissions of officials, all tending to obliterate the distinction between nobles and people. (3) Regulations against superstitions and abuses: *e.g.* against sorcerers, witchcraft, and secret societies, against gambling and opium-smoking, against usury and compound interest, against abortion, suicide, and castration. (4) Judicial and administrative Reforms—relating to the methods of litigation, the regulation of the *corvée*, and of grain-advances to the people, the registration of crops, labour, and produce, the repair of high-roads, and relief to widows and orphans. Amid these attempted reforms, many of which were admirable in theory, and some of which would be excellent in practice, two appear to have been actuated by a more questionable wisdom: viz. a decree rescinding the old law by which the Korean monks (alleged to be the basest and most profligate of the population) were restricted to their monasteries and were prohibited from entering the towns; and a decree legalising the offspring of concubinage, who, under the previous law, were disqualified from holding office, and bore the civil brand of illegitimacy. These decrees were the manifest outcome of the Japanese views respectively of religion and marriage.

Meanwhile the Japanese pushed their influence to a control or readjustment of almost every department of the State. The army was uniformed, drilled, and officered by Japan. The King's Body-guard exchanged the picturesque apparel, which I have before described, for ready-made trousers from Osaka. A new Japanese Post Office was started, with stamps printed in the United States. The telegraphs were taken over by Japan, and the overland line from Söul to Fusan was worked as part of the Japanese Government system, with Japanese forms, words, and stamps. An order was issued that all lands should be surveyed and measured according to Japanese standards, and that taxes should be assessed on the Japanese model. Round the Treaty Ports and in the neighbourhood of the projected railroads land was bought up by Japanese speculators or merchants. The Chinese were treated everywhere with indignity; and persons expressing anti-Japanese sentiments were seized and thrown into prison. The poor King, who at the outset of the war had been kept, dressed as a coolie, in the Japanese camp, but whom it was afterwards found politic to restore, was shorn of all power, state, and income. His establishment was run as part of the new Palace Department, who paid his servants and provided his food. Finally, to such an absurd pitch of bureaucratic triviality was the reforming

[margin: Japanning all round.]

craze carried that the Koreans, with a certain unconscious
appositeness, were ordered to exchange their white garments
for black (made in Japan)[1] and were obliged to smoke short
pipes (also imported from Japan) instead of long ones.
Utopias have as a rule been constructed by scholars in the
harmless seclusion of their studies—a merciful dispensation
for which the world cannot be too grateful; but here was
the imaginative doctrinaire, with his pen in his hand, and
with a posse of soldiers and policemen behind him, running
riot through all the bureaux of state.

It will strike the reader, as it struck all observers, that
the methods above described were a somewhat curious way
of striking off from Korea the fetters of a foreign
dominion—the ostensible purpose of the war— *Pak and the Queen.*
and of re-establishing her independence. This is
the view that was also taken by the Koreans themselves.
The horse can be taken up to the trough; but no amount
of persuasion in the world can compel him to drink if he
is not thirsty. The Koreans had no appetite for reform.
On the contrary, they abominated it in every shape; still
more, when it was offered to them by their hereditary enemies
and recent oppressors, the Japanese. It is quite a mistake
to suppose that, whatever the official expressions of Korean
gratitude, anything but aversion was entertained by the
emancipated themselves for their so-called deliverers. From
the palace to the hovel, the new programme was met with
an obdurate conspiracy of resistance that only a slow-witted
and lethargic people could put forth. In the Court the old
intrigues were rampant. The Queen plotted to get rid of
Pak, and to restore her faithful Mins. Pak counterplotted
to remove the Queen either to another world, or to some

---

[1] In the recent decline of Japanese influence this order has been rescinded, and the old national costume revived.

more retired sphere of activity in this. The Queen heard of the conspiracy and was about to strike, when Pak got wind of her intentions, ran away, jumped on board a Japanese steamer, which was appropriately coasting about off the mouth of the river, and disappeared. He put as long a distance as he could between himself and his beloved country; but in his distant retreat at Washington he must have felt an exquisite triumph upon learning that where he had failed the old Tai Wen Kun had succeeded, and that Her Majesty had ceased to trouble.

The squalid drama of the Palace was reproduced in every grade and circle outside. Attempts were made to assassinate the philo-Japanese ministers, and to burn down their houses. They were obliged to move about escorted by Japanese policemen. The Cabinet itself was obstreperous, and overwhelmed Count Inouye with chronic resignations. It was easy enough to promulgate and post up the reforms, but there was no money in the Treasury with which to carry them out; and no officials willing to execute them. Extortion continued rampant in the provinces; the new administrative machinery fell to pieces; and the people refused to pay taxes. The Tonghaks, who had originally risen against the oppression of the native government, and had accordingly attracted the sympathy of the Japanese, now rose against their self-accredited saviours, and made common cause with their old tyrants against the new masters. Finally the Chinese, with that elasticity of temperament that is indifferent to defeat, began one by one to reappear upon the scene, as shopkeepers, hucksters, and merchants, and were received with enthusiasm. The result of eight months of reform in Korea was bewildered chaos and passionate resentment.

Passive resistance.

The King.

In the month of June the King, with a pathos in which the irony can scarcely have been unconscious, issued, or was ordered to issue, the following decree:

'Since we set about the task of reforming the administration during summer last year, establishing the basis of independence, and swore to Our ancestors and proclaimed the fact to Our people, a year has elapsed, but no result has been attained. Old habits and manners still exist, and administrative orders have not been carried out. The high and low ranks do not know one another, and domestic and foreign troubles are brewing at the same time. The sufferings of the people and the dangers to the country are felt more keenly than ever. Is all this due to Our lack of virtues or to the neglect of Our servants of State? It being Our intention to stir up ourselves, daily see the servants of State, and to consult mutually on State affairs, so as to carry out judiciously and fairly measures conducive to the welfare of the nation, you, Ministers of State, shall strictly observe laws and enforce such measures as will benefit the people, so as to realise our hopes. Viceroys and Local Governors shall also carry out Our commands for reforming abuses and preventing disorders, so as to let Our subjects gratefully submit to us, respect laws, be happy in the enjoyment of their lives and peaceful avocations, and also to let them know that the reform measures are for their own good.'

In fairness to Count Inouye, who is a man of high character and great ability, it should be borne in mind that he had been charged with a task that was beyond human capacity to execute, and which a little greater knowledge of the conditions of the problem would have saved Japan from the mistake of ever committing to him. With how sick a heart he discharged his thankless duties, and with what despondency he regarded the empty result, was obvious when in the course of a short holiday in Japan he unburdened his mind, not merely to his official superiors, but to his countrymen at large, through the medium of the press. In an interview with the *Nichi Nichi Shimbun* in July 1895, he practically

Count Inouye's confession.

admitted the hopelessness of his task, and plaintively reminded the Japanese that Korea was now (owing to their exertions) not a protected but an independent State; that it was not a gold-mine from which Japanese alone had the right to extract nuggets; but that any privilege demanded by them must, under the most-favoured-nation clause of the Treaties, equally be conceded to the subjects of other Powers. And then with a courage that bespoke true statesmanship, he proceeded to read his countrymen a lecture, and to fit on to their heads the cap of self-incurred responsibility. The Japanese in Korea, he said, were selfish, and looked only to their individual gains. They were violent and overbearing in manner to the Koreans, using their fists without provocation, knocking down the natives and cutting them about with swords. They displayed a luxury and a swagger that were offensive to the Koreans. Moreover, they were guilty of commercial dishonesty, jeopardising their trade and destroying confidence by the importation of spurious manufactures. Summing up in words, which relieve me from the task of passing any personal verdict, he said: 'As the Japanese representative I am bound to protect the interests of my fellow countrymen in Korea. But unless they reform themselves, no protection will be of any use to them.'

Since this interesting admission that it is not so much Korea, as Japan in Korea, that needs reforming, the situation has not improved, but has grown steadily worse. The outbreak has occurred in which the Queen lost her life; and the lesson which firsthand experience has burned into the mind of Count Inouye is being gradually realised by his countrymen. The reform of Korea is like the task of Sisyphus. Pushed up to the top with strained muscles and sweating limbs, the relentless

Japanese failure.

stone bumps and crashes down again to the bottom. The
Japanese now know that when, in light-hearted enthusiasm
for reform, they engaged to civilise Korea, the undertaking
was more than they bargained for, and was beyond their
strength. There are signs that the venture will not be
much longer pursued. Already the Japanese Government
has issued an official assurance to the Powers in the following terms :

'The Japanese troops now stationed in Korea are to ensure
tranquillity, to protect our Legation, Consulates, and subjects,
and also to maintain the indispensable lines of communication
with our army, which is still in the occupation of the Liao-tung
Peninsula. The necessity of keeping such troops in Korea will,
however, cease at the same time as the Liao-tung Peninsula is
evacuated. [This has since been begun.] The Japanese Government hope that the Korean Government, having entered upon the
work of reforms, may succeed in maintaining order and in protecting foreigners, even though our troops withdraw. Japan,
having no other designs, does not desire to prolong the maintenance of Japanese troops in Korea, and would be extremely gratified if relieved of such an obligation. In our relations with Korea
our policy is one of non-interference. We will gladly share
equally with other powers the same line of action.'

It is safe to predict that the Japanese reform of Korea,
without Japanese troops to sustain it, will be snuffed
out like a taper in the wind. Within six months there
will not be a trace of it left; and the last state of
the wretched little kingdom will be worse than the first.
Perhaps people will then be able to see why some of
those who, like myself, had been in the country, argued
so strongly for the maintenance of the *status quo*, and, in
the interest of Korea herself, viewed with such unconquerable suspicion the Greek gift of an impossible reform.
Had Japan been at liberty to annex the peninsula, and to
treat it, with her own instruments and in her own way, she

might in time have evolved a new order out of the existing chaos. But this she has been prevented from doing by her own pledges, and by the fear of others. She has cut the single cable by which the crazy little ship rode precariously at anchor in the Far Eastern roadstead; and she has left it to drift, without helmsman and without rudder, upon the stormy waters.

That the recent change in the attitude of Japan has been due to other causes than a tardy recognition of the hopelessness of the struggle will be obvious to those who have followed events on the wider international stage. To fail in Korea, and at the same time only to rear up a more menacing danger outside, would indeed be a disastrous return to Japan for her victory in the war. There is a neighbouring Power, whose interest in Korea has already been described, and who has been watching events with a not wholly unselfish interest. That power could not brook a Japanned Korea, and has let it clearly be known that independence, and not a mere change of protectorates, must be the result, as it was the originally professed object, of the campaign. I hope, in the light of what has happened, that I may be pardoned for quoting the terms of a forecast, upon which I ventured in August 1894, before the war had begun, in a letter to the *Times*:

The Power in the background.

'There is one contingency in which Russia might be tempted out of her philosophic and calculating calm; and that is, the victory of Japan and the substitution upon her Tiumen River boundary of the influence of a young and militant power for the less aggressive and more reliable Conservatism of China. I doubt if Russia would at all welcome Japanese fleets in Gensan and Port Lazareff, or a Korean army reorganised by Japanese officers in the occupation of posts along the northern frontier. Japan must therefore contemplate this additional danger, as the probable price of victory, that she may drive China and Russia into each other's arms, and may only discomfit her ancient adversary at the expense of raising up a far more formidable modern one in his place. And equally, if it is not to the interest of Russia to have in too close proximity to herself the impetuous Chauvinism of Japan, it is not to the interest of Japan to array against her expanding ambitions the premature hostility of Russia. The great future which she anticipates for herself may possibly not suffer, and will clearly, in her own judgment, be confirmed by a war with China. It would be irretrievably compromised if she provoked a vastly more dangerous foe.

How the new issue, thus raised, is likely to affect the fortunes of Korea primarily, and of the Far East in general, the time has not yet come to discuss. Japan has ousted China and is now retiring, for fear of being ousted herself. Meanwhile Korea is the chief sufferer at the hands of her many friends. She supplies the international football that is kicked about between the rival goal-posts of Vladivostok and Nagasaki. Poor forlorn and pathetic victim! Last of the nations and most miserable of peoples! With the achievement of independence her tragic vicissitudes have only entered upon a new phase. It will not be long before we hear of her again.

There remains the question of the effect that has been produced upon the present, and the impetus that may be given to the future of Japan, by the victorious issue of the war. That it has exhilarated the pride and augmented the confidence of her people was only to be expected. 3. Upon Japan. Already sanguine of the efficiency of her naval and military resources, she has seen her ancient enemy collapse at the first contact with her arms. Ambitious of an equal, if not a controlling, voice in the destinies of Farther Asia, she has with little difficulty dethroned from her traditional hegemony the age-long arbiter of the remote East. She has taught her Western tutors the unsuspected lesson, that she has not merely absorbed, but has, in some respects, improved upon their teaching. It would be absurd

2 B

to deny to Japan the legitimate satisfaction of so remarkable a triumph. For my own part I am less disposed to cavil at the sometimes extravagant heights of self-congratulation to which her flattered vanity has soared, than I am to admire the temperate self-restraint with which her statesmen, in the hour of victory, consented to forgo some of its most cherished spoils, because they realised that Japan had already undergone no ordinary strain, and because they feared to compromise that for which they had ventured so much. If the Japanese Government was blamed by many for the precipitancy with which it originally rushed into the war, it may claim to have expiated the offence by the statesmanlike control which it has displayed since its termination.

I have already pointed out that some discount must be made from the apparent brilliancy of the military victory of Japan owing to the inexpressible debility of her foe. If I do not join in the general chorus of panegyric on this point, still less can I follow the reasoning of that cultivated organ of opinion in England which almost from the issue of the first engagement in this war proclaimed that 'the victory of Japan involved the independence of Asia,' 'and that it sounded the death-knell of the European supremacy in that continent, upon which the political and commercial symptoms of the modern world, to a great extent, depend.' There is nothing, we have been told by the same authority, to prevent Japan from stripping Spain, Holland, and Portugal of all their Asiatic possessions. Nay, stimulated by this glorious example, even China may tardily reassert herself, and recover or wrest from Great Britain Siam, Nepaul, and Hyderabad. These speculations appear to me to be tainted by the same academic detachment from the world of fact as are those, which I shall presently discuss, of the late Mr. Pearson. They could not have

The revolt of Asia.

emanated from any critic who had been upon the spot. Because Japan has beaten China, it does not in the least follow that she could beat any single European Power (of those with whom she might conceivably come into collision), much less any combination of a larger number. Because she has acquired Formosa, it by no means follows that she can seize or that she aspires to seize the Philippines or Java. Indeed, almost her first act after the war was to give to Spain a formal pledge of abstention from any interference in the Spanish Seas. In the victory of a young and energetic and well-knit Asiatic power over the notorious invalid of the Far-Eastern world, why should Europe read her own death-sentence in that continent? Nay, a man has but to go to Japan itself to learn the truth of Count Inouye's impressive warning to his own countrymen that a good deal of self-reform will be required before Japan can take in hand the readjustment of the fortunes of others.

These reflections, however, do not preclude the certainty, as a result of the war, of a great increase, in another respect, in the power of Japan. If she does not thereby became a menace to the political influence of Europe in Asia, she may and probably will become a formidable antagonist to British and German trade. Her industrial and mercantile future will receive a decided impetus from this rise in her fortunes. Endowed not merely with an intelligent and enterprising people, but with ample riches, and free from the harassing responsibilities of continental engagements or colonial possessions, there is scarcely any limit that need be set, within a given area, to the commercial expansion of Japan. Every year she becomes more self-providing and less dependent upon others. Six years ago she imported 67 per cent. of her requirements. She now only imports 25 per cent. She has instructed her-

[marginal note: Commercial and industrial expansion.]

self so efficaciously that she can now all but dispense with outside tuition. Her railways were built and run, in the first place, by foreigners. There is at present not a single alien employed upon them. In her cotton mills, where the produce of over half-a-million spindles is challenging the command of the Far-Eastern market, there is a similarly notable absence. In the recent war her soldiers fought with rifles patented and manufactured, not in Europe, but in Japan. Every cartridge, every shot and shell, nay, even the Maxim guns employed, were of Japanese origin. Less than half-a-dozen Europeans are now engaged in the arsenals. When I first visited Japan in 1887, she possessed but a few lines of steamboats, and those for the most part, if not entirely, captained and engineered by Englishmen and Scotchmen. She has now several first-rate lines of steamers, subsidised by the Government, running to every port in the Far East, and wholly officered by natives. Her proximity to the immense and only half-developed market of China, the skill of her artificers, the low rate of wages and the long hours for which they are content to work, give her an advantage with which no European rival can cope. She has a currency which is not fettered by international or imperial exigencies, but which she can regulate to suit her own fiscal needs. I do not mean to say that there is not another side to the picture, or, if the trade of Europe meets with a set-back in these respects, that there are not other channels of recuperation or untapped markets still waiting to be conquered. Japan herself must, for a long time at any rate, be dependent upon Europe for a good deal of the raw material which she proposes to work up. A programme of shipbuilding or of railway construction, or public works, or factories and mills, cannot be carried out without an appeal to European resource and invention. For a while these exchanges may constitute an equipoise. But in the long run Japan may expect to forge ahead of her rivals in the China Seas; and, whatever may have then become of the political balance of power, she will have laid a hand upon the commercial scales that will cause many a moment of disquiet in the counting-houses of the West. In this brilliant and lucrative career, the war with China, which was undertaken with far different objects, may one day be reckoned as marking a very conspicuous stage.

CHAPTER XIII

THE DESTINIES OF THE FAR EAST

Prudens futuri temporis exitum
Caliginosa nocte premit Deus,
Ridetque si mortalis ultra
  Fas trepidat. Quod adest, memento
Componere aequus.
        HORACE: *Carm.* iii. 29.

Summary.

IN the two remaining chapters I propose briefly to sum up the conclusions to which I have endeavoured to lead the readers of this book, and, in so far as they appear to justify so venturesome an enterprise, to cast the horoscope of the future. I desire also to indicate the part that is now being played, or is likely hereafter to be played, on the majestic stage to which I have invited attention, by the Government and the citizens of my own country. In this first portion of my study of the kingdoms of the Far East I have dealt with three States alone—Japan, Korea, and China. Of these, Japan and China are powerful Empires (though in very different senses of the term) whose orbit in the firmament of nations may claim a certain fixity, and whose national existence, in spite of the fact that their political boundaries are liable to modification, is not likely at any time to be submerged. Korea, on the contrary, belongs to a class of States of whom future fixity is the last attribute to be predicated, and before whom an anxious course of vicissitudes, in no degree diminished by the issue

THE DESTINIES OF THE FAR EAST 391

of the recent conflict, opens. Though nominally independent, her territories are still occupied and will probably again be overrun by the armies of one or another of her jealous neighbours. She is too feeble and too corrupt to stand alone. They have successfully interfered to prevent her from leaning upon China. Will Japan be content to let her lean upon Russia? Will Russia acquiesce in her leaning upon Japan? The main result of the war has been to leave Korea, in an even greater degree than it found her, the powder-magazine of the Far East.

The superficial features of Japanese character and politics are known to all. Her nimble-witted and light-hearted people, the romantic environment of her past, and the astonishing rapidity with which she is assimilating all that the West has to teach her, have been praised with an indiscriminate prodigality that has already begun to pall, and has not been without its bad effects upon herself. I conceive that no worse service could have been rendered to Japan than the publication of the last work in English which has been dedicated to her charms by a well-known English writer and poet. These overloaded encomiums not merely cloy the palate; they foster a growing vanity against which the Japanese require to be upon their guard, and which may, unless abated, both provoke and deserve the chastisement of some smart rebuff. Japan is sure enough of a distinguished and even brilliant future, without being told that she has exhausted the sum of all human excellences in the present. Moreover, a time of internal fermentation lies before her in the attempt to graft a purely democratic product on to a stem from which the feudal sap has not been entirely expunged, and to reconcile the widest aspirations of constitutional liberty with the relics of a theocratic *régime*.

The future of Japan.

This struggle will require the fullest measure of sense and self-control, and may, perhaps, not be tided over without crisis and suffering. From such a trial the patriotism of her people and the liberal sentiments of her statesmen are capable of bringing her forth, if not unscarred, at least with vitality unexhausted; and that in the course of the next quarter of a century she will take her place on a level of technical equality with the great Powers of the West may be accepted as certain. The Revision of the Treaties, effected just as these pages originally passed into the printer's hands, will free her from all artificial trammels, and while ratifying, will also test her right to international autonomy.

Japan was frequently blamed before the war for squandering too much money upon armaments, military and naval, and for neglecting the requirements of industrial and commercial expansion. It is true that her resources are capable of very considerable development, and that a prudent finance, already in part inaugurated, will greatly increase both the numbers and the prosperity of her people. But the critics to whom I allude had lost sight of the part which Japan aspires to play in the Far East, and to which her policy of expenditure and organisation has been strictly subordinated. That part is determined by her geographical situation. Placed at a maritime coign of vantage upon the flank of Asia, precisely analogous to that occupied by Great Britain on the flank of Europe, exercising a powerful influence over the adjoining continent, but not necessarily involved in its responsibilities, she sets before herself the supreme ambition of becoming, on a smaller scale, the Britain of the Far East. By means of an army strong enough to defend our shores, and to render invasion unlikely, and still more of a navy

The Great Britain of the Far East.

sufficiently powerful to sweep the seas, she sees that England has retained that unique and commanding position in the West which was won for us by the industry and force of character of our people, by the mineral wealth of these islands, by the stability of our Government, and by the colonising genius of our sons. By similar methods Japan hopes to arrive at a more modest edition of the same result in the East. Like the English, her people are stubborn fighters and born sailors. If she can but intimidate any would-be enemy from attempting a landing upon her shores, and can fly an unchallenged flag over the surrounding waters, while from her own resources she provides occupation, sustenance, clothing, and wages for her people, she will fulfil her *rôle* in the international politics of the future.

And how important a one this may be, those who consider her position in relation both to the Pacific Ocean and to the neighbouring mainland of Asia, in the light that is cast upon it by the ambition of rival Powers, will easily be able to judge. The opening of the Canadian Pacific Railway and Trans-Pacific route on the eastern side; the ultimate completion of the Nicaragua or some other inter-oceanic Canal farther to the south; the maritime ambitions of Russia, already dissatisfied with her base at Vladivostok and thirsting for a Pacific commerce and a Pacific armament; the impetus that will be lent to these desires and the revolution that will be produced in Northern Asia by the Siberian Railway; the emulous zeal with which foreign Powers, England, America, France, and Germany, are snapping up the isles and islets of Oceania; the connection (certain to increase as time advances) between Japan and the British Colonies of the Australasian group—may in the course of the coming century develop a Pacific Question, the existence of which is now not so much as suspected, and the outlines of which can at present be only dimly foreseen. In the solution of such a question Japan, by virtue of her situation, should be capable of playing a considerable part. That she should be free to do so, and should develop the requisite moral force and strength (in both of which she is at present lacking), it is necessary—as I wrote before the war, and see no reason now for altering—that she should hold herself aloof from foreign entanglements, and, above all, that she should not come into sustained or renewed collision with her old and hereditary antagonist, China. She has fought and conquered China; has settled to her own satisfaction and in her own interest the feud of centuries; has demonstrated her military and naval superiority and the reality of her Western tuition; has rounded off her island dominion by the capture of Formosa; and has, wisely for herself, been persuaded to abandon those acquisitions on the Asiatic mainland, which, though they would have placed Peking perpetually at her mercy, would yet have left her a Continental Power, subject to all the harassing and even perilous responsibilities, that, in Asia not less than in Europe, attach to that position. She can now afford to take a wider and more statesmanlike outlook. That the true policy for Japan, ignoring tradition and history and burying national antipathies, is a friendly understanding with China, interested like herself in keeping at a distance the single common peril—namely, the advance of the Muscovite from the north—appears to me self-evident, and is, I believe, appreciated by her own statesmen. Such a solidarity, without taking the form of an offensive and defensive alliance, would be strong enough to preserve the balance of power in the Far East and to prepare the way by which Japan may attain to that still higher place which she yearns to fill among the nations of the world.

THE DESTINIES OF THE FAR EAST 395

The future of China is a problem the very inverse of that involved in the future of Japan. The one is a country intoxicated with the modern spirit, and requiring above all things the stamina to understand the shock of too sudden an upheaval of ancient ideas and plunge into the unknown. The other is a country stupefied with the pride of the past, and standing in need of the very impulse to which its neighbour too incontinently yields. Japan is eager to bury the past; China worships its embalmed and still life-like corpse. Japan wants to be reformed out of all likeness to herself. China declines to be reformed at all. She is a monstrous but mighty anachronism, defiantly planted on the fringe of a world to whose contact she is indifferent and whose influence she abhors; much as the stones of Solomon's Temple look down upon an alley in modern Jerusalem, or as the Column of Trajan rears its head in the heart of nineteenth century Rome.

Future of China.

In the foregoing pages I have depicted in their own country and capital the characteristics of this unlovely but admirable people. But I am not sure that they are not even more wonderful when seen outside their native land. At Hongkong, Hanoi, Cholen, Singapore, Penang, Bangkok, as also at Rangoon and Mandalay on the one side, and at Batavia and Manila on the other, they have established great communities, living contentedly under alien laws, and drawing into their fingers the reins of a multiform and lucrative commerce. Not merely do they absorb and frequently monopolise the retail trades, but they farm the State monopolies; they run big steamships and own immense mills; they float companies with large capital; they own and work productive mines. Under British protection 200,000 of them live serenely in

The Chinese as aliens.

the city of Hongkong, and 180,000 on the island of Singapore. In the adjoining native State of Jahore, 210,000 out of a total population of 300,000 are Chinese. Throughout the Malay States they far outnumber the Malays. In Siam there are said to be between two and three millions of the Yellow Race, or nearly one-third of the entire population. Freed from the exactions and inquisition of their own Government, they develop on foreign soil, and for the edification of foreign commerce, the very qualities which, if applied to the regeneration of their own country, might make her once again the mistress of the Eastern world.

It is sometimes questioned whether this ever-increasing flood of Chinese emigration may not constitute an ultimate danger to the countries which it overruns, and whether the invasion of the hordes of Jinghiz Khan is not capable of a milder twentieth-century reproduction. These apprehensions have recently received a fresh and formidable impetus from the encouragement given to them in the scholarly and remarkable work of the late Mr. Pearson.[1] Therein, supported by much learning, confirmed by ingenious analogies, and rendered attractive by a luminous and agreeable style, may be found developed at length the dismal thesis that the future of Eastern Asia, if not of parts of Central Asia also, is not for the White but for the Yellow Race; and that neither Great Britain, nor France, nor Russia, but China, is the Power into whose hands will pass the predestined sceptre of the Far East. With both the premises and the conclusions of Mr. Pearson's fascinating but melancholy argument I find myself in total disagreement. Before explaining, however, the points and grounds of difference between us, let me summarise Mr. Pearson's propositions as far as possible in his own words.

The theory of Chinese resurrection.

[1] *National Life and Character*: *a Forecast*, by C. H. Pearson.

THE DESTINIES OF THE FAR EAST 397

With the view of sustaining his main and ultimate induction, Mr. Pearson first marshals the evidences, as he conceives them to be, of the power and vitality of China. He points to her recovery of the revolted province of Chinese Turkestan or Kashgaria from Yakub Beg in 1874-87; he says she dominates Korea; and he reminds us that she succeeded in finally stamping out the Mohammedan rebellion in Yunnan. These are the testimonies to her internal organisation and strength. Casting his eyes over a wider range, he next observes the phenomena to which I have already alluded. He sees Chinamen flooding Singapore and the Malay Peninsula, beginning to settle in Borneo and Sumatra, encroaching upon the labour markets of California and Australia, and already supplanting the natives in Hawaii and other islands of the Pacific. He draws attention to the flexibility and versatility of the Chinese character, to their easy adaptation to extremes of climate, to their excellence as labourers, their industry as merchants, and their docility as colonists. Finally, he contemplates the acquisition by the Power, thus endowed by nature, of the resources of modern invention, of a network of railways connecting the great cities of the Empire with each other and with adjoining countries, of telegraphs and steamers, of the use of foreign capital, of large armies drilled and equipped on the European model, of artillery and scientific implements of war, and, above all, the leadership of a really great man. Nay, intoxicated by the enchantment of the picture, he is actually willing to dispense with the last-named advantage :—

<small>Mr. Pearson's arguments in its favour.</small>

'The Chinese do not need even the accident of a man of genius to develop their magnificent future. Ordinary statesmanship, adopting the improvements of Europe, without offending the customs and prejudices of the people, may make them a State which no Power in Europe will dare to disregard; with an army which could march by fixed stages across Asia, and a fleet which could hold its own against any that the strongest of European Powers could afford to keep permanently in Chinese waters.'[1]

Such being the grounds of his confidence in the future of China, Mr. Pearson next proceeds to indicate what in his opinion she may be expected to do. 'On three sides of her lie countries that she may easily seize, over which very often she has some old claim, and in the climate of which her people can live. It is more than probable that some of these will pass under Chinese rule.' Borneo will certainly be hers. 'Expansion towards the south and south-west seems most probable; but she is not debarred either towards the north and west.' Nepal might be wrested from England, parts of Turkestan from Russia, and the Amur Province from the same Power. The danger of this military advance would be still further accentuated if China became a Mohammedan Power.

The new march of the Mongols.

Finally Mr. Pearson sums up his presentment of the triple future that awaits his *protégé*, as a colonising Power, a military Power, and a trading Power, and the corresponding decline that threatens the Caucasian stock, in the following language:—

Lords of the future.

'On the whole, it seems difficult to doubt that the black and yellow belt, which always encircles the globe between the Tropics, will extend its area and deepen its colour with time. The work of the white man in these latitudes is only to introduce order and an acquaintance with the best industrial methods of the West. The countries belong to their autochthonous races; and these, though they may in parts accept the white man as a conqueror and organiser, will gradually become too strong and unwieldy for him to control; or, if they retain him, will do it only with the condition that he assimilates himself to the inferior race. . . . The citizens of the black and yellow races will then be taken up into the social

[1] *National Character*, p. 112.

THE DESTINIES OF THE FAR EAST 399

relations of the white races, will throng the English turf or the
salons of Paris, and will be admitted to intermarriage. . . . Does
any one doubt that the day is at hand when China will have cheap
fuel from her coal-mines, cheap transport by railways and steamers,
and will have founded technical schools to develop her industries?
Whenever that day comes, she may wrest the control of the world's
markets, especially throughout Asia, from England and Germany.
. . . A hundred years hence, when the Chinese, Hindus, and
negroes, who are now as 2 to 1 to the higher races, shall be as 3
to 1 ; when they have borrowed the science of Europe and developed
their still virgin worlds, the pressure of their competition upon the
white man will be irresistible. He will be driven from every
neutral market, and forced to confine himself within his own. . . .
With civilisation equally diffused, the most populous country
must ultimately be the most powerful ; and the preponderance of
China over any rival—even over the United States of America—is
likely to be overwhelming.'

It will be conceded that Mr. Pearson has not erred on the
side of timidity in this forecast, at once so complimentary to
China and so lugubrious for ourselves, and that
the colours of his palette are applied with no Objection of unoccu-
hesitating or piecemeal brush. One objection pied area
alone he admits, and that in order to refute it. at home.
The theory of continued Chinese expansion outside China
proper might seem to be qualified by the enormous unoccupied area at her disposal within. Equivalent in size to
twenty-two, or, as others say, to twenty-six Englands, she
could maintain a population of 650,000,000 or 750,000,000 ;
i.e. she might increase for fifty years before requiring relief
by exodus. In fact, from her superior fertility, China could
support more inhabitants than England to the square mile,
and might duplicate her numbers before she needed to
trouble her neighbours. To which considerations might be
added the conservative genius of Chinese government, and
the discouragement offered to native emigration. This line
of reasoning Mr. Pearson answers by pointing out that

though the Taiping Rebellion forty years ago, which lasted for fourteen years, cost China from twenty to fifty million lives, and though between 1842 and 1882 the nation is calculated to have decreased by thirty millions, yet it was during this very period that she continued to pour her colonists into Siam, Malaysia, the Straits Settlements, America, Peru, and Australia.

I have now summed up, I hope with fairness, Mr. Pearson's argument, and will proceed to show why, in my opinion, it is for the most part unsound. I am conscious, of course, of the extreme fallibility of any individual speculations as to the future, and am quite prepared to believed that *a priori* my own forecast is more likely to be invalidated than one proceeding from so accomplished a scholar as Mr. Pearson. But if the latter writer had, as I believe, never been in China, but only studied the Chinese question from the academic distance of an Australian study; and if, further, I can show his premises to be of questionable validity and authority, there will be some reason for regarding his conclusions with suspicion; the more so that they are, to the best of my knowledge, shared by no contemporary authority who either knows or has resided in China itself.

Reasons for disputing Mr. Pearson.

I will follow Mr. Pearson's reasoning in the order in which he has himself displayed it, premising that much of it has already been answered in anticipation in the pages of this work. The suppression by China of the rebellions in Kashgar and Yunnan justifies no such complimentary inference as Mr. Pearson has drawn. The former depended only upon the personality of a single individual, Yakub Beg, appealing to religious fanaticism and taking advantage of the military weakness of China at a distance of 3500 miles from her base. With the removal by

Alleged successes of China.

poison of the usurper, the movement, almost without fighting, collapsed. Similarly the Taiping and Mohammedan rebellions, so far from testifying to the might of China, demonstrated the full measure of her weakness; for the resources of the Empire were strained almost to breaking point to cope with the double peril, which not less than twenty-five years of fighting were required to suppress. My account of the situation in Korea will have shown that, however creditable to the astuteness of the suzerain Power, China's authority there, even before the war, could scarcely be cited as an evidence of material or military strength. Now that it has ceased altogether to exist, Mr. Pearson loses the support of the Korean prop of his argument, the weight of which, such as it is, must be transferred to the opposite scale.

I next turn to the argument based upon the colonising genius of China, as illustrated in the maritime countries and islands of the Far East, as well as in more distant lands possessing a frontage on the Pacific Ocean. It is assumed that the steady infiltration of Chinese emigrants into these regions, and the control of the labour market which they so rapidly acquire, are the inevitable precursors of a complete political and commercial domination. These anticipations I do not share. Chinese emigration I believe to be dictated by the animal interests of self-maintenance, and by the craving of masculine labour to find an outlet, which is denied to it by the selfish and rapacious tyranny of the Chinese administrative and economic system at home;[1] and to be divorced from any

[1] Since writing these words I have met with a curious confirmation of their accuracy in the report of a Chinese official, who was sent by his Government as Consul-General to Singapore in 1893, to report upon the reasons which induced so many thousand Chinamen to voluntarily expatriate themselves under foreign dominion. He wrote: 'When asked why they do not take

ulterior intent of conquest or dominion. The Marquis Tseng, in his famous article,[1] wrote, or was made to write, as follows :—

'The Chinese have never been an aggressive race. History shows them to have always been a peaceful people, and there is no reason why they should be otherwise in the future. China has none of that land-hunger so characteristic of other nations, and, contrary to what is generally believed in Europe, she is under no necessity of finding in other lands an outlet for a surplus population. Considerable numbers of Chinese have at different times been forced to leave their homes, and push their fortunes in Cuba, Peru, the United States, and the British Colonies; but this must be imputed rather to the poverty and ruin in which they were

---

the opportunity of returning and settling in their native land, their knitted brows and frowning countenances might be observed, and the following complaints were generally made: They said that they feared the so-called "investigations" of their local mandarins; the oppression of the *yamen*-underlings; and the extortions of their clansmen and neighbours, instances of which could be given without number. They complained that those who happened to return home had been maliciously accused as pirates and robbers; as purchasers of contraband in arms and ammunition in order to supply sea pirates; and as buyers and kidnappers of coolie slaves for the purpose of supplying foreign ruffians. Some of them had had their baggage and belongings—the savings of years—forcibly taken away from them and partitioned amongst local ruffians; and some had had their houses pulled down and were forbidden to build on the land of their buying. Alone and unprotected, considered to be strangers and aliens amongst their own kindred, to whom could they apply for help, surrounded as they were on all sides by rapacious hawks, of high and low degree? Hence, having taken a lesson from experience, none of the wealthier Chinese in foreign countries cared to return to the land of their ancestors. Those who did go to China to trade or travel, went either as British or Dutch subjects, under the protection of a foreign Government.' A further confirmation of the same opinion is furnished by a recent lecture of a well-known Dutch Professor, Dr. de Groot, of Leyden, whose countrymen in the East Indies appear to have been seized with a similar panic to Mr. Pearson. He argues in reply that these fears are either baseless or grossly exaggerated, and must be traced in the main to palpable ignorance regarding the chief causes of Chinese emigration, which he limits to the two provinces of Kuangtung and Fukien. These causes he describes as the absence of irrigation and dearth of rain, the primitive condition of agriculture, the discouragement and non-existence of native industries, the superabundance of day-labourers, and the low rate of wages.

[1] 'China, the Sleep and the Awakening.' *Asiatic Quarterly Review*, January 1887.

THE DESTINIES OF THE FAR EAST

involved by the Taiping and Mohammedan rebellions, than to the difficulty of finding the means of subsistence under ordinary conditions.[1] In her wide dominions there is room and to spare for all her teeming population. What China wants is not emigration, but a proper organisation for the equable distribution of the population. In China proper much land has gone out of cultivation, whilst in Manchuria, Mongolia, and Chinese Turkestan there are immense tracts of country which have never felt the touch of the husbandman.'

This reasoning is for the most part true, though it is to be regretted that neither the Marquis Tseng nor any other Chinese statesman seems to have persuaded his Government to deduce from it the only practical lesson, viz. that public works in China would provide that very occupation and outlet for lack of which expatriation is forced upon her citizens.

An examination of the Chinese emigrant communities in British, French, Dutch, or Spanish territories, leads to the same conclusion as to their character and objects. For, on the one hand, the Chinese are by nature tractable, orderly, and content to be governed. They fully appreciate the benefits of a just and organised administration. In a petition which was being signed while I was in Singapore, praying for a continuation of the term of office of the retiring Governor, Sir Cecil Smith, the Chinese population of the colony mentioned, among other grounds of his popularity and of their gratitude, his suppression a few years before of the Chinese Secret Societies, which were as much a curse to themselves as they were a danger to others. On the other hand, the Chinese population in the above-mentioned places is of a two-fold character.

Character of Chinese colonists.

[1] This statement cannot be implicitly accepted, seeing that the emigration of Chinamen to the ports and islands of the Eastern Archipelago, and to Australia and America, had begun long before the Taiping or Mohammedan rebellions, and was the natural consequence of poverty acting upon an overcrowded population.

Either it is composed of a floating element who come down from China to make money for themselves, because there are a better opening and higher wages than at home, but who contemplate as speedy a return as possible to their native country; or it consists of a sedentary population, who never mean to go back at all, because they prefer the city of their adoption, and have married the women of the country. Ugly as is the Chinaman to the European eye, he possesses the gift, unique in the world, of making himself acceptable as a husband to the women of half-a-score of different races. He weds, with equal readiness and satisfaction to both parties, the Korean, the Annamite, the Cambogian, the Siamese. (With the Malays, who are Mohammedans, it is, of course, different.) This connubial facility is an element on the side of order and good conduct, for it establishes him, not merely as a wanderer, but as a contented citizen in the land of Moab. At the same time it severs him, so to speak, from the parent stock; for he loses the connection with the mother country which a Chinese spouse and connections would fortify, while the ensuing generation is hybrid both in origin and sympathy. I doubt, indeed, whether emigrants have ever anywhere established a permanent dominion who did not bring their wives along with them.[1]

---

[1] This sentence has been made the text of a charming essay by Sir Alfred Lyall, entitled 'Permanent Dominion in Asia,' in the *Nineteenth Century* of September 1895. He disputes the generalisation in the following terms: 'On the whole, it seems doubtful, if the case of the English colonies proper be set aside, whether permanent dominion has anywhere been established by emigrants who have brought their wives with them. One might even go further, and contend not only that dominion has rarely been strengthened by the importation of women from home, but also that, in some instances, it may be weakened when a ruling race intermarries strictly within its own nationality, because such exclusiveness tends towards the formation of a caste.' I would answer this contention by the existing cases, quoted by Sir A. Lyall in a different context, of Great Britain in India and of Russia in

Passing from thence to the argument that rests upon the capabilities of China as a great military Power, I have said enough in previous pages of this book to show that in my judgment any such estimate is a delusion. Many European writers appear to think that because China has so many millions of stalwart and tough-limbed sons, she must therefore possess so many hundred thousands of excellent fighting soldiers; and that because she has arsenals, where, under European eyes, she turns out European cannons, projectiles, rifles, cartridges, and powder, she has therefore an organised force capable of being placed in the field against, and of giving serious trouble to, a European army. No such opinion has, I believe, ever been entertained or advanced by a competent critic. There is no country in the world where the military profession is of smaller account, or where the science of warfare is less intelligently studied than in China. The phrase *cedant arma togæ* is there no aspiration for honourable peace, no sigh of satisfaction over the conclusion of a successful campaign, but is the confession of an abiding contempt for the art that prefers the sword to the pen. The Chinese army, under Chinese officers, even with muskets

Military weakness of China.

Asia. There is a Eurasian element in India, but it lends no strength to British dominion. The latter is assured by the presence of a foreign caste, exclusively and matrimonially replenished from home. Since Englishmen took their wives out to India, British power has not become less but more secure. It is true that the governing society is transient and fluctuating. But rapidity of steam-navigation compensates for frequency of change, and there is a constancy of structure in the mass whose molecules are individually detached and fleeting. The Russians in Asia are equally a caste, and though their power of assimilation with Asiatics is notorious, it is not based upon marriage with Asiatic women. Neither in India nor in Asia does the occupation of the governing race amount to permanent settlement, and it may by some be considered premature to speak of it as permanent dominion. But where do we learn that permanence of dominion is necessarily identical with permanence of settlement, or that capacity for assimilation involves marriage with an inferior race? The Roman Empire perished, not because its ruling class was, but because it ceased to remain, a caste.

in its hands and cartridges in its pouches, is an undisciplined rabble of tramps, about as well qualified to withstand a European force as a body of Hyde Park processionists would be to repel a charge of the Life Guards. Whatever the Chinese rank and file have already shown themselves capable of doing under European lead, whatever they might do were such lead repeated in the future,[1] they are, viewed as a national army, a relatively inferior military instrument to the weakest contingent in the force of the feeblest European State. This paragraph, which appeared *ipsissimis verbis* in my original edition, has since then received the crowning confirmation of the war with Japan.

Under these conditions, which might be predicted, in a scarcely less degree, of the naval as well as of the military forces of China, to talk, as Mr. Pearson does, of a Chinese army marching by fixed stages across Asia, or even confining itself to the more humble operation of recovering the adjoining countries which once acknowledged the sovereignty of Peking, appears to me the wildest freak of fancy. No one who had the least acquaintance with the state of the frontier garrisons in Kashgaria, or with the feelings of the Mohammedan population of those regions, could ever speak seriously of China wresting from Russia any portion of Eastern Turkestan. The idea of her marching through Tibet, and across the Himalayas, to re-

Chinese reconquest impossible.

[1] I am not here discussing the contingency, which I have elsewhere contemplated, of the Chinese forces being utilised for purposes of defence, or even ultimately of offence, by an alien Power either in complete or in partial occupation of the country, or placed (in virtue of a compact with the Chinese Government) in control of the military and naval forces of the Empire. Such a use of the Chinese army, which is not so utterly improbable in the far future as to be unworthy of consideration, might invest China with a defensive strength at present undreamed of; and might even (though this is less likely) suggest ideas of expansion. But it is obvious, *ex hypothesi*, that the authority so extended would not be that of Chinese sovereignty, which is the particular point raised by Mr. Pearson's argument.

cover Nepal from Great Britain, is scarcely less fantastic;
while, on the day when Russia is compelled by military or
diplomatic repulse to hand back to her the Amur Province,
it will no longer be possible to return a negative answer to
the question of the American poet—

> 'Is civilisation a failure,
> And is the Caucasian played out?'

To an even more nebulous future, into which not even the
charms of an unfettered imagination will seduce me, belongs
the epoch when, according to Mr. Pearson, Chinese gentlemen will throng the *salons* of Paris and the clubs of Pall Mall; when a Chinese patron of the turf will lead back to the weighing-room a winner of the English Derby; and when the problem of superfluous womanhood will be solved by the apparition at Christian altars of eligible Chinese husbands. {The dream of social apotheosis.}

What Mr. Pearson appears to have lost sight of, in casting
his political horoscope for China, is, on the one hand, the
influence that must inevitably be exercised upon it by the faults as well as the virtues of the national character, by the *morale* of Chinese officialdom, and by the quality of Chinese administration; {Influence of national character.} on the other hand, the lessons of history, which are written in characters so large that he who runs may read. He omits from consideration the Chinese system of government —short-sighted, extortionate, universally corrupt—and the temper of the people, averse from national enterprise, untrained to conquest, devoid of patriotic ardour, content to stagnate. In the face of these obstacles not even the exemplary sobriety of Chinamen, their industrial energy, or their genius for accumulation, can turn that which is a stationary, if not a receding, into a dynamic and aggressive force.

We are led by the teachings of history to the same conclusion. So far from taking naturally to a career of conquest, it is rather in her power of assimilating those by whom she has herself been conquered, that China has displayed her greatest strength. Two and a half centuries ago the millions of China succumbed easily to the assault of a few hundred thousand Tartars, whose yoke they have ever since contentedly borne. Four centuries earlier they had in similar fashion accepted a Mongol master. What the Mongols did, and what the Manchus did, I fail to see why others should not do after them, whose power, as compared with theirs, is in the same ratio as a field-gun to a Roman catapult, or a repeating rifle to the cross-bow. Nay, the work of detrition has already begun and proceeds apace; nor is it the least peculiar feature of Mr. Pearson's daring forecast that it should have been framed in an epoch which, so far from revealing any symptoms of recovered or expanding strength, has, on the contrary, witnessed a steady and still unarrested decline. It is entirely during the last half, and mainly during the last quarter, of a century that Tongking, Annam, and Cochin China have been wrested from the grasp of China by France, that Siam has repudiated her ancient allegiance, that Burma, once a vassal, has been absorbed into the British system, that the Liuchiu Islands, also a tributary State, have been allowed to pass tacitly into the hands of Japan,[1] that Korea, after becoming a playground for the jealous rivalry of foreigners, has now been definitely wrested from the Chinese connection, that the Amur and

Lessons of history.

---

[1] The annexation by Japan of the Liuchiu Islands, which had for centuries accepted the overlordship of China, and had sent an annual Tribute Mission to Peking, was the outcome of the Formosan Expedition in 1874. The Chinese behaved feebly in the matter; and the Japanese, who swaggered and assumed the offensive, won. They then deposed the King, and incorporated the group of 36 islands in the administrative system of the Empire.

Ussuri Provinces have been pusillanimously ceded to Russia.
And yet, in face of this unbroken record of contraction,
against which there is nothing to set but the recovery of
Kulja,[1] we are invited to believe that the Power which
has suffered this continuous diminution is on the threshold
of a mighty revival, and is predestined to overrun the
universe.[2]

Another danger which Mr. Pearson has overlooked, and
which, though it need not seriously affect the national
existence of China, must yet cripple her power
of external advance, is the chance of internal *Danger of rebellion.*
disruption. The items that compose the vast
congeries of peoples and communities still acknowledging
the Chinese sway are but loosely strung together. Even if
we omit from consideration the Tibetans, the Mongolians,
and the enormous mass of Turki and Mussulman subjects,
ever hovering on the brink of revolt, there is in China
proper little or none of that cohesion which is essential

---

[1] China has received an even greater credit than she deserves for this achievement, which was a personal triumph for the diplomacy of the Marquis Tseng. In consenting to the retrocession, which was, after all, the fulfilment of a solemn compact, Russia took very good care to get her *quid pro quo*, which there was nothing in the compact to authorise.

[2] Sir A. Lyall, in the article before cited, answers that, except the districts ceded to Russia, 'these acquisitions made by France and England were independent states, that paid only a formal tribute to Peking and had long ago separated themselves from China, if, indeed, they had ever formed a substantive part of the Empire.' This also was Japan's contention with regard to Korea, when entering upon the recent war. It was not true, however, of Korea ; nor did it hold good of Tongking, for which the Chinese fought as hard as for an integral portion of the Empire ; nor of Upper Burma, in the outlying provinces of which Chinese influence had been so thoroughly recognised that, upon annexing it, the British Government paid the Chinese the diplomatic compliment of continuing the decennial tribute mission to Peking. Each of these countries China either did fight to retain and was beaten, or was too weak to defend and therefore lost. The question of the probable gain to their present owners, which is raised by Sir A. Lyall, is entirely distinct from that of the actual loss sustained by their former suzerains.

to national strength. Each province is an independent unit, with its own government and army, capable in times of convulsion of breaking away without difficulty from the central fabric. No real bond of union connects the northern with the southern portions of the Empire, whose peoples cannot even understand each other's dialect. There are parts of the Empire into which the news of the war with Japan, and of its disastrous consequences (for China) have never yet penetrated. In some of the outlying provinces the lower orders, though lightly taxed, are plunged in chronic penury. The authority of the dynasty is maintained by its sacrosanct associations, by a highly organised and interested official hierarchy, and by the prestige of Peking. But were the capital occupied by an enemy, as it could be with very little difficulty (particularly by an enemy advancing from the north), the Emperor expelled, and the dynasty overturned, it is doubtful whether China would persevere in any protracted resistance, or initiate a policy of revenge. The various elements of disorder scattered throughout the Empire would each find its local focus, and a reign of emulous anarchy and universal dislocation might be expected to ensue.

What then, it may be asked, if this picture of a resuscitated and conquering China be rejected as a brilliant extravaganza of the imagination, is the alternative future that may be anticipated for this extraordinary people? As regards the physical diffusion of the Yellow Race, Mr. Pearson is possibly right. Borneo and Sumatra and New Guinea will be the industrial spoil of her frugal colonists. She may completely swamp the Malays in Malaysia; she may gain a firmer foothold in Siam. Her intrepid sons may cross the ocean and knock at new and unexpected portals. Whether a Manchu Emperor

The real destiny.

THE DESTINIES OF THE FAR EAST 411

handles the vermilion pencil in the halls of the Forbidden City, or whether for the proclamations of the Son of Heaven is substituted the ukase of a Muscovite Tsar, that expansion, like the swelling of the sap within the rind, will continue. But extension of race is not the same thing as extension of empire, and physical multiplication may even be a symptom of political decline. The extinction of China is impossible and absurd. A population of 350,000,000 human souls cannot be extirpated or bodily transferred. On the contrary, I believe it will increase, and swell, and continue to overflow. But in this movement I detect no seed of empire, and I foresee no ultimate peril for the White Race.

On the contrary, I think it may be argued that European administration and protection are essential conditions for the continuance of that very progress which is supposed to constitute their peril. It is in British communities and under the security of British rule that the expansion of Chinese energies has hitherto attained its maximum development. Why is the Yellow Race to turn round and rend its benefactors? Why is it to destroy the very system to secure which it acquiesces in expatriation from its own country, and to erect a reproduction of that from which it has fled? To me it appears no more improbable that Chinamen should continue to accept European domination, in any country to which the overflow of population may propel the emigrant stream, than is the spectacle of their present condition in Hongkong or Singapore. The Yellow belt in the Far East may conceivably snatch from the White the bulk of the spoils of commerce, and the best of the wages of toil; but that it will ever seriously clutch at the keys of empire, or

Race and empire.

challenge the racial dominion of the West, I am quite unable to believe.[1]

There remains a modification, or rather a complete metamorphosis of Mr. Pearson's argument, which some of his disciples, anxious to cover the inglorious retreat enforced by the Chinese collapse, have endeavoured to substitute for the original contention. This is the 'happy thought' that what Mr. Pearson originally said of China may ultimately turn out to be true of Japan, which was barely mentioned by him, and of whose rise to greatness he seems to have been unaware. Japan, according to this hypothesis, is to be the triumphant bearer of the Yellow flag, which she has torn from the hands of China, in the impending campaign against the White ensign in the Asiatic tropics. I am not here concerned to deal minutely with this suggestion, which lies outside of my own argument in this chapter, and which is the outcome of a hasty ratiocination upon the results of the recent war. But I may say in passing that I disbelieve in it for a number of reasons. The Japanese have not, and are not likely for many generations to possess, the requisite numbers. They are lacking in colonising (though certainly not in commercial) energy, and in the hereditary instinct for expansion. Nor in their long and dramatic history is there any indication of capacity to rule or educate subject races of different blood. All their most valuable national properties they have acquired from, not given to, others.

Is Japan the enemy?

---

[1] Sir A. Lyall (*loc. cit.*) meets these conclusions by the hypothesis of a Chinese regeneration, as the result of the war with Japan. Until, however, even a single one of the *ifs* and *mays* is replaced by an *is*, I prefer not to share these dreams.

CHAPTER XIV

GREAT BRITAIN IN THE FAR EAST

> Grave mother of majestic works,
> From her isle-altar gazing down,
> Who, God-like, grasps the triple forks,
> And, king-like, wears the crown.
>
> TENNYSON.

PERHAPS the most gratifying reflection suggested by these observations on the more distant kingdoms of the Asiatic continent is the part that must inevitably be played in their future by this country. The inhabitants of a small island on the face of the northern seas, we exercise, owing to the valour of our ancestors and the intrepid spirit of our merchants, a controlling suffrage in the destinies of the Far East. That influence may, fortunately, be employed in the undivided interests of peace. Friendly relations between ourselves and Japan will assist her in that mercantile and industrial development in which she is following in our own footsteps, at the same time that it will confirm to us the continued command of the ocean routes. A similar attitude towards China will strengthen her in a resistance, for which there is yet time, against the only enemy whom she has real cause to fear, and will facilitate our own commercial access to her territories by land. Warfare with Russia need only ensue from attacks made upon British interests or British territory elsewhere, and assuredly will not be provoked by ourselves.

The rôle of Great Britain.

The possibilities of dispute with France, with which I shall deal in my next volume, are dependent upon her own action, which, if it is confined to the regions at present under her sway, and respects the liberties of intervening States, need awake no protest from England. Whatever the future may bring forth, to this country it cannot fail to be a matter of capital importance, seeing that the Empire of Great Britain, though a European, a Canadian, and an Australian, is before all else an Asiatic dominion. We still are, and have it in our hands to remain, the first Power in the East. Just as De Tocqueville remarked that the conquest and government of India are really the achievements which have given to England her place in the opinion of the world, so it is the prestige and the wealth arising from her Asiatic position that are the foundation stones of the British Empire. There, in the heart of the old Asian continent, she sits upon the throne that has always ruled the East. Her sceptre is outstretched over land and sea. 'God-like,' she 'grasps the triple forks, and, king-like, wears the crown.'

But not only are we politically concerned in the evolution of these complex problems by reason of our Imperial situation in Hindustan: our own fellow-citizens are personal actors in the drama which I have described, and the reflex action which it exercises upon them is a subject of study not less interesting than the part which they play, or are capable of playing, themselves. Englishmen and English influence have been taken to the Far East by one of three purposes—commerce, the diffusion of the faith of Christ, or the responsibilities of empire. In the first category we are the heirs of the Portuguese and the Dutch, of whom the former survive only at the dilapidated port of Macao, while the latter, in their island possessions,

Reflex influence upon England.

lie outside of the track which I have been examining. From the former, too, we inherited the self-imposed duty of carrying the cross which has sent our missionaries into all lands, and which, if it inspires the enthusiasm of Exeter Hall, is a source of not inferior anxiety to Downing Street. In the domain of empire the conquest of India has carried us forward on a tide of inevitable advance that leaves us knocking at the inland door of China and overlapping the northern frontier of Siam. The wars at the end of the last century and in the first half of this, which were part of that Expansion of England which has been so ably portrayed by a contemporary historian, gave us Singapore, which, lying on the ocean highway from West to East, is the greatest coaling station of the Orient, and Hongkong, which is the second port of the British Empire. It has not been without war that we have won even a mercantile entry into those countries at whose Treaty Ports our flag is now in the ascendant, and which have benefited by our intercourse with them not less than we ourselves.

I have shown by figures in the course of this book, in the cases both of Japan and China, that the commercial supremacy of Great Britain in the Far Eastern seas, though sharply assailed by an ever-increasing competition, has not as yet been seriously shaken. When we learn that out of the 3340 vessels that passed through the Suez Canal in 1893, no fewer than 2400 were British, while next on the list came the Germans with 270, the French with 190, and the Dutch with 180, we may form some idea of the extent to which that ascendency is still pushed in Eastern waters. How vital is its maintenance, not merely for the sake of our Empire, but for the sustenance of our people, no arguments are needed to prove. It is only in the

<small>Commercial supremacy of Great Britain.</small>

East, and especially in the Far East, that we may still hope to keep and to create open markets for British manufactures. Every port, every town, and every village that passes into French or Russian hands, is an outlet lost to Manchester, Bradford, or Bombay.

In the commercial competition of the Far East, Germany, as the above returns indicate, comes second, and never loses ground. France is a doubtful third. The real rivalry, however, is rather between Europeans of whatever nationality and the Chinese, whose unrivalled business capacities now seek the widest fields, and, backed up by immense capital and untiring energy, daily steal more ground from beneath the feet of the West. The English merchants complain in some places that their interests are insufficiently cared for and pushed by their consuls or diplomatic representatives; and I have heard of cases in which systematic dilatoriness or contemptuous indifference in high places has seemed to justify some measure of exasperation; although the reply of the impugned authorities is not without force—viz. that they are sent out not to act as touts in behalf of this or that particular enterprise, but to secure fair play to all; and that the prestige acquired with the native functionaries by an attitude of vigilant impartiality in their country's interest is forfeited upon suspicion of acting even as patriotic partisans. The complaint seems, in China at any rate, to have been partly prompted by the success that attended the early efforts of a recent German Minister at Peking in securing contracts for his countrymen, and by alarm at the projected operations of some large financial syndicates who swooped down a few years ago upon Tientsin. These have now retired *re prope infecta*; and I do not myself think that over the whole field of action the charge of

Our rivals.

neglect of British interests is one that has any serious foundation.[1]

At the same time, it is evident that business competition is much keener now than it ever was before. Large fortunes are made with difficulty; the merchant princes and magnificent *hongs* of an earlier day have disappeared; Messrs. Jardine, Matheson & Co. remain almost alone among the great houses whose establishments and operations a generation ago were the talk of the East. Men do not now expect fortunes; they are content with competencies. Wealth is more evenly distributed, and is dislocated by slighter shocks. It may be for this reason that speculation is more indulged in than of yore, and that the share-and-stock market of Hongkong has so many tales of woe to tell. Everywhere the traveller finds the British merchants banded together in a powerful confederacy, possessing strong views, and a very outspoken articulation in the local English press, regarding matters from a somewhat narrow but a very intelligible and a forcibly argued standpoint, and occupied in slowly accumulating the wherewithal which shall enable them some day to return home. The struggles and the

Contraction of business.

[1] When I first published an analogous statement to this in the pages of an English review, I was answered by a British merchant, that what his class complained of was not that British representatives or consuls declined to act as touts for them, but that they did not prevent the representatives of other foreign Powers in the Far East from acting in a similar capacity for their countrymen. This is, I think, expecting a little too much of diplomatic or consular intervention. He further complained of the 'persistent attitude of contemptuous indifference displayed by Parliament towards all commercial matters,' and of the absence of discussions upon questions affecting British Empire and Trade in the Far East. If only my correspondent knew how ignorant is the House of Commons of those subjects, and how perilous is its interference when it begins to dabble in matters which it does not understand, he would hardly deplore an indifference which is at least preferable to partisanship or stupidity. Parliament never did much to help, and will probably, before it ceases, have done a great deal to injure, the Eastern Empire of Great Britain.

interests of these men, who bear the heat and burden of the day in foreign lands, and whose gains, if they are their own, are also their country's, deserve a warmer sympathy than they commonly receive.

As regards the Christian missions, I may sum up my former argument. They are no monopoly either of the Protestant Church or of the English people. In Japan, in Korea, in China, in Tongking, in Annam, in Siam, Roman Catholic missionaries, French or Spanish, but chiefly the former, have been long established, have drawn around themselves native communities amongst whom they reside, and have acquired a numerical hold unquestionably greater than that of their Protestant successors. Among these the English, after the China Wars and the Treaties, took the lead. But an even greater activity is now being displayed by the Americans, who are flooding the Far East with their emissaries, male and female, and are yearly pouring thousands of pounds' worth of human labour into China and Japan. The English missionaries appear on the whole to be more carefully selected and to belong to a superior type. The good done by these men, in the secular aspect of their work, in the slow but sure spread of education, in the diffusion of ungrudging charity, and in the example of pure lives, cannot be gainsaid. On the other hand, it is impossible to ignore the facts that their mission is a source of political unrest and frequently of international trouble; that it is subversive of the national institutions of the country in which they reside, because, while inculcating the Christian virtue of self-respect, it tends to destroy that respect for others which is the foundation of civil society; that the number of converts is woefully disproportionate to the outlay in

[margin note: Christian missions.]

money, brain power, and life; and that, from whatever cause, the missionaries as a class are rarely popular with their own countrymen. Indeed, one of the most striking phenomena of English-speaking society in the countries to which I have referred is the absolute severance of its two main component items, the missionaries and the merchants, neither of whom think or speak over favourably of the other, and who are rarely seen at each other's table. The missionary is offended at what he regards as the mere selfish quest of lucre; the merchant sneers at work which is apt to parade a very sanctimonious expression, and sometimes results in nothing at all. I have come to the conclusion that it is futile either to apportion the blame between the two parties or to hope that any argument can effect a reconciliation. There are, of course, many cases where no such divergence exists, and where a harmony of interest and intercourse prevails; but I have not found them sufficiently numerous to invalidate the general proposition. What may be the future of missionary effort it is impossible to predict; but it would be a service of international value could some means be devised, not of arresting or diverting, but of controlling its operations, which are at present as random as the winds of heaven simultaneously let loose from the Æolus-bag of all the Churches in Christendom.

Everywhere that I have been I have found English life retaining its essential characteristics. The Englishman expatriates himself without a sigh in the pursuit of livelihood, adventure, health or duty. He is too robust to be homesick, too busy to repine. But he keeps up a constant and unbroken communication with home, and is familiar with all that is passing there. For Parliament, perhaps, he cares little, because the

English life in the Far East.

debates are over and forgotten long before they reach him, and because with the bulk of the votes he has no concern; but for the national Flag he cares a great deal. Loyalty is his passion; and the toast of 'The Queen' is drunk with as boisterous a fervour in Far Kathay as at a Unionist banquet in St. James's Hall. Mr. Gladstone would not have been complimented had he been informed of the result of a voluntary poll that was taken among the readers of the principal newspapers, at the time of the last General Election, in Yokohama, Hongkong, and Singapore. In business matters the merchant works on, looks forward, and saves for his decennial holiday; but he means to spend his declining years nowhere else than on his native soil. In the meantime he sustains a perpetual and innocent illusion by an importation of all the adjuncts, and a repetition of most of the habits, of home life. Magnificent club-houses afford a meeting ground for tiffin in the middle of the day, for billiards and smoking when the day's work is over. Some of these institutions, as at Shanghai, Hongkong, and Singapore, are as well furnished with English newspapers and periodicals as any of the palaces of Pall Mall. In his passion for games, which keeps him healthiest of all the foreign settlers in the East, while the German grows fat, and the Frenchman withers, the Englishman plays lawn-tennis under a tropical sun; he has laid out golf links at Hongkong and Chefoo; cricket matches are as frequent and excite as keen an interest as the doings of a county team at home; nay, I have even heard of football and hockey at Singapore, within seventy miles of the Equator. A racecourse must be constructed outside every town where there is a sufficient settlement; the annual race meeting, in which the owner frequently buys or breeds, trains, and rides his own ponies, is one of the events of the year; and the winner of the Hongkong or Shanghai 'Derby' enjoys a more than ephemeral renown. On festive occasions dances reunite the sexes; and, where it is not too hot, riding is a favourite recreation.

Throughout the Far East excellent and well-informed newspapers are owned and edited by Englishmen; and among them *The Japan Daily Mail*, *The North China Daily News*, and the *Straits Times*, as well as several others, would be a credit to the Press of any European country. Their telegraphic information is scanty and bad; but that is the fault of the telegraphic agency upon whom they one and all depend, and whose shortcomings are a byword throughout the East. If these papers frequently attack the local representatives of British government, it must be remembered that Englishmen like to grumble, and that the Press is commonly the mouthpiece of the non-official and mercantile community, who enjoy picking a bone with the salaried servants of Government.

The Press.

The domestic environments of life are not less reminiscent of the old country. The exterior of the house conforms to climatic needs, and spreads itself out in airy verandahs; but the furniture is not seldom imported direct from home. The national love for neatness and decorum appears in the private grounds, the *buuds*, and public gardens of the cities where the English are in the ascendant; and, were every other mark of British influence erased to-morrow, it would always remain a marvel how from a scorching rock had been evolved the Elysian graces of Hongkong.

Domestic life.

Everywhere, too, I have found the Englishman enjoying that reputation for integrity and superiority to chicanery, corruption, or intrigue, which has given him his commanding position in the world. The officials are of a higher type than those by whom other Powers are represented, and are frequently drawn from services specially organised and recruited. Nothing, indeed, is more striking in travel than the character and personality of the men who are sustaining in positions of varied trust the interests of Great Britain in far lands. The larger atmosphere of life and the sense of responsibility seem to free them from the pettinesses of a home existence that is too apt to be consumed in party conflict, and to suggest broader views of men and things. The same high tone exists through the various strata of society and employment, and the clerk behind the counter of the English bank will be no less a gentleman both in birth and education than the Governor in his palace or the Minister in his Legation. I do not think that the same can be said of the Germans, or of the French, or of the Dutch. Commerce has not yet become popular among the upper classes of German society. In France promotion is too frequently the reward of political fidelity, of journalistic service, or of successful Chauvinism, to admit of a continuous evolution of useful public servants. How many of the blunders made by that people in Tongking have been due to the character of the men who in times past have been appointed to positions of importance without the faintest knowledge of the country or qualifications for the post, it would be hard to conjecture.

[English character.]

Similarly, though our rivals and antagonists invariably ascribe our political success and our widespread Empire to a more than ordinary duplicity, I have not found that this impression is anywhere shared by the Eastern Powers with whom, by virtue of our commanding commercial position and the multiplicity of our interests, we are brought into frequent, and sometimes

[British diplomacy.]

contentious, contact. On the contrary, it appears that English Governments compose their disputes, settle their boundaries, and conclude their treaties, with a greater facility than other Powers, and that English consuls are looked up to as the leading men by every section of the community in which they reside, and are frequently appealed to by others as arbiters in matters lying outside their official ken. Though, too, we are credited by France with being the most aggressive of peoples, this accusation does not seem to tally with the voluntary evacuation of Port Hamilton, in deference to the susceptibilities of China and Korea, nor with our conduct in disposing of the vast heritage that came into our hands upon the annexation of Upper Burma, nor with our policy during the recent war, in which we seem to have been the only interested party that secured no pickings from the bone; whilst the charge comes with ill grace from a people who have recently perpetrated the indefensible outrage upon Siam. Similarly, though it frequently appeared in print, particularly in America, that Great Britain alone stood in the way of Treaty Revision in Japan, the facts which I have elsewhere displayed and the signature of the Anglo-Japanese Treaty in July 1894, will have shown the baselessness of the insinuation.

There are certain points in connection with our diplomatic representation in the Far East to which it may not be out of place to call attention. The Foreign Office has sometimes appeared to regard certain of these posts as of only secondary importance, and as refuges for failures elsewhere, or at least for persons possessing no peculiar qualifications. To my mind, there are few more important appointments than those to the Courts of Japan and of China, and, in a somewhat less degree, of Siam; and yet it has in times past occurred that gentlemen

British representatives.

have been appointed to these posts who have no personal acquaintance with the East or knowledge of the problem with which they may require to deal. The reception accorded to Sir N. O'Conor, on his nomination to the British Legation at Peking in 1892, sufficiently indicated the rejoicing of the British community in the Far East at the appointment of a man who really knew both the country to which he was accredited and the business which he would have to transact. There appears to be still an immense opening in the Far East for a diplomatic career. We maintain at Tokio, at Peking, and at Bangkok, a number of so-called Student Interpreters, who, after passing a preliminary examination at home, go out to the East, undergo a steady course of instruction in the language of the country in which they will pass so much of their lives, and thence are drafted into the Consular Service. From their ranks have sprung such men as the late Sir Harry Parkes, whose name is as familiar a household word in Japan and in China as is that of his still-surviving namesake in Australia; Sir. E. Satow, the present British Minister at Tokio; and others whose names will occur to the memory. There is just as great scope for the production of such men, and even greater need for their services now than in bygone days. The Far East demands a knowledge that can only be acquired after years, and a statesmanship that must have been in part nurtured in a local atmosphere. The great position attained by the late Sir William White at Constantinople, starting from a similar origin, may be emulated in countries where also there is an Eastern Question not much less important than the control of the Bosphorus or the ownership of St. Sophia. I would fain hope that among the rising generation may be found some who will be worthy heirs of these great traditions.

In another respect the Foreign Office appears to me to have neglected an elementary part of diplomatic education, and an indispensable adjunct to the smooth working of the diplomatic machine. One would surely expect to find in the British Legation in every foreign country, most of all in the East, a compact, well-chosen, and serviceable library of the best books relating to the country in question, and the political problems which it is likely to suggest. Such libraries were in part collected many years ago. I found the fragments of such a one at Peking, just as I remember routing out from a dusty closet the *débris* of another at Teheran. At Meshed I could not discover a single publication on the Afghan Frontier Question. Similarly, at Bangkok there was not one volume relating to the frontier between Burma, Siam, and China, though a small but excellent literature exists upon the subject, and might at any moment be required for official reference. My impression is that at Tokio there is a similar absence. What is wanted in each case is, not a library of general reference, but a collection of authoritative works, within a limited range, to which recourse can be had at any moment. As soon as the nucleus of such a collection had been formed, a few pounds a year would amply suffice for the necessary increment, which should be carefully selected and sent out from home. The India Office has sometimes extended such a patronage to useful publications, purchasing a certain number of copies, and distributing them among the localities concerned; but I have never heard of the Foreign Office exercising a similarly wise generosity.

Suggested libraries of special reference.

Other diplomatic anomalies, easily removable, if deemed of sufficient importance, have come under my notice while travelling in the Far East. At Peking it might be well were the diplomatic staff of Great Britain to include an Indian officer or *attaché*, so many are the purely Indian questions that come up for discussion with the Tsungli Yamen, upon which there is no one on the spot to throw the necessary light. An even greater desideratum is the appointment of a commercial *attaché* (similar to one or two analogous officials in Europe), who should travel about from post to post in the Far East, and visit the inland districts; and who should report upon the changing taste and style of the native markets and upon the economic products of the country, as well as collect any information that might be of service to British merchants. In days of such acute competition, when the representatives of foreign Powers resort to a more than diplomatic strategy in the interests of their countrymen, no legitimate step should be neglected for the protection and extension of British trade. To the uninstructed eye it further seems a strange anomaly that whilst Japan, China, and Siam are under the Foreign Office, Hongkong, which all but touches the Chinese mainland, and the Straits Settlements, which actually touch Siam, should be under the Colonial Office; while Burma again, which touches both Siam and China, is under the India Office. Perhaps some day we shall arrive at a more rational concentration of interests, possibly even, as has been suggested, at the creation of a new department which shall deal with the British affairs of the Asiatic continent.

<small>Diplomatic anomalies.</small>

Great as is the position which I have depicted as being enjoyed by Great Britain in the Far East, I believe that it will be greater still. The improvement of existing and the creation of new means of communication are rapidly developing a solidarity between the East and the West which our grand-

<small>Future of Great Britain in the Far East.</small>

parents would have deemed impossible. Fusion and not disintegration will be the keynote of the progress of the coming century. There remain now but few countries to which access has not already been gained; though there are several whose political stability is precarious, or whose political boundaries are not determined. As soon, however, as fixity can be predicated of either of these departments— much more, if of both—commercial exploitation will begin. For this object British energy, British capital, and British experience will be required. The Power which has been longest in the field, which enjoys the best geographical position for the distribution of its commerce, or the dissemination of its influence, and which can command the largest resources, must infallibly triumph in any such competition. Our position in India gives us the certain command of the main land-routes and railroads that will lay open the Far East in the not distant future. Our position upon the ocean, if duly safeguarded, should assure to us the control of the maritime highway.[1] Furthermore, the country which has scattered millions in propping up the rotten Republics of

[1] I introduce this qualification because the naval strength of Great Britain in the Far East, *i.e.* in the waters between Singapore and Vladivostok, when compared with the combined fleets of France and Russia, can scarcely be said to possess that incontestable predominance without which security cannot be predicated. In April 1894 the British squadron in the Far East consisted of 2 ironclads (aggregating 11,150 tons), 20 unarmoured vessels, comprising 7 cruisers and 7 gunboats; and 6 torpedo-boats (aggregating 29,850 tons); or a total tonnage of 41,000, with a complement of 3400 men. At the same period the French fleet consisted of 2 ironclads (6350 tons), 1 cruiser, and 20 smaller vessels, mainly gun-boats, as well as 14 river steamers; with a total tonnage of 14,370, or, excluding the river-steamers, 12,050, and a complement of 2580 men. The Russian squadron consisted of 11 vessels, viz. 1 cruiser, 5 sloops, and 5 gunboats, with a total tonnage of 15,510, and a complement of 1650 men. Nor, in speaking of the Russian forces, must sight be lost of the Dobra Volna Flot, or Volunteer Fleet, the principal cruisers of which can carry from 1500 to 2000 troops, and are the swiftest vessels east of Suez. In peace they are used to transport soldiers and stores to Vladivostok. What they would do in war it might be premature to forecast.

the New World may very well repay its age-long debt to the Old by a similar, even if a tardy, service.

Above all will this task be facilitated by the increasing diffusion of the English tongue. Already spoken in every store from Yokohama to Rangoon; already taught in the military and naval colleges of China, and in the schools of Japan and of Siam; already employed in the telegraphic services of Japan, China, and Korea, and stamped upon the silver coins that issue from the mints of Osaka and Canton; already used by Chinamen themselves as a means of communication between subjects from different provinces of their mighty Empire—it is destined with absolute certainty to be the language of the Far East. Its sound will go out into all lands, and its words unto the ends of the world. That this splendid future is no idle dream of fancy, but is capable of realisation at no indefinite period, none who have travelled widely in Eastern Asia will doubt. Moral failure alone can shatter the prospect that awaits this country in the impending task of regeneration.

The English language.

> We sailed wherever ship could sail,
>   We founded many a mighty State;
> Pray God our greatness may not fail
>   Through craven fears of being great!

APPENDIX

I. Treaty of Shimonoseki. (*Signed, April* 17, 1895; *ratified at Chefoo, May* 8, 1895.)

Article I.—China recognises definitively the full and complete independence and autonomy of Korea, and in consequence the payment of tribute and the performance of ceremonies and formalities by Korea to China in derogation of such independence and autonomy, shall wholly cease for the future.

Article II.— China cedes to Japan in perpetuity and full sovereignty the following territories together with all fortifications, arsenals, and public property thereon :

(*a*) The southern portion of the province of Feng-Tien within the following boundaries :—

The line of demarcation begins at the mouth of the River Yalu and ascends that stream to the mouth of the River Anping; from thence the line runs to Feng Huang: from thence to Haicheng, from thence to Ying Kow, forming a line which describes the southern portion of the territory. The places above named are included in the ceded territory. When the line reaches the River Liao at Ying Kow it follows the course of that stream to its mouth, where it terminates. The mid-channel of the River Liao shall be taken as the line of demarcation.

This cession also includes all islands appertaining or belonging to the province of Feng-Tien situated in the eastern portion of the Bay of Liao-Tung and in the northern part of the Yellow Sea.

(*b*) The Island of Formosa, together with all islands appertaining to the said Island of Formosa.

(*c*) The Pescadores Group, that is to say, all islands lying between the 119th and 12th degrees of longitude east of Greenwich and the 23rd and 240th degrees of north latitude.

ARTICLE III.—The alignments of the frontiers described in the preceding Article, and shown on the map, shall be subject to verification and demarcation on the spot by a Joint Commission of Delimitation, consisting of two or more Japanese and two or more Chinese Delegates to be appointed immediately after the exchange of the ratifications of this Act. In case the boundaries laid down in this Act are found to be defective at any point, either on account of topography or in consideration of good administration, it shall also be the duty of the Delimitation Commission to rectify the same.

The Delimitation Commission will enter upon its duties as soon as possible, and will bring its labours to a conclusion within the period of one year after appointment.

The alignments laid down in this Act shall, however, be maintained until the rectifications of the Delimitation Commission, if any are made, shall have received the approval of the Governments of Japan and China.

ARTICLE IV.—China agrees to pay to Japan as a war indemnity the sum of 200,000,000 Kuping Taels. The said sum to be paid in eight instalments. The first instalment of 50,000,000 taels to be paid within six months, and the second instalment of 50,000,000 taels to be paid within twelve months after the exchange of the ratifications of this Act. The remaining sum to be paid in six equal annual instalments as follows: The first of such equal annual instalments to be paid within two years; the second within three years; the third within four years; the fourth within five years; the fifth within six years, and the sixth within seven years, after the exchange of the ratifications of this Act. Interest at the rate of 5 per centum per annum shall begin to run on all unpaid portions of the said indemnity from the date the first instalment falls due.

China, however, shall have the right to pay by anticipation at any time any or all of said instalments. In case the whole amount of said indemnity is paid within three years after the exchange of ratifications of the present Act, all interest shall be waived and the interest for two years and a half or for any less period if then already paid shall be included as a part of the principal amount of the indemnity.

ARTICLE V.—The inhabitants of the territories ceded to Japan, who wish to take up their residence outside the ceded districts, shall be at liberty to sell their real property and retire. For this purpose a period of two years from the date of the exchange of the ratifications of the present Act, shall be granted. At the expiration of that period, those of the inhabitants who shall not have left such territories shall, at the option of Japan, be deemed to be Japanese subjects.

Each of the two Governments shall, immediately upon the exchange of the ratifications of the present Act, send one or more Commissioners to Formosa to effect a final transfer of that Province, and within the space of two months after the exchange of the ratifications of this Act such transfer shall be completed.

ARTICLE VI.—All treaties between Japan and China having come to an end in consequence of war, China engages immediately upon the exchange of the ratifications of this Act, to appoint Plenipotentiaries to conclude, with the Japanese Plenipotentiaries, a Treaty of Commerce and Navigation and a Convention to regulate Frontier Intercourse and Trade. The Treaties, Conventions and Regulations now subsisting between China and European Powers shall serve as a basis for the said Treaty and Convention between Japan and China. From the date of the exchange of the ratifications of this Act until the said Treaty and Convention are brought into actual operation, the Japanese Government, its officials, commerce, navigations, frontier intercourse and trade, industries, ships and subjects, shall, in every respect, be accorded by China most favoured nation treatment.

China makes in addition the following concessions, to take effect six months after the date of the present Act :—

1st.—The following cities, towns, and ports, in addition to those already opened, shall be opened to the trade, residence, industries, and manufactures of Japanese subjects, under the same conditions and with the same privileges and facilities as exist at the present open cities, towns, and ports of China :

1. Shashih, in the Province of Hupeh.
2. Chung King, in the Province of Szechuan.
3. Suchow, in the Province of Kiang Su.
4. Hangchow, in the Province of Chekiang.

The Japanese Government shall have the right to station Consuls at any or all of the above-named places.

2nd. Steam navigation for vessels under the Japanese flag for the conveyance of passengers and cargo, shall be extended to the following places :

1. On the Upper Yangtsze River, from Ichang to Chung King.
2. On the Woosung River and the Canal, from Shanghai to Suchow and Hangchow.

The Rules and Regulations which now govern the navigation of the inland waters of China by foreign vessels shall, so far as applicable, be enforced in respect of the above-named routes, until new Rules and Regulations are conjointly agreed to.

3rd. Japanese subjects purchasing goods or produce in the interior of China or transporting imported merchandise into the interior of China, shall have the right temporarily to rent or hire warehouses for the storage of the articles so purchased or transported without the payment of any taxes or exactions whatever.

4th. Japanese subjects shall be free to engage in all kinds of manufacturing industries in all the open cities, towns, and ports of China, and shall be at liberty to import into China all kinds of machinery, paying only the stipulated import duties thereon.

All articles manufactured by Japanese subjects in China shall, in respect of inland transit and internal taxes, duties, charges, and exactions of all kinds, and also in respect of warehousing and storage facilities in the interior of China, stand upon the same footing and enjoy the same privileges and exemptions as merchandise imported by Japanese subjects into China.

In the event additional Rules and Regulations are necessary in connection with these concessions, they shall be embodied in the Treaty of Commerce and Navigation provided for by this Article.

ARTICLE VII.—Subject to the provisions of the next succeeding Article, the evacuation of China by the armies of Japan shall be completely effected within three months after the exchange of the ratifications of the present Act.

ARTICLE VIII.—As a guarantee of the faithful performance of the stipulations of this Act, China consents to the temporary occupation by the military forces of Japan, of Wei Hai Wei, in the Province of Shantung.

Upon the payment of the first two instalments of the war indemnity herein stipulated for and the exchange of the ratifications of the Treaty of Commerce and Navigation, said place shall be evacuated by the Japanese forces, provided the Chinese Government consents to pledge, under suitable and sufficient arrangements, the Customs Revenue of China as security for the payment of the final instalment of said indemnity.

It is, however, expressly understood that no such evacuation shall take place until after the exchange of the ratifications of the Treaty of Commerce and Navigation.

ARTICLE IX.—Immediately upon the exchange of the ratifications of this Act, all prisoners of war then held shall be restored, and China undertakes not to ill-treat or punish prisoners of war so restored to her by Japan. China also engages to at once release all Japanese subjects accused of being military spies or charged with any other military offences. China further engages not to punish in any manner, nor to allow to be punished, those Chinese subjects who have in any manner been compromised in their relations with the Japanese army during the war.

ARTICLE X.—All offensive military operations shall cease upon the exchange of the ratifications of this Act.

ARTICLE XI.—The present Act shall be ratified by their Majesties the Emperor of Japan and the Emperor of China, and the ratifications shall be exchanged at Chefoo, on the 8th day of the 5th month of the 28th year of Meiji, corresponding to 14th day of the 4th month of the 21st year of Kuang Hsü.

In witness whereof, the respective Plenipotentiaries have signed the same and have affixed thereto the seal of their arms.

Done at Shimonoseki, in duplicate, this 17th day of the 4th month of the 28th year of Meiji, corresponding to 23rd day of the 3rd month of the 21st year of Kuang Hsü.

COUNT ITO HIROBUMI.
VISCOUNT MUTSU MUNEMITSU.
LI HUNG-CHANG.
LI CHING-FONG.

SEPARATE ARTICLES.

ARTICLE I.—The Japanese Military Forces which are, under Article VIII. of the Treaty of Peace signed this day, to temporarily occupy Wei Hai Wei, shall not exceed one Brigade, and from the date of the exchange of the ratifications of the said Treaty of Peace, China shall pay annually one-fourth of the amount of the expenses of such temporary occupation, that is to say, at the rate of 500,000 Kuping Taels per annum.

ARTICLE II.—The territory temporarily occupied at Wei Hai Wei shall comprise the Island of Liu Kung and a belt of land 5 Japanese *ri* wide along the entire coast-line of the Bay of Wei Hai Wei.

No Chinese Troops shall be permitted to approach or occupy any places within a zone 5 Japanese *ri* wide beyond the boundaries of the occupied territory.

ARTICLE III.—The Civil Administration of the occupied territory shall remain in the hands of the Chinese Authorities. But such Authorities shall at all times be obliged to conform to the orders which the Japanese Army of occupation may deem it necessary to give in the interest of the health, maintenance, safety, distribution or discipline of the Troops.

All military offences committed within the occupied territory shall be subject to the jurisdiction of the Japanese Military Authorities.

The foregoing Separate Articles shall have the same force, value, and effect as if they had been word for word inserted in the Treaty of Peace signed this day.

In witness whereof the respective Plenipotentiaries have signed the same and have affixed thereto the seal of their arms.

Done at Shimonoseki, in duplicate, this 17th day of the 4th month of the 28th year of Meiji, corresponding to the 21st year of Kuang Hsü.

COUNT ITO HIROBUMI.
VISCOUNT MUTSU MUNEMITSU.
LI HUNG-CHANG.

II.—IMPERIAL RESCRIPT. (*May* 10, 1895.)

We recently complied with the request of China, and in consequence appointed Plenipotentiaries and caused them to confer with the Plenipotentiaries appointed by China and to conclude a Treaty of Peace between the two Empires.

Since then the Governments of their Majesties the Emperors of Russia and Germany and of the Republic of France have united in a recommendation to our Government not to permanently possess the Peninsula of Feng-Tien, our newly-acquired territory, on the ground that such permanent possession would be detrimental to the lasting peace of the Orient.

Devoted as we unalterably are and ever have been to the principles of peace, we were constrained to take up arms against China for no other reason than our desire to secure for the Orient an enduring peace.

Now, the friendly recommendation of the three Powers was equally prompted by the same desire. Consulting, therefore, the best interests of peace and animated by a desire not to bring upon our people added hardship or to impede the progress of national destiny by creating new complications and thereby making the situation difficult and retarding the restoration of peace, we do not hesitate to accept such recommendation.

By concluding the Treaty of Peace China has already shown her sincerity of regret for the violation of her engagements, and thereby the justice of our cause has been proclaimed to the world.

Under the circumstances, we can find nothing to impair the honour and dignity of our Empire if we now yield to the dictates of magnanimity and, taking into consideration the general situation, accept the advice of the friendly Powers.

Accordingly we have commanded our Government, and have caused them to reply to the three Powers in the above sense.

Regarding the arrangements by which we will renounce the permanent possession of the Peninsula, we have specially commanded our Government that the necessary measures shall be made the subject of future negotiations and adjustment with the Government of China.

Now, the exchange of ratifications of the Treaty of Peace has already been effected; the friendly relations between the two Empires have been re-established, and cordial relations with all other Powers are also strengthened.

We therefore command our subjects to respect our will; to take into careful consideration the general situation; to be circumspect in all things; to avoid erroneous tendencies; and not to impair or thwart the high aspirations of our Empire.

[Imperial Sign Manual].
(Countersigned by all Ministers of State).

INDEX

A

ADDRESSES to the Throne, Japanese, 27, 32-3, 35-6, 62-3.
Alcock, Sir R., 210 n.
Americans in Japan, 46.
—— in Korea, 135, 146, 163, 169, 176, 202, 215.
Amherst, Lord, 268.
Amur, The, 208, 316, 334.
Ancestor Worship in China, 240, 287-8, 344.
—— —— in Korea, 109, 186.
Aoki, Viscount, 59.
Aomori, Rail to, 13.
Army, v. sub Names of Countries.
Arthur, Port, v. Port Arthur.
Asia, Fascination of, 1-6; Influence on Europe of, 2; Individuality of, 3; Contrasts of, 3-4.
Athletics, English, 420.
Audience Question at Peking, The, 264-75.

B

BARROW, Colonel E. G., 39.
Beacons in Korea, 122.
Bell, John, 267 n.
—— Colonel Mark, 278, 330.
Bellonet, M. de, 201.
Black Flags, The, 324.
Brandt, Herr von, 272-3.
'Braves, The,' 323.
Brinkley, Captain, 17.
Broughton Bay, 92.
Broughton, Captain W. R., 92 n.
Buddha, 1, 352.

Buddhism in China, 343-58.
—— in Japan, 49.
—— in Korea, v. sub Monks; and Korean Religion.

C

CAMPBELL, C. W., 88, 100 n, 106.
Canton, 282, 302, 321, 332.
Carles, W. R., 88, 99 n.
Cesarevitch in China, The, 272, 277.
Chang An Sa, 111.
Chang Chih Tung, Viceroy, 318.
Chefoo Convention, The, 223.
Chemulpo, 89, 93-4, 149, 168, 172, 173, 175-6, 200.
Cheng-tu Massacres, 304.
Chia Ching, Emperor, 269.
China, Collapse of, 364-9.
—— The Emperor of, 223, 231, 233, 237-8, 242-6, 272, 348.
—— The Empress Dowager of, 238, 241, 256, 271, 315, 317.
—— Future of, 320, 340-2, 395, 396-412.
—— Results of the War on, 369.
Chinese Administration, 208, 223 n, 261, 282, 338-9, 407.
—— Agriculture, 399, 403.
—— Army, 321-31, 364, 405.
—— Awakening, 311-42.
—— Character, 221-2, 301, 336, 341, 397, 407.
—— Colonists, 395-7 401-4.
—— Customs Service, 178-9, 206, 276.
—— Foreign Policy, 197-207, 264, 275-83.

2 F

Chinese Horses, 221.
—— in Japan, 66.
—— Inns, 221.
—— as Mercenaries, 334, 406 *n*.
—— Minerals, 319.
—— Navy, 331-4.
—— Newspapers, 335, 336 *n*.
—— Officialism, 338-9, 366, 373.
—— Population, 229, 232, 399, 411.
—— Railways, 277, 314-20.
—— Relations with the Powers, 260-83.
—— Religion, 246, 250, 288.
—— Secret Societies, 403.
—— Scenery, 227-8.
—— Trade, 281, 336.
—— Village Life, 228.
—— Women, 242.
Ching, Prince, 262.
Chinnampo, 168 *n*.
Chow Han, 304.
Christianity in China, 283-310.
—— in Japan, 49-50.
—— Korea, 136, 142, 148, 288; and *v. sub* Missionaries.
Chun Chi Chu, The, 223 *n*.
Chun, Prince, 223 *n*, 239.
Clan Government in Japan, 23, 30-1.
Clepsydra at Peking, 248.
Climate of the Far East, 8, and *v. sub* Names of Countries.
Coal Mines in China, 314, 319, 337, 338.
—— —— Japan, 44.
—— —— Korea, 181.
Codes, Japanese, 59, 61-2, 67.
Commerce, *v. sub* Trade.
Confucianism in China, 249, 288, 344 *n*.
—— Korea, 137, 150.
Cremation in China and Japan, 357.

D

DALLET, Père, 87, 96 *n*, 154 *n*, 198 *n*.
Daveluy, Evêque, 96 *n*.
Diamond Mountains, The, 102.

Diet, Japanese, *v. sub* Japanese.
Dockyards, Chinese, 332.
Douglas, Professor R. K., 223 *n*, 261 *n*.
Du Halde, 229.
Dutch in Korea, 87, 97.

E

EAST, The, Books on, 4, 87-8, 305 *n*, 425.
—— The Far, Idiosyncrasies of, 7, 221.
—— Destinies of, 390-412.
East India Company, The, 6 *n*, 168 *n*, 178 *n*.
Elections, Japanese, *v.* Diet.
Elgin, Earl of, 53, 253, 293.
Emperor of China, *v. sub* China.
—— of Japan, *v. sub* Japan.
England in the East, Early appearance of, 6; Importance of, 68; Russian interests and, 213-4, 275-83, 413; Japan and, 215, 413, 423; China and, 210, 214, 225, 264, 275-83, 414; France and, 414; Power of, 414; Diplomacy of, 422; Representatives of, 423-4, 426; Future of, 426-8; Naval strength of, 427 *n*.
English in the Far East, The, 68, 417-22; Character of, 421-2.
—— Language in the Far East, The, 428.
Enomoto, Viscount, 61.
Extra-territoriality in Japan, 53.
—— in Korea, 195 *n*.

F

FAMILY TIES, Strength of Chinese, 240, 346, 351.
Fengshui, The, 233, 302, 317.
Feudalism in Japan, 14, 18, 40, 90, 392.
Foreigners in China, *v.* Missionaries, Treaty Ports, etc.

INDEX 439

Foreigners in Japan, 28, 45-6, 52 *n*, 53, 56, 59-60, 64-5, 67, 69-81.
—— in Korea, 87, 97 *n*, 126, 169-70.
Formosa, 3, 191, 333, 338, 408.
France in the Far East, 9, 43, 215, 279, 414, 416.
Franco-Chinese War (1884), The, 210, 319, 321, 328-9, 333.
Frazer, J. G., 154.
French in China, 279, 292, 294-95.
—— in Korea, 122, 184, 191, 215.
—— in Siam, 423.
Fusan, 89, 90, 189, 212.

G

GARDNER, C. T., 305.
Gensan, 88, 89, 90, 92, 101, 111, 168.
Geo Mun, The, 139.
Germans in Korea, 169, 170, 215.
—— in China, 322.
Ginseng, 168, 179, 199.
Gold in Korea, 181-2.
Gordon, General C. G., 223, 329, 334.
Granville, Earl. 214 *n*.
Gray, Archdeacon, 350 *n*.
'Great Japan Union, The,' 28, 64.
Griffis, W. E., 88, 96, 148, 154 *n*.
Grimaldi, 229 *n*.
Groot, Dr. de, 402 *n*.

H

HAKODATE, 52 *n*.
Hamel, Hendrik, 87 *n*, 97 *n*, 105, 108, 118, 141, 160, 198.
Ham-heung, 105, 113.
Hamilton *v.* Port Hamilton.
Han River, 93, 125, 134, 168, 175, 202.
Hanabusa, 149, 191.
Hankow, 318, 336.
Hanneken, Captain von, 327.
Hara Kiri, 41.

Hart, Sir Robert, 179, 276.
Hideyoshi, 86-7, 90, 190.
Hillier, W. C., 159.
Hongkong, 313, 317, 336, 395, 420-21.
Hong Sal Mun, The, 138.
Hope, Sir J., 210.
House of Representatives in Japan, *v. sub* Japanese Diet.
Hsien Feng, Emperor, 238, 270.

I

IEYASU, 30-1.
Ignatieff, General, 208 *n*.
Imbert, Msgr., 183.
Imperial Rescripts, Japanese, 26, 28.
India, Importance of, 8-9, 414.
Inouye, Count, 21, 22 *n*, 57, 375, 381-82.
Intermarriage of Dominant and Subdued Races, 404.
Islam, Conservatism of, 8.
Ito, Count, 21-3, 27, 29, 33, 36, 62, 68, 196.
Iwakura, 191.
Iyemitsu, 190.

J

Japan Daily Mail, The, 17, 421.
Japan, Democracy in, 17, 30, 32.
—— Effect of the War upon, 381.
—— Emperor of, 26, 30, 33-5.
—— Failure in Korea of, 374-84.
—— Feudalism in, 14, 18, 40, 90.
—— Future of, 18, 30, 31, 386-9, 391-4, 412.
—— Growth of, 13-15, 38, 54.
—— Newspapers in, 17.
—— Passports in, 80.
—— Railways in, 13.
—— Revolution in, The, 24, 30.
Japanese Administration, 24, 30, 32-7.
—— Army, 14, 39-41, 364.
—— Character, 45-8, 194, 196, 412.

Japanese Clans, 30.
—— Codes, 59, 61-2, 67.
—— Constitution, 15, 20, 26, 36, 37, 58.
—— Constitution for Korea, 374-9.
—— Diet, 15-19, 20, 24-9, 32 *n*, 35-7, 58-9, 61-3.
—— Electoral Qualifications, 15 *n*, 19.
—— Finances, 23, 25-6, 42.
—— Imports, 43-4, 387.
—— Land-tax, 24, 55.
—— Law and Law Courts, 14, 56, 60.
—— Losses in War, 365.
—— Manufactures, 43-4.
—— Minerals, 44.
—— Ministers, 16, 21, 35.
—— National Debt, 42.
—— Navy, 14, 30, 31, 38-9.
—— Religions, 49.
—— Reasons for War with China, 362-3.
—— Salaries, 17, 25.
—— Societies, 28, 64.
—— Trade, 43, 53, 55, 177, 386-9.
—— Women, 95.
Jardine, Matheson & Co., Messrs., 417.
Jehol, 256, 268.
Jesuits in China, 247, 255, 266.
Jinghiz, Khan, 2, 230 *n*.
Jinsen or Inchiun, 93 *n*.
Jiyuto Party, The, 25.

K

KAISHINTO PARTY, The, 25.
Kang Hsi, Emperor, 244, 247.
Kashgar, 328, 397, 400, 406.
Keum Kang San, 102, 106, 111.
Kien Lung, Emperor, 244, 249, 251, 253, 255, 267-8, 275.
Kim Ok Kiun, 149 *n*.
Kioto, 13, 49.

Kirin, 251, 315, 321, 323.
Klaproth, 229.
Kobe, 13, 52 *n*.
Korea, 85-217.
—— Area of, 96.
—— British policy towards, 213-215.
—— Chinese in, 93, 97, 115, 118-9, 126, 174, 177, 197, 208, 217.
—— Chinese Resident in, 161, 169, 175, 207.
—— Chinese Suzerainty of, 86, 120, 139, 149, 161, 189, 190, 192, 189-207.
—— Climate of, 90, 98, 109.
—— Crown Prince of, 143, 148, 154, 159.
—— Effects of the Chino-Japanese War on, 372.
—— Europeans in, 87-8, 97 *n*, 169-70.
—— Future of, 174, 176, 182, 391.
—— Independence of, 201-2, 203, 214-5, 373-6.
—— Japanese policy towards, 48, 139, 150, 152, 190-7, 363, 381-4.
—— —— in, 22 *n*, 86, 90, 91, 92, 139, 149, 152, 167, 172, 176, 177, 178, 187, 189, 190, 192, 194.
—— King of, 85, 109, 140-1, 147-52, 158-9, 167, 203, 204, 375.
—— Name of, 85.
—— Obstacles to the advance of, 98, 168, 174, 176.
—— Queen of, 148, 151, 153-4, 379-80.
—— Rivers of, 175.
—— Russia and, 92, 154, 176, 178, 208-13, 214 *n*.
—— Seclusion of, 85-7.
—— Situation of, 189, 216.
Korean Administration, 98, 99, 100, 116, 165-7.
—— Agriculture, 113, 174.
—— Alphabets, 97.

INDEX

Korean Amusements, 130, 134, 135.
—— Aristocracy, 98, 100, 157-8.
—— Army, 140, 144, 160-1, 163-4, 212, 378.
—— Banks, 173.
—— Character, 94, 95, 97-8, 100, 101, 103, 104, 187.
—— Classes, 98-100, 112-3, 133.
—— Currency, 171-3.
—— Customs Service, 167, 179-80.
—— Dancing-girls, 130.
—— Dress, 94, 95, 107, 126, 127, 129-30, 131-3, 157.
—— Education, 171.
—— Envoys, 204-5.
—— Examinations, 166.
—— Executions, 140.
—— Harbours, 89-94, 213.
—— Hats, 94, 131-3.
—— Horses, 110, 115.
—— Houses, 112-13, 124.
—— Implements, 136.
—— Inns, 116-7.
—— Language, 97.
—— Memorial Tablets, 115.
—— Minerals, 180-3.
—— Mints, 172-3.
—— Ministers, 155-6.
—— Monarchy, 154.
—— Monasteries, 102-6, 378.
—— Mourners, 132.
—— Music, 105.
—— Navigation, 175-6.
—— Officialism, 28.
—— Paper, 134.
—— Peasant-life, 112-4.
—— Population, 94-6.
—— Produce, 168, 174, 177.
—— Race, 94, 96-7.
—— Railways, 176.
—— Rebellions, 147-54, 192, 206, 210.
—— Reforms made by Japan, 374.
—— Religion, 86, 104, 107, 108, 137.
—— Resistance to Japan, 379-82.

Korean Revenue, 165, 167-8.
—— Roads, 110, 174.
—— Scenery, 89, 91, 92, 94, 102, 104-5.
—— Smuggling, 168, 177, 179-80.
—— Spirit-worship, 108.
—— Sport, 110-12.
—— Stone-throwing, 135.
—— Superstitions, 108-9.
—— Telegraphs, 122, 207, 212.
—— Temples, 86, 107.
—— Tombs, 115.
—— Trade, 170-80.
—— Travel, 100-3, 109-10, 116.
—— Women, 95, 98, 113, 129, 130-1.
Kowtow, The, 265, 275.
Kuang Hsu, Emperor, 238, 240, 271, 273.
Kublai Khan, 230 *n*, 247.
Kulja, 209, 264, 278, 329, 419.
Kung, Prince, 238-9, 262.
Kurile Islands, 47.
Kutien, Massacres at, 301.

L

LANG, Captain, 327.
Lay, H. N., 331.
Lazareff, Port, 92, 209 *n*.
Liao-Tung Peninsula, The, 279, 332, 365, 383.
Libraries on Eastern Questions, Consular, 425.
Li Hung Chang, Viceroy, 149, 169, 179, 197, 202, 204, 205, 206, 208, 211, 223-7, 314-5, 317, 322, 323, 329.
Liturgy, Buddhist, 355.
Liu Ming Chuan, 319.
Liuchiu Islands, The, 408.
Lowell, P., 88.
Lyall, Sir A., 404, 409, 412.

M

MACAO, 414.
Macartney, Earl of, 229 *n*, 268, 275.

Macartney, Sir H., 263.
Maitreya, 251, 352, 354.
Malay Peninsula, 395, 396, 397.
Mandarins, v. Chinese Officialism.
Mapu, The Korean, 98, 110.
Marco Polo, 230 n, 248.
Massacres in China, v. sub Missionaries; Kutien, Tientsin, Cheng-tu, Wuhsueh.
Maubant, M., 183.
Michie, A., 305 n.
Mikado, v. sub Japan, Emperor of.
Ming Tombs, The, 257-8.
Missionaries in China, 247, 255, 283, 310, 418.
―― in Japan, 46, 50, 418.
―― in Korea, 87, 132, 142, 183-7, 418.
Mitford, A. B., 41 n.
Mixed Residence in Japan, 64-5, 67.
Mokpo, 168.
Monasteries and Monks in China, 343-58.
―― ―― in Korea, 102-6, 140.
Moriyama, 191.
Morrison, Rev. R., 285.
Moukden, 315, 316, 323.
Mouravieff, General, 208 n.
Mutel, Msgr., 185.
Mutsu, Viscount, 22 and n, 28, 374.

N

NAGASAKI, 14, 52 n.
Naktong River, The, 175.
Nam San, 121-2.
Nanking, 118, 282, 320, 321.
Napoleon, Fascination of the East for, 2.
Nature-Worship in Korea, 104-5.
Newchwang, 185, 282, 315.
Newspapers, v. sub Names and Countries.
―― English, of the East, 421.
Ni Taijo, 119, 198.
Niigata, 52 n.

Novoe Vremya, The, 210, 211.

O

O'CONOR, Sir N. R., 175, 216, 273, 424.
Officers, Chinese, v. Chinese Army.
Okubo, 191.
Okuma, Count, 23, 25, 58.
Oliphant, L., 210.
Opium Question, The, 283.
Oppert, E., 96 n.
Osaka, 52, 173, 428.

P

PACIFIC OCEAN, Access to the, 394.
―― Question of the, 395.
Paik-tu-san, 104-5.
Pak Yong Hio, 137, 376, 379-80.
Pamirs, Chinese and the, 277.
Parkes, Sir Harry, 60 n, 96 n, 202, 262 n, 424.
Party Government in Japan, v. Diet.
Pearson, C. H. (*National Life and Character: A Forecast*), 396-412.
Pechili, Gulf of, 222.
Peiho River, The, 222.
Peking, 118, 120, 127, 183, 198, 199, 221, 227-259, 370.
―― Audience Halls at, 266-275.
―― Bells of, 248, 253.
―― British Legation at, 259.
―― Drum and Bell Towers of, 248-9.
―― Examination Building at, 248.
―― Ground Plan of, 232.
―― Hall of the Classics at, 250
―― Lama Temples of, 250-2.
―― Observatory at, 247-8.
―― Palace at, 237, 253, 255, 266, 267, 269, 270.
―― Parks near, 258.
―― Population of, 229.
―― Streets of, 127, 234-7.
―― Summer Palace at, 253-5, 269, 294.

INDEX

Peking, Temple of Confucius at, 249.
—— —— of Heaven at, 244-5.
—— Traditions of, 232.
—— Walls of, 230-3.
—— Wedding Customs in, 236.
Peking Gazette, The, 241, 271, 335.
Perry, Commodore, 52.
Pillars of Korea, Memorial, 136-7.
Ping Yang, Battle of, 325.
Port Arthur, 197, 315, 332, 365.
—— Hamilton, 207, 210, 214-5, 423.
—— Lazareff, 92, 209 *n*, 213, 384.
Pouk San, 121, 140.
Printing in the East, 97 *n*.
Prjevalski, General, 278, 330.
Pyong-yang, 92, 175, 181-2, 197.

Q

Quelpart, 87, 214.

R

Railway, The Siberian, 277, 279, 316.
Railways in China, 314-20.
—— in Japan, 13.
—— in Korea, 176.
Rosebery, Earl of, 68, 214 *n*, 226.
Ross, Rev. J., 88, 185.
Russian Policy, 178, 208-13, 276-80.
—— —— forecast in 1894 of, 384.
—— —— towards China, 208-13, 277-80, 409.
Russians in Korea, 92, 154, 176, 178, 208.
Ryong-San, 168, 175.

S

Saghalin, 3.
Saigo of Satsuma, 192.
Sak Wang Sa, 119, 139.
Sakyamuni, 346.
Salisbury, Lord, 59, 308.
Sam Kok San, 122, 140.
San Kuo Chih, The, 138.
Satow, Sir E. M., 97 *n*, 424.
Satsuma Clan, Inflence in Japanese Navy of the, 30-1.

Satsuma Rebellion, 22, 31, 41 *n*, 192.
Scherzer, M., 198 *n*.
Sen Kuang Kio, The, 137.
Shanghai, 46, 178, 313, 321.
Shang-ti, 246, 289.
Shan-hai-kuan, 256, 314.
Shimonoseki, 13, 39, 52, 282 *n*.
—— Treaty of, 429-5.
Shufeldt, Commodore, 202.
Shun Chih, Emperor, 266.
Siberian Railway, The, 277, 279, 316.
Siuen, Emperor, 249.
Singapore, 396, 397, 415, 420.
Soshi, Japanese, 28.
Smith, Sir C., 403.
Söul, 87 *n*, 89, 101, 109, 118-164.
—— Arsenal at, 164.
—— Beacons at, 122-3.
—— Big Bell of, 135.
—— Court at, 156-9.
—— Ground Plan of, 125.
—— Houses in, 123, 126-7.
—— Mint at, 172-3.
—— Pagoda at, 136.
—— Palaces at, 140-6, 156, 161.
—— Population of, 123-4.
—— Royal Procession in, 160, 162-3.
—— Streets of, 124, 125, 134.
—— Temples in, 137-8.
—— Walls and Gates of, 119-21, 138-9.
—— Warehouses in, 136.
Steamship Lines in the East, 175, 178, 212.
Sternburg, Baron Speck von, 322 *n*.
Student Interpreters, 424.
Sungpu Murders, The, 306.
Syel Chong, 97.
Szechuan Riots, The, 306.

T

Taijo Tai Woang, 135.
Taiping Rebellion, The, 223, 299, 400.
Tai Wen Kun, The, 135, 142, 148-51, 184, 206, 374, 380.

Taku, 222, 293, 314, 324.
Tariff Reform in Japan, 44.
Temples, Chinese, 353-5.
Tientsin, 211, 222, 268, 322, 324.
—— Treaty of (1858), 292-4.
—— Convention (1885), 192-3, 205-6.
—— Massacres (1870), 186, 222, 263.
Tigers, Korean, 111-2.
Ting, Admiral, 367.
Tiumen River, The, 208, 384.
Tokaguto, The, 186, 380.
Tokio, 13, 14, 52 *n*.
Tonghaks, *v*. Tokaguto.
Trade in the Far East, British, 6, 43, 177, 415-18.
—— with China, British, 281, 415.
—— with Japan, British, 43, 70-81.
—— with Korea, British, 177, 213.
—— French, in the Far East, 43, 281, 415.
—— German, in the Far East, 281, 415.
—— Japanese, 43-4, 177, 387-9.
—— Korean, 168-9, 176-9.
Treaties, Texts of; (1) Anglo-Japanese (1894), 70-81; (2) Shimonoseki, 429-35.
—— British, with China, 269, 292.
—— —— with Japan, 51, 68-9, 70-81.
—— —— with Korea, 60 *n*, 169, 178.
—— French, with China, 294.
—— Japanese, with Korea, 90 *n*, 168, 191-2.
—— —— with Mexico, 65.
—— Russian, with Korea, 169, 212.
—— —— with China, 208 *n*.
Treaty ports of China, 276, 282.
—— —— Japan, 13, 52, 66.
—— —— Korea, 88-94, 168.
Treaty Revision in Japan, 23, 27, 28, 46, 51-69, 391.
Tseng, Marquis, 207, 223, 225, 311, 331, 402.
Tsi An, Empress, 238.

Tsungli Yamen, The, 201, 214, 223, 260-4.
Tsushima Islands, 210.
Tung Chih, Emperor, 238, 271.
Tungchow, 316.
Tzu-chin-cheng, The, 232.

V

VARAT, Ch., 96 *n*.
Verbiest, F., 247.
Vladivostok, 47, 89, 92, 175, 178, 209, 316.

W

WADE, Sir T., 271, 344 *n*.
Wall, The Great, 256-7, 314.
War, Chino-Japanese (1894), 194-7, 361-89.
Wei Hai Wei, 197, 332, 367, 369.
Weltevree, Jan Jansson, 87 *n*.
Whampoa, 293.
Williams, Dr. W., 257, 271.
Witchcraft in Korea, 108.
Woosung, 293, 314.
Wuhsueh Massacres, 304.

Y

YAKUB BEG, 328, 397.
Yalu River, The, 105, 111, 175, 197, 365.
—— Battle of, 365.
Yamagata, Count, 22 and *n*, 58.
Yamens, Korean, 99-101.
Yang-hwa-chin, 134, 168.
Yellow Races, Future of the, 341, 396-412.
Yellow Sea, The, 89.
Yen-king, 230 *n*.
Yezo, 64.
Yokohama, 13, 52 *n*.
Younghusband, Capt. G. J., 41 *n*, 278.
Yuan Shih Kai, 207.
Yung Lo, Emperor, 249, 258.
—— Bells of, 253.
Yunnan Rebellion, The, 328, 397.

7

www.ingramcontent.com/pod-product-compliance
Lightning Source LLC
Chambersburg PA
CBHW051846300426
44117CB00006B/284